THE
POWER
OF THE
WORD

THE POWER OF THE WORD

SAVING DOCTRINES
FROM THE
BOOK OF MORMON

ROBERT L. MILLET

DESERET BOOK COMPANY
SALT LAKE CITY, UTAH

Variations of chapters 2, 4, 6, 10, 13, 14, and 17 were delivered as lectures at symposia sponsored by the BYU Religious Studies Center. Used by permission.

Variations of chapters 3, 15, and 16 were delivered at the Sidney B. Sperry Symposia sponsored by BYU Religious Education. Used by permission.

Chapter 9 was delivered at the tenth annual CES Religious Educators' Symposium. Used by permission of the Corporation of the President.

Chapter 19 first appeared in the *Journal of Book of Mormon Studies,* vol. 2, no. 2, fall 1993. Used by permission.

Library of Congress Cataloging-in-Publication Data

Millet, Robert L.
   The power of the word : saving doctrines from the Book of Mormon / Robert L. Millet.
     p.   cm.
   Includes index.
   ISBN 0-87579-826-8
   1. Book of Mormon—Criticism, interpretation, etc. 2. Church of Jesus Christ of Latter-day Saints—Doctrines. 3. Mormon Church—Doctrines. I. Title.
BX8627.M55   1994
289.3'22—dc20   93-44307
                                                    CIP

Printed in the United States of America

10 9   8   7   6   5   4   3   2

And now, as the preaching of the word had a great tendency to lead the people to do that which was just—yea, it had had more powerful effect upon the minds of the people than the sword, or anything else, which had happened unto them—therefore Alma thought it was expedient that they should try the virtue of the word of God. (Alma 31:5.)

———

Thus we see that the gate of heaven is open unto all, even to those who will believe on the name of Jesus Christ, who is the Son of God. Yea, we see that whosoever will may lay hold upon the word of God, which is quick and powerful, which shall divide asunder all the cunning and the snares and the wiles of the devil, and lead the man of Christ in a strait and narrow course across that everlasting gulf of misery which is prepared to engulf the wicked. And land their souls, yea, their immortal souls, at the right hand of God in the kingdom of heaven, to sit down with Abraham, and Isaac, and with Jacob, and with all our holy fathers, to go no more out. (Helaman 3:28–30.)

———

Now, if the Book of Mormon is true, our acceptance of it will lead to salvation in the highest heaven. On the other hand, if we say it is true when in fact it is not, we are thereby leading men astray and surely deserve to drop down to the deepest hell. The time is long past for quibbling about words and for hurling unsavory epithets against the Latter-day Saints. These are deep and solemn and ponderous matters. We need not think we can trifle with sacred things and escape the wrath of a just God. Either the Book of Mormon is true, or it is false; either it came from God, or it was spawned in the infernal realms. It declares plainly that all men must accept it as pure scripture or they will lose their souls. It is not and cannot be simply another treatise on religion; it either came from heaven or from hell. And it is time for all those who seek salvation to find out for themselves whether it is of the Lord or of Lucifer. (Bruce R. McConkie, "What Think Ye of the Book of Mormon?" *Ensign,* November 1983, p. 73.)

———

Success in righteousness, the power to avoid deception and resist temptation, guidance in our daily lives, healing of the soul—these are but a few of the promises the Lord has given to those who will come to His word. Does the Lord promise and not fulfill? Surely if He tells us that these things will come to us if we lay hold upon His word, then the blessings can be ours. And if we do not, then the blessings may be lost. However diligent we may be in other areas, certain blessings are to be found only in the scriptures, only in coming to the word of the Lord and holding fast to it as we make our way through the mists of darkness to the tree of life. (Ezra Taft Benson, "The Power of the Word," *Ensign,* May 1986, p. 82.)

CONTENTS

Contents

Preface

The title of this book is drawn from the title of an address prepared by President Ezra Taft Benson for a priesthood leadership meeting at the time of the April 1986 general conference of the Church. In that significant message (published in the May 1986 *Ensign*), a modern prophet spoke of the challenges facing the membership of the Church now and in the future; of the growing power of Satan in a wayward and wandering world; and of the natural fear and discouragement that follow in the wake of such things. He also drew our attention to the fact that Nephi, in navigating the strait and narrow path along the way to the tree of life, was able to stay on course through holding fast to the rod of iron. That rod of iron, President Benson reminded us, is the word of God.

"Not only will the word of God lead us to the fruit which is desirable above all others," President Benson declared, "but in the word of God and through it we can find the power to resist temptation, the power to thwart the work of Satan and his emissaries." He also observed: "The word of God, as found in the scriptures, in the words of living prophets, and in personal revelation, has the power to fortify the Saints and arm them with the Spirit so they can resist evil, hold fast to the good, and find joy in this life." (P. 80.)

This book has been prepared with the assurance that few things are of greater worth, few things bring greater dividends in this life, than prayerfully searching and pondering the scriptures, particularly the Book of Mormon, Another Testament of Jesus Christ. The essays in this volume, *The Power of the Word,* represent articles, book chapters, symposium addresses, and special lectures that I have prepared and delivered during the past ten years. It has been my delight and privilege to teach all of the Standard Works of the Church and to research and write on each of them as I have worked as a faculty member in Religious Education at Brigham Young University. But my greatest area of focus, my deepest passion and love, has been the Book of Mormon. In the Book of Mormon my soul finds rest and peace. To the Book of Mormon I always seem to return. From the Book of Mormon I invariably draw upon illustrations and doctrinal clarifications, no matter the book of scripture under consideration.

I have no other desire than to bear witness of the truthfulness and eternal relevance of the Book of Mormon. To the degree that persons who read what follows are motivated to turn to the pure word, to the scriptural text itself, and be transformed by the power of that word—to that degree this work will have fulfilled its purpose. Because one's knowledge is so very cumulative, because so much of what we know and understand is dependent upon what we have learned from others, it is impossible to express appreciation to all who have assisted me in my study of the gospel, and especially my study of the Book of Mormon. I express special thanks to my friends and colleagues Larry E. Dahl, Joseph F. McConkie, Robert J. Matthews, and Monte S. Nyman, men who love the Book of Mormon, who declare its doctrines with sincere persuasion, and at whose side I have enjoyed the privilege of teaching. This book is not an official publication of The Church of Jesus Christ of Latter-day Saints or of Brigham Young University. Though I have sought in my writing to be in harmony with the holy scriptures and the teachings of the latter-day apostles and prophets, the book is a private endeavor, and the conclusions drawn from the evidence cited are my own. I do, however, believe them to be true.

I have great confidence in the power of the word—the power of the written or spoken word of God or his servants—to penetrate the hearts of men and women (2 Nephi 33:1), to speak to us through the medium of memory and convince us of the error of our ways (Alma 37:8), and to lead us to faith on the name of Christ and to a life thereafter that the scriptures characterize as firm and steadfast (Helaman 15:7–8). I have especial confidence in the unique language, logic, and transforming power of the Book of Mormon. Mine is an overwhelming desire to "try the virtue of the word of God" (Alma 31:5), to trust in the Lord's ability to communicate with the people of this final dispensation through this ancient but ever-pertinent voice that speaks to us, one and all, from the dust.

A Spiritual Odyssey with the Book of Mormon

I know with a certainty that defies all doubt that the Book of Mormon is true. But I have not always felt that way. As a young missionary, I was particularly attracted to the Doctrine and Covenants. For some reason I found myself reading it again and again, memorizing favorite passages and keeping careful notes on which doctrines were found in which sections. A number of my companions and I quizzed one another on the Doctrine and Covenants as we walked along lonely roads or as we tracted from one door to another. I did read the Book of Mormon a couple of times while on my mission, but I did so more out of duty than enjoyment. I had a testimony that Joseph Smith was indeed a prophet of God and that the work he set in motion was divine; but for reasons that I cannot explain, I simply had not had a personal experience with the Book of Mormon.

After returning home from my mission and transferring to Brigham Young University, I took a class in the Pearl of Great Price and was stirred intellectually and spiritually. I began to sense, more than I ever had before, the depth and breadth and reach of the restored gospel. Courses in the Doctrine and Covenants rekindled my excitement about the revelations given through the Prophet Joseph Smith. A semester before I was to graduate, I discovered that two courses in the Book of Mormon were required for graduation. I dutifully enrolled, though my heart wasn't in it. I somehow made it through the classes, received B grades in both, but was still unenthusiastic about the scripture known as the stick of Joseph.

After completing my master's degree at BYU, I began work with the Church Educational System and soon thereafter took several graduate courses in religion. I studied LDS theology, LDS church history, the Gospels, the life and letters of Paul, and the general epistles and the Apocalypse. I focused much of my personal study on the teachings and translation work of Joseph Smith, particularly his inspired translation of the Bible. All this time I believed the Book of Mormon was true, but I had become no more than distantly acquainted with it.

It was while I was working in the southern states area of the Church Educational System that I began to unstick the pages in the first section of my triple combination. In 1982 I read and relished the final volume in Elder Bruce R. McConkie's masterwork on the Messiah. I began to notice in *The Millennial Messiah*[1] how often Elder McConkie turned to the Book of Mormon for doctrine, for interpretation, and for prophetic pronouncements. It was uncanny. He really used the Book of Mormon! This was especially the case when it came to discussing the destiny of the house of Israel as revealed in the promises made to the ancient fathers and their posterity. When I finished my second reading of *The Millennial Messiah*, I knew that I must turn my attention to the Book of Mormon.

It was as if all things were in readiness. The pages exploded with feeling and meaning for me. I had known the Book of Mormon story for many years. When I was a young boy, my family had read and even listened to recordings of the Book of Mormon. But now it was different. Nephi came alive. Jacob seemed to be someone I had known but forgotten about. And Alma the Younger was larger than life. In short, I fell in love with the *story* of the Book of Mormon. I felt the need to read it through, time after time, to get straight in my mind who was who and where they went and what they did. In the months and years that followed this experience, I became intimately acquainted with those voices from the dust, voices that now seemed not to be whispering but rather shouting to me that what they had to say was real and true. The witness had come like fire into my heart that the Book of Mormon was a sacred record of a people who had once inhabited the Americas.

My first phase of discovery—the truthfulness and relevance of the story of the Book of Mormon—soon merged into another phase. Over the years, I had heard more than one of the General Authorities remark that the Book of Mormon was the doctrinal standard for the Church; that in spite of the marvelous revealed truths contained in the Bible, the Doctrine and Covenants, and the Pearl of Great Price, it was to the Book of Mormon that we turn primarily to understand the *doctrine* of Christ. I had certainly heard them say that, but I wasn't sure. Now suddenly my eyes began to be opened to that reality. It became clear that if we were to understand the Fall, the book of Genesis or even the book of Moses (the accounts of the Fall) would be far less helpful than 2 Nephi

2 or Alma 42. If we wanted to gain deeper insight into the Atonement, it was to 2 Nephi 9 and Alma 34 that we should turn, rather than to the Gospels. It began to dawn upon me that the teachings of Lehi, Nephi, Jacob, Mormon, and the risen Lord on the destiny of Israel far excelled in detail and spirit those of Isaiah, Jeremiah, and Ezekiel. And so on and so on. As a teacher I found myself illustrating principles more and more often from the personalities and events (the story) of the Book of Mormon, and I also felt driven to teach and explain sacred matters (the doctrine) more frequently from the Nephite record.

It was several years after I had come to recognize the infinite worth of the Book of Mormon as a doctrinal refuge and a source for theological understanding that I began to realize another phase of my own spiritual odyssey with this unusual scriptural record. That third phase might be called *personal encounter*. I loved the story more than ever. I treasured the doctrine. But now I sensed that the prophet-writers were speaking directly to me, not only so that I might understand specific doctrinal matters but also that I might more fully conform my personal life with their teachings. For example, my study of the Fall now seemed to be an invitation from Lehi or Nephi or Benjamin or Abinadi to recognize my own fallen nature and seek to put off the natural man. My search of the scriptures pertaining to the Atonement now became a pattern and an invitation to come unto Christ and be changed, to become a new creature of the Holy Ghost. In short, I now found myself driven beyond doctrinal understanding to personal engagement with things of holiness. The Book of Mormon became more than a book about religion; it *was* religion. The Book of Mormon was not simply something to be read and studied, though such activities were a necessary beginning; it was something to be *lived*. The Book of Mormon was not simply a collection of teachings about which we should speak (though we certainly needed to speak the word), but also something that we needed to do (see D&C 84:57).

Perhaps it is in this context that I have come to appreciate why the Book of Mormon has a spirit all its own. I love the Bible, both the Old and New Testaments. I cherish the Doctrine and Covenants and Pearl of Great Price and enjoy teaching about them more than I can say. But the Book of Mormon is different. The other books of scripture—especially the books of modern scripture—are true and from God, and they convey a remarkable spirit. But the Book of Mormon is different. More than any other other book, it is Christ centered and gospel centered. It leads men and women to the Lord and motivates them to do good. There is a language, a logic, and a discernment that flow into the lives of those who drink deeply from it. Within the reach of all those who become serious students of its pages and precepts is an interpretive key that opens hidden treasures of knowledge. God was and is its author and its ultimate editor. It was written and compiled by men who knew the Lord and had personally partaken of his goodness and grace, men with seeric vision who saw our day and prepared the record with our obstacles, our challenges, and our personal difficulties in mind (see Mormon 8:35; 9:30). It is in this sense that the Book of Mormon is everlastingly relevant and perpetually pertinent. It speaks directly to us because it was written directly to us.

In the words of Elder Bruce R. McConkie, "Men can get nearer to the Lord; can have more of the spirit of conversion and conformity in their hearts; can have stronger testimonies; and can gain a better understanding of the doctrines of salvation through the Book of Mormon than they can through the Bible." Further: "More people will flock to the gospel standard; more souls will be converted; more of scattered Israel will be gathered; and more people will migrate from one place to another because of the Book of Mormon than was or will be the case with the Bible." Finally: "There will be more people saved in the kingdom of God—ten thousand times over—because of the Book of Mormon than there will be because of the Bible."[2] Similarly, President Ezra Taft Benson, then president of the Quorum of the Twelve, observed that "the spirit, as well as the body, is in need of constant nourishment. Yesterday's meal is not enough to sustain today's needs. So also an infrequent reading of 'the most correct of any book on earth,' as Joseph Smith called it, is not enough." Then President Benson uttered this profound fact: "Not all truths are of equal value, nor are all scriptures of the same worth."[3]

I feel a tremendous love for the Book of Mormon. A spirit akin to coming home after a long vacation settles over me whenever I pick up the Book of Mormon and begin reading. It speaks peace to my mind and heart. The Spirit of the Lord has borne witness to my soul that the Book of Mormon is not only true but faithful; its precepts are as current as they are consistent, as sanctifying as they are soothing. I know that a modern prophet, Joseph Smith, has been raised up to reveal anew the way of life and salvation. And God be praised that that "choice seer" has been the means of translating and thus making available an ancient record of a fallen people, a blessing in the form of sacred scripture, a divine message whose import can hardly be measured and whose total impact is yet to be seen and felt by earth's inhabitants.

Notes

1. Bruce R. McConkie, *The Millennial Messiah: The Second Coming of the Son of Man* (Salt Lake City: Deseret Book Co., 1982).
2. Bruce R. McConkie, address to Church Educational System, 18 August 1978.
3. Ezra Taft Benson, in Conference Report, October 1984, p. 6.

CHAPTER 2

The Condescension of God

The Prophet Joseph Smith stated in 1841 that a man could get "nearer
to God by abiding by" the precepts of the Book of Mormon "than by
any other book."[1] Those who have made the Book of Mormon more
than casual reading know of the truthfulness of the Prophet's declaration; they can testify with President Ezra Taft Benson that the serious
study of this sacred volume can bring "spiritual and intellectual unity
to [one's] whole life."[2] The Book of Mormon has been preserved and
prepared with our day in mind. Prophets and noble men who wrote on
the plates knew of our day, sensed and saw our challenges, and were
fully aware of the sublime strength that the Nephite-Jaredite record
could be in a troubled and uncertain world (see Mormon 8:35; 9:30).
The Book of Mormon has been given to bring men and women to
Christ—to point them toward the reality of his existence, to bear witness of his divine Sonship, and to demonstrate how the peace that
comes through a remission of sins here and the ultimate peace through
salvation hereafter are to be had through calling on his holy name and
in no other way. The Book of Mormon brings men to Christ because it
is a masterful revelation of him, an additional witness (with the New
Testament) that he "hath abolished death, and hath brought life and
immortality to light through the gospel" (2 Timothy 1:10). It is indeed
"another testament of Jesus Christ."[3]

THE NEED FOR ANOTHER TESTAMENT

In a revelation given at the time of the organization of the restored
Church, the Lord explained that the Book of Mormon had been given
for the purpose of "proving to the world that the holy scriptures are
true" (D&C 20:11). Presumably the expression *the holy scriptures* refers
to the Bible. That is to say, the Nephite record has been delivered to this
final dispensation to establish the truthfulness of the biblical record; or,
in the words of Mormon, "this [the Book of Mormon] is written for the
intent that [we] may believe [the Bible]" (Mormon 7:9). The Book of
Mormon establishes clearly that the Bible is the "book of the Lamb of

6

Chapter 2—The Condescension of God

God" (1 Nephi 13:28); that Old and New Testament characters such as Adam and Eve, Noah, Abraham, Moses, David, Solomon, John the Baptist, and John the Beloved were real persons through whom God fulfilled his purposes; that the miracles and wonders described in the Bible (for example, crossing the Red Sea, healings through looking upon the brazen serpent, displacing the Canaanites from the promised land) are genuine manifestations of divine power.

Most important, the Book of Mormon attests that Jehovah, the God of ancient Israel, truly became the Son of the Highest; that Jesus of Nazareth came to earth through birth and took upon himself a physical body; that he submitted to the throes of mortality; and that he lived a sinless life, took upon himself the sins of all mankind on conditions of repentance, was crucified, died, and rose again three days later into glorious immortality. In other words, the Book of Mormon is another testament of the *gospel*, the glad tidings that deliverance from death and hell and endless torment is available through the infinite Atonement and by obedience to the laws and ordinances of the gospel (see 3 Nephi 27:13–21).

In a time when men are eager to acknowledge Jesus of Nazareth as a great teacher, as a model of morality and decency, and as the prototype of purity and peaceful living—but who in the same breath deny his divinity—the prophets of the Book of Mormon boldly declare that Jesus is the Christ, the Eternal God; that he has power to forgive sins, power over life and death, and that as the Holy One of Israel he is the "keeper of the gate," the Eternal Judge of both quick and dead. It has become fashionable among some biblical scholars during the last century to undertake "the quest for the historical Jesus," seeking through form-critical methods to peel away the traditions of the centuries concerning the God-Man until they would arrive, as some suppose, at a simple picture of the lowly Nazarene. However, in the words of F. F. Bruce: "Perhaps the most important result to which Form Criticism points is that, no matter how far back we may press our researches into the roots of the gospel story, no matter how we classify the gospel material, we never arrive at a nonsupernatural Jesus."[4] The Book of Mormon saves us "the quest." It attests that Jesus was God before he came to earth and was the promised Messiah and Savior on earth.

LEHI AND NEPHI: A REMARKABLE VISION

Sometime after Nephi and his brothers had returned from their journey to Jerusalem to get Ishmael and his family, Lehi announced, "I have dreamed a dream; or, in other words, I have seen a vision" (1 Nephi 8:2). In the words of a modern apostle: "All inspired dreams are visions, but all visions are not dreams. Visions are received in hours of wakefulness or of sleep and in some cases when the recipient has passed into a trance; it is only when the vision occurs during sleep that it is termed a dream."[5] Lehi, a visionary man and designated prophet of God, declared that he had been the recipient of a prophetic revelation. The dream, which most Latter-day Saints have read numerous times, is a literary masterpiece and a doctrinal gem. In a personal way, the dream provided Lehi with a forum for family instruction: the great patriarch expressed deep concern that his elder sons, Laman and Lemuel, would not pay the price sufficient to press forward on the strait and narrow path which led to the tree of life, and thus would never know of the consummate joys associated with full participation in the plan of the Father (1 Nephi 8:3–4, 12–18).

In a more general way, the dream provided a vivid description of four main groups of people, types and representations of all walks of life, persons with varying spiritual aptitudes and diverse degrees of sensitivity toward things of righteousness. This part of the dream (1 Nephi 8:21–33) might well be called "the parable of the path." It has fascinating similarities to the parable of the soils in the New Testament (Matthew 13:3–8, 18–23) and stresses the differences in spiritual receptivity. According to Lehi's vision, to navigate the path and arrive securely at the tree of life, one is required to hold tenaciously to the rod (word of God), pass safely through the mists of darkness (temptations of the devil), avoid detours from the path, which might lead to the waters of filthiness (depths of hell) beneath the path,[6] and ignore the taunting voices of ridicule of those situated in the great and spacious building (the pride and wisdom of the world).

Nephi explained that he was desirous to "see, and hear, and know" of the same things that his father had experienced in vision. Knowing full well that God was no respecter of persons, that the Almighty constantly reveals the things of eternity to those who seek him in faithfulness and in truth, and, in Nephi's own words, "believing that the Lord was able to make them known unto me, as I sat pondering in mine heart I was caught away in the Spirit of the Lord, yea, into an exceedingly high mountain, which I never had before seen, and upon which I never had before set my foot" (1 Nephi 10:17–11:1). Mountains are frequently the meeting places between God and men; they serve as nature's temples, the point of intersection between the finite and the infinite. As is so often the case, Nephi's meditation upon the things of the Spirit resulted in a heavenly manifestation (compare D&C 76:11–19; 138:1–11); he received the same vision his father had received.

Nephi's rendition of his vision, given to us in 1 Nephi 11–14, is obviously a much more extensive account than that which Lehi delivered in 1 Nephi 8. It is a vision not only of the tree of life but also a glimpse of the future destiny of the world, a vision not unlike that given to the brother of Jared, Enoch, Moses, and John the Revelator. And yet, Nephi himself explained to us later: "I, Nephi, am forbidden that I should write the remainder of the things which I saw and heard; wherefore the things which I have written sufficeth me; and I have written but a small part of the things which I saw. And *I bear record that I saw the things which my father saw*, and the angel of the Lord did make them known unto me" (1 Nephi 14:28–29; italics added).

Nephi's words, spoken here at the end of the vision, seem to imply not simply that his vision comprehended or circumscribed that of his father (and thus he had seen what his father saw *and much more*), but rather that they had beheld the same vision. Let us note here that Nephi had earlier observed (1 Nephi 1:16–17) that the opening chapters of the small plates would be devoted to an abridgment of some of his father's experiences (now 1 Nephi 1–8), while he would soon come to devote the remainder of his record to an account of his own life (see, for example, 1 Nephi 10:1). Lehi spoke "all the words of his dream or vision" to his family, "which," Nephi hastened to add, *"were many"* (1 Nephi 8:36; italics added). In 1 Nephi 8, therefore, we are introduced to the vision of the tree of life, an obvious abridgment of Lehi's much lengthier spiritual experience. We turn, however, to subsequent chapters—chapters 11, 12, and 15—for Nephi's commentary and explanation of the vision and the specific symbolism involved.

NEPHI'S GUIDES IN THE VISION

Having been caught away to a high mountain for instruction, Nephi was asked by a personage whom he calls "the Spirit," "What desirest thou?" Nephi answered promptly, "I desire to behold the things which my father saw" (1 Nephi 11:1–3). Then followed a series of questions, answers, and visual explanations to the young Nephite seer. Having been shown the vision of the tree, the same which Lehi had beheld, Nephi was asked, "What desirest thou?" to which he responded, "To know the interpretation thereof—for I spake unto him as a man speakest; for *I beheld that he was in the form of a man*; yet nevertheless, *I knew that it was the Spirit of the Lord*; and he spake unto me as a man speaketh with another" (1 Nephi 11:9–11; italics added). One is faced right away with an interesting theological question: Is Nephi's guide, designated by him as "the Spirit of the Lord," the premortal Christ (the individual spirit personage who became Jesus Christ in mortality) or the Holy Ghost?

If this is a personal appearance of the Holy Ghost to a man, it is indeed a singular occasion, so far as our scriptural accounts are concerned.[7] In addressing this issue some years ago, Sidney B. Sperry suggested the latter alternative—that the "Spirit of the Lord" refers to the Holy Ghost—based upon the following textual evidence.[8] First, we read of Nephi's desires to "see, and hear, and know of these things, *by the power of the Holy Ghost*." He further testified that the Holy Ghost gave authority for his words (see 1 Nephi 10:17–22; italics added). Second, Nephi used phrases such as "the Spirit said," "the Spirit cried," and "I said unto the Spirit" (1 Nephi 11:2, 4, 6, 8, 9), all of which sound very much like references to the Holy Ghost rather than to Jehovah. Third, Nephi never spoke of the Lord Jesus Christ as the "Spirit of the Lord" when the Master appeared to him on other occasions (see 1 Nephi 2:16; 2 Nephi 11:2–3). Fourth, the phrase *Spirit of the Lord* occurs some forty times in the Book of Mormon, and in every case reference seems to be to either the Holy Ghost or to the Light of Christ. Examples of this would be 1 Nephi 1:12, where Lehi, having read from the book delivered to him, was filled with the "Spirit of the Lord"; 1 Nephi 13:15, where the "Spirit of the Lord" was poured out upon the Gentiles in preparation for the establishment of the American nation; Mosiah 4:3, where the "Spirit of the Lord" came upon the people of King Benjamin and they experienced a remission of sins and its subsequent joy; and, of course, those references wherein the expression *Spirit of the Lord* is used after the mortal ministry of Jesus Christ and could only mean the Holy Ghost (for example, Mormon 2:26; 5:16; Moroni 9:4).

"The Holy Ghost undoubtedly possesses personal powers and affections," wrote Elder James E. Talmage; "these attributes exist in Him in perfection. . . . That the Spirit of the Lord is capable of manifesting Himself in the form and figure of man, is indicated by the wonderful interview between the Spirit and Nephi, in which He revealed Himself to the prophet, questioned him concerning his desires and belief, instructed him in the things of God, speaking face to face with the man."[9]

After explaining to the Holy Ghost that he sought the meaning behind the representation of the tree of life, Nephi "looked as if to look upon" the Spirit, "and [he] saw him not; for he had gone from before [his] presence" (1 Nephi 11:12). Nephi was then caught away into vision again, this time beholding many of the cities of the Holy Land, specifically Nazareth of Galilee. The heavens were opened to Nephi, and "an angel came down and stood before" him (verse 14). This angel, whose identity is not given, became Nephi's guide and instructor throughout the remainder of his panoramic vision, providing both prophetic sight and doctrinal insight into such future matters as the coming of Jesus Christ to both hemispheres; the formation of the great and abominable church; the journey of Columbus and the establishment of the American nation under divine direction; the plain and precious truths taken away and kept back from the Bible; the spread of the great and abominable church and the church of the Lamb to all nations of the earth; and the winding-up scenes preparatory to the coming of the Lord in glory.

THE CONDESCENSION OF GOD

Nephi's attention was drawn specifically to Nazareth of Galilee. There he "beheld a virgin, and she was exceedingly fair and white."[10] The angel then asked Nephi a penetrating question: "Knowest thou the condescension of God?" (1 Nephi 11:13–16.) To condescend is literally to "go down with" or to "go down among." It is "the act of descending to a lower and less dignified state; or waiving the privileges of one's rank and status; of bestowing honors and favors upon one of lesser stature or status."[11] The angel's question might be restated thus: "Nephi, do you fathom the majesty of it all? Can your mortal mind comprehend the infinite wonder and grandeur of the marvelous love made manifest by the Father and the Son?" Nephi answered: "I know that he loveth his children; nevertheless, I do not know the meaning of all things" (1 Nephi 11:17). One of the remarkable discoveries of those who come to know him who is Eternal is that God's infinity as the Almighty does not preclude either his immediacy or his intimacy as a loving Father of spirits. Enoch learned this precious lesson during his ministry (see Moses 7:28–32), and Nephi evidenced his knowledge of the same principles.

The "condescension of God" described in 1 Nephi 11 seems to be twofold: the condescension of God the Father (verses 16–23) and the condescension of God the Son (verses 24–36). "Without overstepping the bounds of propriety by saying more than is appropriate," Elder Bruce R. McConkie wrote, "let us say this: God the Almighty; the Maker and Preserver and Upholder of all things; the Omnipotent One . . . elects, in his fathomless wisdom, to beget a Son, an Only Son, the Only Begotten in the flesh. God, who is infinite and immortal, condescends to step down from his throne, to join with one who is finite and mortal in bringing forth, 'after the manner of the flesh,' the Mortal Messiah."[12] In the words of President Ezra Taft Benson: "The Church of Jesus Christ of Latter-day Saints proclaims that Jesus Christ is the Son of God in the most literal sense. The body in which He performed His mission in the flesh was sired by that same Holy Being we worship as God, our Eternal Father. Jesus was not the son of Joseph, nor was He begotten by the Holy Ghost. He is the Son of the Eternal Father!"[13]

The condescension of God the Son consists in the coming to earth of the great Jehovah, the Lord God Omnipotent, the God of the ancients. The 1830 edition of the Book of Mormon contains the following words from the angel to Nephi: "Behold, the virgin whom thou seest is the *mother of God*, after the manner of the flesh" (1 Nephi 11:18; italics added). The angel later said unto Nephi regarding the vision of the Christ child, "Behold the Lamb of God, yea, *the Eternal Father !*" (1 Nephi 11:21; italics added; compare 1 Nephi 13:40, 1830 edition). Later in the same vision of the ministry of Christ, the angel spoke, saying, "Look! And I looked," Nephi added, "and beheld the Lamb of God, that he was taken by the people; yea, *the everlasting God* was judged of the world; and I saw and bear record" (1 Nephi 11:32; italics added). In the 1837 edition of the Book of Mormon, Joseph Smith the Prophet changed these verses to read "the mother of *the Son of* God," "the *Son of the* Eternal Father," and "the *Son of the* everlasting God," respectively (italics added). It would appear that the Prophet made these textual alterations to assist the Latter-day Saints in fully understanding the meaning of the expressions.[14]

Some persons are eager to point up these changes as illustrative of Joseph Smith's changing views on the doctrine of the Godhead, an example of pre- and post-1835 theology. They would suppose that Joseph was tied to a type of "trinitarianism" before his theology "developed" over time and thus would place (inappropriately) the Book of Mormon within that developmental process. Such a conclusion is both unwarranted and incorrect. For one thing, the Book of Mormon writers make scores of references to the distinct identities of Jesus Christ and his Father.[15] One need only read Nephi's words in 2 Nephi 25, regarding the necessity of the Jews believing in Christ and worshipping the Father in his name (see verse 16) to appreciate the distinctness of the members of the Godhead in the minds of Nephite prophets. In addition, in 2 Nephi 31 we note the constant reference to the words of the Father as opposed to the words of the Son. In the chapter now under consideration, 1 Nephi 11, we read in verse 24 these words: "And I looked, and I beheld *the Son of God* going forth among the children of men; and I saw many fall down at his feet and worship him" (italics added; see also verse 7; Alma 5:50). The Prophet Joseph Smith's alterations in previous verses—mother of *the Son of* God and *the Son of* the Eternal Father—are perfectly consistent with the description of Christ in verse 24.[16]

Mary was indeed the "mother of God," and Jesus Christ was the "Eternal Father," the "everlasting God" (compare Mosiah 15:4; 16:15; Alma 11:38–39). The condescension of God the Son thus consists in the fact that the Eternal One would "descend from his throne divine" (*Hymns*, 1985, no. 193), be born in the most humble of circumstances, become among the most helpless of all creation—a human infant—and submit to the refining influences of mortal life. An angel further explained the condescension of God the Son to King Benjamin: "The time cometh, and is not far distant," he prophesied, "that with power, the Lord Omnipotent who reigneth, who was, and is from all eternity to all eternity, shall come down from heaven among the children of men, and shall dwell in a tabernacle of clay." Further, Jehovah, the God of creation, "shall suffer temptations, and pain of body, hunger, thirst, and fatigue, even more than man can suffer, except it be unto death" (Mosiah 3:5, 7). The condescension of the Son—his ministry among the unenlightened, his suffering and death, followed by the persecution and death of his anointed servants—is described by Nephi in 1 Nephi 11:27–36.

Inextricably tied to the concept of the Incarnation, of the condescension of the Great God, is the awful irony of the suffering and atonement of our Lord. He who was sinless was persecuted and put to death by sinners whom he came to save. He who was sinless became, as it were, the great sinner. In Paul's words, God the Father has "made him to be sin for us, who knew no sin" (2 Corinthians 5:21). He who deserved least of all to suffer suffered most—more than mortal mind can fathom. He who had brought light and life—the more abundant life (John 10:10)—was rejected by the powers of darkness and death. As Joseph Smith taught the members of the School of the Prophets in Kirtland, Jesus Christ is called the *Son* of God because he "descended in suffering below that which man can suffer; or, in other words, suffered greater sufferings, and was exposed to more powerful contradictions than any man can be."[17] All this Nephi saw in vision, including the persecution and deaths of the Twelve Apostles after the crucifixion and ascension of the Master (1 Nephi 11:24–36).

THE TREE OF LIFE

After Nephi had explained that he desired to see the things his father had seen, the Spirit asked what appears, at first blush, to be a most unusual question: "Believest thou that thy father saw the tree of which he hath spoken?" Nephi answered the query: "Yea, thou knowest that I believe all the words of my father" (1 Nephi 11:3–5). One wonders about the Spirit's question: Why did he not ask Nephi if he believed that his father had seen a large and spacious building, or mists of darkness, or a strait and narrow path, or a rod of iron? The fact is, faith is not exercised in trees, and the Spirit of the Lord was not simply inquiring into Nephi's knowledge of a form of plant life. Indeed, it was not a belief in the tree that would qualify Nephi for the manifestation to follow; nor was this the concern of the Spirit. The tree was obviously a doctrinal symbol, a "sign" that pointed beyond itself to an even greater reality. Yet the tree was of marvelous importance, for it was the symbol, even from the time of the Edenic paradise, of Jesus Christ's central and saving role and of the glorified immortality to be enjoyed by the faithful through his atoning sacrifice. Nephi's vision was to be more than an involvement with an abstract concept called the "love of God" (1 Nephi 11:22); it was a messianic message, a poignant prophecy of him toward whom all men press forward on that strait and narrow path that leads to life eternal.

"My soul delighteth in proving unto my people," Nephi would later say, "the truth of the coming of Christ; for, for this end hath the law of Moses been given; and *all things which have been given of God* from the beginning of the world, unto man, *are the typifying of him*" (2 Nephi 11:4; italics added; compare Moses 6:63). In reference to this verse, Elder Bruce R. McConkie wrote: "It follows that if we had sufficient insight, we would see in every gospel ordinance, in every rite that is part of revealed religion, in every performance commanded of God, in all things Deity gives his people, something that typifies the eternal ministry of the Eternal Christ."[18] It is just so with the vision enjoyed by Lehi and Nephi: it is Christ centered and to be fully appreciated only by focusing attention upon him who is the author of salvation. Consider the following:

1. After Nephi had certified his belief in the fact that his father saw the tree, the Spirit "cried with a loud voice, saying: Hosanna to the Lord, the most high God; for he is God over all the earth, yea, even above all. And *blessed art thou Nephi, because thou believest in the Son of the most high God*; wherefore, thou shalt behold the things which thou hast desired" (1 Nephi 11:6; italics added). Note that the guide rejoiced over Nephi's *faith in Christ*, not simply in his belief in a tree.

2. The words of the Spirit continue: "And behold this thing shall be given unto thee for *a sign*, that after thou hast beheld *the tree* which bore the fruit which thy father tasted, thou shalt also behold *a man* descending out of heaven, and him shall ye witness; and after ye have witnessed him ye shall bear record that *it is the Son of God*" (1 Nephi

11:7; italics added). The Spirit here began to unfold the typology to Nephi. The tree was given "for a sign," as a symbolic representation of a man, even he whose branches provide sacred shade and shelter from the scorching rays of sin and ignorance.

3. Consider Nephi's description of the tree: "The beauty thereof was far beyond, yea, exceeding of all beauty; and the whiteness thereof did exceed the whiteness of the driven snow" (1 Nephi 11:8). Whiteness generally symbolizes purity. Jesus of Nazareth was the purest of pure, for he lived without spot or blemish, the only mortal to achieve moral perfection through never wandering from the path of righteousness (see 2 Corinthians 5:21; Hebrews 4:15; 1 Peter 2:22).

4. After Nephi had been asked concerning his knowledge of the condescension of God and had then seen Mary "carried away in the Spirit for the space of a time," he "looked and beheld the virgin again, bearing a child in her arms." Nephi's account continues: "And the angel said unto me: Behold the Lamb of God, yea, even the Son of the Eternal Father! Knowest thou the meaning of the tree which thy father saw?" That is, while looking at the Christ child, it is as if the angel were summing up, bringing Nephi back to the point where he had begun—the deeper significance of the tree. Essentially Nephi was asked, "Now, Nephi, do you finally understand the meaning of the tree? Now do you understand the message behind the sign?" And he answered: "Yea, *it is the love of God*, which sheddeth itself abroad in the hearts of the children of men; wherefore, it is the most desirable above all things." The angel then added by way of confirmation: "Yea, and the most joyous to the soul" (1 Nephi 11:19–23; italics added). Nephi's answer was perfect: it was an understanding given by the power of the Holy Ghost. Again, the tree represented more than an abstract emotion, more than a vague (albeit divine) sentiment. It was the greatest manifestation of the love of God—the gift of Christ. "For God so loved the world," Jesus explained to Nicodemus, "that he gave his only begotten Son, that whosoever believeth in him should not perish, but have everlasting life" (John 3:16). That love is made manifest and is extended to all men through the Atonement—it "*sheddeth* itself abroad in the hearts of the children of men"—through, appropriately, the blood *shed* in Gethsemane and on Golgotha.[19]

There is no ceiling to the number of saved beings, no limit to the love of the Father that can be received by all who qualify for the fulness of salvation. "And again," Moroni spoke to the Savior, "I remember that thou hast said that thou hast loved the world, even unto the laying down of thy life for the world." Continuing, Moroni added, "And now I know that this love which thou hast had for the children of men is charity" (Ether 12:33–34). Those who partake of the powers of Christ through repentance gain the blessings mentioned in regard to the people of King Benjamin. "O have mercy," they had pleaded in prayer at the conclusion of the king's mighty sermon, "and apply the atoning blood of Christ that we may receive forgiveness of our sins, and our hearts may be purified; for we believe in Jesus Christ, the Son of God." As a result of their sincere petition, "the Spirit of the Lord came upon them, and they were filled with joy, having received a remission of their sins, and having peace of conscience" (Mosiah 4:2–3).

5. Finally, we attend carefully to Nephi's words regarding the tree: "And it came to pass that I beheld that the rod of iron, which my father had seen, was the word of God, which led to *the fountain of living waters, or to the tree of life*; which waters are a representation of the love of God; and I also beheld that the tree of life was a representation of the love of God" (1 Nephi 11:25; italics added). The "fountain of living waters," or "waters of life"—linked to the tree of life very often in the literature of the ancient Near East (compare Revelation 22:1–2)[20]—would seem to symbolize the cooling draft available through him alone whose words and works are as an oasis in the desert of the world. "Whosoever drinketh of the water that I shall give him shall never thirst," Jesus said to the Samaritan woman; "but the water that I shall give him shall be in him a well of water springing up into everlasting life" (John 4:14). Finally, in dramatizing the sins of Judah in Lehi's day, the Lord Jehovah spoke to Jeremiah: "For my people have committed two evils; they have forsaken *me the fountain of living waters*, and hewed them out cisterns, broken cisterns, that can hold no water" (Jeremiah 2:13; italics added).

CONCLUSION

It has wisely been observed that what a person thinks of Christ will largely determine what kind of a person he will be. How then could one utilize his time more profitably than by seriously studying the Book of

Mormon, a book whose primary purpose is to reveal and testify of Jesus Christ? We learn from its title page that the Book of Mormon has been preserved and delivered through prophets to us in this day for "the convincing of the Jew and Gentile that JESUS is the CHRIST, the ETERNAL GOD, manifesting himself unto all nations" (compare 2 Nephi 26:12). True to its central theme, and with Christocentric consistency, the Nephite prophets talk of him, preach of him, prophesy of him, and rejoice in him, that all of us might know to what source we may look for a remission of our sins (see 2 Nephi 25:26). Salvation is in Christ. Of that central verity the Book of Mormon leaves no doubt. "And my soul delighteth in proving unto my people," Nephi exulted, "that save Christ should come all men must perish. For if there be no Christ there be no God; and if there be no God we are not, for there could have been no creation. *But there is a God,*" Nephi boldly proclaimed, *"and he is Christ"* (2 Nephi 11:6–7; italics added). The witness has been borne, and thus the testament is in force.

NOTES

1. Joseph Smith, *Teachings of the Prophet Joseph Smith*, sel. Joseph Fielding Smith (Salt Lake City: Deseret Book Co., 1976), p. 194.
2. Ezra Taft Benson, in Conference Report, April 1975, p. 97.
3. This appropriate subtitle for the Book of Mormon was announced to the Church by Elder Boyd K. Packer in the 152d Semiannual General Conference of the Church. See Conference Report, October 1982, p. 75.
4. F. F. Bruce, *The New Testament Documents: Are They Reliable?* (Grand Rapids, Michigan: William B. Eerdmans Publishing Co., 1974), p. 33.
5. Bruce R. McConkie, *Mormon Doctrine*, 2d ed. (Salt Lake City: Bookcraft, 1966), p. 208.
6. For a discussion of the "gulf" separating the righteous in paradise from the wicked in hell (see 1 Nephi 12:18; 15:28; 2 Nephi 1:13; Helaman 3:29), see Robert L. Millet and Joseph Fielding McConkie, *The Life Beyond* (Salt Lake City: Bookcraft, 1986), pp. 21–24, 179.
7. It may be that the Holy Ghost appeared in person at the baptism of Jesus, but there is no reference to his conversing with anyone. See Matthew 3:13–17; *Teachings of the Prophet Joseph Smith*, pp. 275–76.
8. Sidney B. Sperry, *Answers to Book of Mormon Questions* (Salt Lake City: Bookcraft, 1967), pp. 27–30; see also Sperry's *Book of Mormon Compendium* (Salt Lake City: Bookcraft, 1968), pp. 116–18.
9. James E. Talmage, *The Articles of Faith* (Salt Lake City: Deseret Book Co., 1975), pp. 159–60. See also Marion G. Romney, in Conference Report, April 1974, p. 131.
10. "Can we speak too highly of her whom the Lord has blessed above all women? There was only one Christ, and there is only one Mary. Each was noble and great in

Chapter 2—The Condescension of God

preexistence, and each was foreordained to the ministry he or she performed. We cannot but think that the Father would choose the greatest female spirit to be the mother of his Son, even as he chose the male spirit like unto him to be the Savior" (Bruce R. McConkie, *The Mortal Messiah: From Bethlehem to Calvary*, 4 vols. [Salt Lake City: Deseret Book Co., 1979–81], 1:326–27, n. 4).

11. Bruce R. McConkie, "Knowest Thou the Condescension of God?" in *Brigham Young University Speeches of the Year*, 16 December 1969 (Provo, Utah: Brigham Young University Press, 1969), pp. 3–4.

12. Bruce R. McConkie, *The Mortal Messiah*, 1:314–15.

13. Ezra Taft Benson, *Come unto Christ* (Salt Lake City: Deseret Book Co., 1983), p. 4.

14. It may also be that Joseph Smith altered these verses to make certain that no reader—member or nonmember—would confuse the Latter-day Saint understanding of the Father and the Son with that of other Christian denominations, particularly the Roman Catholic Church. See an article by Oliver Cowdery, "Trouble in the West," in *Latter Day Saints' Messenger and Advocate*, I (April 1835), p. 105.

15. For a more detailed discussion on the roles of both members of the Godhead, see my paper titled "The Ministry of the Father and the Son," delivered at the First Annual Book of Mormon Symposium (1985), in Paul R. Cheesman, ed., *The Book of Mormon: The Keystone Scripture* (Provo: BYU Religious Studies Center, 1988) pp. 44–72.

16. Joseph Smith spoke the following just eleven days before his death: "I have always declared God to be a distinct personage, Jesus Christ a separate and distinct personage from God the Father, and that the Holy Ghost was a distinct personage and a Spirit: and these three constitute three distinct personages and three Gods" (*Teachings*, p. 370).

17. Joseph Smith, *Lectures on Faith* (Salt Lake City: Deseret Book Co., 1985), 5:2.

18. Bruce R. McConkie, *The Promised Messiah: The First Coming of Christ* (Salt Lake City: Deseret Book Co., 1978), p. 378.

19. It is instructive to consider the language used in this verse: the love of God that "*sheddeth* itself abroad," instead of "*spreadeth* itself abroad," as we might expect Nephi to have said.

20. See John M. Lundquist, "The Common Temple Ideology of the Ancient Near East," in *The Temple in Antiquity*, ed. Truman G. Madsen (Provo, Utah: Religious Studies Center, Brigham Young University, 1984), pp. 53–76.

The Brass Plates: Past, Present, and Future

The Book of Mormon bears testimony of the critical nature of record keeping and particularly of the necessity for scriptural records in the development and preservation of a civilization. One of the earliest but most poignant lessons of the Nephite record is the power of scriptural sources to prevent a nation from dwindling and perishing through both illiteracy and unbelief (1 Nephi 4:13; Omni 1:17). King Benjamin explained to his sons that "were it not for these [brass] plates, which contain these records and these commandments, we must have suffered in ignorance, even at this present time, not knowing the mysteries of God" (Mosiah 1:3). Alma likewise explained to his son Helaman that the brass plates "have enlarged the memory of this people, yea, and convinced many of the error of their ways, and brought them to the knowledge of their God unto the salvation of their souls" (Alma 37:8).

The brass plates are an integral part of the story and message of the Book of Mormon. Nephi killed a man to obtain possession of the plates and was instructed that in so doing he had helped to achieve righteous purposes (1 Nephi 4:13). The brass plates contained the Pentateuch and law of Moses, thus tying the Nephites to their Old World kinsmen in both cultural practice and belief (1 Nephi 4:15–16). The brass plates contained, in addition, a listing of the fathers back through Joseph of old (1 Nephi 5:14), thus linking the Lehite colony genealogically with Abraham, Isaac, and Jacob and thereby perpetuating the patriarchal covenant (the "promises made to the fathers") in a new hemisphere. Finally, the brass plates contained a more extensive account of Old Testament peoples and events (1 Nephi 13:23), precious remnants of which are to be found in the Book of Mormon and in the Prophet Joseph Smith's translation of the King James Version of the Bible.

Inasmuch as there has been little serious research published on the nature and content of the brass plates, this chapter will seek to (1) show relationships between these plates and the Old Testament record as we now have it; and (2) accent some of the particular contributions of the writings of the brass plates to our understanding of peoples and events of antiquity, noting especially how it is that many of those contributions compare with the Joseph Smith Translation (JST), an additional latter-day revelatory source of knowledge of biblical matters.

BIBLICAL MATTERS IN THE BOOK OF MORMON

Book of Mormon prophets make numerous references to what we would call Old Testament matters. There can be no doubt that the knowledge of many of these things came through the information contained on the brass plates. We definitely know this to be true in those instances wherein the brass plates or the prophets of the brass plates are mentioned specifically. We might also suppose that in those cases in which the brass plates are not mentioned but in which new or unique details are given in the Book of Mormon pertaining to biblical events, the speakers or writers are drawing upon an additional source, of which the brass plates are a prime candidate. At the same time, we cannot overlook the very real possibility that oral or written traditions of events or experiences of biblical antiquity were perpetuated from the beginning of Nephite history by those—such as Lehi or his family—who would have been a part of and thus aware of Israelite history. Finally, we must keep in mind that the prophets in the Book of Mormon may have on occasion received an independent revelation from the Lord regarding the lives and works of their prophetic predecessors.

There are a number of occasions in the Book of Mormon story in which individuals refer to or quote from other records containing information about biblical persons or events. It is conceivable that some of these records were copied from the brass plates, while other documents were of ancient origin or came by special revelation. "And now there are many records kept of the proceedings of this people," Mormon wrote, "by many of this people, which are particular and very large, concerning them. But behold, a hundredth part of the proceedings of this people . . . cannot be contained in this work. But behold, there are many books and many records of every kind, and they have been kept chiefly by the Nephites" (Helaman 3:13–15). Surely this statement of Mormon would have reference to scriptures; it is inconceivable that the one set of brass plates was the only scriptural record available to the Nephite people.

Just before his death, Abinadi took occasion to read to the priests of Noah the Ten Commandments from a scriptural source; it may well be that he read also from Isaiah's greatest messianic prophecy (Mosiah 12:11–24; 14:1–12). Likewise, "when Aaron [the son of Mosiah] saw that the king [the father of Lamoni] would believe his words, *he began from the creation of Adam, reading the scriptures unto the king*" (Alma 22:12; italics added). Alma and Amulek taught the gospel with power to the people of Ammonihah, and as a result of their preaching, many believed their words "and began to repent, and to *search the scriptures*." The reaction of the hardhearted of the city was, however, unrestrained in its evil intensity: "And they brought their wives and children together, and whosoever believed or had been taught to believe in the word of God they caused that they should be cast into the fire; and they also brought forth their records which contained the holy scriptures, and cast them into the fire also, that they might be burned and destroyed by fire" (Alma 14:1, 8; italics added).

We will now consider some illustrations of biblical characters or events discussed in the Book of Mormon and will later note particular insights from the brass plates.

• Both Lehi and Alma spoke of *Adam, Eve*, and the events surrounding the expulsion from the Garden of Eden (2 Nephi 2:18–25; Alma 12:22–27; 42:2–10).

• Amulek made brief mention to the people of Ammonihah of *Noah* and the flood (Alma 10:22).

• Amaleki alluded to the escape of the Jaredites at the time of the *Tower of Babel* and the confusion of tongues (Omni 1:22).

• Jacob taught the people concerning *Abraham* and explained that the sacrifice of Isaac was but a type and shadow of the coming sacrifice of the Lord Jesus Christ (Jacob 4:5). Alma spoke of Abraham paying tithes to Melchizedek (Alma 13:15), while Nephi, the son of Helaman, made reference to Abraham's messianic prophecies (Helaman 8:16–17).

• Alma spoke at some length about the successful ministry of the great high priest *Melchizedek* and how it was that this man established peace in the land of Salem (Alma 13:14–19).

• Captain Moroni related many of the words of *Jacob* (Israel) before the latter's death and focused upon Jacob's prophecies regarding the destiny of his seed (Alma 46:24–26).

• Lehi quoted many of the prophecies of *Joseph* of old regarding Moses, the Savior, and a choice latter-day seer (2 Nephi 3).

• *Moses* is an ancient prophetic personality to whom the Nephite prophets made repeated allusion in the Book of Mormon; sayings and events from the life of the great lawgiver were constantly utilized as object lessons in their teachings. Nephi spoke of the command to Moses to lead the children of Israel out of Egyptian bondage (1 Nephi 17:24); Israelite rebellion against Moses (1 Nephi 17:30, 42); Moses and the brazen serpent (2 Nephi 25:20; see also Alma 33:19; Helaman 8:14–15); and Moses' prophecies of the coming Messiah (1 Nephi 22:20–21). Abinadi spoke of the commandments given to Moses on the mount and of Moses' messianic utterances (Mosiah 12:33; 13:33). The prophet-editor Mormon stated that Abinadi's face shone with the glory of God even as Moses' face had shone when Moses descended from the holy mount (Mosiah 13:5). Finally, Mormon wrote that the prophet Alma was "taken up by the Spirit, or buried by the hand of the Lord, even as Moses" (Alma 45:19).

• Nephi spoke to Laman and Lemuel of the *conquest* of the land of Canaan by the Israelites and of how the Lord allowed the children of Israel to displace the "children of the land" (1 Nephi 17:32–34).

• *David and Solomon* are mentioned in the Book of Mormon but not in positive terms. Jacob warned the Nephites against attempting to justify their immoralities via reference to the practices of David and Solomon, each of whom eventually displeased the Lord through taking unauthorized plural wives (Jacob 1:15; 2:23–24). Nephi also instructed his readers that he had built a temple. It was "after the manner of the temple of Solomon save it were not built of so many precious things," and yet "the manner of the construction was like unto the temple of Solomon" (2 Nephi 5:16).

• The Nephite prophets quoted extensively from *Isaiah* because (1) this prophet's love for and testimony of the Savior are so evident; and (2) Isaiah spoke so eloquently of the scattering, gathering, and destiny of the house of Israel, of which the Nephites were an important branch (1 Nephi 19:23; 2 Nephi 6:4–5).

THE NATURE OF THE BRASS PLATES

There is no specific reference in the Book of Mormon about the origins of the brass plates. Nephi explained that "Laban also was a descendant of Joseph, wherefore he and his fathers had kept the records [the brass plates]" (1 Nephi 5:16). Exactly how long before the time of Laban the brass records were begun is unknown. The record was probably kept in the tribe of Ephraim of Joseph, and thus Laban may well have been of the tribe of Ephraim (See Genesis 48:5, 13–20; 1 Chronicles 5:1–2). In suggesting how it was that the families of Ephraim and Manasseh (of whom Ishmael and Lehi were descendants) came to settle in Jerusalem, Sidney B. Sperry wrote:

"The Northern Kingdom of Israel fell to the Assyrians when its capital of Samaria capitulated to Sargon II in 722 B.C. The forebears of Laban may have fled to Jerusalem to prevent the sacred records from falling into alien hands. Lehi's grandfather or great-grandfather may have left his northern home for Jerusalem in order to prevent his children from intermarrying and making religious compromises with the foreigners brought into the land by the Assyrians." Brother Sperry then asked the following question in regard to this matter: "What happened to the keeping of sacred records when the Israelites became sharply divided on political grounds—so much so that the two nations were enemies?" He then suggested an answer:

> The prophets in both nations probably paid little attention to the political lines of division, but it is improbable that all of them had their words recorded in the scriptures of both nations. From the time of the division until the fall of the Northern Kingdom in 722 B.C., the brass plates may well have been the official scripture of the ten tribes. It is probable that some prophets wrote on these plates whose writings may not have been recorded on the records kept in Judah. Were Zenos, Zenock, Neum, and Ezias (1 Nephi 19:10; Helaman 8:20) among them? They were all Hebrew prophets known to the Nephites, but their names do not appear in our current Old Testament. It is also possible that the writings of some prophets in Judah were not placed on the brass plates during the period under consideration, but of this we have no way of knowing.[1]

The fact that Lehi's genealogy could be traced back to Joseph— specifically to Manasseh (Alma 10:3)—also implies that the record had its origins in the northern kingdom, rather than in Judah in the south (1 Nephi 3:3, 12; 5:14–16). In one of the prophecies of Zenos are found these words: "And *as for those who are at Jerusalem* . . ." (1 Nephi 19:13; italics added), suggesting that Zenos was speaking from somewhere other than the south. Further, note Mormon's words concerning the prophets Zenos and Zenock: "Behold, I say unto you, Yea, many have testified of these things [signs surrounding the death of Christ] at the coming of Christ, and were slain because they testified of these things. Yea, the prophet Zenos did testify of these things, and also Zenock spake concerning these things, because *they testified particularly concerning us, who are the remnant of their seed*" (3 Nephi 10:15–16; italics added). This passage is a fairly convincing statement that Zenos and Zenock were both of the tribe of Joseph.

The nonbiblical prophets mentioned in the Book of Mormon (whose prophecies we suppose were drawn from the brass plates) are named as Zenos, Zenock, Neum, and Ezias. Other than the fact that they lived "since the days of Abraham" (Helaman 8:19), we know very little, if anything, about these men—their backgrounds, places of residence, and time of their ministries—and are only aware of their existence because their words or works are in many cases mentioned in passing by Nephite leaders. Of *Ezias* we know only that he prophesied of the coming of the Messiah (Helaman 8:20). *Neum* spoke prophetically of the crucifixion of the Son of God (1 Nephi 19:10). *Zenock* bore repeated witness of the Savior: that redemption would come only in and through the atoning sacrifice and death of Christ (Helaman 8:18–20; 3 Nephi 10:16); that he would be lifted up by wicked men (1 Nephi 19:10); and that the anger of the Father was kindled against those who do not recognize the cost of the Lord's atonement. Note Zenock's words: "Thou art angry, O Lord, with this people, because they will not understand thy mercies which thou hast bestowed upon them because of thy Son." Because of the poignancy of Zenock's messianic witness, he was put to death (Alma 33:15–17).

We have more details of the oracles of the prophet *Zenos* than any of the other nonbiblical prophets of the brass plates. Nephi and Jacob quoted Zenos extensively (1 Nephi 19, 22; Jacob 5), and Alma utilized the words of Zenos on worship and prayer in speaking to the Zoramites (Alma 33:3–11). "I do not think I overstate the matter," said Elder Bruce R. McConkie, "when I say that next to Isaiah himself—who is the prototype, pattern, and model for all the prophets—there was not a greater prophet in all Israel than Zenos. And our knowledge of his inspired writings is limited to the quotations and paraphrasing summaries found in the Book of Mormon."² Nephi, the son of Helaman, explained that because of Zenos' testimony of the Redeemer, Zenos was slain by unbelievers (Helaman 8:19). Particular doctrinal contributions of these prophets to our understanding of ancient times will be considered later in this chapter.

THE BRASS PLATES: AN EGYPTIAN RECORD

In explaining to his sons the importance of record keeping (and especially the importance of the brass plates in the preservation of the Nephites), King Benjamin said, "For it were not possible that our father, Lehi, could have remembered all these things, to have taught them to his children, except it were for the help of these plates; for *he having been taught in the language of the Egyptians therefore he could read these engravings*, and teach them to his children" (Mosiah 1:4; italics added). It is difficult to know exactly what is meant when King Benjamin indicated that the brass plates were written in Egyptian. In speaking on this matter, one Latter-day Saint scholar has written that the plates "were almost certainly not started until after the flood and the tower of Babel, as there was no Egyptian language before these events. The brass plates were probably not started until after the Israelites went down into Egypt in the days of Joseph, although the writers on these plates may have had access to records that had been written earlier."³

First of all, perhaps the phrase "language of the Egyptians" in the above verse means the same thing that Nephi meant when he spoke of the language of his father (and thus the language of the Book of Mormon) as consisting of "the learning of the Jews and the language of the Egyptians" (1 Nephi 1:2). That is to say, the Nephite record reflected the Hebrew culture and background of the Jews but was written in Egyptian characters.⁴ In the present context, then, the brass plates may have been records of Hebrew prophets and their prophecies, all recorded in an Egyptian script. According to Sperry:

> Every reader of the Nephite record has observed the large number of quotations of the text of Isaiah, which were taken from the brass plates. Now it must be remembered that Isaiah was a Hebrew prophet and an advisor at the royal court in Jerusalem. Were his sermons given in Egyptian? Common sense says not. Otherwise we have to assume that they were translated into Egyptian and copied on the brass plates. . . .

Chapter 3—The Brass Plates: Past, Present, and Future

> Doesn't it seem unreasonable to believe that the sermons of the Hebrew prophets, down to and including Jeremiah (1 Nephi 5:13), which were delivered in Hebrew, would be translated into Egyptian and then copied onto the brass plates—itself a record kept for the benefit of Hebrews? . . . The Hebrew scriptures on the brass plates evidently became well known in the Nephite nation, but nowhere is the statement made that they were translated from Egyptian into the Nephite language—that is, into Hebrew.

Professor Sperry then remarked: "The writer is frank to say that he sees little evidence that our present English text of the Book of Mormon betrays having been translated from an Egyptian original; on the other hand traces of a Hebrew original seem abundant."[5]

Secondly, it may be that only a portion of the brass plates was written in Egyptian. We know that the Israelites spent centuries in Egyptian bondage. Joseph, the great-grandson of Abraham, spent a total of ninety-three years in Egypt and surely would have become proficient in the language of the Pharaohs. Moses, the author-editor of the Pentateuch, spent the first forty years of his life in Egypt and "was learned in all the wisdom of the Egyptians" (Acts 7:22). "We . . . suppose that [Moses] copied or condensed the historical portions of Genesis from the writings of Noah, Melchizedek, Abraham, and the patriarchs. The fourteenth and fiftieth chapters of Genesis, both as restored by Joseph Smith, must have been written respectively by Melchizedek and Joseph (the son of Jacob) in the first instance."[6] A second possibility, then, is that the first five books of Moses were written in Egyptian and that the historical books and prophecies of such notable personalities as Isaiah and Jeremiah were given and recorded in Hebrew. Lehi's knowledge of Egyptian would thus have allowed him to read and pass on the sacred knowledge contained in Moses' first five books—the story of the birth and development of the nation of Israel.

In speaking to his rebellious brothers, Nephi declared: "It is wisdom in God that we should obtain these records [brass plates], that we may preserve unto our children the language of our fathers" (1 Nephi 3:19). In the light of the discussion above, it may be that the Nephites felt the need to preserve the Hebrew language, the Egyptian language (script), or both. So far as the Lehite colony was concerned, such a preservation would serve to do more than remind this American branch of Israel of its illustrious past—it would, as indicated earlier, prove essential in maintaining both intellectual and spiritual literacy (1 Nephi 4:13; Omni 1:17).

SOME SPECIFIC CONTRIBUTIONS TO BIBLICAL UNDERSTANDING

We will now consider a number of passages from the Book of Mormon wherein details concerning specific biblical peoples or events are elucidated. We will note those that come directly from the brass plates, and also attend to those others whose sources are not given directly.

As an important part of his prophetic experience, Nephi was shown in vision the coming forth of the Bible—a book that "proceedeth out of the mouth of a Jew," even "a record of the Jews, which contains the covenants of the Lord" as well as "many of the prophecies of the holy prophets" (1 Nephi 13:23). He also beheld that many plain and precious truths and many matters of eternal import were kept back by a great and abominable church whose motives were malicious (verse 34). It is in the context of this vision of the future that Nephi's angelic guide made the instructive observation that the Bible "*is a record like unto the engravings which are on the plates of brass, save there are not so many*" (verse 23; italics added). It is from this statement, as well as from a number of examples in the Book of Mormon of singular and unique extra-biblical contributions, that we conclude that the plates of brass were more extensive than the Bible and thus contained materials that have not survived the centuries and the precarious transmission process of biblical manuscripts.

1. *The Ministry of the Messiah*. One of the marvels of the Restoration is the divine perspective provided by the flood of intelligence that has come through the Prophet Joseph Smith and his successors. Among the gems of truth that have been revealed to the Latter-day Saints is the nature of Christ's eternal gospel, the realization that Christian prophets have taught Christian doctrines and administered Christian ordinances since the days of Adam. A revelation given at the time of the organization of the restored Church explained that "as many as would believe and be baptized in [Christ's] holy name, and endure in faith to the end, should be saved—not only those who believed after he came in the meridian of time, in the flesh, but *all those from the beginning, even as many as were before he came*, who believed in the words of the holy prophets, who spake as they were inspired by the gift of the Holy Ghost,

who truly testified of him in all things, should have eternal life" (D&C 20:25–26; italics added).

In this regard, Elder McConkie noted that "what interests us more than the books included on the brass plates is the tone and tenor and general approach to the gospel and to salvation that they set forth. *They are gospel oriented and speak of Christ and the various Christian concepts which the world falsely assumes to have originated with Jesus and the early apostles.*"[7] Whereas the biblical prophecies of the Christ are missing, or at best veiled, the prophets of the brass plates are bold in testifying of the coming of Jesus Christ and are specific as to his ministry. Note the words of Nephi concerning the time of the death of Christ:

> And the God of our fathers, who were led out of Egypt, out of bondage, and also were preserved in the wilderness by him, yea, the God of Abraham, and of Isaac, and the God of Jacob, yieldeth himself, according to the words of the angel, as a man, into the hands of wicked men, to be lifted up, according to the words of Zenock, and to be crucified, according to the words of Neum, and to be buried in a sepulchre, according to the words of Zenos, which he spake concerning the three days of darkness, which should be a sign given of his death. . . .
>
> For thus spake the prophet [Zenos?]: The Lord God surely shall visit all the house of Israel at that day, some with his voice, because of their righteousness, unto their great joy and salvation, and others with the thunderings and the lightnings of his power, by tempest, by fire, and by smoke, and vapor of darkness, and by the opening of the earth, and by mountains which shall be carried up.
>
> And all these things must surely come, saith the prophet Zenos. And the rocks of the earth must rend; and because of the groanings of the earth, many of the kings of the isles of the sea shall be wrought upon by the Spirit of God, to exclaim: The God of nature suffers. (1 Nephi 19:10–12.)

Zenos and Zenock presented a view of the Godhead that is consistent with the knowledge revealed to the Prophet Joseph Smith and that therefore established the distinct personalities of the Father and the Son and the separate functions of each. This knowledge, restored through the Book of Mormon, reaffirms that the correct idea of the nature of God was had anciently. Alma and his missionary colleagues had been working strenuously to build faith in Christ within the hearts of their listeners, the Zoramites. The poorer Zoramites, having been dismissed from the synagogues because of their poverty, desired to know how they were to plant the seed of faith in Jesus Christ when in fact they had no place to assemble. Alma assured these people that appropriate worship of God does not require an elaborate hall of assembly nor presuppose a particular setting. He then said: "If ye suppose that ye cannot worship God [as you are now], ye do greatly err, and *ye ought to search the scriptures*; if ye suppose that they have taught you this, ye do not understand them."

Alma then proceeded to quote at length from Zenos a sermon dealing with worship and prayer. This beautiful statement is itself a prayer and dramatizes the fact that God is eager to hear all prayers—all uttered in the wilderness, in the fields, in closets, in houses, and prayers offered by the rejected and disconsolate. Indeed, Zenos testified unto the Lord: "Thou are merciful unto thy children when they cry unto thee, to be heard of thee and not of men." And then, emphasizing the centrality of Jesus as the Advocate and Mediator for men, Zenos continued: "And thou didst hear me because of mine afflictions and my sincerity; and *it is because of thy Son that thou hast been thus merciful unto me*, therefore I will cry unto thee in all mine afflictions, for in thee is my joy; for *thou hast turned thy judgments away from me, because of thy Son*." Alma asked the Zoramites, "Do ye believe those scriptures which have been written by them of old?" Alma then quoted from a written record of Zenock, who said: "Thou art angry, O Lord, with this people, because they will not understand *thy mercies which thou hast bestowed upon them because of thy Son*" (Alma 33:1–16; italics added).

2. *The Destiny of Israel.* One of the prominent themes of the prophet Zenos (as given in the Book of Mormon) was the scattering and gathering and destiny of the house of Israel. Zenos, like the Nephites who came after him, taught clearly that the rejection of Christ and his gospel leads to the scattering of persons and nations, while the acceptance of the true Messiah and true Church results in being gathered by the Lord into the true fold (2 Nephi 9:1–2; 10:3–7). We cannot help but suppose that Nephi, who "makes a better exposition of the scattering and gathering of Israel than do Isaiah, Jeremiah, and Ezekiel combined,"[8] was greatly influenced in his views on this doctrinal matter by the writings of Zenos. In 1 Nephi 19, Nephi refers to the prophecies of Zenos regarding the rejection of the Messiah by the Jews:

"And as for those who are at Jerusalem, saith the prophet, they shall be scourged by all people, because they crucify the God of Israel, and turn their hearts aside." Because they have turned their hearts aside, he continues, "they shall wander in the flesh, and perish, and become a hiss and a byword, and be hated among all nations." They shall remain in this scattered state, Zenos taught, until they repent and receive their Lord and Redeemer. "Then will [the Lord] remember the covenants which he made to their fathers," the patriarchal promises made to Abraham, Isaac, Jacob, and their posterity (1 Nephi 19:13–16).

There is no finer statement in all of holy writ as to God's infinite love and patience with Israel than the allegory of Zenos (Jacob 5). Jacob, the brother of Nephi, delivered this metaphorical marvel—unfolded this "mystery" (see Romans 11:25; 16:25; Ephesians 3:3)—to his people as a means of dramatizing Jehovah's tender regard for his chosen people over the millennia of their existence. "How merciful is our God unto us," Jacob exclaimed in retrospect, "for he remembereth the house of Israel, both roots and branches; and he stretches forth his hands unto them all the day long." In pleading fashion, Jacob applied the symbolism of the allegory and encouraged his people to "cleave unto God as he cleaveth unto you" (Jacob 6:4–5). It may well be that Paul the apostle was drawing upon his knowledge of the allegory of Zenos when he wrote his epistle to the Saints at Rome:

> And if some of the branches be broken off, and thou, being a wild olive tree, wert graffed [grafted, or "come to the knowledge of the true Messiah"—1 Nephi 10:14] in among them, and with them partakest of the root and fatness of the olive tree;
>
> Boast not against the branches. But if thou boast, thou bearest not the root, but the root thee.
>
> Thou wilt say then, The branches were broken off [that is, the natural branches of the house of Israel have been scattered because of their lack of loyalty to the truth], that I might be graffed in.
>
> Well; because of unbelief they were broken off, and thou standest by faith. Be not highminded, but fear:
>
> For if God spared not the natural branches, take heed lest he also spare not thee. (Romans 11:17–21.)

The very fact that Jacob chose to take the time (and provide the space) on the small plates to record this lengthy allegory—constituting by far the longest chapter in the Book of Mormon—is a witness to the critical nature of the undergirding message contained therein. Zenos' masterwork helps to demonstrate convincingly to the house of Israel "what great things the Lord hath done for their fathers; and that they may know the covenants of the Lord, that they are not cast off forever" (title page of Book of Mormon).

3. *Nephi, Malachi, and Zenos.* In the midst of his prophetic commentary upon the writings of Isaiah (Isaiah 48–49), Nephi said: "For behold, saith the prophet, the time cometh speedily that Satan shall have no more power over the hearts of the children of men; *for the day soon cometh that all the proud and they who do wickedly shall be as stubble; and the day cometh that they must be burned*" (1 Nephi 22:15, italics added). Later in Nephi's sermonizing we find Nephi discussing the wicked, "in fine, all those who belong to the kingdom of the devil." These are they, according to Nephi, "who need fear, and tremble, and quake; they are those who must be brought low in the dust; *they are those who must be consumed as stubble*; and this is according to the words of the prophet. And the time cometh speedily that *the righteous must be led up as calves of the stall*, and the Holy One of Israel must reign in dominion, and might, and power, and great glory" (1 Nephi 22:23–24; italics added; compare Malachi 4:1).

A number of years later, Nephi prophesied concerning the coming of the Savior to the Americas: "Wherefore, *all those who are proud, and that do wickedly, the day that cometh shall burn them up, saith the Lord of Hosts, for they shall be as stubble*." The righteous, on the other hand, "are they which shall not perish. But *the Son of righteousness shall appear unto them; and he shall heal them*, and they shall have peace with him" (2 Nephi 26:4, 8–9; italics added). Again, note Malachi's words: "*But unto you that fear my name shall the Sun of righteousness arise with healing in his wings; and ye shall go forth, and grow up as calves of the stall*" (Malachi 4:2, italics added). Inasmuch as Nephi's oracle was uttered some two hundred years before the time of Malachi, how do we explain the similarity of language? Elder Bruce R. McConkie taught in 1984:

> Our understanding of the prophetic word will be greatly expanded if we know how one prophet quotes another, usually without acknowledging his source.
> Either Isaiah or Micah copied the prophetic words of the other relative to the mountain of the Lord's house being established in the last days with all nations flowing thereto. Their ministries overlapped, but we assume that the lesser Micah copied from the greater

Isaiah and then appended some words of his own about the Millennial Era.

Some unnamed Old Testament prophet, who obviously was Zenos, as the Book of Mormon testifies, spoke of the day when the wicked would be destroyed as stubble; when the righteous would be "led up as calves of the stall;" when Christ should "rise from the dead, with healing in his wings;" and when the Holy One of Israel would then reign on earth.

Malachi, who lived more than two hundred years after Nephi, uses these very expressions in his prophetic writings. *Can we do other than conclude that both Nephi and Malachi had before them the writings of Zenos?*

Once the Lord has revealed his doctrine in precise language to a chosen prophet, there is no reason why he should inspire another prophet to choose the same words in presenting the same doctrine on a subsequent occasion. It is much easier and simpler to quote that which has already been given in perfection. We are all commanded—including the prophets among us—to search the scriptures and thereby learn what other prophets have presented.[9]

4. *The Writings of Isaiah.* Nephi taught his people from the plates of brass "that they might know concerning the doings of the Lord in other lands, among people of old." He indicated to his readers that he read at length from the Pentateuch, but in order that he "might more fully persuade them to believe in the Lord their Redeemer" he did read unto them "that which was written by the prophet Isaiah; for I did liken all scriptures unto us, that it might be for our profit and learning" (1 Nephi 19:22–23).

Two of Isaiah's central messages are (1) the coming ministry of the Messiah; and (2) the destiny of the house of Israel. Just before beginning a long section of chapters in Isaiah (Isaiah 2–14; 2 Nephi 12–24), Nephi wrote concerning Isaiah's witness of the Savior: "And now I, Nephi, write more of the words of Isaiah, for my soul delighteth in his words. For I will liken his words unto my people, and I will send them forth unto all my children, for he verily saw my Redeemer, even as I have seen him. And my brother Jacob, also has seen him as I have seen him." Nephi then concluded: "Wherefore, by the words of three, God hath said, I will establish my word" (2 Nephi 11:2–3). In this regard, one Latter-day Saint scholar has suggested that of more than 400 verses in the Book of Mormon quoting Isaiah, 391 deal in some way with Jesus Christ—his mission or attributes.[10]

33

Jacob taught in regard to Isaiah's second major theme: "And now, behold, I would speak unto you concerning things which are, and which are to come; wherefore, I will read you the words of Isaiah. . . . And now," Jacob continued, "the words which I shall read are they which Isaiah spake concerning all the house of Israel; wherefore, they may be likened unto you [the Nephites], for ye are of the house of Israel. And there are many things which have been spoken by Isaiah which may be likened unto you, because ye are of the house of Israel" (2 Nephi 6:4–5).

Even a superficial perusal of the Book of Mormon (brass plates) text of Isaiah reveals many differences from the Authorized Version. "The text of Isaiah in the Book of Mormon," wrote Sidney B. Sperry, "is not word for word the same as that of the King James Version."

> Of 433 verses of Isaiah in the Nephi record, Joseph Smith modified about 233. Some of the changes made were slight, others were radical. However, 199 verses are word for word the same as the old English version. We therefore freely admit that Joseph Smith may have used the King James Version when he came to the text of Isaiah on the gold plates. As long as the familiar version agreed substantially with the text on the gold plates, he let it pass; when it differed too radically he translated the Nephite version and dictated the necessary changes.[11]

In regard to the differences between the two texts, Brother Sperry also noted:

> The version of Isaiah in the Nephite scripture hews an independent course for itself, as might be expected of a truly ancient and authentic record. It makes additions to the present text in certain places, omits material in others, transposes, makes grammatical changes, finds support at times for its unusual readings in the ancient Greek, Syriac, and Latin versions, and at other times no support at all. In general, it presents phenomena of great interest to the student of Isaiah.[12]

The resurrected Lord gave additional stress to the importance of Isaiah when he said to the righteous Nephites: "A commandment I give unto you that ye search these things diligently; for great are the words of Isaiah. For surely he spake as touching all things concerning my people which are of the house of Israel; therefore it must needs be that he must speak also to the Gentiles. And all things that he spake have been and shall be, even according to the words which he spake" (3 Nephi 23:1–3).

5. *The Prophecies of Jacob (Israel).* There are additional occasions in which the Book of Mormon clarifies or expands our vision with regard to antiquity. As indicated earlier, in many of these passages quoted or referred to by the prophets we learn knowledge gained from the brass plates. In other passages, while the source of the information is not given, we suppose that the supplementary truths were taken from either the brass plates or some similar record. The next two biblical episodes are examples of the latter situation.

General Moroni sought the support of the members of the Church in preparing themselves to defend their rights and families against Lamanite aggressions. After General Moroni prepared the title of liberty and encouraged the people to enter into a solemn covenant to keep the commandments and defend their liberties, the members "cast their garments at the feet of Moroni, saying: We covenant with our God, that we shall be destroyed . . . if we shall fall into transgression; yea, he may cast us at the feet of our enemies, even as we have cast our garments at thy feet to be trodden under foot, if we shall fall into transgression." Moroni then reminded the people that they were descendants of Joseph of old, the one whose "coat of many colors" had been rent by his scheming brothers. He caused them to acknowledge that should they prove disloyal to the Lord and his commandments, their garments and freedoms would likewise be rent from them by their enemies, the Lamanites. Moroni then recounted an important prophetic moment from the life of Jacob, the father of Joseph—a moment that is nowhere to be found in our present Old Testament account.

> Yea, let us preserve our liberty as a remnant of Joseph; yea, let us remember the words of Jacob, before his death, for behold, he saw that a part of the remnant of the coat of Joseph was preserved and had not decayed. And he said—Even as this remnant of garment of my son hath been preserved, so shall a remnant of the seed of my son be preserved by the hand of God, and be taken unto himself, while the remainder of the seed of Joseph shall perish, even as the remnant of his garment.
>
> Now behold, this giveth my soul sorrow; nevertheless, my soul hath joy in my son, because of that part of his seed which shall be taken unto God.
>
> Now behold, this was the language of Jacob.

35

Moroni then observed to the Nephites that at least a partial fulfillment of this prophecy of Jacob was to be seen in the faithfulness and waywardness of the Nephite nation—those who kept the commandments would be preserved while those who dissented from the truth would be rent by their enemies (Alma 46:11–27; compare a prophecy by Zenos in Helaman 15:11 concerning the restoration of the Lamanites).

6. *Moses and the Brazen Serpent.* A final example to consider concerns the rebellion of the children of Israel as "they journeyed from mount Hor by the way of the Red Sea, to compass the land of Edom." The constant murmuring of the people of Israel against Moses was punished by the Lord: "And the Lord sent fiery [poisonous] serpents among the people, and they bit the people; and much people of Israel died." Following the supplications of the people for forgiveness and intercession, Moses was instructed by the Lord: "Make thee a fiery serpent, and set it upon a pole: and it shall come to pass, that every one that is bitten, when he looketh upon it, shall live." The report of this incident from the Pentateuch ends simply: "And Moses made a serpent of brass, and put it upon a pole, and it came to pass, that if a serpent had bitten any man, when he beheld the serpent of brass, he lived" (Numbers 21:4–9).

Nephi, in speaking to Laman and Lemuel, added a minute but fascinating detail to the above story. Having explained that Jehovah had led Israel out of Egyptian bondage, Nephi observed: "And [the Lord] did straiten them in the wilderness with his rod; for they hardened their hearts, even as ye have; and the Lord straitened them because of their iniquity. *He sent fiery flying serpents among them;* and after they were bitten he prepared a way that they might be healed; and the labor which they had to perform was to look" (1 Nephi 17:40–41; italics added). Nephi supplied the additional detail that the venomous snakes were fiery *flying* serpents. One scholar who is not a Latter-day Saint has explained:

> We are . . . told of the results of the Lord's anger: venomous snakes are sent (lit. "fiery serpents," cf. KJV; their bite caused the burning sensation of a serious infection). Many kinds of snakes whose bite is dangerous to man and beast are still found in the Sinai peninsula and in the desert south of Palestine. . . . Among the venomous snakes is also the "flying serpent" of Isaiah 14:29; 30:6 (NIV, "darting serpent"), a tree serpent that is still found in Arabia and

Egypt, and which in the popular imagination has become some kind of dragon.[13]

Nephi also pointed out that "because of the simpleness of the way, or the easiness of it, there were many who perished" (1 Nephi 17:41; Alma 37:46). Alma contributed to our understanding of the event the idea that "there were many who were so hardened that they would not look, therefore they perished. Now the reason they would not look is because they did not believe that it would heal them" (Alma 33:20). These particulars are lacking in our presently accepted biblical story.

Of deeper significance yet is the fact that the episode in Numbers is shown via the Book of Mormon to be a marvelous type, an actual historical reality pointing in symbolic fashion beyond itself to an even greater and more profound reality. Alma explained that prophets from the beginning had borne fervent witness of the coming of Christ. "Behold," Alma added, "he was spoken of by Moses; yea, and behold a *type was raised up in the wilderness*, that whosoever would look upon it might live. And many did look and live" (Alma 33:19; italics added). An even stronger statement was made by Nephi, the son of Helaman, as he spoke of Moses' messianic testimony:

> Yea, did he not bear record that the Son of God should come? *And as he lifted up the brazen serpent in the wilderness, even so shall he be lifted up who should come* [see John 3:14].
>
> And as many as should look upon that serpent should live, even so as many as should look upon the Son of God with faith, having a contrite spirit, might live, even unto that life which is eternal. (Helaman 8:14–15; italics added.)

THE BRASS PLATES AND JOSEPH SMITH'S TRANSLATION OF THE BIBLE

As noted earlier, Nephi saw in vision the time when plain and precious truths, as well as many covenants of the Lord, would be taken from the Bible. Fortunately, however, Nephi learned that by means of the truths contained in the Book of Mormon, as well as "other books, which [would come] forth by the power of the lamb" (1 Nephi 13:39), a major doctrinal restoration would commence and thereby bring back that which had been lost. Latter-day Saints would certainly acknowledge the revelations and instructions contained in the Doctrine and

Covenants as fulfilling this prophecy. In addition, Joseph Smith's translation of the Bible (JST) is a godsend to the last dispensation, a means by which ancient scripture has been restored and clarified in modern times. To Sidney Rigdon, the primary scribe in the Bible translation, the Lord explained in 1830 that "the scriptures shall be given, even as they are in mine own bosom, to the salvation of mine own elect" (D&C 35:20).

I have written elsewhere of my conviction regarding the JST as a restoration of ancient texts or events.[14] At this point it is worth noting that there is a fascinating similarity in subject and specific language between the brass plates and the JST. In the words of Robert J. Matthews: "It is very clear that the JST, having received the touch of restoration through the hand of the Prophet of God, resembles the doctrinal content of the brass plates more fully than does the Bible."[15] We will now consider several specific examples wherein the texts of the two works will be compared.

1. *The Fall of Lucifer.* One of the most profound doctrinal sections of the Book of Mormon is a father-son discussion between Lehi and Jacob. For our purposes, the account begins as follows: "And I, Lehi, according to the things which I have read, must needs suppose that an angel of God, *according to that which is written*, had fallen from heaven; wherefore, he became a devil, having sought that which was evil before God. And because he had fallen from heaven, and had become miserable forever, he sought also the misery of all mankind" (2 Nephi 2:17–18; italics added). Biblical references to the fall of Lucifer in premortal times are, of course, scarce (Isaiah 14; Revelation 12) and are only to be recognized and understood as a result of modern revelation on the subject.

The Joseph Smith Translation of Genesis 3:1–5 (also known in our canon of scripture as Moses 4:1–4) is an account of the Grand Council in Heaven during which the plan of the Father was discussed by the spirits, Jehovah was selected and acknowledged as the Savior and Chief Advocate of the plan, and Lucifer was cast from heaven for rebelling against the will of Almighty Elohim. Lehi pointed out that the diabolical one "became a devil, having sought that which was evil before God" (2 Nephi 2:17). The JST is remarkably specific about his malevolent motives: "He came before me [God], saying—Behold, here am I, send me, I will be thy son, and I will redeem all mankind, that one soul shall not be lost, and surely I will do it; wherefore give me thine honor" (Moses 4:1). Regarding Lehi's observation that Satan had "sought also the misery of all mankind" (2 Nephi 2:18), we note from the JST that "he became Satan, yea, even the devil, the father of all lies, to deceive and to blind men, and to lead them captive at his will, even as many as would not hearken to my voice" (Moses 4:4).

2. *Creation, Fall, and Atonement.* From the same chapter in the Book of Mormon (2 Nephi 2), we are able to learn invaluable truths through Lehi's teachings concerning the plan of salvation. Lehi explained to Jacob that "if Adam had not transgressed he would not have fallen, but he would have remained in the Garden of Eden. And *all things which were created must have remained in the same state in which they were after they were created; and they must have remained forever, and had no end*" (2 Nephi 2:22; italics added). The great Nephite patriarch is here alluding to the paradisiacal and Edenic state, the *spiritual* state—a state in which things were not yet subject to death—(see also Alma 11:45; D&C 88:27; 1 Corinthians 15:44)—that existed with regard to man and all forms of life on earth before the Fall. From the Prophet Joseph Smith's inspired translation of Moses' account of the Creation, we learn a similar truth. In speaking of the things on the earth in the morn of creation, the Lord said that "it was spiritual in the day that I created it; for *it remaineth in the sphere in which I, God, created it*" (JST, Genesis 2:11; Moses 3:9; italics added).

Being in an immortal, spiritual state, Adam and Eve "*would have had no children,*" Lehi added, "wherefore they would have remained in a state of innocence, having no joy, for they knew no misery; doing no good, for they knew no sin." After acknowledging the hand of the Omniscient One in the plan of life, Lehi concluded that "*Adam fell that men might be; and men are that they might have joy*" (2 Nephi 2:23–25; italics added). The JST provides an expanded biblical account of Adam and Eve's retrospective thinking in regard to the events in the Garden of Eden. Having learned by the ministry of angels (see Alma 12:29–32; JST, Genesis 4:5–8 [Moses 5:5–8]) of the mission of Messiah and the redemption possible through repentance, Adam blessed God, began to prophesy concerning all the families of the earth, and expressed gratitude for the eternal benefits of the Fall. "And Eve, his wife, heard all these things

39

and was glad, saying: *Were it not for our transgression we never should have had seed, and never should have known good and evil, and the joy of our redemption, and the eternal life which God giveth unto all the obedient"* (JST, Genesis 4:9–11; Moses 5:9–11; italics added). It was Enoch who later observed simply that *"because that Adam fell, we are"* (JST, Genesis 6:49; Moses 6:48; italics added).

Jacob, drawing upon the teachings of his father (and thus the doctrines on the brass plates), taught, "For as death hath passed upon all men, to fulfill the merciful plan of the great Creator, there must needs be a power of resurrection, and *the resurrection must needs come unto man by reason of the fall; and the fall came by reason of transgression*; and because man became fallen they were cut off from the presence of the Lord" (2 Nephi 9:6; italics added). This language is unmistakably close to the divine directive to Adam contained in the inspired translation of Genesis: "Therefore I give unto you a commandment, to teach these things freely unto your children, saying: That *by reason of transgression cometh the fall,* which fall bringeth death, and inasmuch as ye were born into the world by water, and blood, and the spirit, which I have made, and so became of dust a living soul, even so ye must be born again into the kingdom of heaven" (JST, Genesis 6:61–62; Moses 6:58–59; italics added).

3. *The Origin of Secret Combinations.* In the book of Helaman we are introduced to one Kishkumen, the originator among the Nephites of a secret band of men bent upon wealth and power. After the death of Kishkumen, this secret combination continued its escapades of evil under Gadianton and thereafter came to be known as the Gadianton robbers (Helaman 1–2). In writing of this abominable group, Mormon observed that "those secret oaths and covenants [of the Gadianton bands] did not come forth unto Gadianton from the records which were delivered unto Helaman [Alma had been commanded to keep the particulars of these oaths from public knowledge; see Alma 37:27–32]; but behold, they were put into the heart of Gadianton by that same being who did entice our first parents to partake of the forbidden fruit—*Yea, that same being who did plot with Cain, that if he would murder his brother Abel it should not be known unto the world.* And he did plot with Cain and his followers from that time forth" (Helaman 6:26–27; italics added).

The biblical account of the murder of Abel is extremely brief, only six verses long (Genesis 4:3–8), and the only motive for murder is implied—jealousy as a result of the Lord's acceptance of Abel's sacrifice. Further, there is no mention of Satan's involvement in the story. From the JST we gain an insight into Cain's personality as a result of his response to the counsel of his parents and the Lord: "Who is the Lord that I should know him?" We learn further that "Cain loved Satan more than God" and thereby chose to follow the devil and thus reject divine counsel. Cain entered into an oath of secrecy with Satan and became "master of this great secret, that I may murder and get gain. Wherefore Cain was called Master Mahan ["Master Mind"], and he gloried in his wickedness." Others entered into league with Lucifer and perpetuated this perversity. "For, from the days of Cain, there was a secret combination, and their works were in the dark"; therefore, we learn that "the works of darkness began to prevail among all the sons of men" (JST, Genesis 5:5–42; Moses 5:16–55).

4. *The Prophecies of Joseph.* In delivering his parting counsel to his son Joseph, the prophet Lehi took occasion to quote (or read) from the writings of the patriarch Joseph, the one who had been sold into Egypt. In discussing this record, Nephi observed: "And now, I Nephi, speak concerning the prophecies of which my father hath spoken, concerning Joseph, who was carried into Egypt. For behold, he truly prophesied concerning all his seed. And the prophecies which he wrote, there are not many greater. And he prophesied concerning us, and our future generations; and they are written upon the plates of brass" (2 Nephi 4:1–2). Joseph's prophecies (as contained in the Book of Mormon via the brass plates) consist of predictions concerning such matters as (1) the ministry of Moses as a seer and deliverer; (2) the ministry of a "choice seer" of the lineage of Joseph to be raised up in the last days— Joseph Smith; (3) the "growing together" of the writings of Joseph and Judah in order to confound false doctrines, lay down contentions, and establish peace among and bring knowledge to the descendants of Joseph; (4) the choice latter-day seer to be named after his father, his father's name being Joseph; (5) that which comes forth by the hands of the latter-day seer to bring many to salvation; (6) Moses to be given a spokesman; (7) a spokesman to be provided for the representative of the fruit of the loins of Joseph;[16] and (8) many in the last days to remember the covenants of the Lord unto the ancient fathers (2 Nephi 3).

These prophecies of Joseph have no biblical counterpart whatso-ever. The JST contains an account of these prophecies with many verses almost identical to that given in the Book of Mormon. Additional details contained in the JST are (1) the Messiah is known as Shiloh (Genesis 49:10); and (2) the name of the spokesman of Moses is to be Aaron. It is interesting to note that in the JST account there is no mention of a scribe for the "choice seer" of the latter days (JST, Genesis 50:24–35).

5. *Abraham's Knowledge of the Messiah*. Nephi, the son of Helaman, taught clearly that "all the holy prophets, from [Moses'] days even to the days of Abraham," bore fervent witness of the coming of Jesus Christ, the Lord Omnipotent. Nephi then exclaimed: "Yea, and behold, *Abraham saw of his coming, and was filled with gladness and did rejoice*" (Helaman 8:16–17; italics added). Though we have biblical episodes wherein Abraham heard the voice of the Lord and received revelations, we have no single account on record where the "father of the faithful" beheld the Savior in vision. And yet there is evidence in the New Testament of this very thing. Jesus, in speaking to those who opposed him and who claimed special status via their Abrahamic descent, said: "*Your Father Abraham rejoiced to see my day: and he saw it, and was glad*" (John 8:56; italics added). It would appear, therefore, that Abraham had such a prophetic vision but that the episode has been lost from our present biblical collection.

A marvelous restoration of an ancient event is found in the Prophet's translation of the fifteenth chapter of Genesis. The Lord Jehovah had just explained to Abraham concerning his eventual land inheritance in Canaan:

> And Abram said, Lord God, how wilt thou give me this land for an everlasting inheritance?
> And the Lord said, Though thou wast dead, yet am I not able to give it thee?
> And if thou shalt die, yet thou shalt possess it, for the day cometh, that the Son of Man shall live; but how can he live if he be not dead? [reference here seems to be to the doctrine and promise of resurrection] he must first be quickened.
> And it came to pass, that *Abram looked forth and saw the days of the Son of Man, and was glad*, and his soul found rest, and he believed in the Lord; and the Lord counted it unto him for righteousness. (JST, Genesis 15:9–12; italics added.)

Chapter 3—The Brass Plates: Past, Present, and Future

6. *The Ministry of Melchizedek.* In speaking to the people in the city of Ammonihah, Alma and Amulek preached sound and powerful doctrine on such vital matters as the Creation, Fall, Atonement, and Resurrection (Alma 11–12). Then Alma began a sermon on the priesthood and stressed the importance of the high priesthood in attaining the rest of the Lord. As an example of those who had been faithful in times past in magnifying callings in the priesthood (and had thereby been sanctified by the Spirit; see D&C 84:33), Alma referred to Melchizedek and the people of Salem. "Now this Melchizedek," he observed, "was a king over the land of Salem; and his people had waxed strong in iniquity and abomination; yea, they had all gone astray; they were full of all manner of wickedness." Alma then explained that Melchizedek "did establish peace in the land in his days; therefore *he was called the prince of peace,* for he was the king of Salem; and he did reign under his father." And then by way of summary, Alma stated: "Now, there were many before him, and also there were many afterwards, but none were greater; therefore, of him they have more particularly made mention" (Alma 13:1–19; italics added).

It seems that on some scriptural record, the writers prior to Alma had made mention of this king of Salem and had given enough detail of his successful ministry to allow Alma to utilize him as a notable example of what could be done via righteousness. As is commonly known, however, such detail is not to be had in our present Bible. There is passing reference to Melchizedek in Genesis 14 as well as a strange allusion to Melchizedek by Paul in Hebrews 7:3 (Melchizedek is identified as being "without father, without mother, without descent, having neither beginning of days, nor end of life"); but we must turn to the JST to learn specifically of this ancient character. In this inspired restoration we learn that Melchizedek "was a man of faith, who wrought righteousness," one ordained after that order of priesthood that "came, not by man, nor the will of man; neither by father nor mother; neither by beginning of days nor end of years; but of God." This account explains that those who were faithful to the covenant of the high priesthood obtained an oath from God, an immutable promise from the Almighty, that they would have power to subdue the elements and even come up into the presence of God. "And men having this faith, coming up unto this order of God, were," like Enoch the ancient prototype, "translated and taken up

43

into heaven. And now, Melchizedek was a priest of this order; therefore he obtained peace in Salem, and was called the Prince of peace. And his people wrought righteousness, and obtained heaven, and sought for the city of Enoch which God had before taken" (JST, Genesis 14:26–34).

CONCLUSION

Latter-day Saints love the Bible. They cherish the doctrine and stories contained in the Old and New Testaments and feel a deep sense of kinship with the ancients through this book of books. The Bible has done more to enlighten and lift mankind than any other book in earth's history. A modern apostle has taught:

> There are no people on earth who hold the Bible in such high esteem as we do. We believe it, we read and ponder its sayings, we rejoice in the truths it teaches, and we seek to conform our lives to the divine standard it proclaims. But we do not believe, as does evangelical Christianity, that the Bible contains all things necessary for salvation; nor do we believe that God has now taken upon himself the tongue of the dumb which no longer speaks, nor reveals, nor makes known his will to his children.
>
> Indeed, we know that the Bible contains only a sliver, a twig, a leaf, no more than a small branch at most, from the great redwood of revelation that God has given in ages past. There has been given ten thousand times ten thousand more revelation than has been preserved for us in our present Bible. It contains a bucket, a small pail, a few draughts, no more than a small stream at most, out of the great ocean of revealed truth that has come to men in ages more spiritually enlightened than ours.[17]

God has not, however, left us with the Bible alone. Honest truth seekers now have access to timely and timeless truths—a treasure house of knowledge—verities not available to those who are content with what they already have. By means of the record known as the brass plates, that ancient source now available to the world only through the Book of Mormon, we are able to glimpse into the distant past and extract valuable insights to be had in no other way.

As the people of the Church and the world become ready to receive additional light and truth in this regard, more revelation will be forthcoming. After searching the brass plates "from the beginning," Lehi was "filled with the Spirit, and began to prophesy concerning his seed—that *these plates of brass should go forth to all nations, kindreds, tongues, and people who were of his seed.* Wherefore, he said that these plates of brass should never perish; neither should they be dimmed any more by time" (1 Nephi 5:17–19; italics added). One of the ways by which the seed of Lehi is, has been, and will be exposed to the message on the plates of brass is certainly the Book of Mormon. By means of this sacred volume, we are better able to grasp many of the veiled or deficient details in our present Bible.

There is, of course, another way by which the knowledge on the brass plates is to be disseminated—far more extensive in its scope—than through the Book of Mormon. As a part of the "doctrinal restoration"— the unfolding of intelligence and power that began in the spring of 1820 and will continue throughout the Millennium—the brass plates themselves will be restored to the earth and knowledge thereon will be available to all who love the Lord and find joy in his gospel verities. That is to say, "someday the Lord will raise up a prophet, who will also be a seer and a translator, to whom he will give the brass plates that they may be translated for the benefit and blessing of those in all nations."[18] And what a glorious day that will be! Alma's prophetic words to Helaman concerning the destiny of the brass plates show that this record will be sought after and received by more than the seed of Lehi. According to Alma, the brass plates were to be "kept and handed down from one generation to another" among the Nephites "and be kept and preserved by the hand of the Lord" until eventually *they shall go forth unto every nation, kindred, tongue, and people, that they shall know of the mysteries contained therein*" (Alma 37:4; italics added).

Notes

1. Sidney B. Sperry, *The Problems of the Book of Mormon* (Salt Lake City: Bookcraft, 1964), pp. 43–44.
2. Bruce R. McConkie, "The Doctrinal Restoration," in *The Joseph Smith Translation: The Restoration of Plain and Precious Things*, ed. Monte S. Nyman and Robert L. Millet (Provo: Religious Studies Center, Brigham Young University, 1985), p. 17.
3. Daniel H. Ludlow, *A Companion to Your Study of the Book of Mormon* (Salt Lake City: Deseret Book Co., 1976), p. 173.
4. See Sidney B. Sperry, *Book of Mormon Compendium* (Salt Lake City: Bookcraft, 1968), p. 33; John L. Sorenson, *An Ancient American Setting for the Book of Mormon* (Salt Lake City: Deseret Book Co., 1985), pp. 74–76; Bruce R. McConkie, *A New Witness for the Articles of Faith* (Salt Lake City: Deseret Book Co., 1985), p. 448.
5. Sidney B. Sperry, *Our Book of Mormon* (Salt Lake City: Bookcraft, 1947), p. 32.

6. McConkie, *New Witness for the Articles of Faith*, p. 402.

7. McConkie, "Doctrinal Restoration," p. 17; italics added.

8. See Bruce R. McConkie, in Conference Report, October 1983, p. 106.

9. McConkie, "Doctrinal Restoration," pp. 17–18; see also McConkie, *New Witness for the Articles of Faith*, p. 402.

10. Monte S. Nyman, *Great Are the Words of Isaiah* (Salt Lake City: Bookcraft, 1980), p. 7.

11. Sperry, *Problems of the Book of Mormon*, p. 92.

12. Ibid., p. 97; see also Hugh Nibley, *Since Cumorah* (Salt Lake City: Deseret Book Co., 1967), pp. 137–52.

13. A. Noordtzij, *Numbers: Bible Student's Commentary*, trans., Ed van der Maas (Grand Rapids, Michigan: Zondervan Publishing House, 1983), p. 186; for an extended treatment of the incident in Numbers 21, see Robert L. Millet, "Lessons in the Wilderness," in *Studies in Scripture, Vol. 3: The Old Testament, Genesis to 2 Samuel*, ed. Kent P. Jackson and Robert L. Millet (Sandy, Utah: Randall Book Co., 1985), pp. 197–200.

14. See Robert L. Millet, "Joseph Smith's Translation of the Bible: A Historical Overview," in Nyman and Millet, *The Joseph Smith Translation*, pp. 23–49.

15. From "The JST: Historical Source and Doctrinal Companion to the D&C," Church Educational System Ninth Annual Religious Educators' Symposium (The Doctrine and Covenants and History of the Church), 15 August 1985, typescript, p. 19.

16. Elder Bruce R. McConkie has provided a fascinating explanation of 2 Nephi 3:18 regarding the latter-day spokesman. According to Elder McConkie, the person of the lineage of Joseph who would be raised up to write the record of Joseph (the Book of Mormon) is Mormon; the spokesman of the word is Joseph Smith (see *A New Witness for the Articles of Faith*, p. 426).

17. Bruce R. McConkie, "The Bible: A Sealed Book," Eighth Annual Church Education System Religious Educators' Symposium—New Testament Supplement (Salt Lake City: The Church of Jesus Christ of Latter-day Saints, 1984), p. 2.

18. McConkie, "Doctrinal Restoration," p. 16; see also *Mormon Doctrine*, 2d ed. (Salt Lake City: Bookcraft, 1966), p. 103; *The Millennial Messiah: The Second Coming of the Son of Man* (Salt Lake City: Deseret Book Co., 1982), p. 113.

Portrait of an Anti-Christ

President Ezra Taft Benson has instructed that "the Book of Mormon brings men to Christ through two basic means":

> First, it tells in a plain manner of Christ and His gospel. It testifies of His divinity and of the necessity for a Redeemer and the need of our putting trust in Him. It bears witness of the Fall and the Atonement and the first principles of the gospel, including our need of a broken heart and a contrite spirit and a spiritual rebirth. It proclaims we must endure to the end in righteousness and live the moral life of a Saint.
>
> Second, *the Book of Mormon exposes the enemies of Christ.* It confounds false doctrines and lays down contention (See 2 Nephi 3:12.) It fortifies the humble followers of Christ against the evil designs, strategies, and doctrines of the devil in our day. *The type of apostates in the Book of Mormon is similar to the type we have today.* God, with his infinite foreknowledge, so molded the Book of Mormon that we might see the error and know how to combat false educational, political, religious, and philosophical concepts of our time.[1]

Jacob ends a lengthy recitation of and a brief commentary on the allegory of Zenos by pleading with his readers to receive and pay heed to the words of the prophets and traverse carefully that strait and narrow gospel path. "Finally," he concludes, "I bid you farewell, until I shall meet you before the pleasing bar of God, which bar striketh the wicked with awful dread and fear" (Jacob 6:13). This would appear to be a farewell statement, an indication to the reader that Jacob had initially planned to close his record at that point. Subsequently, however, he had an experience worthy of inclusion in a record that would come forth to a cynical and highly secular world—his encounter with Sherem the anti-Christ.

PORTRAIT OF AN ANTI-CHRIST

There are certain characteristics of an anti-Christ, certain patterns of belief and practice that we might expect to find among those who, like Sherem, are bent upon overthrowing the doctrine of Christ. A review of some of these identifying characteristics follows.

They deny the need for Jesus Christ. The first and perhaps the most obvious characterization of an anti-Christ is that he or she denies the reality of or necessity for Jesus Christ. The anti-Christ has partaken of that spirit of rebellion that resulted in the expulsion of a third part of all the children of the Eternal Father in the premortal world. Prior to the meridian of time, the anti-Christ contended that there would be no Christ and that no man had the ability to speak authoritatively concerning future things.

Of Sherem, the Nephite record states that "he began to preach among the people, and to declare unto them that there should be no Christist. . . . that he might overthrow the doctrine of Christ" (Jacob 7:2). The doctrine of Christ is the gospel, the glad tidings that deliverance from death and hell and endless torment is available through the atoning work of Jesus Christ the Lord (see Jacob 7:6; 2 Nephi 31:3; 3 Nephi 27:13–22; D&C 76:40–42). Frequently, as we shall see, the message of the anti-Christ is a denial of man's fallen condition and thus of his need for anyone or anything to liberate him from the mire of mortality.

They use flattery to win disciples. "And [Sherem] preached many things which were flattering unto the people" (Jacob 7:2). To flatter is to soothe or satisfy, to make people feel comfortable. It is to whisper in their ears that all is well. To flatter is also to raise false hopes of an anticipated reward or acquisition.[2] Nehor, a different type of anti-Christ, thus taught that "all mankind should be saved at the last day. . . for the Lord had created all men, and had also redeemed all men; and, in the end, all men should have eternal life" (Alma 1:4).

Characteristically, anti-Christs are worldly-wise; they are properly trained for their persuasive ministry. Sherem was "learned, that he had a perfect knowledge of the language of the people; wherefore, he could use much flattery, and much power of speech, according to the power of the devil" (Jacob 7:4). Anti-Christs are usually glib of tongue and nimble of speech. They are sinister students of human behavior, knowing how to persuade and dissuade, how to attract attention and create a following, and how to make their listeners feel secure and at ease in their carnality. An anti-Christ is ostensibly refined, schooled in rhetoric, and polished in homiletics. He is a peerless preacher of perversion. In Faustian fashion the anti-Christ has sold his soul to the devil: his power is not his own; he is but the pawn of him who in the end does not support his own (see Alma 30:60).

They accuse the Brethren of teaching false doctrine. The devil and his disciples are neither shy nor hesitant about accomplishing their purposes. Some among the legions of Beelzebub are subtle and cunning; others are direct, assertive, and aggressive. Sherem goes directly to the prophet of the Lord—to Jacob—to gain a hearing in an effort to gain a convert. Satan would always rather capture a spiritual general than one of lesser rank. And be it remembered that the Lord himself was not immune from personal confrontation with the evil one (see Matthew 4) and that Christ in turn said to Peter, the chief apostle, "Simon, Simon, behold, Satan hath desired to have you, that he may sift you as wheat" (Luke 22:31). And thus it is that Sherem "sought much opportunity" (Jacob 7:6) to engage Jacob the prophet.

Sherem accused Jacob of perverting the gospel and of uttering false prophecies concerning the coming of Jesus Christ (see Jacob 7:7). Surely some Nephites who were in tune with the Spirit must have discerned in Sherem the spirit of one who "accused" the brethren (Revelation 12:10) and who was guilty of evil speaking of the Lord's anointed. "That man who rises up to condemn others," Joseph Smith taught, "finding fault with the Church, saying that they are out of the way, while he himself is righteous, then know assuredly, that that man is in the high road to apostasy; and if he does not repent, will apostatize, as God lives."[3] Sherem was on a course that would take him directly to hell.

They have a limited view of reality. When a person refuses to exercise faith—to have a hope in that which is unseen but true (see Alma 32:21)—he thereby denies himself access to the spiritual world, another realm of reality. His vision of things is at best deficient and at worst perverse; he does not see things "as they really are" (Jacob 4:13; see D&C 93:24). He is a scientist with insufficient data; his methodology is limited by his approach, and his conclusions must surely be suspect.

Sherem's naturalistic view of reality precluded his appreciation of the unseen and his desire to apprehend the unknown. Those who rely exclusively upon human sensory experience and human reason to come to the truth cannot find a place in their tightly enclosed epistemological system for such matters as spirit and revelation and prophecy. In responding to Jacob's testimony that Christ shall come as the fulfillment of the Law, Sherem said, "This is blasphemy; for *no man knoweth* of such things; for *he cannot tell of things to come.*" Further, "If there should be a Christ, I would not deny him; but *I know that there is no Christ,* neither has been nor ever will be" (Jacob 7:7–9; italics added). If we were to paraphrase Sherem's argument, it might be stated as follows: "If there should be a Christ—here and now, one that I could see and feel and hear, one who requires no faith or hope—then I would not deny him; I would believe." This, of course, is not true. The unbelievers and the faithless have hardened their hearts to the point that most of the time they deny or rationalize even tangible evidence (see 1 Nephi 16:38; Helaman 16:21). It is usually the case that proof is the last thing that those demanding it really want. The louder the shouts for evidence, the less the inclination to accept it.

The doubter—the one whose faith centers in that which may be seen and heard and felt through natural means only—errs grossly through generalizing beyond his own experiences. What he has not experienced he assumes no one else can. Because he does not know, no one knows (compare Alma 30:48); because he is past feeling, surely no one else has felt; because he lacks internal evidence concerning the coming of a Messiah, unquestionably the evidence amassed by every believing soul is either insufficient or naively misinterpreted. Those who dare not believe dare not allow others to believe.

They have a disposition to misread and thereby misrepresent the scriptures. Those whose motives are impure are not entitled to that which the scriptures call "pure knowledge" (D&C 121:42), knowledge from a pure source. They are unable to comprehend the scriptures in their true light, to perceive and then incorporate the purity of their messages into their own impure lives. Such persons are frequently guilty of wresting the scriptures, of distorting their true meanings and thus doing violence to that which was intended by the inspired writers. "Behold, the scriptures are before you," Alma said to the spiritually unstable people of Ammonihah; "If ye will wrest them it shall be to your own destruction" (Alma 13:20; compare 2 Peter 3:16). Those who wrest the scriptures do not understand them (see D&C 10:63); they have little sacred structure for their lives and wander far astray from that gospel path that must be traversed with care and caution (see Alma 41:1).

Sherem professes to know and to believe in the scriptures, but lacking that elevated perspective and learning that come not only by study but also by faith, he is unable to discern the undergirding message of the scriptures (see Jacob 7:10–11)—that all things bear witness of the Holy One of Israel, that all things which have been "given of God from the beginning of the world, unto man, are the typifying of him" (2 Nephi 11:4; see also Moses 6:63). Devoid of that divine influence that constitutes the spirit of prophecy and revelation, Sherem cannot possess the testimony of Jesus (see Revelation 19:10).

Those who have become more than distant acquaintances with the words of scripture begin to see things as God sees them: they gain "the mind of Christ" (1 Corinthians 2:16) and are thereby able to have "great views of that which is to come" (Mosiah 5:3). They are able to see a providential pattern in all things, to sift through the sands of the fleeting and the ephemeral and to treasure that which is eternal. Sherem, on the other hand, seems to have been afflicted with a means-end sickness, an obsession with the here and now but a refusal to look beyond the present to greater and grander ends. In accusing Jacob of preaching false doctrine, Sherem tells him that "ye have led away much of this people that they pervert the right way of God, and keep not the law of Moses which is the right way; and convert the law of Moses into the worship of a being which ye say shall come many hundred years hence" (Jacob 7:7). Sherem, like the priests of Noah, believed that the Law was all-sufficient (see Mosiah 12:31–32), that salvation would come through observance of the Law without any reference whatsoever to Christ the Lawgiver. It is strange indeed that Sherem would argue for the sufficiency of the law of Moses when, in fact, the law was given by God to point people toward the coming of Christ. Sherem's dispute was not, then, with Jacob alone on this issue, for Nephi had taught similar doctrine many years earlier (see 2 Nephi 11:4; 25:24–25). The irony and inconsistency of Sherem's argument is seen in his use of revelation—the law of Moses—to deny the principle of further revelation—the revelation of the Father in the person of Jesus Christ. Like many of his modern counterparts, Sherem was a master of scriptural manipulation: his was not a search for truth; he read with a jaundiced eye for self-justification, not sanctification.

They are sign seekers. Like most anti-Christs, Sherem insisted that Jacob prove by demonstrable evidence that his was a true position—he demanded a sign (Jacob 7:13; compare Alma 30:43). Miracles or wonders or gifts of the Spirit always follow true believers; indeed, they are one of the signs of the true Church and evidence that the power of God is operating among his people. And yet Jesus taught that it is an "evil and adulterous generation [that] seeketh after a sign" (Matthew 12:39). Joseph Smith added that this principle "is eternal, undeviating, and firm as the pillars of heaven; for whenever you see a man seeking after a sign, you may set it down that he is an adulterous man."[4]

Why is this so? How does a disposition to seek after signs relate to seeking after carnal pleasures? Simply stated, those who have given themselves up to their lusts, who desire that which will satiate the flesh, and who have exhausted their passions in their search for the sensual also seek physical manifestations of spiritual sensations. They demand proof! Unable to recognize and acknowledge eternal certainties, they insist that the truths associated with the area with which they are least familiar—the spiritual—be manifest and translated into that realm they have come to know more surely than any other—the fanciful and the physical. The adulterous are those who worship at the altar of appetite, whose thresholds for gratification are ever rising and who thereby demand something extraordinary to establish the truthfulness of a claim. Ironically, this claim may be verified only by the quiet and unobtrusive whisperings of the Spirit. Spiritual blindness and the spirit of adultery are thus common companions. Of this fascinating but pathetic phenomenon, Elder Neal A. Maxwell has written:

> First of all, the people of the world cannot presume to command God to provide them with signs. A person can neither be a disciple and command the Master nor can he require "perpetual renewal of absolute proof." Some behave, however, as if they would set forth the conditions under which they will believe—complete with specifications; they then invite God to bid on their specifications! . . . Sign seekers, like adulterers, often do have a clear preference for *repeated* sensation. Those who do not understand why adultery is intrinsically wrong will also fail to understand why faith is a justified requirement laid upon us by God. We are to walk by faith and to overcome by faith (see D&C 76:53). . . . By contrast, the faithful,

who are intellectually honest but are confronted with new and present challenges, sing of the Lord, "We've proved Him in days that are past." . . . Those who are adulterous have also a strong preference for "now" rather than for eternity. Impatience and incontinence, quite naturally, team up.

Such erring individuals or generations also have a strong preference for meeting the needs of "me" over attending to others, a lifestyle which speeds selfishness on its endless, empty journey.

By making demands of God, the proud would attach conditions to their discipleship. But discipleship requires of us unconditional surrender to the Lord. Hence the proud neither understand nor really love God. Therefore they violate the first commandment by seeing God as a sign provider upon request; as a function, not a tutoring father.[5]

Sign seekers have one thing going for them when it comes to convincing an audience: the servants of the Lord will not stoop to cheap theatrics to win the hearts of observers. In fact, "faith cometh not by signs, but signs follow those that believe. Yea, signs come by faith, not by the will of men, nor as they please, but by the will of God" (D&C 63:9–10). That is to say, signs and miracles fan the flame already burning in the hearts of believers. Seldom will God perform a notable miracle through his legal administrators to titillate sign seekers. And sign seekers know enough about the Lord and the prophetic past to know this. Simply stated, the anti-Christ demands a sign because he knows that the Lord does not generally give them in that manner. Unfortunately for Sherem (as we shall see), once in a great while the Lord does choose to make bare his mighty arm in response to the taunting imps of uncleanness, but such cases entail the Lord's wrath and condemnation of the thrill seekers.

THE POWER OF JACOB'S TESTIMONY

There are few greater prophets than Jacob, the son of Lehi. He was one of the mighty apostles of the Book of Mormon. As a special witness of Christ, he bore a perfect testimony and was true to his calling. It was to a very young Jacob that father Lehi said:

> Jacob, my firstborn in the wilderness, *thou knowest the greatness of God;* and he shall consecrate thine afflictions for thy gain.
> Wherefore, thy soul shall be blessed, and thou shalt dwell safely with thy brother, Nephi; and thy days shall be spent in the service

of thy God. Wherefore, *I know that thou art redeemed,* because of the righteousness of thy Redeemer; for thou hast beheld that in the fulness of time he cometh to bring salvation unto men.

And *thou hast beheld in thy youth his glory;* wherefore, thou art blessed even as they unto whom he shall minister in the flesh; for the Spirit is the same, yesterday, today, and forever. And the way is prepared from the fall of man, and salvation is free. (2 Nephi 2:2–4; italics added.)

In speaking of Jacob's witness of the coming Messiah, Nephi declared: "I, Nephi, write more of the words of Isaiah, for my soul delighteth in his words . . . , for he verily saw my Redeemer, even as I have seen him. And *my brother, Jacob, also has seen him as I have seen him;* wherefore, I will send their words forth unto my children to prove unto them that my words are true" (2 Nephi 11:2–3; italics added).

Having described Sherem's power of persuasion, Jacob noted: "And he had hope to shake me from the faith, notwithstanding the many revelations and the many things which I had seen concerning these things; for I truly had seen angels, and they had ministered unto me. And also, I had heard the voice of the Lord speaking unto me in very word, from time to time; wherefore, I could not be shaken" (Jacob 7:5). Jacob here provides a marvelous pattern for steadfastness in the face of spiritual persecution and intellectual challenge. Only when we have drunk deeply of the waters of life—when we have been grounded in revealed theology, rooted in genuine spiritual experience, and established in the things of God—can we hope to withstand the burning rays of doubt and the scorching thirst of skepticism.

To be able to bear witness of the truth in the face of ridicule, and to give no heed to the enticing and otherwise convincing voices of the worldly-wise is, according to President Joseph F. Smith, to have entered into the "rest of the Lord," to have partaken of the spiritual rest and peace that are "born from a settled conviction of the truth."[6] To enter the rest of the Lord "means entering into the knowledge and love of God, having faith in his purpose and in his plan, to such an extent that we know we are right, and that we are not hunting for something else, we are not disturbed by every wind of doctrine, or by the cunning and craftiness of men who lie in wait to deceive." To enter into the rest of the Lord is to enjoy "rest from doubt, from fear, from apprehension of danger, rest from the religious turmoil of the world."[7]

Chapter 4—Portrait of an Anti-Christ

After Enos, the son of Jacob, had prayed without ceasing; after he had wrestled in mighty supplication to the God of his fathers; after he had searched and pondered and inquired with a fervor known only to the spiritually hungry—then the voice of the Lord came to him, announced that his sins were forgiven, and regenerated his soul. "And after I, Enos, had heard these words, *my faith began to be unshaken in the Lord*" (Enos 1:11; italics added). Again we note that it is through being introduced into the realm of the sacred that one is able to proceed confidently and unimpeded when confronted by the profane.

The Lord explained to Joseph Smith and Sidney Rigdon in our day—at a time when the Church was under attack by those bent on its overthrow—that "there is no weapon that is formed against you shall prosper; and if any man lift his voice against you he shall be confounded in mine own due time" (D&C 71:9–10). We see this promise literally fulfilled in the ministry of Jacob, particularly in his encounter with Sherem. "But behold, the Lord God poured in his Spirit into my soul," Jacob wrote, "insomuch that I did confound him in all his words" (Jacob 7:8). To say that Jacob *confounded* Sherem is to say that he threw him into disorder; perplexed him; terrified, dismayed, astonished, or stupefied him.[8] The power of God resting upon his servant Jacob both disarmed and disabled Sherem.

It was at the climax of his encounter with this anti-Christ that Jacob testified powerfully of the reality and necessity of Jesus Christ and again affirmed the depth of his own knowledge of the things of the Spirit (compare Alma 30:37–44):

> Believest thou the scriptures? [Jacob asked Sherem.] And [Sherem] said, Yea.
>
> And [Jacob] said unto him: Then ye do not understand them; for they truly testify of Christ. Behold, I say unto you that none of the prophets have written, nor prophesied, save they have spoken concerning this Christ.
>
> And this is not all—it has been made manifest unto me [note that Jacob first appeals to the testimonies of earlier prophets and then bears his own witness; compare Alma 5:43–48], for *I have heard and seen; and it also has been made manifest unto me by the power of the Holy Ghost;* wherefore, I know if there should be no atonement made all mankind must be lost. (Jacob 7:10–12; italics added.)

THE WOEFUL END OF SIGN SEEKERS

In a modern revelation, the Lord explained that "signs come by faith, unto mighty works, for without faith no man pleaseth God; and with whom God is angry he is not well pleased; wherefore, unto such he showeth no signs, only in wrath unto their condemnation" (D&C 63:11). Indeed, when God does choose to manifest his power by means of the miraculous—and it is seldom—the curious sign seeker is often surprised and stunned by what is brought to pass: the sign is usually a divine judgment upon the sign seeker. After Korihor had been struck dumb by the power of God through Alma, the chief judge asked Korihor: "Art thou convinced of the power of God? *In whom did ye desire that Alma should show forth his sign? Would ye that he should afflict others, to show unto thee a sign?* Behold, he has showed unto you a sign; and now will ye dispute more?" (Alma 30:51; italics added). Elder George A. Smith recounted one incident from the history of the restored Church in which Joseph Smith dealt with a sign seeker:

> When the Church of Jesus Christ of Latter-day Saints was first founded, you could see persons rise up and ask, "What sign will you show us that we may be made to believe?" I recollect a Campbellite preacher who came to Joseph Smith . . . and said that he had come a considerable distance to be convinced of the truth. "Why," said he, "Mr. Smith, I want to know the truth, and when I am convinced, I will spend all my talents and time defending and spreading the doctrines of your religion, and I will give you to understand that to convince me is equivalent to convincing all my society, amounting to several hundreds." Well, Joseph commenced laying before him the coming forth of the work, and the first principles of the Gospel, when [the minister] exclaimed, "O this is not the evidence I want, the evidence that I wish to have is a notable miracle; I want to see some powerful manifestation of the power of God, I want to see a notable miracle performed; and if you perform such a one, then I will believe with all my heart and soul, and will exert all my power and all my extensive influence to convince others; and if you will not perform a miracle of this kind, then I am your worst and bitterest enemy." "Well," said Joseph, "what will you have done? Will you be struck blind, or dumb? Will you be paralyzed, or will you have one hand withered? Take your choice, choose which you please, and in the name of the Lord Jesus Christ it shall be done." "That is not the kind of miracle I want," said the preacher.

Chapter 4—Portrait of an Anti-Christ

"Then, sir," replied Joseph, "I can perform none, I am not going to bring any trouble upon any body else, sir, to convince you."[9]

After Jacob had borne his powerful apostolic witness, Sherem replied, "Show me a sign by this power of the Holy Ghost, in the which ye know so much. And [Jacob] said unto him: What am I that I should tempt God to show unto thee a sign *in the thing which thou knowest to be true?* Yet thou wilt deny it, because thou art of the devil." Then Jacob said: "Nevertheless, not my will be done; but if God shall smite thee, let that be a sign unto thee that he has power, both in heaven and in earth; and also, that Christ shall come" (Jacob 7:13–14; italics added). It is interesting to note that Jacob, like his Master and other humble servants endowed with the Spirit, discerned the true intents of Sherem's heart (see Matthew 9:4; 12:25; Luke 9:47; Alma 18:16, 18). Further, Jacob perceived, as is often the case (see Alma 11:24; 30:42), that the antagonist already knew that what the servant of the Lord was preaching was true and that he, the anti-Christ, was fighting the truth and thus sinning against the light.

Jacob then writes: "And it came to pass that when I, Jacob, had spoken these words, the power of the Lord came upon him, insomuch that he fell to the earth. And it came to pass that he was nourished for the space of many days" (Jacob 7:15). Sherem was struck down dramatically, even as Korihor (Alma 30) and Ananias and Sapphira were (Acts 5); his heresies were stopped, his perverse teachings silenced, and his flattering ways revealed for what they truly were. From the account it appears that from then until the time of his death, Sherem was unable to care for himself; Jacob 7:15 states that he "was nourished for the space of many days." Surely he was nourished in the sense that his physical needs were met—he was fed and clothed and sheltered.

Further, to *nourish* is to encourage, to educate, and to instruct.[10] It may be that Sherem was taught the gospel, was reproved and corrected in his doctrine, and was "nourished by the good word of God" (see Jacob 6:7; compare Alma 39:10). This act alone demonstrates Christianity at its highest and discipleship at its deepest—a group of Saints who had been the object of a very unchristian intellectual attack now providing succor for him who had formerly wielded the sword of Satan and had specialized in subtlety. This passage demonstrates one of the marvels of Christianity: the ability to truly love an enemy and to return good for evil. No true Christian takes delight in any person's demise, even if that person happens to be an anti-Christ, an avowed enemy to the cause of truth. The Saints of all ages pray for the defeat of evil and the overthrow of bitterness and opposition (see D&C 109:24–33), but they seek also to forgive and forget and welcome home the wandering prodigal. They leave judgment in the hands of the keeper of the gate, the Holy One of Israel (2 Nephi 9:41).

Life's starkest reality is death. And death is the great moment of truth. In the words of Elder Bruce R. McConkie, death is "a subject which strikes dread—even terror—into the hearts of most men. It is something we fear, of which we are sorely afraid, and from which most of us would flee if we could."[11] Even the most hardened atheists and the most elusive agnostics face what they believe to be the end with fear and trembling. Sherem, in the knowledge that he was about to face his God, sought to purge his soul of duplicity. He spoke plainly unto the people "and denied the things which he had taught them, and confessed the Christ, and the power of the Holy Ghost, and the ministering of angels. And he spake plainly unto them, that he had been deceived by the power of the devil [compare Alma 30:53]. And he spake of hell, and of eternity, and of eternal punishment" (Jacob 7:17–18). These are doctrines that would normally be scoffed at by the learned and ignored by the sophisticated. Sherem now spoke of these things because they weighed upon his mind: hell and eternal punishment were, to him, no longer religious rhetoric, but reality.

Sherem's final words are both poignant and pathetic: "I fear lest I have committed the unpardonable sin, for I have lied unto God; for I denied the Christ, and said that I believed the scriptures; and they truly testify of him. And because I have thus lied unto God I greatly fear lest my case shall be awful; but I confess unto God" (Jacob 7:19). Although the ultimate fate of Sherem is not known to us, this we do observe: deathbed repentance does not have within it the seeds of everlasting life. "It is the will of God," Joseph Smith observed, "that man should repent & serve him in health & in the strength & power of his mind in order to secure his blessings & not wait untill [sic] he is called to die."[12] It would appear that Sherem's sin was not unpardonable—that he will not be numbered among the sons of perdition—for he still possessed a soul capable of repentance, which disposition is wholly alien to a son of perdition.[13] Confession at any time is to be commended, even just prior to death. But true repentance consists not only in confessing sins but also in forsaking forbidden behavior and attitudes and in keeping the commandments thereafter (see D&C 1:32). It is well that Sherem acknowledged his lies and professed a belief in the scriptures and the coming of Christ before his demise; his situation would, however, have been far more positive had he not been compelled to believe.

A Warning to Our Day

The Book of Mormon "was written for our day," President Benson has taught us. "The Nephites never had the book; neither did the Lamanites of ancient times. It was meant for us. Mormon wrote near the end of the Nephite civilization. Under the inspiration of God, who sees all things from the beginning, he abridged centuries of records, choosing the stories, speeches, and events that would be most helpful to us."[14] Mormon's son, Moroni, having witnessed the coming forth of the Book of Mormon in a day of pride and envy and wars and pollutions, said: "Behold, I speak unto you as if ye were present, and yet ye are not. But behold, Jesus Christ hath shown you unto me, and I know your doing" (Mormon 8:35).

With this in mind—with the voice of the Nephite prophets crying out to us and stressing the eternal relevance of their messages, with the clear witness burning in our souls that the Book of Mormon is an ancient book that exposes modern falsehoods and modern anti-Christs—President Ezra Taft Benson has challenged the Saints as follows:

> Now, we have not been using the Book of Mormon as we should. Our homes are not as strong unless we are using it to bring our children to Christ. Our families may be corrupted by worldly trends and teachings unless we know how to use the book to expose and combat the falsehoods in socialism, organic evolution, rationalism, humanism, and so forth. . . . Social, ethical, cultural, or educational converts will not survive under the heat of the day unless their taproots go down to the fulness of the gospel which the Book of Mormon contains.[15]

The Book of Mormon thus attests that anti-Christs are to be found in every age; that doubt and skepticism are ever with us, at least as long as Satan reigns on this planet and as long as people of the earth value the accolades of their cynical constituency more than the quiet acceptance of the Lord and his people; but that certitude and peace and power are the fruits of personal spiritual experience and the keys to remaining steadfast in the face of opposition and challenge.

One of the most effective ways to teach faith in Christ is through reading the scriptural accounts of persons who have evidenced great faith, then patterning our lives after them. Similarly, an indispensable guide in discovering the path of repentance and the miracle of forgiveness is the way of spiritual regeneration and holiness set forth in the labors and ministries of the Saints of earlier dispensations. In our own day there exists no more credible and critical source for discerning and exposing the spirit of anti-Christ than the scriptures, especially the Book of Mormon; nor is there any better formula for remaining untroubled and unhindered in our course than that put forward in the example of Jacob, who had received many revelations, had been ministered to by angels, knew well the voice and dictation of the Spirit, was a student of holy writ, and had spent many quiet hours in spiritual struggle and mighty prayer (see Jacob 7:5, 8, 11, 22). When the moment of significant confrontation came to him—just as it has or will come to individual Latter-day Saints—he stood steadfast and immovable, firm in the faith of his beloved Redeemer. Only when we are built upon the rock of Christ and anchored and settled in true doctrine and personal spiritual experience will we have the strength and capacity to perceive the perverse or engage the diabolical. In the words of Helaman, "when the devil shall send forth his mighty winds, yea, his shafts in the whirlwind, yea, when all his hail and his mighty storm shall beat upon you, it shall have no power over you to drag you down to the gulf of misery and endless wo, because of the rock upon which ye are built, which is a sure foundation, a foundation whereon if men build they cannot fall" (Helaman 5:12).

NOTES

1. Ezra Taft Benson, *A Witness and a Warning* (Salt Lake City: Deseret Book Co., 1988), p. 3; italics added.

2. Noah Webster, *American Dictionary of the English Language,*. facsimile of the 1828 edition (San Francisco: Foundation for American Christian Education, 1967), s.v. "flattery."

3. Joseph Smith, *Teachings of the Prophet Joseph Smith*, sel. Joseph Fielding Smith (Salt Lake City: Deseret Book Co., 1976), pp. 156–57.

Chapter 4—Portrait of an Anti-Christ

4. Smith, *Teachings*, p. 157; compare p. 278.

5. Neal A. Maxwell, *Sermons Not Spoken* (Salt Lake City: Bookcraft, 1985), pp. 58–59.

6. Joseph F. Smith, *Gospel Doctrine* (Salt Lake City: Deseret Book Co., 1971), p. 126.

7. Ibid., p. 58.

8. Webster, *American Dictionary,* s.v. "confound.*"*

9. George A. Smith, in *Journal of Discourses,* 26 vols. (London: Latter-day Saints' Book Depot, 1854–86), 2:236.

10. Webster, *American Dictionary,* s.v. "nourish.*"*

11. In Conference Report, October 1976, pp. 157–60.

12. *The Words of Joseph Smith,* eds. Andrew F. Ehat and Lyndon W. Cook (Provo, Utah: BYU Religious Studies Center, Brigham Young University, 1980), p. 107.

13. Smith, *Teachings*, p. 358.

14. Benson, *Witness and a Warning*, p. 19.

15. Ibid., p. 6.

CHAPTER 5

"Adam Fell That Men Might Be"

We cannot fully understand or appreciate the glorious doctrine of atonement unless we grasp the fact that Adam and Eve fell and until we recognize the very real effects of that fall upon all of us. And it is to the scriptures of the Restoration that we turn to envision what took place in Eden in those earliest days of earth's history. In this chapter, we shall briefly discuss our first parents' choice to partake of the forbidden fruit and bring mortality into being.

THE PARADISIACAL CREATION

We state as an article of faith that in the Millennium "the earth will be renewed and receive its paradisiacal glory" (Articles of Faith 1:10). Reasoning in reverse, and knowing that during the thousand years of peace the earth will exist in a terrestrial glory, we can conclude that life on the Edenic earth was of a terrestrial order. This state was indeed paradisiacal. Man knew his God and walked and talked with him. Adam was, as Joseph Smith taught, "Lord or governor of all things on earth," at the same time enjoying direct communication with his Maker, "without a vail to separate between."[1]

The accounts of the Creation from the records of Moses and Abraham depict the placement of Adam, Eve, and all forms of life in a physical state. They had substance. They were tangible. And yet they were what the scriptures describe as being *spiritual*. That is, they were immortal, or perhaps more correctly, *amortal*, not subject to death (see 1 Corinthians 15:44; Alma 11:45; D&C 88:27). The nature of things in Eden before the Fall can therefore be described as physical-spiritual: physical and tangible in its makeup but not subject to the decaying and deteriorating effects of death. In the words of President Joseph Fielding Smith:

> The account of creation in Genesis was not a spirit creation, but it was in a particular sense, a spiritual creation. This, of course, needs some explanation. The account in Genesis, chapters one and two, is the account of the creation of the physical earth. The

account of the placing of all life upon the earth, up and until the fall of Adam, is an account, in a sense, of the spiritual creation of all of these, but it was also a physical creation. When the Lord said he would create Adam, he had no reference to the creation of his spirit for that had taken place ages and ages before when he was in the world of spirits and known as Michael.[2]

Elder Orson Pratt observed: "Man, when he was first placed upon this earth, was an immortal being, capable of eternal endurance; his flesh and bones, as well as his spirit, were immortal and eternal in their nature; and it was just so with all the inferior creation."[3] More specifically, President Joseph Fielding Smith, then president of the Quorum of the Twelve, wrote: "Adam [and, by extension, all of the animal creation] had no blood in his veins before the fall. Blood is the life of the mortal body." After Adam partook of the forbidden fruit, blood became "the life-giving fluid in Adam's body, and was inherited by his posterity. Blood was not only the life of the mortal body, but also contained in it the seeds of death which bring the mortal body to its end. Previously the life force in Adam's body, which is likewise the sustaining power in every immortal body, was the spirit."[4]

Inasmuch as blood did not become a part of the physical organization of animal life until after the Fall, death was held in abeyance. The revelations attest that by reason of transgression came the Fall, and through the Fall came death (2 Nephi 9:6; compare Moses 6:59). In addition, because blood is the medium of mortality and thus the means by which mortal life is propagated, before the Fall there was no procreation. That is to say, the command to our first parents and to all forms of life to multiply and replenish the earth (Moses 2:22, 28) could not be obeyed until man had fallen and until blood had entered the human and animal systems.

It is in light of these principles of truth that Lehi explained to Jacob that "if Adam had not transgressed he would not have fallen, but he would have remained in the garden of Eden." That is to say, if the nature of things had not changed, Adam and Eve would still be there today, six thousand years later, in their Edenic and terrestrial state, and the plan of salvation would have been placed on hold for all of us. "And all things which were created must have remained in the same state in which they were after they were created"—that is, in their paradisiacal and amortal condition—"and they must have remained forever, and

THE POWER OF THE WORD

had no end. And they would have had no children; wherefore they would have remained in a state of innocence, having no joy, for they knew no misery; doing no good, for they knew no sin. But behold, all things have been done in the wisdom of him who knoweth all things" (2 Nephi 2:22–24). Truly, as Eve declared, "Were it not for our transgression we never should have had seed, and never should have known good and evil, and the joy of our redemption, and the eternal life which God giveth unto all the obedient" (Moses 5:11). In summary, then, "Adam fell that men might be; and men are, that they might have joy" (2 Nephi 2:25). Or as Enoch testified, "Because that Adam fell, we are" (Moses 6:48).

PARTAKING OF THE FORBIDDEN FRUIT

Let us back up for a moment and consider in more detail the nature of Adam and Eve's offense in Eden. We have generally spoken of the task facing Adam and Eve as a choice between what appear to be competing commandments—the command to multiply and replenish the earth and the prohibition against partaking of the fruit of the tree of knowledge of good and evil. We have usually tried to reconcile what seems to be a difficult situation by suggesting that such a dilemma required moral agency and thus shifted the burden for choice upon Adam and Eve. This is true enough. But let me suggest another approach to this matter. It seems that God was saying to our first parents: "Of every tree of the garden thou mayest freely [that is, without consequence] eat, but of the tree of the knowledge of good and evil, thou shalt not [freely, not without consequence] eat of it, nevertheless, thou mayest choose for thyself, for it is given unto thee; but, remember that I forbid it, for in the day thou eatest thereof thou shalt surely die" (Moses 3:17).

In other words, the only question to be decided by Adam and Eve was whether they desired to remain the Garden of Eden. If they did—and there were certainly many things to recommend staying there—then they were not to partake of the forbidden fruit. For if they partook of the fruit, the Lord forbade them to stay in the garden. Or, as President Joseph Fielding Smith put it: "The Lord said to Adam, here is the tree of the knowledge of good and evil. If you want to stay here then you cannot eat of that fruit. If you want to stay here then I forbid you to eat it. But you may act for yourself and you may eat of it if you want to."[5]

Truly the Latter-day Saints view the scenes in Eden with an optimism that is uncharacteristic of the Christian world. We believe that Adam and Eve went into the Garden of Eden to fall; that the Fall was God-ordained and God-intended; that it was as much a part of the fore-ordained plan of salvation as was the very atonement of Christ; and that the Fall "had a twofold direction—downward, yet forward. It brought man into the world and set his feet upon progression's highway."[6] "It was Eve," Elder Dallin H. Oaks observed, "who first transgressed the limits of Eden in order to initiate the conditions of mortality. Her act, whatever its nature, was formally a transgression but eternally a glorious necessity to open the doorway toward eternal life. Adam showed his wisdom by doing the same."[7]

We speak of our first parents' actions in Eden as a *transgression*, and not as a sin (see Articles of Faith 1:2). Indeed, the Nephite prophets were consistent in their expressions that Adam's act was a transgression (see 2 Nephi 2:22; 9:6; Mosiah 3:11; Alma 12:31). The Prophet Joseph Smith taught that "Adam did not commit sin in eating the fruits, for God had decreed that he should eat and fall."[8] "Just why the Lord would say to Adam that he forbade him to partake of the fruit of that tree is not made clear in the Bible account," President Joseph Fielding Smith stated, "but in the original as it comes to us in the book of Moses it is made definitely clear. It is that the Lord said to Adam that if he wished to remain as he was in the garden, then he was not to eat the fruit, but if he desired to eat it and partake of death he was at liberty to do so. So really it was not in the true sense a transgression of a divine commandment. Adam made the wise decision, in fact the only decision that he could make."[9] Elder Oaks has also explained: "Some acts, like murder, are crimes because they are inherently wrong. Other acts, like operating without a license, are crimes only because they are legally prohibited. Under these distinctions, the act that produced the Fall was not a sin—inherently wrong—but a transgression—wrong because it was formally prohibited. These words [*transgression* and *sin*] are not always used to denote something different, but this distinction seems meaningful in the circumstances of the Fall."[10] President Smith expressed his views on this matter as follows: "I am very, very grateful for Mother Eve. If I ever get to see her, I want to thank her for what she did and she did the most wonderful thing that ever happened in this world and that was to place herself where Adam had to do the same thing that she did or they would have been separated forever. . . . They had to partake of that fruit or you wouldn't be here. I wouldn't be here. No one would have been here except Adam and Eve; and they would have stayed there and been there today and been there forever. . . . Adam and Eve did the very thing they had to. I tell you, I take my hat off to Mother Eve."[11]

LIMITATIONS ON OUR KNOWLEDGE

I seldom begin any discussion of the Creation or the Fall in one of my classes without setting forth at least three disclaimers:

1. Everything has not been revealed. All of the data are not in. Even with the inspired material in the books of Moses and Abraham and in the temple endowment, we are not yet in a position to answer all the questions that might arise from a discussion of these matters. Elder Bruce R. McConkie thus stated that "our knowledge about the Creation is limited. We do not know the how and why and when of all things. Our finite limitations are such that we could not comprehend them if they were revealed to us in all their glory, fulness, and perfection. What has been revealed is that portion of the Lord's eternal word which we must believe and understand if we are to envision the truth about the Fall and the Atonement and thus become heirs of salvation."[12]

2. We cannot always tell which items are literal and which are figurative. That is, we do not always know when the scriptures are giving us symbolic imagery or when they provide a record of literal events. We know, for example, that there was an Adam and an Eve, that there was a Garden of Eden, and that the Fall was an actual historical event. But what of the "rib story?" Was Eve really created from Adam's rib, or is the scripture pointing to a greater doctrinal reality? And what of the trees in the garden and the fruit? Elder McConkie has written: "As to the fall, the scriptures set forth that there were in the Garden of Eden two trees. One was the tree of life, which figuratively refers to eternal life; the other was the tree of knowledge of good and evil, which figuratively refers to how and why and in what manner mortality and all that appertains to it came into being. . . . Eve partook without full understanding [see 1 Timothy 2:14]; Adam partook knowing that unless

he did so, he and Eve could not have children and fulfill the commandment they had received to multiply and replenish the earth." In short, to say that Adam and Eve partook of the forbidden fruit is to say that they "complied with whatever the law was that brought mortality into being."[13]

3. We do not know how much Adam and Eve knew and understood prior to their fall. Like all of us, the knowledge of their premortal existence was veiled. In that sense, then, they were required, as are we, to walk by faith. But unlike us, they walked and talked with God, held immediate communion with him, and were taught by him. They lived for a time in a state of naive innocence, but at the same time Adam was appointed as lord or governor over the earth.

In one sense it is as important for us to know what we do *not* know as it is to know what we know. To argue or debate or quarrel over what the Lord has chosen to leave unclear for the time being is foolish and certainly unproductive. We know there was a Creation. We know there was a Fall. We know there was an Atonement. These are the three pillars of eternity. We do not, however, have a complete understanding of all the particulars of these three transcendent events. In regard to the Fall, it should be sufficient for us to know that Adam and Eve and all forms of life are required to partake of the fruits of mortality before we can partake of the fruits of immortality in the Resurrection. Further, men and women cannot partake of the fruit of the tree of life—that is, gain eternal life—while they remain in their sins; mortal man simply cannot inherit immortal glory. It is as though the Lord places cherubim and a flaming sword to guard the way of celestial glory so that we may surely understand that no unclean thing can enter his presence. Repentance and redemption always and forevermore precede exaltation.

Thus, as Alma taught, "if it were possible that our first parents could have gone forth and partaken of the tree of life they would have been forever miserable, having no preparatory state; and thus the plan of redemption would have been frustrated, and the word of God would have been void, taking none effect" (Alma 12:26). Or, in the words of Moroni: "Do ye suppose that ye shall dwell with [God] under a consciousness of your guilt? Do ye suppose that ye could be happy to dwell with that holy Being, when your souls are racked with a consciousness of guilt that ye have ever abused his laws? Behold," he continues, "I say unto you that ye would be more miserable to dwell with a holy and just God, under a consciousness of your filthiness before him, that ye would to dwell with the damned souls in hell" (Mormon 9:3–4).

CONCLUSION

We have so much. The Lord has been more than gracious and kind to us in making known those marvelous truths that pertain to the plan of life and salvation. We love the Bible and feel to rejoice in the testimony of Jesus that flows from the pens of its writers, but we know that it is to Joseph Smith and the scriptures of the Restoration that we turn to learn many of the mysteries of godliness that were taken from the Bible before it was compiled. From the Book of Mormon, the Joseph Smith Translation of the Bible, and the Doctrine and Covenants, we know that the Creation, the Fall, and the Atonement represent one grand doctrinal package. As Elder McConkie explained at Brigham Young University:

> Now this atoning sacrifice of the Lord Jesus Christ—grand and infinite, glorious and eternal as it is—does not stand alone. It is not simply a sudden blaze of light in a universe of darkness and despair. It is not by itself alone a great sun rising in celestial splendor to dispel the gloom of endless night. It is not merely a manifestation of the grace of an infinite God toward his fallen children.
>
> However much the atonement may be and is all these things— and more!—yet it does not stand alone. It is not a child born without parents. It has roots; it has a reason for being; it came because other events called it forth.
>
> The atonement is part of the eternal plan of the Father. It came at the appointed time, according to the will of the Father, to do for man that which could not have been done in any other way. The atonement is the child of the fall, and the fall is the father of the atonement. Neither of them, without the other, could have brought to pass the eternal purposes of the father.[14]

Moroni bore witness that Christ our Lord—he who is also known as the God of Abraham, Isaac, and Jacob—is that God of miracles "who created the heavens and the earth, and all things that in them are. Behold, he created Adam, and by Adam came the fall of man. And because of the fall of man came Jesus Christ, even the Father and the Son; and because of Jesus Christ came the redemption of man. And because of the redemption of man, which came by Jesus Christ, they are brought back into the presence of the Lord" (Mormon 9:11–13).

NOTES

1. Joseph Smith, *Lectures on Faith* (Salt Lake City: Deseret Book Co., 1985), 2:12.

2. Joseph Fielding Smith, *Doctrines of Salvation*, 3 vols., comp. Bruce R. McConkie (Salt Lake City: Bookcraft, 1954–56), 1:76.

3. Orson Pratt, in *Journal of Discourses*, 26 vols. (London: Latter-day Saints' Book Depot, 1854–86), 1:281.

4. Joseph Fielding Smith, *Man: His Origin and Destiny* (Salt Lake City: Deseret Book Co., 1954), pp. 362, 376–77.

5. Joseph Fielding Smith, address given at the Salt Lake LDS Institute of Religion, 14 January 1961.

6. Orson F. Whitney, in *Cowley and Whitney on Doctrine*, comp. Forace Green (Salt Lake City: Bookcraft, 1963), p. 287.

7. Dallin H. Oaks, in Conference Report, October 1993; also in *Ensign*, November 1993, p. 73.

8. Joseph Smith, *The Words of Joseph Smith*, ed. Andrew F. Ehat and Lyndon W. Cook (Provo: BYU Religious Studies Center, 1980), p. 63; spelling and punctuation modernized.

9. Joseph Fielding Smith, in *Improvement Era*, April 1962, p. 231.

10. Oaks, in Conference Report, October 1993; also in *Ensign*, November 1993, p. 73; see also Smith, *Doctrines of Salvation* 1:114.

11. Joseph Fielding Smith, *Take Heed to Yourselves* (Salt Lake City: Deseret Book Co., 1966), pp. 291–92; see also Conference Report, October 1967, pp. 121–23.

12. Bruce R. McConkie, "Christ and the Creation," *Ensign*, June 1982, p. 10.

13. Bruce R. McConkie, *A New Witness for the Articles of Faith* (Salt Lake City: Deseret Book Co., 1985), p. 86; see also "Christ and the Creation," p. 15.

14. Bruce R. McConkie, "The Three Pillars of Eternity," in *1981 BYU Speeches of the Year* (Provo, UT: BYU Publications, 1981), pp. 28–29.

CHAPTER 6

Putting Off the Natural Man

President Ezra Taft Benson has observed: "Just as a man does not really desire food until he is hungry, so he does not desire the salvation of Christ until he knows why he needs Christ. No one adequately and properly knows why he needs Christ until he understands and accepts the doctrine of the Fall and its effect upon all mankind. And no other book in the world explains this vital doctrine nearly as well as the Book of Mormon."[1]

Indeed, serious and careful study of the Fall in the Book of Mormon can drive people to their knees, bringing them to acknowledge their own weaknesses and thus their need for the Lord's redemption. The Atonement is necessary because of the Fall, and unless people sense the effects of Eden—both cosmologically and personally—they cannot comprehend the impact of Gethsemane and Calvary. In this chapter, we will attend primarily to a doctrinal message about humanity that was delivered to King Benjamin by an angel of God. At the same time we will consider related passages in the Book of Mormon that bear upon and amplify this timeless truth—that the natural man is an enemy to God and a foe to all righteousness.

THE SETTING

Benjamin the prophet-king had warred a good warfare, had finished his course, and was prepared to render an accounting of his earthly stewardship to his people and to God. In the strength of God he had led his people to victory over their enemies. In the company of holy and just men he had confounded false prophets and teachers, spoken the word of truth with power and authority, perpetuated the record of Nephi, and established peace in the land of Zarahemla (see Omni 1:25; Words of Mormon 1:12–18). His garments were clean, and his conscience was void of offense.

King Benjamin called his oldest son, Mosiah, to succeed him and asked him to summon the people to a large conference at the temple (1) to announce his retirement and the appointment of Mosiah to serve in his stead, (2) to account to his people concerning his reign and ministry, and (3) to give to them a name, "that thereby they may be distinguished above all the people which the Lord God hath brought out of the land of Jerusalem; . . . a name that never shall be blotted out, except it be through transgression" (Mosiah 1:11–12). His sermon, contained in what we know as Mosiah 2–5, is one of the most eloquent and profound in all of holy writ, a timely treatise not for slothful servants but a dispensation of the "mysteries of God" (Mosiah 2:9) to some of the most "diligent people" whom God had led out of Jerusalem (1:11). It is also a timeless message to those in any age who have kept the commandments of God or who strive to do so. It points the way to the Master by unfolding in plainness and clarity the doctrines of the fall of man and the atonement of Christ. It sets forth the proper foundation—a theological foundation—for service, for Christian compassion, and for kindness, so that human works become the Lord's works—enduring testimonies of that Lord whose they are.

THE DOCTRINE OF THE FALL

The gospel, or plan of salvation, is designed, according to President Brigham Young, for "the redemption of fallen beings."[2] The existence of a plan of deliverance indicates that there must be something from which we need to be redeemed. This is a hard doctrine, one which strikes at the heart of man-made religions and suggests the need for revealed religion. People too often attempt to temper the doctrine of the Fall, to soften its effects. Yet the Fall is a companion doctrine to the Atonement. In fact, there are no serious or extended treatments of the Atonement in the Book of Mormon that are not somehow connected, whether directly or by obvious implication, with the Fall.

We know that because Adam and Eve transgressed by partaking of the forbidden fruit they were cast from the Garden of Eden and from the presence of the Lord, which is spiritual death. As a result came blood, sweat, toil, opposition, bodily decay, and, finally, physical death. Elder Orson F. Whitney taught that the Fall was "a step forward—a step in the eternal march of human progress."[3] Even though the Fall was a vital part of the great plan of the Eternal God—as much a foreordained act as Christ's intercession—our state, including our relationship to and contact with God, changed dramatically. Early in the Nephite record,

Lehi "spake concerning the prophets, how great a number had testified of . . . [the] Redeemer of the world. Wherefore, all mankind were in a lost and in a fallen state, and ever would be save they should rely on this Redeemer" (1 Nephi 10:5–6). Again, the coming of the Messiah presupposes the need for redemption.

Joseph Smith wrote to John Wentworth, "We believe that men will be punished for their own sins, and not for Adam's transgression" (Articles of Faith 1:2). The Lord affirms this principle in his statement to Adam: "I have forgiven thee thy transgression in the Garden of Eden" (Moses 6:53). This declaration must, however, be understood in the proper doctrinal context. Although God forgave our first parents their transgression, although there is no "original sin" entailed upon Adam and Eve's children, and although "the Son of God hath atoned for original guilt, wherein the sins of the parents cannot be answered upon the heads of the children" (Moses 6:54), we must not conclude that all is well.

To say that we are not condemned by the fall of Adam is not to say that we are unaffected by it. Jehovah explained to Adam, "Inasmuch as thy children are conceived in sin, even so when they begin to grow up, sin conceiveth in their hearts, and they taste the bitter, that they may know to prize the good" (Moses 6:55). We do not believe, as did John Calvin, in the moral depravity of humanity. We do not believe, as did Martin Luther, that human beings, because of intrinsic carnality and depravity, do not even have the power to choose good over evil. And we do not believe that children are born in sin and thus inherit the so-called sin of Adam, either by sexual union or by birth. Rather, children are conceived in sin, meaning that, first, they are conceived into a world of sin, and second, conception is the vehicle by which the effects of the Fall (not the original guilt, which God has forgiven) are transmitted to Adam and Eve's posterity. To be sure, there is no sin in sexual union within the bonds of marriage, nor is conception itself sinful. Rather, through conception the flesh originates; through the process of becoming mortal, one inherits the effects of the fall of Adam—both physical and spiritual.

To say that we are not punished for the transgression of Adam is not to say that we are not subject to or affected by it. In fact, Lehi taught Jacob that in the beginning God "gave commandment that all men must repent; for he showed unto all men that they were lost, because of the transgression of their parents" (2 Nephi 2:21; compare Alma 22:14). Thus we all need to repent, because we all have inherited Adam and Eve's fallen nature, which includes the ability and the propensity to sin. "We know that thou art holy," the brother of Jared confessed to the Almighty, "and dwellest in the heavens, and that we are unworthy before thee; *because of the fall our natures have become evil continually*; nevertheless, O Lord, thou hast given us a commandment that we must call upon thee, that from thee we may receive according to our desires" (Ether 3:2; italics added).

Again, conception, which clothes us in the flesh, is the mechanism of transmission, the means by which Adam and Eve's fallen nature (both physical and spiritual death) is transferred from generation to generation. The propensity for and susceptibility to sin are implanted in our nature at conception, just as death is. Both death and sin are present only as potentialities at conception, and therefore neither is fully evident at birth. Death and sin do, however, become actual parts of our nature as we grow up. A nature prone to sin comes spontaneously, just as death does. In the case of little children, the results of this fallen nature (sinful actions and dispositions) are held in abeyance by virtue of the Atonement until children reach the age of accountability. When children reach that age, however, they become subject to spiritual death and must thereafter repent and come unto Christ by covenant and through the ordinances of the gospel.

The teachings of modern apostles and prophets confirm the testimony of ancient Book of Mormon prophets. Elder Bruce R. McConkie summarized the effects of the Fall as follows:

> Adam fell. We know that this fall came because of transgression, and that Adam broke the law of God, became mortal, and was thus subject to sin and disease and all the ills of mortality. We know that the effects of his fall passed upon all his posterity; *all inherited a fallen state*, a state of mortality, a state in which spiritual and temporal death prevail. In this state all men sin. *All are lost. All are fallen.* All are cut off from the presence of God. . . . Such a way of life is inherent in this mortal existence. . . .
>
> Death entered the world by means of Adam's fall—death of two kinds, temporal and spiritual. Temporal death passes upon all men when they depart this mortal life. It is then that the eternal spirit steps out of its earthly tenement, to take up an abode in a realm

where spirits are assigned, to await the day of their resurrection. *Spiritual death passes upon all men when they become accountable for their sins. Being thus subject to sin they die spiritually;* they die as pertaining to the things of the Spirit; they die as pertaining to the things of righteousness; they are cast out of the presence of God. It is of such men that the scriptures speak when they say that the natural man is an enemy to God.[4]

"I have learned in my travels," the Prophet Joseph Smith observed, "that man is treacherous and selfish, but few excepted."[5] "Men have been ever prone to apostasy," President John Taylor pointed out. "Our fallen nature is at enmity with a godly life."[6]

THE NATURAL MAN

In setting forth the doctrine of the Atonement, King Benjamin taught the lesson that is the focus of this chapter: "The natural man is an enemy to God," he said, "and has been from the fall of Adam, and will be, forever and ever, unless he yields to the enticings of the Holy Spirit, and putteth off the natural man and becometh a saint through the atonement of Christ the Lord" (Mosiah 3:19). What is King Benjamin saying about humanity? What is the natural man, and how may he be characterized?

Simply stated, natural men and women are unregenerated beings who remain in their fallen condition, living without God and godliness in the world. They are unredeemed creatures without comfort, beings who live by their own light. On the one hand, natural men and women may be people bent on lechery and lasciviousness; they may love Satan more than God, and therefore they are "carnal, sensual, and devilish" (Moses 5:13). After having preached to and pleaded with his son Corianton, and after having taught him that "wickedness never was happiness," Alma said, "And now, my son, all men that are in a state of nature, or I would say, in a carnal state, are in the gall of bitterness and in the bonds of iniquity." Now note how such persons are enemies to God: "They are without God in the world, and they have gone contrary to the nature of God; therefore, they are in a state contrary to the nature of happiness" (Alma 41:10–11).

In the same vein, Abinadi warned the priests of Noah of that day wherein natural men and women—in this case the vile and wicked— would receive their just rewards:

> And then shall the wicked be cast out, and they shall have cause
> to howl, and weep, and wail, and gnash their teeth; and this because
> they would not hearken unto the voice of the Lord; therefore the
> Lord redeemeth them not.
>
> For they are carnal and devilish, and the devil has power over
> them; yea, even that old serpent that did beguile our first parents,
> which was the cause of their fall. (Mosiah 16:2–3.)

And then Abinadi explained how the Fall opened the way for
people to reject the Spirit and choose sin: "Which [Fall] was the cause
of all mankind becoming carnal, sensual, devilish, knowing evil from
good, subjecting themselves to the devil. Thus all mankind were lost;
and behold, they would have been endlessly lost were it not that God
redeemed his people from their lost and fallen state" (Mosiah 16:3–4).

At this point we might be prone to sit back, let out a sigh of relief,
and offer gratitude to God that because of the atoning work of Christ
the battle is over. But Abinadi continued his warning: "But remember
that he that persists in his own carnal nature, and goes on in the ways
of sin and rebellion against God, remaineth in his fallen state and the
devil hath all power over him. Therefore he is as though there was no
redemption made, being an enemy to God; and also is the devil an
enemy to God" (Mosiah 16:5). Sons of perdition experience this exclusion to its fullest at the time of the Judgment, while all others except
celestial candidates will experience much of it. We should here attend
carefully to the fact that the phrase "persists in his own carnal nature"
implies that individuals, in spite of the Atonement, have such a nature
in which to persist. Further, "*remaineth* in his fallen state" does not simply mean to get into a fallen state through sin. It is true that the scriptures affirm that one becomes "carnal, sensual, and devilish" through
loving Satan more than God, through willful disobedience to the commandments (Moses 5:13; 6:49). But to be a fallen being is not necessarily to be a carnal, sensual, and devilish being. One becomes fallen by
coming into mortality; a fallen person becomes carnal, sensual, and devilish by defying the truth and sinning against it.

On the other hand, natural men and women need not be what we
would call degenerate. They may well be moral and upright men and
women, bent upon goodness and benevolence. However, they operate
in and are acclimated to the present fallen world. Such persons do not
enjoy the enlivening powers of the Holy Ghost: they have not received

the revealed witness of the truth, and they have not enjoyed the sanctifying powers of the blood of Christ. Although their behavior is proper and appropriate according to societal standards, these natural men and women have not hearkened sufficiently to the Light of Christ to be led to the covenant gospel (Mosiah 16:2; see also D&C 84:45–48). "The whole world lieth in sin," the Savior declared in a modern revelation, "and groaneth under darkness and under the bondage of sin. And by this you may know they are under the bondage of sin, because they came not unto me" (D&C 84:49–50). More specifically, with regard to those outside the restored gospel, the Lord states, "There are none that doeth good except those who are ready to receive the fulness of my gospel, which I have sent forth unto this generation" (D&C 35:12).

And what of the members of The Church of Jesus Christ of Latter-day Saints? Are any of us natural men or women? We certainly qualify for that title if we are guilty of gross wickedness, if we have sinned against gospel light and have not thoroughly repented. And yes, we are relatively guilty, too, if we persist in a nature that leads us to exist in twilight when we might bask in the light of the Son. In 1867, President Brigham Young declared to the people of the Church:

> There is no doubt, if a person lives according to the revelations given to God's people, he may have the Spirit of the Lord to signify to him His will, and to guide and to direct him in the discharge of his duties, in his temporal as well as his spiritual exercises. I am satisfied, however, that in this respect, we live far beneath our privileges.[7]

Members of the Church who refuse to climb toward greater spiritual heights, who have no inclination to further anchor themselves in the truth, who have become satisfied with their present spiritual state—these are they who are natural men and women, persons generally of goodwill who do not understand that through their smugness and complacency they are aiding and abetting the cause of the enemy of all righteousness. "Fallen man," C. S. Lewis perceptively observed, "is not simply an imperfect creature who needs improvement: he is a rebel who must lay down his arms."[8]

What are some broad characteristics of natural men and women? Consider the following:

1. *They are unable or unwilling to perceive spiritual realities.* Paul explained that "the natural man receiveth not the things of the Spirit

of God: for they are foolishness unto him: neither *can* he know them, because they are spiritually discerned" (1 Corinthians 2:14; italics added). In exulting over the Lord's infinite mercy—in His willingness to snatch His children from evil and forgive their sins—Ammon said: "What natural man is there that knoweth these things? I say unto you, there is none that knoweth these things, save it be the penitent" (Alma 26:21). "No man has seen God at any time in the flesh, except quickened by the Spirit of God," a modern revelation teaches. "Neither can any natural man abide the presence of God, neither after the carnal mind" (D&C 67:11–12; compare Moses 1:11). "How difficult it is to teach the natural man," Brigham Young declared, "who comprehends nothing more than that which he sees with the natural eye!" President Young went on to say:

> How hard it is for him to believe! How difficult would be the task to make the philosopher, who, for many years, has argued himself into the belief that his spirit is no more after his body sleeps in the grave, believe that his intelligence came from eternity, and is as eternal, in its nature, as the elements, or as the Gods. Such doctrine by him would be considered vanity and foolishness, it would be entirely beyond his comprehension. It is difficult, indeed, to remove an opinion or belief into which he has argued himself from the mind of the natural man. Talk to him about angels, heavens, God, immortality, and eternal lives, and it is like sounding brass, or a tinkling cymbal to his ears; it has no music to him; there is nothing in it that charms his senses, soothes his feelings, attracts his attention, or engages his affections, in the least; to him it is all vanity.[9]

2. *They are fiercely independent.* Joseph Smith taught that "all men are naturally disposed to walk in their own paths as they are pointed out by their own fingers, and are not willing to consider and walk in the path which is pointed out by another, saying, This is the way, walk ye in it, although he should be an unerring director, and the Lord his God sent him."[10] Seeking to be independent, natural men and women ironically end up conforming to the trends of the day. Natural men and women, at least those who have "the carnal mind," are "not subject to the law of God" (Romans 8:7) but are rather subject to their own whims, passions, and desires. C. S. Lewis remarked that "until you have given up yourself to [the Lord] you will not have a real self. Sameness is to be found most among the most 'natural' men, not among those who sur-

render to Christ. How monotonously alike all the great tyrants and conquerors have been: how gloriously different are the saints."[11]

Samuel the Lamanite expressed the tragic end of those whose natural view of reality causes them to spend their days climbing the wrong ladder:

> But behold, your days of probation are past; ye have procrastinated the day of your salvation until it is everlastingly too late, and your destruction is made sure; yea, for ye have sought all the days of your lives for that which ye could not obtain; and ye have sought for happiness in doing iniquity, which thing is contrary to the nature of that righteousness which is in our great and Eternal Head. (Helaman 13:38.)

In the words of a Protestant counselor:

> Fallen man has taken command of his own life, determined above all else to prove that he's adequate for the job. And like the teen who feels rich until he starts paying for his own car insurance, we remain confident of our ability to manage life until we face the reality of our own soul. . . . To put it simply, people want to run their own lives. Fallen man is both terrified of vulnerability and committed to maintaining independence. . . . The most natural thing for us to do is to develop strategies for finding life that reflect our commitment to depending on our own resources.[12]

3. *They are proud, overly competitive, reactionary, and externally driven.* Natural men and women—be they the irreverent and ungodly or the well-meaning but spiritually unregenerate—are preoccupied with self and obsessed with personal aggrandizement. Their lives are keyed to the rewards of this ephemeral sphere; their values derive solely from pragmatism and utility. They take their cues from the world and the worldly. The central feature of pride, as President Ezra Taft Benson warned the Latter-day Saints, is enmity—enmity toward God and enmity toward man. The look of natural men and women is neither up (to God) nor over (to their fellow humans), except as the horizontal glance allows them to maintain a distance from others. "Pride is essentially competitive in nature," President Benson explained. "We pit our will against God's. When we direct our pride toward God, it is in the spirit of 'my will and not thine be done.' . . . The proud cannot accept the authority of God giving direction to their lives. . . . The proud wish God would agree with them. They aren't interested in changing their

opinions to agree with God's." With regard to other people, the proud "are tempted daily to elevate [themselves] above others and diminish them." There is no pleasure, as C. S. Lewis says, in "having something," only in "having more of it than the next man." In short, "Pride is the universal sin, the great vice. . . . [It] is the great stumbling block to Zion."[13]

4. *They yield themselves to the harsh and the crude.* The Spirit of the Lord has a calming and quieting influence upon those who cultivate it and enjoy its fruits. As a sanctifier, the Holy Ghost "expands, and purifies all the natural passions and affections. . . . It inspires virtue, kindness, goodness, tenderness, gentleness and charity."[14] On the other hand, as President Spencer W. Kimball declared, the natural man—the person who lives without this divine refinement—"is the 'earthly man' who has allowed rude animal passions to overshadow his spiritual inclinations."[15]

FREQUENT REACTIONS TO THE DOCTRINE

As indicated earlier, the doctrine of the natural man is a hard doctrine, one that is not only misunderstood but also frequently denied. Reactions to the idea that the natural man is an enemy to God are numerous. Some of these we will now consider.

1. *We all enjoy the Light of Christ.* One rejoinder to this doctrine is that every person who comes into the world is endowed by God with the Light of Christ. Although it is true that the Light of Christ is a gift and endowment from God, this is a doctrine that requires some explanation, for it is necessary to distinguish between two aspects of the Light of Christ. On the one hand, there is the natural or physical light or law by which the sun, moon, and stars operate—the light by which we see and the means by which human, animal, and plant life abound (D&C 88:6–13, 50). On the other hand, there is what might be called a redemptive dimension of the Light of Christ, a light that we must receive, a voice to which we must hearken before we are led to the higher light of the Holy Ghost and are thereby redeemed from our fallen state. Because we have our agency, we can choose to accept or reject this light. Whether such redemptive light takes the form of reason or judgment or conscience, we must exercise some degree of faith to enjoy its benefits. Thus, although it is true that the Spirit gives light to

all of us, it only spiritually enlightens and redeems those of us who hearken to it (see D&C 84:42–50).

2. *The spirit of humankind is good.* Those who contend that humans are basically good, that their inherent inclination is to choose righteousness, enjoy quoting a statement by Brigham Young in which he seems to take quite a different view of who and what the natural man is:

> It is fully proved in all the revelations that God has ever given to mankind that they naturally love and admire righteousness, justice and truth more than they do evil. It is, however, universally received by professors of religion as a Scriptural doctrine that man is naturally opposed to God. This is not so. Paul says, in his Epistle to the Corinthians, "But the natural man receiveth not the things of God," but I say it is the unnatural "man that receiveth not the things of God." . . . That which was, is, and will continue to endure is more natural than that which will pass away and be no more. The natural man is of God.[16]

There is no question, in light of the belief in human depravity held by so many in the nineteenth century, that the doctrines of the Restoration were a refreshing breeze in a dry and arid spiritual climate. The revelation that God had forgiven Adam and Eve of their transgression, as well as the corollary principle that little children who die before the time of accountability are saved, served to set the Latter-day Saints apart from much of the Christian world and certainly painted a more positive and optimistic picture of human nature. The scriptures teach that we lived before we came here, that we are all the sons and daughters of God and that our spirits literally inherited from our exalted Sire the capacity to become like him (Abraham 3:22–23; D&C 76:23–24, 58–59). These are all true doctrines. When understood they can do much to lift our sights toward the glorious and the ennobling.[17]

Such beliefs, however, do not invalidate the burden of scripture—that there was a fall and that the Fall takes a measured and meaningful toll upon earth's inhabitants. Obviously President Young used the phrase "natural man" differently from the way that Benjamin or Paul used it. His reference is to the spirit of man, the willing and striving eternal agent who is a child of God. His point is a good one: human beings can choose good as well as evil and can, through the proper exercise of their God-given agency, stand as spiritual beings before the Almighty. And yet our spirits can be and are influenced by our physical bodies, inasmuch as the latter are subject to our present fallen state. President Brigham Young taught:

> Now, I want to tell you that [Satan] does not hold any power over man, only so far as the body overcomes the spirit that is in a man, through yielding to the spirit of evil. The spirit that the Lord puts into a tabernacle of flesh, is under the dictation of the Lord Almighty; but the spirit and body are united in order that the spirit may have a tabernacle, and be exalted; and the spirit is influenced by the body, and the body by the spirit.
>
> In the first place the spirit is pure, and under the special control and influence of the Lord, but the body is of the earth, and is subject to the power of the devil, and is under the mighty influence of that fallen nature that is on the earth. If the spirit yields to the body, the devil then has power to overcome both the body and spirit of that man.[18]

On another occasion, President Young taught that "there are no persons without evil passions to embitter their lives. Mankind are revengeful, passionate, hateful, and devilish in their dispositions. This we inherit through the fall, and the grace of God is designed to enable us to overcome it."[19]

3. *Little children are innocent.* Latter-day Saints too often become concerned and confused about the scriptural statement that children are conceived in sin (see Moses 6:55) and ask, "Are children pure?" The answer to this question is always a resounding "Yes!" No one disputes that. The real issue is *why* children are pure. Two possibilities suggest themselves: (1) the Greek or humanistic response is that children are pure because human nature is pure, prone toward the good; while (2) the Christian gospel response is that children are pure because of the Atonement, because Jesus Christ declared them so. To paraphrase the words of Lehi, children are redeemed because of the righteousness of our Redeemer (see 2 Nephi 2:3). Benjamin, declaring the words of the angel, said, "And even if it were possible that little children could sin they could not be saved." That is, if Christ required children to be responsible for those actions or deeds that are ostensibly wrong and sinful, they could not be saved, had there been no atonement. "But I say unto you," Benjamin explains, "they are blessed; for behold, as in Adam, or by nature, they fall, even so the blood of Christ atoneth for their sins" (Mosiah 3:16).

The revelations state that little children "cannot sin, for power is not given unto Satan to tempt little children, until they begin to become accountable before me" (D&C 29:47). All of us know of deeds performed by little children that may only be described as evil. I am aware of a seven-year-old who in an act of rage killed his brother. The act of murder is a heinous sin. But in this case the child's action is not counted as sin. Why? Because, in the words of God, "Little children are redeemed from the foundation of the world through mine Only Begotten" (D&C 29:46). Christ explained that "the curse of Adam is taken from [children] in me, that it hath no power over them" (Moroni 8:8). Little children are subject to the effects of the Fall, just as all of us are; they are not, however, held accountable for their actions. In summary, little children are saved without any preconditions—without faith, repentance, or baptism. Their innocence is decreed and declared by and through the tender mercies of an omni-loving Lord. Children are innocent through the Atonement, but not because there is no sin in their nature.

4. *Joseph Smith taught that we are gods in embryo.* Some people believe that Joseph Smith and the Latter-day Saints progressed or evolved beyond the doctrine of the Fall, that the message of the Book of Mormon was later quietly but surely superseded by the purer pronouncements in the King Follett sermon. To me such views are groundless and misleading. It was in 1841 that the Prophet made his now-famous statement about the correctness and power of the Book of Mormon.[20] Only the night before the Prophet's martyrdom,

> Hyrum Smith read and commented upon extracts from the Book of Mormon, on the imprisonments and deliverance of the servants of God for the Gospel's sake. Joseph bore a powerful testimony to the guards of the divine authenticity of the Book of Mormon, the restoration of the Gospel, the administration of angels, and that the kingdom of God was again established upon the earth.[21]

That scene in Carthage certainly bespeaks more than sentimental attachment on the part of the Prophet to the scriptural record—and to the doctrines it put forward—that had come to light through his instrumentality almost two decades earlier. The fact is, on some occasions Joseph Smith spoke of the nobility of humankind, and on some occasions he spoke of the carnality of humankind.[22] To conclude that the Prophet taught only of humankind's nobility—or, for that matter, that he taught only of humankind's ignobility—is to misrepresent his broader theological view.

Conclusion

During his speech at the temple, King Benjamin explained that

men drink damnation to their own souls except they humble themselves and become as little children, and believe that salvation was,
and is, and is to come, in and through the atoning blood of Christ,
the Lord Omnipotent.

For the natural man is an enemy to God, and has been from the
fall of Adam, and will be, forever and ever, unless he yields to the
enticings of the Holy Spirit, and putteth off the natural man and
becometh a saint through the atonement of Christ the Lord, and
becometh as a child, submissive, meek, humble, patient, full of love,
willing to submit to all things which the Lord seeth fit to inflict
upon him, even as a child doth submit to his father. (Mosiah
3:18–19.)

We do not put off the natural man by living longer. We do not
change our natures by simply attending meetings and being involved
in the work of the Church. The Church is a divine organization. It
administers the saving gospel. The transformation from the natural state
to the spiritual state, however, is accomplished only through the mediation and atonement of Jesus Christ, through the power of the Holy
Ghost. No one goes from death to life without that enabling power we
call the grace of God. Programs to develop self-control, plans to modify
human behavior, and schemes directed toward the shaping of more
appropriate actions have fallen and will forever fall far short of the mark
that Christ has set. These programs are at best deficient and at worse
perverse. In the language of President Ezra Taft Benson:

The Lord works from the inside out. The world works from the
outside in. The world would take people out of the slums. Christ
takes the slums out of people, and then they take themselves out of
the slums. The world would mold men by changing their environment. Christ changes men, who then change their environment.
The world would shape human behavior, but Christ can change
human nature.[23]

Those who are born again or born from above—who die as to the
things of unrighteousness and begin to live again as pertaining to the
things of the Spirit—are like little children. First and foremost, these
people are, like children, clean and pure. Through the atoning blood of
Christ, they have had their sins remitted and have entered the realm of

divine experience. Putting off the natural man involves putting on Christ. As Paul counseled the Saints in his day, those who put off the "old man" are "renewed in the spirit of [their] mind." They "put on the new man, which after God is created in righteousness and true holiness" (Ephesians 4:22–24) and "which is renewed in knowledge after the image of him that created him" (Colossians 3:10).

We shall spend all our days seeking to subdue the flesh and put off the natural man; this is the challenge of mortality. "Will sin be perfectly destroyed?" Brigham Young asked. "No, it will not, for it is not so designed in the economy of Heaven."

> Do not suppose that we shall ever in the flesh be free from temptations to sin. Some suppose that they can in the flesh be sanctified body and spirit and become so pure that they will never again feel the effects of the power of the adversary of truth. Were it possible for a person to attain to this degree of perfection in the flesh, he could not die neither remain in a world where sin predominates. Sin has entered into the world, and death by sin. I think we shall more or less feel the effects of sin so long as we live, and finally have to pass the ordeals of death.[24]

Zion is built "in process of time" (Moses 7:21); it is only by patience and long-suffering that the Saints of the Most High become a holy people.

There is great virtue in truth and great power in the proclamation of the truth. President Ezra Taft Benson repeatedly warned the Saints of the condemnation, scourge, and judgment that rest upon the Church because of our neglect of the Book of Mormon (see D&C 84:54–61). He has, however, reminded us that the condemnation can be lifted through serious study and consistent application of the teachings and patterns for living provided in that sacred volume. "I am deeply concerned," he once said, "about what we are doing to teach the Saints at all levels the gospel of Jesus Christ as completely and authoritatively as do the Book of Mormon and Doctrine and Covenants. By this I mean teaching the 'great plan of the Eternal God,' to use the words of Amulek (Alma 34:9)."

> Are we using the messages and the method of teaching found in the Book of Mormon and other scriptures of the Restoration to teach this great plan of the eternal God? . . .
> The Book of Mormon Saints knew that the plan of redemption

must start with the account of the fall of Adam. In the words of Moroni, "By Adam came the fall of man. And because of the fall of man came Jesus Christ, . . . and because of Jesus Christ came the redemption of man." (Mormon 9:12.)

We all need to take a careful inventory of our performance and also the performance of those over whom we preside to be sure that we are teaching the "great plan of the Eternal God" to the Saints.

Are we accepting and teaching what the revelations tell us about the Creation, Adam and the fall of man, and redemption from that fall through the atonement of Christ?[25]

As stated earlier, just as we do not desire food until we are hungry, so the living waters can bless our lives only to the degree to which we acknowledge our fallen condition, seek diligently to put off the natural man, and receive deliverance from sin through repentance. "It requires all the atonement of Christ," President Brigham Young noted, "the mercy of the Father, the pity of angels and the grace of the Lord Jesus Christ to be with us always, and then to do the very best we possibly can, to get rid of this sin within us, so that we may escape from this world into the celestial kingdom."[26] In the words of C. S. Lewis, the animation and renovation of human character "is precisely what Christianity is about. This world is a great sculptor's shop. We are the statues and there is a rumor going round the shop that some of us are some day going to come to life."[27] When we do so, as individuals and as a people, to quote a modern prophet, "a new day will break and Zion will be redeemed."[28]

NOTES

1. Ezra Taft Benson, *A Witness and a Warning* (Salt Lake City: Deseret Book Co., 1988), p. 33.

2. Brigham Young, in *Journal of Discourses*, 26 vols. (London: Latter-day Saints' Book Depot, 1854–86), 1:1.

3. Orson F. Whitney, in Conference Report, April 1908, p. 90.

4. Bruce R. McConkie, *The Promised Messiah: The First Coming of Christ* (Salt Lake City: Deseret Book Co., 1978), pp. 244, 349–50; italics added.

5. Joseph Smith, *Teachings of the Prophet Joseph Smith,* sel. Joseph Fielding Smith (Salt Lake City: Deseret Book Co., 1976), p. 30.

6. John Taylor, *The Mediation and Atonement* (Salt Lake City: Deseret News, 1892), p. 197.

7. Young, in *Journal of Discourses*, 12:104.

8. C. S. Lewis, *Mere Christianity* (New York: Macmillan, 1960), p. 59.

9. Young, in *Journal of Discourses*, 1:2.

10. Smith, *Teachings*, pp. 26–27.

11. Lewis, *Mere Christianity*, p. 190.

12. Larry Crabb, *Inside Out* (Colorado Springs, Colorado: NavPress, 1988), pp. 15–16, 54.

13. Ezra Taft Benson, in Conference Report, April 1989, pp. 4, 6–7.

14. Parley P. Pratt, *Key to the Science of Theology* (Salt Lake City: Deseret Book Co., 1970), p. 61.

15. Spencer W. Kimball, in Conference Report, October 1974, pp. 159–63.

16. Young, in *Journal of Discourses*, 9:305.

17. Smith, *Teachings*, p. 193.

18. Young, in *Journal of Discourses*, 2:255–56; compare Smith, *Teachings*, pp. 181, 187, 189, 226.

19. Ibid., 8:160.

20. Smith, *Teachings*, p. 194.

21. Joseph Smith, *History of The Church of Jesus Christ of Latter-day Saints*, 7 vols, 2d ed. rev., ed. B. H. Roberts (Salt Lake City: The Church of Jesus Christ of Latter-day Saints, 1932–51), 6:600.

22. Smith, *Teachings*, pp. 26–27, 30, 196, 249–50, 252, 258, 303, 315, 328.

23. Benson, in Conference Report, October 1985, p. 6.

24. Young, in *Journal of Discourses*, 10:173.

25. Benson, *Witness and a Warning*, pp. 32–33.

26. Young, in *Journal of Discourses*, 11:301.

27. C. S. Lewis, *Mere Christianity*, p. 140.

28. Benson, *Witness and a Warning*, p. 66.

CHAPTER 7

Redemption through the Holy Messiah

Jacob, son of Lehi, preceded his powerful discussion of the atonement of Christ by a brief encounter with the writings of Isaiah, a statement of "things which are, and which are to come" (2 Nephi 6:4; compare Jacob 4:13). Having been asked by Nephi to read the words of Isaiah to his people, Jacob stressed that "the words which I shall read are they which Isaiah spake concerning all the house of Israel; wherefore, they may be likened unto you, for ye are of the house of Israel" (2 Nephi 6:5).

After quoting Isaiah 49:22–26 regarding the establishment of the ensign in the last days and the manner in which the gospel banquet is to be served by the Gentiles to the Lamanites and the Jews in the final dispensation, Jacob provided appropriate commentary on these otherwise difficult passages. Jacob then quoted Isaiah 50:1 and 52:1–2. Without undertaking a verse-by-verse commentary, we simply acknowledge that Isaiah's message is directed toward the promise of an eventual return of the scattered remnants of Israel. Although Israel has "sold herself" through repeated transgression and rejected her God and his everlasting covenant, and although the people of the covenant have been disloyal to the royal within them, yet the decree is sure: Jehovah has not and will not cast them off forever. The Omnipotent One has power to do all things: "O house of Israel, is my hand shortened at all," he asked, "that it cannot redeem, or have I no power to deliver" the exiles to their Lord and to their lands? (2 Nephi 7:1–2.)

Through the marvelous work and a wonder of the last days—the restoration of the gospel through the Prophet Joseph Smith—the "Lord shall comfort Zion, he will comfort all her waste places." Because the heavens will have been opened, "a law shall proceed" from God to his people, and, in his words, "I will make my judgment to rest for a light for the people" (2 Nephi 8:3–4; compare Isaiah 2:3). His promise is fixed and his word is faithful: Israel shall be gathered. Thus, "the redeemed of the Lord shall return" to that Lord, "and come with singing unto Zion," unto the Lord's true church; "and everlasting joy and holiness shall be upon their heads" (2 Nephi 8:6, 11; compare 9:2).

THE DOCTRINE OF REDEMPTION FROM DEATH

Jacob's understanding of the plan of salvation was grounded in the teachings of his father, based upon what Lehi had learned through revelation and from his study of the brass plates (see 2 Nephi 2:17). Further, Jacob himself had enjoyed the ministry and instruction of angels and the revelations of heaven (see 2 Nephi 2:4; 10:3). His was a clear conception of and a firm commitment to his Lord and Savior, a quiet but powerful assurance that God had a plan for the redemption and salvation of his children.

The Book of Mormon affirms the antiquity of the doctrine of redemption from death and specifically suggests that the knowledge of the resurrection of Christ and of all people is much older than scholars have supposed. It did not originate with Job (see Job 19:25–26), with Ezekiel (see Ezekiel 37), or during the Babylonian captivity. It was known in the Adamic dispensation that salvation was to be had through the sufferings, death, and resurrection of Jesus Christ (see Moses 6:51–60). Enoch likewise "looked and beheld the Son of Man lifted up on the cross, after the manner of men." He further beheld the meridian of time wherein "the saints arose, and were crowned at the right hand of the Son of Man, with crowns of glory" (Moses 7:55–56). Abraham, the father of the faithful, was also privileged to understand the redemptive labors of the Lord Jesus Christ (see JST, Genesis 15:9–12).

Jacob acknowledged that many of his people had searched the scriptures to better understand these matters, to know of things to come; "wherefore," he added, "I know that ye know that our flesh must waste away and die; nevertheless, in our bodies we shall see God" (2 Nephi 9:4). Jacob taught that death has passed upon all men as a vital part of the merciful plan of the great Creator (2 Nephi 9:6). From God's perspective, life and death are not opposites but points on an eternal spectrum.

Adam's fall brought death. Christ's suffering and death brought life. Adam is thus the father of mortality, Christ the father of immortality.[1] Having experienced spiritual death—being cut off from the presence of God and dying as to things of righteousness (see Alma 12:16; 40:26; 42:9; Helaman 14:18; D&C 29:41)—Adam and his posterity were in need of a universal life force, an infinite atoning power, to deliver them from the grasp of death and hell and to open the door once again to eternal life. Indeed, Christ's atonement is infinite in a number of ways. First, it is infinite in that it circumvents the ever-present mortal commonality—physical death. "Save it should be an infinite atonement," Jacob explained, "this corruption could not put on incorruption." In such an eventuality, "this flesh must have laid down to rot and to crumble to its mother earth, to rise no more" (2 Nephi 9:7).

Second, the atonement of Christ is infinite in the sense that its influence extends to all of the worlds Christ created. The gospel of Jesus Christ is "the glad tidings . . . that he came into the world, even Jesus, to be crucified for the world, and to bear the sins of the world, and to sanctify the world, and to cleanse it from all unrighteousness; that *through him all might be saved whom the Father had put into his power and made by him*" (D&C 76:40–41; italics added; compare Moses 1:32–35). Joseph Smith, in his poetic version of the Vision of the Glories (D&C 76), wrote of the outreach of our Lord's saving grace: "I heard a great voice, bearing record from heav'n, / He's the Savior, and only begotten of God— / By him, of him, and through him, the worlds were all made, / Even all that careen in the heavens so broad, / *Whose inhabitants, too, from the first to the last,* / *Are sav'd by the very same Savior of ours;* / And, of course, are begotten God's daughters and sons, / By the very same truths, and the very same pow'rs."[2] In a related way, the Atonement is infinite in the sense that it covers all sins (with the exception of murder and the sin against the Holy Ghost) and thus makes redemption possible for all people (see Articles of Faith 1:3).

Third, the Savior's atonement is infinite in the sense that he is an infinite being. Jesus was able to do for us what we simply could not have done for ourselves. To begin with, his was a sinless offering, an act performed by one who was "in all points tempted like as we are, yet without sin" (Hebrews 4:15). In addition, and perhaps most important, Christ was able to do what he did—to suffer in Gethsemane and on Calvary, as well as to rise from the tomb in glorious immortality—because of who and what he was. Jesus of Nazareth was a man, a son of Mary, from whom he inherited mortality—the capacity to know pain and sorrow, to struggle with the flesh, and, finally, to die. Jesus the Christ was also the son of Elohim, the Eternal Father. From that exalted being Jesus inherited the powers of immortality—the power over death, the capacity to live forever. In the purest sense, the sacrifice of Jesus Christ was a voluntary offering. "Therefore doth my Father love me," Jesus said, "because I lay down my life, that I might take it again. No man taketh it from me, but I lay it down of myself. I have power to lay it down [mortality], and I have power to take it again [immortality]. This commandment have I received of my Father" (John 10:17–18). Amulek also bore witness of the Messiah; he testified that Jesus would be "the Son of God, yea, infinite and eternal" (Alma 34:14).

THE WISDOM AND MERCY OF THE GREAT PLAN

Jacob's depth of appreciation and feelings of awe for the Savior knew no bounds. He "felt to sing the song of redeeming love" (Alma 5:26), to lift his voice in praise toward that Lord who has redeemed us. "O the wisdom of God," he exulted, "his mercy and grace! For behold, if the flesh should rise no more our spirits must become subject to that angel who fell from before the presence of the Eternal God, and became the devil, to rise no more. And our spirits must have become like unto him, and we become devils, angels to a devil, to be shut out from the presence of our God, and to remain with the father of lies, in misery, like unto himself" (2 Nephi 9:8–9).

When the preceding verses are pondered, pertinent theological questions arise: Why would the spirits of men be subject to Satan if there had been no resurrection? Why would they become "devils, angels to a devil"? What if a man had lived a good life, a commendable and noble life—why would such a one be subject to Satan in the world of spirits? The answers to these queries lie in an appreciation for the central role of the resurrection of Christ in the overall plan of life and salvation. Joseph Smith was asked: "What are the fundamental principles of your religion?" He answered: "The fundamental principles of our religion are the testimony of the Apostles and Prophets, concerning Jesus Christ, that He died, was buried, and rose again the third day, and ascended into heaven; and *all other things which pertain to our religion are only appendages to it.*"[3] Simply stated, if Christ did not rise from the grave—as he stated he would do—then he was not the promised Messiah. If Christ has not the power to save the body from death, then he surely has not the power to save the spirit from hell. If he did not break the bands of death in the Resurrection, then our hope of deliverance from sin through the Atonement is futile and unfounded. "Our spirits, stained with sin," wrote Elder Bruce R. McConkie, "unable to cleanse themselves, would be subject to the author of sin everlastingly; we would be followers of Satan; we would be sons of perdition."[4]

"If Christ be not raised," Paul explained to the Corinthians, "your faith is vain; *ye are yet in your sins*" (1 Corinthians 15:17; italics added). In Jacob's language, if the flesh should rise no more, each of us—guilty of some degree of sin—would have no hope for a union of spirit and body and likewise no hope for repentance and forgiveness. We would thus become like unto the devil: we would be spirits forever and damned beings in eternity.

It should be understood, however, that Jacob's whole spiritual scenario is hypothetical. His system of reasoning is created to produce a deeper appreciation for the glorious fact that our Lord *did* suffer and bleed and die; that he *did* take up his body on the third day; that in a way incomprehensible to us, the effects of our Lord's rise to newness of life pass upon all mankind; and that he has, in reality, made escape possible from the awful monster of death—the grave—and hell—the abode of the wicked in the world of spirits after death (see 2 Nephi 9:10–13). Through the resurrection of Christ and of all people, the sting of death is removed. Through individual repentance and the miracle of forgiveness, the victory of the grave is snatched away by the Lord of the living and the dead (see 1 Corinthians 15:54–56). Our Master has thereby "abolished death, and . . . brought life and immortality to light through the gospel" (2 Timothy 1:10).[5]

THE DOCTRINE OF ETERNAL JUDGMENT

As noted earlier, the gospel is the "glad tidings" of the atoning mission of our Lord and the plan whereby all people may take full advantage of that atonement (see D&C 76:40–41). The "principles of the gospel" are those doctrines and ordinances of salvation the knowledge and application of which make it possible for us to rise above carnality and a sinful state and thus prepare for an eventual inheritance with God. The principles of the gospel are faith in Jesus Christ, repentance, baptism by immersion for the remission of sins, laying on of hands for the gift of the Holy Ghost, enduring to the end, resurrection, and eternal judgment[6] (see, for example, 2 Nephi 31; 3 Nephi 27). The latter two doctrines—resurrection and judgment—are among the major topics of the Book of Mormon prophets.

The Book of Mormon attests to the order of things hereafter: at death we enter the world of spirits and experience a "partial judgment"[7] (see Alma 40:11–14). Thereafter we are resurrected, judged, and consigned to our eternal reward. Jacob taught that after resurrection, all people "must appear before the judgment-seat of the Holy One of Israel," who is Jesus Christ. "And then cometh the judgment, and then must they be judged according to the holy judgment of God" (2 Nephi 9:15). This final judgment will take place at the end of the Millennium. Those who have been righteous on earth shall receive a righteous body and inherit the reward of the righteous. Those, on the other hand, who have sowed seeds of wickedness on earth shall reap condemnation and never know or partake of the fruit of the tree of life. The devil and his angels, those who are filthy—including the sons of perdition (see D&C 88:35, 102)—"shall be filthy still" after the Resurrection. These "shall go away into everlasting fire, prepared for them; and their torment is as a lake of fire and brimstone, whose flame ascendeth up forever and ever and has no end" (2 Nephi 9:16).[8]

For the righteous, the final judgment will be a formality; they will already have received their celestial, resurrected bodies and will know of their eternal destiny. These are they who have "believed in the Holy One of Israel, they who have endured the crosses of the world, and despised the shame of it." They stood firm in the midst of the tauntings and enticements echoing from that great and spacious building and were undeterred from their appointed task. These shall inherit that kingdom promised to them on a conditional basis before the world was (see 2 Nephi 9:18). For the wicked, however, the Judgment will be a moment of confrontation, a time of soul stirring and forthright acknowledgment that the ways of the Lord are just.

The Lord Jehovah is the perfect judge, "for he knoweth all things, and there is not anything save he knows it" (2 Nephi 9:20). In discussing the inevitability of the final judgment, Jacob implored, "Prepare your souls for that glorious day when justice shall be administered unto the righteous, even the day of judgment, that ye may not shrink with awful fear" (2 Nephi 9:46). "O then, my beloved brethren, come unto the Lord, the Holy One. Remember that his paths are righteous. Behold, the way for man is narrow, but it lieth in a straight course before him, and the keeper of the gate is the Holy One of Israel; and he employeth no servant there; and there is none other way save it be by the gate; for he cannot be deceived, for the Lord God is his name" (2 Nephi 9:41). A knowledge of our Lord's mercy, an appreciation for his divine justice, and an awareness of his infinite love also suggest to the soul that he waits at the gate, not only to certify us but also to welcome us.

CHRIST SUFFERED FOR ALL

In speaking of the coming of the Messiah, Jacob said, "Wherefore, as I said unto you, it must needs be expedient that Christ—for in the last night the angel spake unto me that this should be his name[9]—should come among the Jews, among those who are the more wicked part of the world; and they shall crucify him—for thus it behooveth our God, and there is none other nation on earth that would crucify their God." Jacob further added the detail that "because of priestcrafts and iniquities, they at Jerusalem [would] stiffen their necks against him, that he be crucified." This rejection of the Lord by the Jews would lead to their being "scattered among all nations" until "the day cometh that they shall believe" in Christ. Then has the Lord "covenanted with their fathers [Abraham, Isaac, and Jacob] that they shall be restored in the flesh, upon the earth, unto the lands of their inheritance" (2 Nephi 10:3–7).

Jacob taught that Jesus would come into the world "that he may save all men if they will hearken unto his voice; for behold, he suffereth the pains of all men, yea, the pains of every living creature, both men, women, and children, who belong to the family of Adam" (2 Nephi 9:21). This is one of the first places in the Book of Mormon record where the nature of Christ's redemptive suffering is discussed. Because the effects of Adam's fall were universal, the effects of the atonement must be universal. Because every son and daughter of Adam and Eve would be subject to sin and death, so also must the atonement of Christ provide escape from the damning influences of sin and the possible dissolution of death.

In Gethsemane and again on the cross,[10] our Savior descended in suffering below all things (see 2 Corinthians 8:9; Ephesians 4:8–10; D&C 19:2; 88:6). In a way incomprehensible to the finite mind, the Infinite

One took upon him the effects of the sins of all humanity. He who had been the sinless one now became the great sinner; the Father "made him to be sin for us," even he "who knew no sin" (2 Corinthians 5:21; compare Galatians 3:13; Hebrews 2:9). He who had always walked in the light of his God was in the darkness alone; he who had basked constantly in the glory of his Father's Spirit now knew, for the first time, the painful reality associated with alienation from things divine.[11]

An angel explained to King Benjamin, "[Christ] shall suffer temptations, and pain of body, hunger, thirst, and fatigue, even more than man can suffer, except it be unto death; for behold, blood cometh from every pore, so great shall be his anguish for the wickedness and the abominations of his people" (Mosiah 3:7). In a modern revelation, Christ graphically described the bitterness of his suffering:

> I command you to repent—repent, lest I smite you by the rod of my mouth, and by my wrath, and by my anger, and your sufferings be sore—how sore you know not, how exquisite you know not, yea, how hard to bear you know not.
>
> For behold, I, God, have suffered these things for all, that they might not suffer if they would repent;
>
> But if they would not repent they must suffer even as I;
>
> Which suffering caused myself, even God, the greatest of all, to tremble because of pain, and to bleed at every pore, and to suffer both body and spirit—and would that I might not drink the bitter cup, and shrink—
>
> Nevertheless, glory be to the Father, and I partook and finished my preparations unto the children of men. (D&C 19:15–19; compare 18:11.)

"Can we," asked a modern apostle, "even in the depths of disease, tell Him anything at all about suffering? In ways we cannot comprehend, our sicknesses and infirmities were borne by Him [see Alma 7:11–12] even before they were borne by us. The very weight of our combined sins caused Him to descend below all. We have never been, nor will we be, in depths such as He has known. Thus His atonement made perfect His empathy and His mercy and His capacity to succor us, for which we can be everlastingly grateful."[12] Our Savior would undergo all of this, Jacob prophesied about 550 B.C., "that the resurrection might pass upon all men, that all might stand before him at the great and judgment day" (2 Nephi 9:22).

One of the eternal verities taught clearly and persuasively in the

Chapter 7—Redemption through the Holy Messiah

Book of Mormon is that the atonement of Christ is extended toward those who were without gospel law while on earth and had no opportunities to participate in the ordinances of salvation. "Where there is no law given," Jacob explained, "there is no punishment; and where there is no punishment there is no condemnation." This is true because "the atonement satisfieth the demands of his justice upon all those who have not the law given to them, . . . and they are restored to that God who gave them breath, which is the Holy One of Israel" (2 Nephi 9:25–26; compare Mosiah 3:11; Moroni 8:22).

One of the unconditional benefits of the Atonement is the decree that no person in all eternity will be denied a blessing that is beyond his or her control to enjoy; no person will be condemned for not observing a commandment or participating in an ordinance of which he or she was ignorant. God knows all things. He, and he alone, can adjudicate humanity, for he alone knows the thoughts and intents of the human heart (see D&C 6:16). The divine word is sure: "All who have died without a knowledge of this gospel, who would have received it if they had been permitted to tarry, shall be heirs of the celestial kingdom of God; also all that shall die henceforth without a knowledge of it, who would have received it with all their hearts, shall be heirs of that kingdom." The principle undergirding this doctrine is then stated as follows: "For I, the Lord, will judge all men according to their works, *according to the desire of their hearts*" (D&C 137:7–9; italics added; compare Alma 41:3). Elder Dallin H. Oaks illustrated this principle as follows:

> When someone genuinely wanted to do something for my father-in-law but was prevented by circumstances, he would say: "Thank you. I will take the good will for the deed." Similarly, I believe that our Father in heaven will receive the true desires of our hearts as a substitute for actions that are genuinely impossible.
>
> Here we see [a] contrast between the laws of God and the laws of men. It is entirely impractical to grant a *legal* advantage on the basis of an intent not translated into action. "I intended to sign that contract" or "We intended to get married" cannot stand as the equivalent of the act required by law. If the law were to give effect to intentions in lieu of specific acts, it would open the door for too much abuse, since the laws of man have no reliable means of determining our innermost thoughts.
>
> In contrast, the *law of God* can reward a righteous desire because

an omniscient God can discern it. As revealed through the prophet of this dispensation, God "is a discerner of the thoughts and intents of the heart." (D&C 33:1.) If a person refrains from a particular act because he is genuinely unable to perform it, but truly would if he could, our Heavenly Father will know this and can reward that person accordingly.[13]

JACOB'S LIST OF WARNINGS

Having spoken at length of Jesus Christ and the Atonement, Jacob then turned his attention to the condemnation of specific sins and uttered a series of woes—harsh warnings to the Saints. First of all, he gave stern warning to the person who sins against light, who "has all the commandments of God, like unto us, and that transgresseth them, and that wasteth the days of his probation." Of such a one Jacob said, "Awful is his state!" (2 Nephi 9:27.) Those who have access to the light are expected to walk in that light, "for of him unto whom much is given much is required; and he who sins against the greater light shall receive the greater condemnation" (D&C 82:3). Amulek would likewise counsel the Zoramites some five hundred years hence: "I beseech of you that ye do not procrastinate the day of your repentance until the end; for after this day of life, which is given us to prepare for eternity, behold, if we do not improve our time while in this life, then cometh the night of darkness wherein there can be no labor performed" (Alma 34:33; compare Helaman 13:38).

Jacob also warned against the worship of riches, promising that those who despise the poor and persecute the meek shall eventually find that their riches will perish with them (see 2 Nephi 9:30; compare Mosiah 4:23). He also warned against the following:

1. The spiritually deaf who will not hear the word of the Lord and the spiritually blind who refuse to see things as they really are, who are described in a modern revelation as "walking in darkness at noon-day" (see 2 Nephi 9:31–32; D&C 95:6).

2. "The uncircumcised of heart," those who may appear clean outwardly—whose actions seem to accord with the prescribed patterns of living—but whose hearts are corrupt, whose minds lust after the things of this world (see 2 Nephi 9:33; compare Romans 2:29).

3. Liars, who shall spend their days after this life in hell and shall thereafter go to the telestial kingdom (see 2 Nephi 9:34; D&C 76:103–6).

4. Murderers, for they are worthy of death themselves and shall inherit the least of the kingdoms of glory hereafter (see 2 Nephi 9:35; Genesis 9:6; Revelation 21:8; 22:15; D&C 42:19; 76:103).

5. The immoral, who "shall suffer the wrath of God on earth," even "the vengeance of eternal fire" when the Savior returns. These shall be "cast down to hell and suffer the wrath of Almighty God" in the world of spirits and shall eventually come forth to dwell in the telestial kingdom (see 2 Nephi 9:36; D&C 76:103–6).

6. Those who worship idols, who rivet their attention and focus their affections upon anything other than the true and living God, for such persons please and play into the hands of Satan and will eventually find themselves in the hands of a jealous God (see 2 Nephi 9:37).

President Ezra Taft Benson has taught that "the two groups in the Book of Mormon that seemed to have the greatest difficulty with pride are the 'learned and the rich.'"[14] It is of the former group—those who are proud because of their learning—that Jacob chose to particularize a woe: "O that cunning plan of the evil one!" Jacob said. "O the vainness, and the frailties, and the foolishness of men! When they are learned they think they are wise, and they hearken not unto the counsel of God, for they set it aside, supposing they know of themselves, wherefore, their wisdom is foolishness and it profiteth them not. And they shall perish" (2 Nephi 9:28). Whenever any people—particularly members of the household of faith—refuse to acknowledge the true Source of all knowledge and wisdom, but choose instead to worship at the shrine of intellect; or whenever they develop an unhealthy allegiance to the philosophies and disciplines of men—but set at naught or ignore entirely the revealed word—then such persons are on the road to spiritual destruction. For the present they are "ever learning, [but] never able to come to the knowledge of the truth" (2 Timothy 3:7). One day they shall learn of the evils they have perpetrated among their fellow beings and the irreparable damage they have done to their own souls. President Joseph F. Smith explained:

> Among the Latter-day Saints, the preaching of false doctrines disguised as truths of the gospel, may be expected from people of two classes, and practically from these only; they are:
> First—The hopelessly ignorant, whose lack of intelligence is due to their indolence and sloth, who make but feeble effort, if indeed any at all, to better themselves by reading and study; those who are

afflicted with a dread disease that may develop into an incurable malady—laziness.

Second—The proud and self-vaunting ones, *who read by the lamp of their own conceit;* who interpret by rules of their own contriving; *who have become a law unto themselves,* and so pose as the sole judges of their own doings. *More dangerously ignorant than the first.*[15]

Jacob's advice is timeless; adopting his perspective will prevent a multitude of sins: "To be learned is good if [we] hearken unto the counsels of God" (2 Nephi 9:29). In short, the key to a person's spiritual success is the eye: "If your eye be single to my glory," the Lord told the Latter-day Saints, "your whole bodies shall be filled with light, and there shall be no darkness in you; and that body which is filled with light comprehendeth all things" (D&C 88:67). To use Jacob's simple but pointed language, "to be carnally-minded is death, and to be spiritually-minded is life eternal" (2 Nephi 9:39).

CONCLUSION

Jacob, son of Lehi, was a gifted philosopher, a profound theologian, and a mighty preacher of righteousness. He was a sensitive seer who enjoyed the gift of discernment, rejoiced in the spirit of prophecy and revelation with which the Lord had blessed him, and spoke to his people, the Nephites, in terms of their true needs (see 2 Nephi 9:48). An underlying theme to all his writings was a call to the members of the Church—the house of Israel—to gather to Christ, to "reconcile yourselves to the will of God, and not to the will of the devil and the flesh" (2 Nephi 10:24). Further, his was an open invitation (like Isaiah's): "Every one that thirsteth, come ye to the waters," the waters of life available through the gospel of Jesus Christ. "Come," he pleaded, "buy wine and milk without money and without price" (2 Nephi 9:50). That is, come to salvation, which is free (see 2 Nephi 2:4; compare Isaiah 55:1–2), freely available, knowing full well that "after ye are reconciled unto God, that it is only in and through the grace of God that ye are saved" (2 Nephi 10:24). His desire? That the Saints of Most High would center their lives and focus their actions upon those things that soothe and sanctify the soul, that they would never labor in secondary causes, in endeavors of doubtful worth or questionable productivity (see 2 Nephi 9:51). Jacob's desire for his people, and for all of God's children alike, is the same as that of all of the Lord's anointed servants: "Wherefore, may God raise you from death by the power of the resurrection, and also from everlasting death by the power of the atonement, that ye may be received into the eternal kingdom of God, that ye may praise him through grace divine" (2 Nephi 10:25).

NOTES

1. Jacob's language is unmistakably similar to that of the language of God to Adam, as found in Joseph Smith's translation of Genesis: "Therefore I give unto you a commandment," the Lord said to our first father, "to teach these things [the plan of salvation] freely unto your children, saying: That by reason of transgression cometh the fall, which fall bringeth death, . . . even so ye must be born again into the kingdom of heaven" (Moses 6:58–59; JST, Genesis 6:61–62). Note the similarity to Jacob's teachings, based, it would appear, upon the brass plates: "There must needs be a power of resurrection, and the resurrection must needs come unto man by reason of the fall; and the fall came by reason of transgression" (2 Nephi 9:6).

2. See *Times and Seasons* (February 1, 1843), 4:82–83; italics added; see also Bruce R. McConkie, *Mormon Doctrine*, 2d ed. (Salt Lake City: Bookcraft, 1966), p. 65.

3. Joseph Smith, *Teachings of the Prophet Joseph Smith*, sel. Joseph Fielding Smith (Salt Lake City: Deseret Book Co., 1976), p. 121; italics added.

4. Bruce R. McConkie, *A New Witness for the Articles of Faith* (Salt Lake City: Deseret Book Co., 1985), p. 130.

5. For an insightful comment on the central importance of the resurrection of Christ, see Smith, *Teachings*, p. 62.

6. "The Doctrines of the Resurrection of the Dead and the Eternal Judgment are necessary to preach among the first principles of the Gospel of Jesus Christ" (Smith, *Teachings*, p. 149).

7. See Joseph F. Smith, *Gospel Doctrine* (Salt Lake City: Deseret Book Co., 1971), pp. 448–49.

8. "A man is his own tormentor and his own condemner. Hence the saying, They shall go into the lake that burns with fire and brimstone. The torment of disappointment in the mind of man is as exquisite as a lake burning with fire and brimstone. I say, so is the torment of man" (Smith, *Teachings*, p. 357; compare pp. 310–11).

9. It is a remarkable thing to discover that, indeed, this is the first time in the Book of Mormon that the name-title *Christ* is given for the Redeemer. Before this he is known by numerous titles, such as Messiah, Holy One of Israel, Shepherd, Lamb of God, Son of the Eternal Father, Savior, and Lord. It is difficult to know exactly what Jacob had in mind here. Did he mean that this was the first occasion when he came to know that the name of the Holy One of Israel, the Messiah, would be Christ? Did he mean that the angel had simply confirmed in his mind the specific name of the Messiah, something the Nephites already knew? The question is largely one of language: we know the Lord Jehovah as *Jesus Christ,* names that mean literally "the Lord is salvation" and "the Messiah or anointed one," respectively. The exact name by which Christ was known to other peoples of the past (and of different languages)—including the Nephites—is unknown to us. The complete name-title *Jesus Christ* is given for the first time by Nephi in 2 Nephi 25:19. For a more detailed discussion of this matter,

see Theodore M. Burton, *God's Greatest Gift* (Salt Lake City: Deseret Book Co., 1976), pp. 153–55.

10. While Jesus was on the cross, between the sixth and ninth hours (between noon and 3:00 P.M.), all the agonies of Gethsemane returned (see James E. Talmage, *Jesus the Christ*, 3d ed. [Salt Lake City: The Church of Jesus Christ of Latter-day Saints, 1916], p. 661; Bruce R. McConkie, *The Mortal Messiah: From Bethlehem to Calvary*, 4 vols. [Salt Lake City: Deseret Book Co., 1979–81], 4:224–25).

11. President Brigham Young taught that it was the withdrawal of the Father's Spirit that caused Jesus to sweat blood (see *Journal of Discourses* [London: Latter-day Saints' Book Depot, 1854–86], 3:205–6).

12. Neal A. Maxwell, *Even As I Am* (Salt Lake City: Deseret Book Co., 1982), pp. 116–17.

13. Dallin H. Oaks, "The Desires of Our Hearts," in *Brigham Young University 1985–86 Devotional and Fireside Speeches* (Provo: Brigham Young University Publications, 1986), p. 30.

14. Ezra Taft Benson, in Conference Report, April 1986, p. 6.

15. Joseph F. Smith, *Gospel Doctrine,* p. 373; italics added.

CHAPTER 8

The New Birth

The Book of Mormon is an invitation to come unto Christ. It is a divine invitation to come unto the Holy Messiah and partake of his goodness and grace. It is a consummate invitation to come unto the Lord of Life and be changed. Indeed, one who chooses Christ chooses to be changed. The plan of salvation is not just a program bent on making bad men good and good men better; it is a system of salvation that seeks to renovate society and transform the whole of humankind. The Church of Jesus Christ of Latter-day Saints is a divine institution; it is led by prophets and apostles, men with seeric vision. The Church is, however, only a means to an end, the vehicle that administers the saving gospel. The great challenge in life is for men and women to receive the everlasting gospel, participate in the ordinances of salvation, live worthy of the powers of godliness, put off the natural man, and grow in righteousness so that they might enjoy a mature spiritual union with that Lord whose they are.

It is a rich blessing to belong to "the only true and living church upon the face of the whole earth" (D&C 1:30). Yet membership in the Church is not enough; we are neither saved nor damned as congregations. Salvation is not found in occupying the right pew. Alma reported the Lord as saying that all citizens of the earthly kingdom "must be born again; yea, born of God, changed from their carnal and fallen state, to a state of righteousness, being redeemed of God, becoming his sons and daughters; and thus they become new creatures; and unless they do this, they can in nowise inherit the kingdom of God" (Mosiah 27:25–26). Given the importance of the new birth and the confusion often surrounding its true nature, it will be helpful to a proper understanding of this subject if we here identify at least some of the basic doctrinal concepts associated with it.

BAPTISM: OF WATER AND OF THE SPIRIT

The baptism of water is accomplished through immersion by one having authority, thereby allowing the initiate to demonstrate his or her acceptance of the atonement of the Lord our Redeemer: one goes down into the "watery grave" in remembrance of Christ's death and burial; one comes forth out of the water in remembrance of his coming forth from the tomb unto resurrected glory. "Know ye not," Paul asked the Romans, "that so many of us as were baptized into Jesus Christ were baptized into his death? Therefore we are buried with him by baptism into death: that like as Christ was raised up from the dead by the glory of the Father, even so we also should walk in newness of life. For if we have been planted together in the likeness of his death, we shall be also in the likeness of his resurrection" (Romans 6:3–5).

When a person is confirmed a member of the Church, he or she is directed to "receive the Holy Ghost." This is an imperative statement, a command. There is no salvation save the command be heeded. Through the new member's living worthy of the companionship of the Holy Ghost, the second part of the baptismal ordinance—the rebirth of the Spirit—begins. Scripturally this process is called the "baptism of fire"; the Holy Ghost is a sanctifier who burns dross and iniquity out of the soul as if by fire. Thus the remission of sins comes only after the reception and cleansing influence of the Holy Ghost. That is, only after water baptism may one be "wrought upon and cleansed by the power of the Holy Ghost" (Moroni 6:4). Nephi explained: "Wherefore, do the things which I have told you I have seen that your Lord and your Redeemer should do; for, for this cause have they been shown unto me, that ye might know the gate by which ye should enter. For the gate by which ye should enter is repentance and baptism by water; and then cometh a remission of your sins by fire and by the Holy Ghost" (2 Nephi 31:17).

Elder Bruce R. McConkie wrote: "Sins are remitted not in the waters of baptism, as we say in speaking figuratively, but when we receive the Holy Ghost. It is the Holy Spirit of God that erases carnality and brings us into a state of righteousness. We become clean when we actually receive the fellowship and companionship of the Holy Ghost."[1] "You might as well baptize a bag of sand as a man," said Joseph Smith, "if not done in view of the remission of sins and getting of the Holy Ghost. Baptism by water is but half a baptism, and is good for nothing without the other half—that is, the baptism of the Holy Ghost."[2]

Entering into the kingdom of God through repentance and baptism is properly referred to as a "rebirth," for thereby we become as children in the household of faith. The godly anguish and suffering of the repentant soul could be likened to the pain experienced by the mother in labor. The elements common to the process of birth are water, blood, and spirit. The amniotic fluid that surrounds the child prior to birth is a watery substance that aids in the development of the infant. The water of the baptismal font serves as a medium through which spiritual development begins. Blood is the medium through which saving nutrients and life-giving substances are passed to the child. Likewise, it is through the blood of Christ that the benefits of the Atonement are extended to man and the saving principles of the gospel are made a part of his life. Just as the individual spirit gives life to the infant body, even so the reception of the Holy Ghost begins a "quickening in the inner man" (see Moses 6:59–61, 64–65). It follows, therefore, that if one receives the ordinance of water baptism but fails to live worthy of the enlivening and sanctifying influences of the Holy Ghost, he has not been "born again"; he is, in effect, stillborn as to the things of the Spirit. "Now I say unto you," Alma implored, "that ye must repent, and be born again; for the Spirit saith if ye are not born again ye cannot inherit the kingdom of heaven" (Alma 7:14).

SEEING AND ENTERING THE KINGDOM

A large segment of Christianity believes that being born again consists in receiving the sacraments of the church. Another segment feels that being born again is to have a personal spiritual experience with the Lord. Truth takes a road between them both. Joseph Smith expressed it thus: "Being born again, comes by the Spirit of God through ordinances."[3] That is, both ordinances and spiritual experiences are requisite for the change described in scripture as the new birth.

Jesus said to Nicodemus: "Except a man be born again, he cannot *see* the kingdom of God." Nicodemus, rather foolishly, asked: "How can a man be born when he is old? Can he enter the second time into his mother's womb, and be born?" Unperturbed, Jesus responded: "Verily, verily, I say unto thee, Except a man be born of water and of the Spirit, he cannot *enter* into the kingdom of God" (John 3:3–5; italics added). Joseph Smith explained: "It is one thing to *see* the kingdom of God, and another thing to *enter* into it. We must have *a change of heart to see* the

kingdom of God, and *subscribe the articles of adoption to enter therein*."[4]
To *see* the kingdom of God is to recognize that church in one's day
which is the Lord's church; to sense and feel the truthfulness of its pronouncements and the authenticity of its priesthood; and to acknowledge that those who present the gospel message are true servants of
God. One comes to *see* the kingdom—that is, to recognize the truths of
salvation—as the Holy Ghost grants to him the eye of faith. One enters
the kingdom, as the Prophet explained, through subscribing to the *articles of adoption*, the first principles and ordinances of the gospel—faith in
Jesus Christ, repentance, baptism, and the reception of the Holy Ghost.
These allow one to be legally adopted into the family of the Lord Jesus
Christ and into the church and kingdom of God on earth.

In further discussing the new birth—and particularly the importance of seeing and entering the kingdom—the Prophet observed:

> The birth here spoken of [John 3:3–5] was not the gift of the
> Holy Ghost, which was promised after baptism, but was a portion
> of the Spirit, which attended the preaching of the gospel by the
> elders of the Church. The people wondered why they had not pre-
> viously understood the plain declarations of scripture, as explained
> by the elder, as they had read them hundreds of times. When they
> read the Bible [now] it was a new book to them. *This was being born
> again to see the kingdom of God.* They were not in it, but could see it
> from the outside, which they could not do until the Spirit of the
> Lord took the veil from their eyes. It was a change of heart, but not
> of state. Though Cornelius [Acts 10] had seen an holy angel, and on
> the preaching of Peter the Holy Ghost was poured out upon him
> and his household, they were only born again to see the kingdom of
> God. Had they not been baptized afterwards they would not have
> been saved.[5]

There are numerous illustrations in the Book of Mormon wherein
individuals and groups came to see the kingdom as a preparation for
entering therein. In the eleventh chapter of Alma, Amulek stood to offer
a corroborating witness to that of Alma. He was challenged by the crafty
lawyer Zeezrom. With great power and persuasion, Amulek bore testimony of the fatherhood of Christ, of his role as the Creator and
Redeemer, and of the glory of the resurrection and judgment that come
through Christ's mediation and atonement (verses 26–46). By the time
Alma stood again to speak, Zeezrom had become "convinced more and
more of the power of God." More specifically, he was "convinced that

Chapter 8—The New Birth

Alma and Amulek had a knowledge of him, for he was convinced that they knew the thoughts and intents of his heart." At this point "Zeezrom began to inquire of them diligently, that he might know more concerning the kingdom of God." His questions changed; they were more poignant and sincere (see Alma 12:8). His appreciation for who Alma and Amulek were, as well as Whom and what they represented, also began to grow. In short, Zeezrom was being born again to see the kingdom of God. Thereafter he repented and joined Alma's missionary force. And so it was with King Lamoni and his father. As Ammon and Aaron preached the gospel and unfolded the scriptures and delineated the doctrines of the Creation, the Fall, and the Atonement, the Lamanite leaders began to see things in a new light, things as they really are. They had been born again to see (see Alma 17–22).

A CHANGE OF ATTITUDE AND CHARACTER

Those who have been born again have "crucified the old man of sin"; they who are "in Christ" represent a "new creation" of the Holy Ghost (see Romans 6:6; 2 Corinthians 5:17). One who is born again does not continue in sin (see JST, 1 John 3:8), for such a one has "no more disposition to do evil, but to do good continually" (Mosiah 5:2). To be born again is to be converted. "Membership in the church and conversion are not necessarily synonymous," said President Marion G. Romney. "Being converted . . . and having a testimony are not necessarily the same thing. . . . A testimony comes when the Holy Ghost gives the earnest seeker a witness of the truth. A moving testimony vitalizes faith; that is, it induces repentance and obedience to the commandments. Conversion, on the other hand, is the fruit of, or the reward for, repentance and obedience. . . . Conversion is effected by divine forgiveness, which remits sins. . . . Thus he is converted to a newness of life. His spirit is healed."[6]

Elder Orson Pratt explained the cleansing powers of the Holy Ghost:

> Water baptism is only a preparatory cleansing of the believing penitent . . . whereas, the baptism of fire and the Holy Ghost cleanses more thoroughly, by renewing the inner man, and by purifying the affections, desires, and thoughts which have long been habituated in the impure ways of sin. Without the aid of the Holy Ghost, a person would have but very little power to change his

105

mind, at once, from its habituated course, and to walk in newness of life. . . . So great is the force of habit, that he would, without being renewed by the Holy Ghost, be easily overcome, and contaminated again with sin. Hence, it is infinitely important that the affections and desires should be, in a measure, changed and renewed, so as to cause him to hate that which he before loved, and to love that which he before hated. To thus renew the mind of man is the work of the Holy Ghost.[7]

Such renewal is evident in the case of King Lamoni. After the message of salvation had been declared, King Lamoni was overwhelmed and spiritually subdued by what he had heard and felt. "And he began to cry unto the Lord, saying: O Lord, have mercy; according to thy abundant mercy which thou hast had upon the people of Nephi, have upon me, and my people. And now, when he had said this, he fell unto the earth, as if he were dead." His family mourned over him, supposing that he had died. But Ammon knew better, for "he knew that king Lamoni was under the power of God; he knew that the dark veil of unbelief was being cast away from his mind, and the light which did light up his mind, which was the light of the glory of God, which was a marvelous light of his goodness—yea, *this light had infused such joy into his soul, the cloud of darkness having been dispelled, and that the light of everlasting life was lit up in his soul,* yea, he knew that this had overcome his natural frame, and he was carried away in God" (Alma 18:41–43; 19:6; italics added).

The infusion of light and joy here spoken of is also known as a "quickening in the inner man." In describing the spiritual renewal of father Adam in the opening dispensation of this world's history, Moses wrote: "And it came to pass, when the Lord had spoken with Adam, our father, that Adam cried unto the Lord, and he was caught away by the Spirit of the Lord, and was carried down into the water, and was laid under the water, and was brought forth out of the water. And thus he was baptized, and the Spirit of God descended upon him, and thus he was born of the Spirit, and became quickened in the inner man" (Moses 6:64–65). To be born again is to gain a heightened sensitivity to things that matter.

For example, since much of the time the Holy Ghost works with members of the Church through their consciences, to be born again is to gain a deeper sensitivity to right and wrong, to enjoy greater manifestations of the gift of discernment, to develop more refined and educated desires. Since being born again consists in being adopted into the royal family and thus gaining godly attributes and qualities, experiencing the new birth entails feeling a deeper compassion and empathy for those who mourn or suffer or reach out for succor. The quickening in the inner man peels away the film and facade of sin, makes unnecessary the rigors and taxing labors of ostentation and superfluity; those who are born again see things clearly and sharply and are able to sift and sort out the sordid or even the subsidiary. They have less inclination to labor in secondary causes and have a consuming but patient passion to occupy themselves with that which brings light and life and love. They come to treasure the simple pleasures in life and rejoice in the goodness of their God. Joseph Smith taught that "the nearer man approaches perfection, the clearer are his views, and the greater his enjoyments, till he has overcome the evils of his life and lost every desire for sin."[8]

NEW KNOWLEDGE, NEW INSIGHTS, NEW DIRECTIONS

The Holy Ghost is a revelator, and he makes known the things of God to those who are ready to bear them. The Holy Ghost reveals matters that man cannot teach nor man's wisdom convey (see 1 John 2:27; Moroni 10:5; D&C 43:15–16). President Brigham Young said that the Holy Ghost reveals heaven's treasures to its disciples. "It shows them things past, present, and to come. It opens the vision of the mind, unlocks the treasures of wisdom, and they begin to understand the things of God. . . . They comprehend themselves and the great object of their existence."[9] The Spirit brings certitude and conviction and banishes the darkness of doubt. Cyprian, a great defender of the faith after the apostolic period, spoke of his own conversion. "Into my heart," he recounted, "purified of all sin, there entered a light which came from on high and then suddenly, and in a marvelous manner, I saw certainty succeed doubt."[10] "To know God our Eternal Father and Jesus Christ, whom he sent," President Marion G. Romney explained, "one must, as did the Apostles of old, learn of them through the process of divine revelation. One must be born again."[11]

Those persons who have been born again begin to see things in perspective, from an elevated perspective, from an eternal perspective; they have "great views of that which is to come" (Mosiah 5:3). It is not that they never have questions or doubts; rather, they know for a certainty, by the power of the Holy Ghost, that the fundamental verities of the faith are true—that God is in his heaven, that the church and kingdom of God have been restored to earth with all necessary keys and powers, and that those who have been chosen and anointed to lead the Church are divinely called. Questions and uncertainties are placed on the shelf. They may not immediately disappear, but they do not disturb. As President John Taylor explained, the Holy Ghost "is not something that affects the outward ear alone; it is not something that affects simply his judgment, but it affects his inner man; it affects the spirit that dwells within him; it is part of God imparted unto man, if you please, giving him an assurance that God lives."[12] Those who have been born of the Spirit are not free from the vicissitudes of this life; rather, because they have gained new vision, they have gained new strength, new resources with which to deal with their challenges.

SONS AND DAUGHTERS OF JESUS CHRIST

Those who are born again are received into a new family: they become the sons and daughters of Jesus Christ. As the Savior and foreordained Messiah, Jesus Christ became the "author of eternal salvation unto all them that obey him" (Hebrews 5:9), and the Father's gospel became his by adoption; thus we know it as the gospel of Jesus Christ. Things on earth are patterned after that which is in heaven. God dwells in the family unit. Those who accept the gospel of Jesus Christ enter the family of Jesus Christ, take upon them the family name, and thus become inheritors of family obligations and family privileges. All must be born into the family of Christ by conversion. Because the hearts of the Saints are changed through faith on his name, they become the sons and daughters of their Lord.

This was the testimony of King Benjamin. After he had delivered his masterful discourse on atonement and service and had called for his people to put off the natural man through putting on Christ, the people renewed their baptismal covenant and promised to keep the commandments of God to the best of their abilities. "And now, these are the words which king Benjamin desired of them; and therefore he said unto them: Ye have spoken the words that I desired; and the covenant which ye have made is a righteous covenant" (Mosiah 5:6). And then come these words:

> And now, *because of the covenant which ye have made ye shall be called the children of Christ, his sons, and his daughters; for behold, this day he hath spiritually begotten you; for ye say that your hearts are changed through faith on his name; therefore, ye are born of him and have become his sons and his daughters.*
>
> And under this head ye are made free, and there is no other head whereby ye can be made free. There is no other name given whereby salvation cometh; therefore, I would that ye should take upon you the name of Christ, all you that have entered into the covenant with God that ye should be obedient unto the end of your lives. (Verses 7–8; italics added.)

The Savior, in speaking to those of our day, said: "Hearken unto the voice of the Lord your God, while I speak unto you . . . ; for verily I say unto you, *all those who receive my gospel are sons and daughters in my kingdom*" (D&C 25:1; italics added; compare 39:4). "Thus it is that the saints are born of Christ because they have been born of the Spirit; they are alive in Christ because they enjoy the companionship of the Spirit, and they are members of his family because they are clean as he is clean."[13] Those who have given strict heed to the words of the prophets are thus known as the "seed of Christ," persons who are "heirs of the kingdom of God," those "for whom he has died" (see Mosiah 15:11–12). Alma the Younger attested:

> I have repented of my sins, and have been redeemed of the Lord; behold I am born of the Spirit.
>
> And the Lord said unto me: Marvel not that all mankind, yea, men and women, all nations, kindreds, tongues and people, must be born again; yea, born of God, changed from their carnal and fallen state, to a state of righteousness, being redeemed of God, becoming his sons and daughters;
>
> And thus they become new creatures; and unless they do this, they can in no wise inherit the kingdom of God. (Mosiah 27:24–26.)

THE NEW BIRTH: A LIFETIME PROCESS

Though the new birth is a result of a definite time of decision—a desire for the things of righteousness—it is usually a quiet but powerful process. It is true that certain individuals such as Alma (see Mosiah 27; Alma 36), Paul (see Acts 9), or King Lamoni (see Alma 18–19) underwent dramatic and miraculously sudden conversions. They were born again through a singular experience. And no doubt others, even in our day, change from weakness to strength in a wondrous fashion. These, however, are exceptions rather than the rule. There are few sudden disciples, few instant Christians. The Holy Ghost generally makes Saints out of sinners "in process of time." Of Christ our Prototype the revelations attest: "He received not of the fulness at first, but continued from grace to grace, until he received a fulness" (D&C 93:13). Elder Bruce R. McConkie taught:

> A person may get converted in a moment, miraculously. That is what happened to Alma the younger. He had been baptized in his youth, he had been promised the Holy Ghost, but he had never received it. He was too worldly-wise; he went off with the sons of Mosiah to destroy the church. . . . Alma was in this state, and then this occasion occurred when a new light came into his soul, when he was changed from his fallen and carnal state to a state of righteousness. In his instance the conversion was miraculous, in the snap of a finger, almost. . . . But that is not the way it happens with most people. With most people conversion is a process; and it goes step by step, degree by degree, level by level, from a lower state to a higher, from grace to grace, until the time that the individual is wholly turned to the cause of righteousness. . . . And the conversion process goes on, until it is completed, until we become, literally, as the Book of Mormon says, saints of God instead of natural men.[14]

On another occasion Elder McConkie taught: "We are born again when we die as pertaining to unrighteousness and when we live as pertaining to the things of the Spirit. But that doesn't happen in an instant, suddenly. That . . . is a process. *Being born again is a gradual thing, except in a few isolated instances that are so miraculous that they get written up in the scriptures. As far as the generality of members of the Church are concerned, we are born again by degrees, and we are born again to added light and added knowledge and added desires for righteousness as we keep the commandments.*"[15] President Ezra Taft Benson also explained that "we must be careful, as we seek to become more and more godlike, that we do not become discouraged and lose hope. Becoming Christlike is a lifetime pursuit and very often involves growth and change that is slow, almost imperceptible." Then, after mentioning the sudden spiritual transformations of such notables as Alma the Younger, Paul, Enos, and King Lamoni, he added: "But we must be cautious as we discuss these remarkable examples. *Though they are real and powerful, they are the exception more than the rule.* For every Paul, for every Enos, and for every King Lamoni, there are hundreds and thousands of people who find the process of repentance much more subtle, much more imperceptible. Day by day they move closer to the Lord, little realizing they are building a godlike life. They live quiet lives of goodness, service, and commitment. They are like the Lamanites, who the Lord said, 'were baptized with fire and with the Holy Ghost, and they knew it not' (3 Nephi 9:20)."[16]

Birth is but a beginning—the journey of faith lies ahead. It was never intended that those of the household of faith remain children forever, even children of Christ. When the members of the Church receive the ordinances of salvation and then live so as to enjoy the promptings, guidance, and sanctifying powers of the Holy Ghost; when they take upon themselves the name of Christ, forsake the ways of the world, and are born again into the family kingdom of their Savior and Redeemer—when they do these things they qualify themselves for richer and higher privileges and spiritual opportunities. They then receive the blessings of the temple, particularly the new and everlasting covenant of marriage. Latter-day Saints who keep these supernal covenants will gain power to become the sons and daughters of God, meaning the Father. They become joint heirs or co-inheritors with Christ to all that the Father has: they are entitled to the blessings of the Firstborn, and thus "they are they who are the church of the Firstborn. . . . Wherefore, as it is written, they are gods, even the sons of God" (D&C 76:54, 58).[17]

CONCLUSION

The Prophet Joseph Smith, like his Master, Jesus Christ, spoke forthrightly of the need for spiritual change. "Except a man be born again," he said, "he cannot see the kingdom of God. This eternal truth settles the question of all men's religion. *A man may be saved, after the judgment, in the terrestrial kingdom, or in the telestial kingdom, but he can never see the celestial kingdom of God, without being born of water and the Spirit.* . . . He can never come unto Mount Zion, and unto the city of the living God, the heavenly Jerusalem, and to an innumerable company of angels; to the general assembly and Church of the Firstborn, which are written in heaven, and to God the judge of all, and to the spirits of just men made perfect, and to Jesus the Mediator of the new covenant, *unless he becomes as a little child, and is taught by the Spirit of God.*"[18]

The Holy Ghost is the midwife of salvation. He is the agent of the new birth, the sacred channel and power by which men and women are changed and renewed, made into new creatures. This new birth, which comes in process of time, brings membership in the family of God: such persons are redeemed from the Fall, reconciled to the Father through the Son, made worthy of the designation of sons and daughters of Jesus Christ and, thereafter upon continued faithfulness, sons and daughters of God the Father. They come to see and feel and understand things that the spiritually inert can never know. They become participants in the realm of divine experience.

Notes

1. Bruce R. McConkie, *A New Witness for the Articles of Faith* (Salt Lake City: Deseret Book Co., 1985), p. 290; see also p. 239.

2. Joseph Smith, *Teachings of the Prophet Joseph Smith,* sel. Joseph Fielding Smith (Salt Lake City: Deseret Book Co., 1976), p. 314.

3. Ibid., p. 162.

4. Ibid., p. 328; italics added.

5. Reported by Daniel Tyler in *"Recollections of the Prophet Joseph Smith,"* pp. 93–94, as cited in Hyrum L. Andrus and Helen Mae Andrus, comps., *They Knew the Prophet* (Salt Lake City: Bookcraft, 1974), p. 50; italics added.

6. Marion G. Romney, in Conference Report, October 1963, p. 24.

7. Orson Pratt, "The Holy Spirit," in *Writings of an Apostle* (Salt Lake City: Mormon Heritage Publishers, 1976), pp. 56–57.

8. Smith, *Teachings,* p. 51.

9. Brigham Young, in *Journal of Discourses,* 26 vols. (London: Latter-day Saints' Book Depot, 1854–86), 3:368.

10. Cited by Harold B. Lee, *Stand Ye in Holy Places* (Salt Lake City: Deseret Book Co., 1974), p. 57.

11. Romney, in Conference Report, October 1981, pp. 18, 20.

12. John Taylor, in *Journal of Discourses,* 11:23.

13. Bruce R. McConkie, *New Witness for the Articles of Faith,* p. 285.

14. From an address at a BYU First Stake Conference, 11 February 1968; see also Lee, *Stand Ye in Holy Places,* pp. 58–61.

15. Bruce R. McConkie, "Jesus Christ and Him Crucified," in *1976 BYU Devotional Speeches of the Year* (Provo: BYU Press, 1977), pp. 399–401.

16. Ezra Taft Benson, "A Mighty Change of Heart," *Ensign,* October 1989, pp. 2–5.

17. See Bruce R. McConkie, *Doctrinal New Testament Commentary,* 3 vols. (Salt Lake City: Bookcraft, 1970), 2:474–75.

18. Smith, *Teachings,* p. 12.

The Fatherhood and Sonship of Christ

One of the most fascinating and doctrinally significant sections of the Book of Mormon is the ministry of the Nephite prophet Abinadi. Sent by the Lord to declare repentance to King Noah, his wayward priests, and the wicked people in the land of Nephi, Abinadi was bold in pointing out the sins of the day; his testimony is particularly important in establishing the central verity that salvation is in Christ, that only in and through his atoning sacrifice could man hope for peace here and eternal life hereafter. This chapter will concentrate upon some of the key doctrinal contributions of Abinadi's sermon.

THE LAW OF MOSES AND THE ATONEMENT

Nephi and his brothers were instructed early in the Lehite experience to return to Jerusalem to procure the plates of brass. Lehi knew that his people "could not keep the commandments of the Lord according to the law of Moses, save they should have the law. And [he] also knew that the law was engraven upon the plates of brass" (1 Nephi 4:15–16). From the beginning of Nephite history, the writers made it extremely clear that the people were expected to observe the law of Moses. According to Nephi, his people "did observe to keep the judgments, and the statutes, and the commandments of the Lord in all things, *according to the law of Moses*" (2 Nephi 5:10; italics added). But what does this expression mean? Did they participate in the intricate system of sacrificial ritual described in Leviticus? In daily sacrifices? In the dietary laws? In the health practices?

We learn from the Book of Mormon itself and from subsequent teachings of Joseph Smith that the Nephite nation was composed of people whose lineages could be traced to three separate tribes of Israel: Lehi and his family were of Joseph, and specifically of Manasseh (see 1 Nephi 5:14; Alma 10:3); Ishmael was of the tribe of Ephraim;[1] and Mulek, the son of Zedekiah, was of the tribe of Judah (see Helaman 6:10). Inasmuch, then, as there were no Levites among the Nephites, we may assume that those holding authority presided and officiated by virtue of the higher priesthood. President Joseph Fielding Smith explains:

> The Nephites did not officiate under the authority of the Aaronic Priesthood. They were not descendants of Aaron, and there were no Levites among them. There is no evidence in the *Book of Mormon* that they held the Aaronic Priesthood until after the ministry of the resurrected Lord among them. . . . [The] higher priesthood can officiate in every ordinance of the gospel, and Jacob and Joseph, for instance, were consecrated priests and teachers after this order.[2]

The Nephites thus offered sacrifices by virtue of the Melchizedek Priesthood, the same authority by which sacrifices would have been offered from the days of Adam to the days of Moses and Aaron. Elder B. H. Roberts has written the following in this regard:

> That [the] higher priesthood was competent to act in administering the ordinances under what is known as the law of Moses, is evident from the fact that it so administered before the Aaronic or Levitical priesthood proper was given; and the fact that there was given to the household of Aaron and the tribe of Levi a special priesthood, by no means detracts from the right and power of the higher or Melchizedek priesthood to officiate in the ordinances of the law of Moses; for certainly the higher order of priesthood may officiate in the functions of the lower, when necessity requires it.[3]

Having the higher priesthood and the fulness of the gospel, the Nephites were thus able to see the law in its true light, as a great means to an even greater end. For those like the faithful Nephites who understood the timeless—retroactive and proactive—dimension of the Atonement, and thus had come to believe in Christ "as though he already was" (Jarom 1:11), the law of Moses had, in their words, become dead unto them (see 2 Nephi 25:25). The Law, grand and helpful though it might be, was but the prophecy; Jesus Christ himself was the fulfillment. How, then, would a people keep the law of Moses—a lesser law administered by a lesser priesthood—if they already had the everlasting gospel? According to a modern apostle, "We know the Nephites offered sacrifices and kept the law of Moses. Since they held the Melchizedek Priesthood and there were no Levites among them, we suppose their sacrifices were those that antedated the ministry of Moses [for example, the sacrifice of Adam in Moses 5] and that, since they had the fulness of the gospel itself, *they kept the law of Moses in the sense that they con-*

formed to its myriad moral principles and its endless ethical restrictions." Further, "there is, at least, no intimation in the Book of Mormon that the Nephites offered the daily sacrifices required by the law or that they held the various feasts that were part of the religious life of their Old World Kinsmen."[4]

Abinadi, identified by Mormon simply as "a man among them" (Mosiah 11:20), was sent by the Lord to proclaim against the iniquity and immorality of the people in the land of Nephi. His life was threatened; he left town for a period of two years and then returned in disguise to deliver the remainder of his doctrinally based prophecy. He predicted the violent death of King Noah and further spoke of the famine and pestilence that would be sent as a result of the iniquities of the people in the area (see Mosiah 11:21–12:7).

Abinadi was brought before Noah and his high priests for questioning. One of the priests asked, "What meaneth the words which are written, and which have been taught by our fathers?" (Mosiah 12:20). The beautiful passage in question is from Isaiah 52:7: "How beautiful upon the mountains are the feet of him that bringeth good tidings, that publisheth peace." One cannot help but wonder about the motivation behind the question. Did the high priest actually desire understanding of the verses? Or, rather, was he essentially saying: "I thought that the prophet Isaiah had said that blessed are those who declare *good* tidings and bring *peaceful* salutations. Why is your message so negative, so pessimistic, and why are you so prone to such gloomy prophecy?"

Abinadi nevertheless treated the questioner with enough respect to suggest a direct answer; the answer would, however, not be given at the moment (see Mosiah 15:11–18), for Abinadi had questions of his own to ask. "Are you priests, and pretend to teach this people, and to understand the spirit of prophesying, and yet desire to know of me what these things mean?" He then accused the priests of perverting the ways of the Lord. How did they do so? "If ye understand these things," Abinadi explained, "ye have not taught them." They had not been wise, he continued, for they had not applied their hearts to understanding (see Mosiah 12:17–27).

Abinadi asked, "What teach ye this people?" They answered, "We teach the law of Moses." "If ye teach the law of Moses," the prophet countered pointedly, "why do ye not keep it?" And then he followed up with questions that seem to summarize (consistent with Elder McConkie's statement above) what it meant for the people to keep the Law: "Why do ye set your hearts upon riches? Why do ye commit whoredoms and spend your strength with harlots, yea, and cause this people to commit sin?" (Mosiah 12:27–29.) In short, "Why are your lives not in harmony with the moral and ethical truths delivered by God and taught by Moses to the children of Israel? Why do you not even keep the Ten Commandments?"

One of the major doctrinal misunderstandings of errant individuals and groups in the Book of Mormon is the notion that the law of Moses is an end in itself, is all-sufficient, and that it has efficacy, virtue, and force enough to bring salvation. Sherem the anti-Christ sought to shake Jacob in his faith. This cunning one said: "I have heard and also know that thou goest about much, preaching that which ye call the gospel, or the doctrine of Christ." He continued: "And ye have led away much of this people that they pervert the right way of God, and keep not the law of Moses which is the right way; and convert the law of Moses into the worship of a being which ye say shall come many hundred years hence. And now behold, I, Sherem, declare unto you that this is blasphemy" (Jacob 7:6–7; italics added). We find a similar mentality among the priests of Noah. Abinadi asked: "And what know ye concerning the law of Moses? Doth salvation come by the law of Moses?" The priests "answered and said that salvation did come by the law of Moses" (Mosiah 12:31–32).

Herein is a subtle truth clouded in error. True it is that if the people from Moses to Christ had kept the Ten Commandments, had kept the ethical statutes laid down in the Law, had observed the ordinance of sacrifice—*all with an eye single to the glorious coming and atonement of the Messiah*—they would have departed this life with the peaceful assurance of exaltation that comes by the power of the Spirit to those who endure in faith. In the words of Elder McConkie: "Just as our conformity to gospel standards, while dwelling as lowly mortals apart from our Maker, prepares us to return to his presence with an inheritance of immortal glory, so the Mosaic standards prepared the chosen of Israel to believe and obey that [preparatory] gospel by conformity to which eternal life is won."[5] But salvation is not in the Law alone, not in the type but in that which is known as the antitype, that toward which the type points.

Chapter 9—The Fatherhood and Sonship of Christ

That symbol is of maximum worth which points beyond itself to a greater reality. Salvation comes through the law of Moses when individuals and congregations look beyond the Law to the Lawgiver, and thus to that life which only he can provide. Thus Abinadi remarked: "I know if ye keep the commandments of God ye shall be saved; yea, if ye keep the commandments which the Lord delivered unto Moses in the mount of Sinai" (Mosiah 12:33). Abinadi then began to read unto the wicked leaders the word of the Lord contained in the twentieth chapter of Exodus—the Ten Commandments (see Mosiah 12:34–13:24).

Having focused his listeners' minds upon the commandments, Abinadi returned to his discussion of the place of the law of Moses. He acknowledged the present expediency of keeping the Law but also observed that "the time shall come when it shall no more be expedient to keep the law of Moses." He continued: "And moreover, I say unto you, that salvation doth not come by the law alone; and were it not for the atonement, which God himself shall make for the sins and iniquities of his people, that they must unavoidably perish, notwithstanding the law of Moses" (Mosiah 13:27–28).

Drawing upon the same principle and relating it to our own day, Elder Bruce R. McConkie taught in 1984:

> Now let us suppose a modern-day case. Suppose we have the scriptures, the gospel, the priesthood, the Church, the ordinances, the organization, even the keys of the kingdom—everything that now is down to the last jot and tittle—and yet there is no atonement of Christ. What then? Can we be saved? Will all our good works save us? Will we be rewarded for all our righteousness?
>
> Most assuredly we will not. We are not saved by works alone, now matter how good; we are saved because God sent his Son to shed his blood in Gethsemane and on Calvary that all through him might ransomed be. We are saved by the blood of Christ.
>
> To paraphrase Abinadi: "Salvation doth not come by the Church alone: and were it not for the atonement, given by the grace of God as a free gift, all men must unavoidably perish, and this notwithstanding the Church and all that appertains to it."[6]

Abinadi concluded his sermon on the Law by giving to the wicked priests (and, of course, to us) one of the most comprehensive statements in all of scripture on the nature and purpose of the law of Moses. Because of the failure of the children of Israel in the days of Moses to receive the blessings of the higher priesthood and the sanctifying powers associated with the everlasting gospel, God elected to give to them a preparatory gospel. He provided a "law of carnal commandments" (D&C 84:27; see also Hebrews 7:16), "yea, even a very strict law; . . . a law which they were to observe strictly from day to day, to keep them in remembrance of God and their duty towards him" (Mosiah 13:29–30). In a sense, the law of Moses was given as a sort of "spiritual busywork," a system and pattern of life that would keep the people constantly involved. In addition, "all these things were types of things to come" (Mosiah 13:31), similitudes of the coming Savior and Redeemer. This latter statement by Abinadi is of infinite worth, for the symbolic and typical nature of the Law is nowhere taught in our present Old Testament. In the Nephite record this same testimony is given again and again (see, for example, 2 Nephi 11:4; 25:24–25; Jacob 4:5; Jarom 1:11; Mosiah 3:15; Alma 25:16; 34:14). Unfortunately, the people of Israel "did not all understand the law; and this because of the hardness of their hearts; for they understood not that there could not any man be saved except it were through the redemption of God" (Mosiah 13:32).

God's Suffering Servant

The prophet Isaiah spoke—like so many before him and so many after—of the condescension of the Great God, of the incarnation of the Eternal One, of the coming to earth of the Great Jehovah (compare 1 Nephi 11; Mosiah 3:5–9; Alma 34:10, 14). Surely if we had a complete record of all the messianic testimonies of those designated as the Lord's spokesmen, we would find in their messages a similar prophetic pattern: a witness that "God himself should come down among the children of men, and take upon him the form of man" (Mosiah 13:34). Jesus was indeed the Suffering Servant (see Acts 8:26–35).

Abinadi, like "all the prophets who have prophesied ever since the world began" (Mosiah 13:33), continued his message by delivering a testimony of the coming Christ. In Mosiah 14, he quoted from Isaiah's marvelous messianic pronouncement (see Isaiah 53); in Mosiah 15 he offered an inspired prophetic commentary upon Isaiah's words. We will now consider the meaning and import of but a few of the words of this messianic psalm.

1. "For he [Jesus Christ] shall grow up before him [the Father] as a tender plant, and as a root out of a dry ground" (Isaiah 53:2; Mosiah

14:2). Jesus of Nazareth, though the literal son of God and thus posses-sor of the very powers of immortality, was to undergo the throes of mor-tality, including the tender and helpless years of infancy and childhood characteristic of all children. He would grow as a root in the arid and parched ground of apostate Judaism. This root-stock or "stem of Jesse" would develop in a sterile and barren religious soil, in the midst of great learning but gross spiritual darkness.

2. "He hath no form nor comeliness; and when we shall see him, there is no beauty that we should desire him" (Isaiah 53:2; Mosiah 14:2). The Son of God was not to be known or recognized by any out-ward beauty; rather, those with an eye of faith would know by the wit-ness of the Spirit who it was that ministered among them.

3. "He is despised and rejected of men; a man of sorrows, and acquainted with grief" (Isaiah 53:3; Mosiah 14:3). What mortal man could know the loneliness that the Sinless One knew? Who among us can comprehend the awful irony associated with rejection by his own townspeople (see Luke 4:16–30; John 7:5) and by his own nation—the Jews? (see Matthew 23:37). Who can comprehend our Lord's soul cry, "My God, my God"? (Matthew 27:46; compare Matthew 26:42; Luke 22:41–44).

4. "Surely he has borne our griefs, and carried our sorrows" (Isaiah 53:4; Mosiah 14:4). There is no pain nor sorrow about which the Suf-fering Servant is ignorant; he who descended below all things became aware of mortal suffering through personal experience and thus became one who is "touched with the feeling of our infirmities" (Hebrews 4:15). Abinadi would later describe the Savior as one "having the bowels of mercy; being filled with compassion towards the children of men" (Mosiah 15:9). In the words of Alma, the son of Abinadi's student, the Savior "will take upon him their infirmities, that his bowels may be filled with mercy, according to the flesh, that he may know according to the flesh how to succor his people according to their infirmities" (Alma 7:12).

5. "But he was wounded for our transgressions, he was bruised for our iniquities" (Isaiah 53:5; Mosiah 14:5). Note that in Abinadi's com-mentary upon this passage, he speaks of the Master "standing betwixt them [the children of men] and justice; having broken the bands of

death, taken upon himself their iniquity and their transgressions, having redeemed them, and satisfied the demands of justice" (Mosiah 15:9).

6. "The chastisement of our peace was upon him; and with his stripes we are healed" (Isaiah 53:5; Mosiah 14:5). He who was the Prince of Peace and who had never known that loss of peace that follows in the wake of backward steps or moral detours became vicariously in Gethsemane and on Calvary "sin for us" (2 Corinthians 5:21). He bore on his own shoulders the vicarious but vicious load of a world's sins and thereby came to know for himself the consequence of sin—the loss of the Father's Spirit. "At the very moment," taught President Brigham Young, "at the hour when the crisis came for [Christ] to offer up his life, the Father withdrew Himself, withdrew His Spirit. . . . That is what made him sweat blood. If he had the power of God upon him, he would not have sweat blood; but all was withdrawn from him, . . . and he then pled with the Father not to forsake him."[7] Because Christ suffered, we need not suffer as he did. "For behold, I, God, have suffered these things for all, that they might not suffer if they would repent" (D&C 19:16).

7. "And he made his grave with the wicked, and with the rich in his death" (Isaiah 53:9; Mosiah 14:9). In this verse we gain an even stronger appreciation for the remarkable detail of the prophecy of Isaiah quoted by Abinadi. Jesus was indeed put to death "with the wicked," literally crucified between two thieves (see Luke 23:32). At the same time, he was buried "with the rich" in the sense that he was placed in a tomb owned by a wealthy man, Joseph of Arimathea (see John 19:38–42).

8. "Yet it pleased the Lord to bruise him" (Isaiah 53:10; Mosiah 14:10). This is a verse that requires careful consideration. God our Eternal Father loved his Only Begotten and, like any parent, surely anguished with the pain of his child. And yet, as infinitely painful as it must have been for Elohim, the hours of agony were necessary—they were a part of that plan of the Father of which Jehovah had been the chief advocate and proponent in premortality. Indeed it was needful that the "Lamb slain from the foundation of the world" be slain, in order that life and immortality might be brought to light. And thus "it pleased the Lord [the Father] to bruise him," in the sense that Jesus carried out to the fullest the will of the Father, in spite of the pain associated with the implementation of the terms and conditions of that will.

"Oh," Elder Melvin J. Ballard said, "in that moment when He might have saved His Son, I thank Him and praise Him that He did not fail us, for He had not only the love of His Son in mind, but He also had love for us. I rejoice that He did not interfere, and that His love for us made it possible for Him to endure to look upon the sufferings of His Son and give Him finally to us, our Savior and our Redeemer. Without Him, without His sacrifice, we would have remained, and would never have come glorified into His presence. And so this is what it cost, in part, for our Father in heaven to give the gift of His Son unto men."[8]

9. "When thou shalt make his soul an offering for sin, he shall see his seed" (Isaiah 53:10; Mosiah 14:10). Abinadi's commentary upon this passage is, in part, as follows: "Behold I say unto you, that *whosoever has heard the word of the prophets, yea,* all the holy prophets who have prophesied concerning the coming of the Lord—I say unto you, that *all those who have hearkened unto their words,* and believed that the Lord would redeem his people, and have looked forward to that day for a remission of their sins, I say unto you, that *these are his seed, or they are the heirs of the kingdom of God.*

"For these are they whose sins he has borne; these are they for whom he has died, to redeem them from their transgressions. And now, are they not his seed?" (Mosiah 15:11–12; italics added.)

When he had finished his work on Calvary, the Lord of the living and the dead entered the world of spirits. Having made his soul "an offering for sin" in Gethsemane and on the cross, the Master was greeted in Paradise by his seed, "an innumerable company of the spirits of the just," the righteous dead from the days of Adam to the meridian of time. To these persons—his seed—he taught the principles of his gospel and prepared them to come forth in a glorious resurrection (see Mosiah 14:10; D&C 138:12–19).

"But Isaiah's prophecy and Abinadi's interpretation speak only of those who have been and not of those who shall yet believe and who shall gain the adoption of sonship in a future day. A clear awareness of this fact is essential to a full understanding of what Isaiah and Abinadi really mean."[9]

10. "He shall prolong his days, and the pleasure of the Lord shall prosper in his hand" (Isaiah 53:10; Mosiah 14:10). This prophecy was certainly not fulfilled in Christ's mortal life, for the Lord gave up his life

as a ransom for many while yet in his prime. Its pure fulfillment, therefore, is to be seen in the Savior's rise from death into an immortal, resurrected state. His days, like the days of all those who die and are thereafter raised from the grave, are now prolonged everlastingly. In the words of Abinadi: "They are raised to dwell with God who has redeemed them; thus they have eternal life through Christ, who has broken the bands of death" (Mosiah 15:23).

THE MINISTRY OF CHRIST AS THE FATHER AND THE SON

Elohim is the Father of the spirits of all men, including Jesus Christ (see Hebrews 12:9; Numbers 16:22) and is thus the ultimate object of our worship (see 2 Nephi 25:16; Jacob 4:5; D&C 19:29). Elohim is our Father because he gave us life—provided a spirit birth for each of us. Jesus Christ is also known by the title of Father and is so designated in scripture.[10] An appreciation for the ways in which Christ is known as Father will do much toward clarifying the beautiful but rather difficult scriptural passage contained in the fifteenth chapter of Mosiah—Abinadi's sermon concerning the Father and the Son.

First of all, Jesus Christ is known as Father by virtue of his role as the Creator. Ages before he ever became mortal, he was directly involved in creation. Under the direction of his Father, he became the creator of worlds without number (see Moses 1:31–33; 7:30) and was thereby known as the Lord Omnipotent long before he tabernacled the flesh. Because of this creative role, Jehovah/Christ is appropriately known in the Book of Mormon as "the Father of heaven and earth, the Creator of all things from the beginning" (Mosiah 3:8; compare 2 Nephi 25:12; Alma 11:39; 3 Nephi 9:15).

Secondly, Christ is Father through spiritual rebirth. As the Savior and foreordained Messiah, Jesus Christ became the "author of eternal salvation unto all them that obey him" (Hebrews 5:9), and the Father's gospel became his by adoption—the gospel of Jesus Christ. Things on earth are patterned after that which is in heaven. God dwells in the family unit, and so the order of heaven is patriarchal. Those on earth who accept the gospel of Jesus Christ enter the family of Jesus Christ, take upon them the family name, and thus become inheritors of family obligations and family privileges. Because one was not originally a member of the family of the Lord Jesus Christ prior to the time of accountability (or conversion), he must be adopted into that family; one must "subscribe the articles of adoption"—have faith in Christ, repent of all sins, be baptized by immersion by a legal administrator, and receive and enjoy the gift of the Holy Ghost—that is, meet the legal requirements of the kingdom of God to properly qualify for and be received into the new family relationship.[11] The Book of Mormon prophets clearly taught the absolute necessity for spiritual rebirth. Even as one may enter mortality only through mortal birth, so also may one qualify for life in the spiritual realm—eternal life—only after spiritual rebirth, through being born again as to things of righteousness (see Mosiah 5:1–15; 15:11–12; 27:23–27; Alma 5:14; 3 Nephi 9:16–17; Ether 3:14).

The Master explained to a group in his Palestinian ministry, "I am come in my Father's name" (John 5:43). Our Lord acted and spoke on behalf of the Almighty Elohim and is therefore known as Father by divine investiture of authority, meaning that "the Father-Elohim has placed his name upon the Son, has given him his own power and authority, and has authorized him to speak in the first person as though he were the original or primal Father."[12] This principle is clearly operative in the accounts of prophets in the Pearl of Great Price (see Moses 1:4–6, 32–33; 6:51–52) as well as in the Doctrine and Covenants. In fact, in the latter book of scripture there are occasions in which the Lord chooses to speak as both Christ and Elohim in the same revelation (see D&C 29:1, 42; 49:5, 28). What better way is there to establish firmly in the minds of the Saints that the words of Jehovah are the very same words of Elohim, that they have the same mind and thoughts, that they are totally and completely one?

One of the powerful witnesses of the Book of Mormon is that Jesus Christ is Father because Elohim has literally invested his Son with his own attributes and powers. "This is a matter of his Eternal Parent investing him with power from on high so that he becomes the Father because he exercises the power of that Eternal Being."[13] As already indicated, one of the grandest messianic sermons ever delivered was Abinadi's defense before King Noah and his wicked priests, particularly that portion constituting chapter fifteen of Mosiah. The first five verses of this chapter are especially poignant and may be understood in light of the previous discussion on the ministry of Christ as the Father and the

Son. A number of key doctrinal matters are given in verses one through five:

1. God himself—Jehovah, the God of ancient Israel—will come to earth, take a physical body, and bring to pass redemption for all men.

2. Because Jehovah/Jesus Christ will have a physical body and dwell in the *flesh*—like every other mortal son and daughter of God—he will be known as the *Son* of God. On the other hand, because he will be conceived by the power of God and will thus have within him the powers of the *Spirit,* he will be known as the *Father.* This same doctrine is given in a modern revelation through the Prophet Joseph Smith (see D&C 93:4, 12–14).

3. The will of the Son is to be swallowed up in the will of the Father. That is, the *flesh* will become subject to the *Spirit,* the mortal subject to the immortal. "I seek not mine own will," Jesus explained, "but the will of the Father which hath sent me" (John 5:30; compare 6:38). In short, Jesus will do what the Father would have him do.

4. Thus Christ will be both the Father and the Son. He will be called the Father because he was conceived by the power of God and inherited all of the divine endowments, particularly immortality, from his exalted Sire. He will be called the Son because of the flesh—his mortal inheritance from his mother, Mary. Therefore Christ will be both *flesh* and *spirit,* both *man* and *God,* both *Son* and *Father.* And they—the Son and the Father, the man and the God, the flesh and the spirit—are to be blended wondrously in one being, Jesus Christ, "the very Eternal Father of heaven and of earth." The testimony of Abinadi is surely consistent with the message of Paul—in Christ "dwelleth all the fulness of the Godhead bodily" (Colossians 2:9).

Because men must believe this dimension of the "doctrine of Christ" to be saved—the doctrine that the Lord Omnipotent, the Pre-existing One, shall take a mortal and then an immortal body in working out the infinite and eternal Atonement—Satan has labored incessantly to deny and stamp out the true message and messengers whose focus is the Messiah. Indeed, teaching the condescension of the Great God proved costly to many of the Lord's messengers. Lehi almost lost his life (see 1 Nephi 1:20). Zenos and Zenock were put to death (see Alma 33:14–17; compare 21:9–10; Helaman 8:12–23). After Abinadi had delivered his message, he too was put to death for his testimony of the Christ. Note Limhi's description of the martyrdom, as given to Ammon:

> And a prophet of the Lord have they [King Noah and his wicked followers] slain; yea, a chosen man of God, who told them of their wickedness and abominations, and prophesied of many things which are to come, yea, even the coming of Christ.
>
> And *because he said unto them that Christ was the God, the Father of all things, and said that he should take upon him the image of man,* and it should be the image after which man was created in the beginning; or in other words, he said that man was created after the image of God, and that God should come down among the children of men, and take upon him flesh and blood, and go forth upon the face of the earth—
>
> *And now, because he said this, they did put him to death.* (Mosiah 7:26–28; compare 17:7–8; italics added.)

THE DOCTRINE OF THE RESURRECTION

The Book of Mormon provides a remarkably clear definition of resurrection—the eternal union of spirit and body—a definition which is painfully deficient in the Bible. Latter-day Saints understand the biblical allusions to resurrection largely because these matters are so plainly taught in the Nephite record, particularly in the sermons of such prophetic personalities as Abinadi (see Mosiah 15), Amulek (see Alma 11), and Alma (see Alma 40).

It is from Abinadi that we learn of a "first resurrection," meaning (in his words) a resurrection of those righteous persons "that have been, and who are, and who shall be, even until the resurrection of Christ." This would entail "the resurrection of all the prophets, and all those that have believed in their words, or all those that have kept the commandments of God." These enjoy "eternal life through Christ, who has broken the bands of death" (Mosiah 15:21–23).

We know from modern revelation that the first resurrection consists of the resurrection of both celestial and terrestrial bodies (see D&C 76:50–80, 85; 88:100–101). But there is a difference between those resurrected in the *"morning* of the first resurrection" and those resurrected in the *"afternoon* of the first resurrection." "Those being resurrected with celestial bodies," writes Elder Bruce R. McConkie, "whose destiny is to inherit a celestial kingdom, will come forth in the *morning* of the first resurrection. Their graves shall be opened and they shall be caught up to meet the Lord at his Second Coming." Concerning the resurrection of terrestrial beings, Elder McConkie states: "This is the *afternoon* of the first resurrection; it takes place after our Lord has ushered in the millennium. Those coming forth at that time do so with terrestrial bodies and are thus destined to inherit a terrestrial glory in eternity."[14]

Abinadi chose to discuss only the former category. He gave specific examples of those who shall have eternal life and thus come forth in the first resurrection. Of these are the following two groups:

1. "They that have died before Christ came, in their ignorance, not having salvation declared unto them" (Mosiah 15:24). We know from the vision of the three degrees of glory (see D&C 76) that "they who died without law"—the heathen nations (D&C 76:72; see also 45:54)—shall come forth in a terrestrial resurrection and thus will not have eternal life. Abinadi's statement would seem, therefore, to have reference to "all who have died without a knowledge of this gospel, who would have received it if they had been permitted to tarry," or "all that shall die henceforth without a knowledge of it, who would have received it with all their hearts." His testimony is firm: our God is both omniscient and omni-loving, and will judge all men mercifully and justly—by the desires of the heart, as well as by the works in the flesh (D&C 137:7–9; compare Alma 41:3).

2. "And little children also have eternal life" (Mosiah 15:25). A central message of the plan of redemption is that little children are whole from the foundation of the world, that they enjoy the tender mercies of God through the Atonement, that those who die before the age of accountability are saved in the celestial kingdom of God (see Moses 6:54; Mosiah 3:16; Moroni 8:10–23; D&C 29:46; 137:10). The Prophet Joseph Smith and some of his successors taught that little children who die shall come forth from the grave as they lie down, as children, shall be nurtured by loving and righteous parents, and shall go on to enjoy the highest and grandest blessings of exaltation associated with the everlasting continuation of the family unit.[15]

Abinadi then discussed briefly those who do not come forth in the first resurrection—those identified in modern revelation as heirs of the telestial kingdom (see D&C 76:81–106). These are they who rebel against the Lord and die in their sins, those who have known the commandments but refused to keep them. For these there is no celestial redemption, no salvation in the highest heaven, for our God is a God of justice as well as a God of mercy (see Mosiah 15:26–27; Alma 42).

OVERCOMING THE NATURAL MAN THROUGH CHRIST

Abinadi quoted Isaiah (52:8–10) and spoke of the great millennial day, "a time [to] come when all shall see the salvation of the Lord . . . and shall confess before God that his judgments are just" (Mosiah 16:1; see also Mosiah 15:28–31). This marvelous Nephite prophet then delivered profound truths consistent with those verities that would soon be pronounced by the angel to King Benjamin: the essential doctrinal fact that the natural man—the wicked man, the unillumined and unassisted man—is an enemy to God and to the plan of happiness; he is essentially working at cross purposes to the Lord's divine design. "Thus all mankind were lost," Abinadi added, and "would have been endlessly lost were it not that God redeemed his people from their lost and fallen state" (Mosiah 16:4; see also Mosiah 16:2–5). Had there been no atonement of Christ, the effects of the fall of Adam would be devastatingly permanent. Nothing that we could do on our own could make up the difference. But Christ will come, deliverance is available from death, hell, and endless torment, and man need not remain in his carnal ways or sinful state. Our Deliverer "is the light and the life of the world," Abinadi exulted, "yea, a light that is endless, that can never be darkened; yea, and also a life which is endless, that there can be no more death" (Mosiah 16:9).

Abinadi chose to return to an earlier theme—the purpose behind the law of Moses—to conclude his remarks. His counsel to the priests of Noah was simple but stern: "Therefore, if ye teach the law of Moses, also teach that it is a shadow of those things which are to come—teach them that redemption cometh through Christ the Lord, who is the very Eternal Father. Amen" (Mosiah 16:14–15).

CONCLUSION

Having delivered his majestic messianic prophecy and called the wicked to repentance, Abinadi, like his prophetic partner Stephen (see Acts 7), submitted to a cruel death at the hands of cruel men (see Mosiah 17). It is not easy to die, even to die for one's testimony, but the taste of death is so much sweeter to those whose lives and words bear fervent witness of Him whose servants they are. Occasionally in the overall scheme of things, the Lord asks certain of his representatives to shed their own blood in a martyr's death, that their testament might be in full force (see D&C 135:5; Hebrews 9:16–17).

And so the testator was dead. But the testament lived on. "Faith comes by hearing the word of God," Joseph Smith taught, "through the testimony of the servants of God; that testimony is always attended by the Spirit of prophecy and revelation."[16] Sometime during Abinadi's sermon a heart was touched and a witness planted as to the truthfulness of his words; a "young man . . . believed the words which Abinadi had spoken" (Mosiah 17:2). And because of the power of the word, the power of a single human testimony, the course of events in the Nephite story would never be the same.

NOTES

1. See Erastus Snow, in *Journal of Discourses,* 26 vols. (London: Latter-day Saints' Book Depot, 1854–86), 23:184.
2. Joseph Fielding Smith, *Doctrines of Salvation,* 3 vols., comp. Bruce R. McConkie (Salt Lake City: Bookcraft, 1954–56), 3:87; see also Joseph Fielding Smith, *Answers to Gospel Questions,* 5 vols. (Salt Lake City: Deseret Book Co., 1957–66), 1:123–26.
3. B. H. Roberts, *New Witness for God,* 3 vols. (Salt Lake City: Deseret News, 1909), 2:220–21.
4. Bruce R. McConkie, *The Promised Messiah: The First Coming of Christ* (Salt Lake City: Deseret Book Co., 1978), p. 427; italics added.
5. McConkie, *Promised Messiah,* p. 416; compare *The Mortal Messiah: From Bethlehem to Calvary,* 4 vols. (Salt Lake City: Deseret Book Co., 1979–81), 1:74.
6. Bruce R. McConkie, "What Think Ye of Salvation by Grace?" *Brigham Young University 1983–84 Fireside and Devotional Speeches* (Provo: Brigham Young University Press, 1984), p. 48.
7. Brigham Young, in *Journal of Discourses,* 3:206.
8. *Melvin J. Ballard—Crusader for Righteousness* (Salt Lake City: Bookcraft, 1966), p. 137.
9. McConkie, *Promised Messiah,* pp. 360–61.
10. "The Father and the Son: A Doctrinal Exposition of the First Presidency and the Twelve, 30 June 1916," in James E. Talmage, *The Articles of Faith* (Salt Lake City: The Church of Jesus Christ of Latter-day Saints, 1924), pp. 466–73.
11. Joseph Smith, *Teachings of the Prophet Joseph Smith,* sel. Joseph Fielding Smith (Salt Lake City: Deseret Book Co., 1976), p. 328; see also Orson Pratt, "The Kingdom of God," in *Orson Pratt's Works* (1848–51; reprint, Salt Lake City: Parker Pratt Robison, 1965), pp. 46–48.
12. McConkie, *Promised Messiah,* p. 63.

13. Ibid., p. 371.

14. McConkie, *Mormon Doctrine,* 2d ed. (Salt Lake City: Bookcraft, 1966), p. 640.

15. Smith, *Teachings,* pp. 199–200; compare pp. 196–97; Bruce R. McConkie, "The Salvation of Little Children," *Ensign,* April 1977, pp. 5–6.

16. Smith, *Teachings,* p. 148.

The Holy Order of God

To the wayward people of Ammonihah, Amulek had delivered a poignant testimony of Christ as God, had borne witness of the necessity of repentance, and had held out the hope of redemption from sin and death through the merits and mercy of the coming Messiah (see Alma 11:26–46). Alma then delivered a companion and confirming witness of the reality of the Savior and the manner in which men and women can, through faith, pass from death unto eternal life. "Therefore," he said, quoting the Lord to the ancients, "whosoever repenteth, and hardeneth not his heart, he shall have claim on mercy through mine Only Begotten Son, unto a remission of his sins; and these shall enter into my rest." Alma then pleaded: "And now, my brethren, seeing we know these things, and they are true, let us repent, and harden not our hearts, . . . but let us enter into the rest of God, which is prepared according to his word" (Alma 12:34, 37). It is in the context of Alma's discussion of how the Saints can, through applying the atoning blood of Christ, enter into the rest of God, that Alma begins a discussion of the holy order of God. His discussion is a deep and ponderous and insightful prophetic declaration as to how, through the blessings of the priesthood, the people of God—those called and prepared from the foundation of the world—may be sanctified from sin and enjoy the "words of eternal life" in this mortal sphere, all in preparation for eternal life with God and holy beings hereafter (see Moses 6:59).

THE PRIESTHOOD AMONG THE NEPHITES

Before we undertake a serious consideration of Alma 13, let us turn our attention to the matter of priesthood among the Nephites. From the days of Adam to the time of Moses, the high priesthood was administered through what we know as the patriarchal order, a patriarchal theocracy whereby the will of God in heaven was made known to the inhabitants of earth through worthy high priests who governed their families in both civil and ecclesiastical matters.[1] When the children of Israel proved unworthy and unwilling to receive the highest blessings of the gospel, including the fulness of the priesthood and the privilege of seeing the face of God, Jehovah took from the midst of Israel the fulness of the high priesthood. He also took Moses, the man on earth who held the priesthood keys, or the right of presidency (see JST, Exodus 34:1–2; JST, Deuteronomy 10:1–2; D&C 84:19–27). There were men among the people of the covenant who held the Melchizedek Priesthood after Moses was translated—including the sons of Aaron and the seventy elders of Israel—but they had been ordained to the same previously. President Joseph Fielding Smith stated that after this time in Israel,

> the common people, the people generally, did not exercise the functions of priesthood in its fulness, but were confined in their labors and ministrations very largely to the Aaronic Priesthood. The withdrawal of the higher priesthood was from the people as a body, but the Lord still left among them men holding the Melchizedek Priesthood, with power to officiate in all its ordinances, so far as he determined that these ordinances should be granted unto the people. Therefore, Samuel, Isaiah, Jeremiah, Daniel, Ezekiel, Elijah, and others of the prophets held the Melchizedek Priesthood.[2]

Because there were no Levites in the colony of Lehi (the Nephites and Mulekites were of the tribes of Joseph and Judah, respectively), we assume that the Aaronic Priesthood was not among the Nephites, at least not until the coming of Jesus to the Americas. The titles *priests* and *teachers* (see 2 Nephi 5:26; Jacob 1:17–18; Alma 45:22) thus appear to describe ministerial duties in the higher priesthood rather than offices in the Aaronic Priesthood.[3] In seeking to understand the nature of authority among the Nephite branch of Israel, we turn to a capsule statement by Joseph Smith: "All Priesthood is Melchizedek but there are different portions or degrees of it. That portion which brought Moses to speak with God face to face was taken away; but that which brought the ministry of angels remained." The latter-day seer then added this important detail: *"All the prophets had the Melchizedek Priesthood and were ordained by God himself."*[4] Lehi was a prophet. Nephi and Jacob were prophets. Mosiah, Benjamin, Alma, Samuel, Mormon, and Moroni all wore the prophetic mantle and held the Melchizedek Priesthood. Surely what the Lord said to Nephi, son of Helaman, was true in regard to others of the Nephite oracles who had the keys of power: "Behold, I give unto you power, that whatsoever ye shall seal on earth shall be sealed in heaven;

and whatsoever ye shall loose on earth shall be loosed in heaven; and thus shall ye have power among this people" (Helaman 10:7; compare D&C 132:39). To what degree all male persons among the Nephites held the priesthood, how and under what circumstances it was conferred, and the nature of priesthood organization between 600 B.C. and 34 A.D. are not clear from the account in the Book of Mormon.

The Nephites were Christians. They were Former-day Saints who enjoyed transcendent spiritual blessings. They had the veil parted and saw the visions of heaven. They knew the Lord, enjoyed his ministration, and received from him the assurance of eternal life. They built temples (see 2 Nephi 5:16; Jacob 1:17; 2:2, 11; Mosiah 1:18; Alma 10:2; 16:13; 26:29; 3 Nephi 11:1), not to perform work for the dead, for such was not done until the ministry of Christ to the world of spirits, but to receive the covenants and ordinances of exaltation. During the Nephite "mini-millennium" and, we would suppose, during those prior periods of Nephite history when the people qualified themselves for such, "they were married, and given in marriage, and were blessed *according to the multitude of the promises which the Lord had made unto them*" (4 Nephi 1:11; italics added). These were the promises made to Abraham, Isaac, and Jacob, the promise of the gospel, the priesthood, and eternal life (see D&C 2; Abraham 1:2–3; 2:8–11).

THE CALLING OF HIGH PRIESTS ANCIENTLY

In beginning his discussion of foreordination to the priesthood, Alma said, "And again, my brethren, I would cite your minds forward to the time when the Lord God gave these commandments unto his children" (Alma 13:1). His use of the word *forward* is unusual, especially in light of the fact that he will speak of people in the past; we would normally say *backwards*. But actually *forward* can also mean toward the beginning, toward the front, "[n]ear or at the forepart."[5] The commandments mentioned here seem to be those referred to in Alma 12. Alma had stated, "Wherefore, [God] gave commandments unto men" after Adam and Eve were cast out of the Garden of Eden, "after having made known unto them the plan of redemption, that they should not do evil, the penalty thereof being a second death, which was an everlasting death as to things pertaining unto righteousness" (Alma 12:31, 32).

Alma noted "that the Lord God ordained priests, after his holy order, which was after the order of his Son, to teach these things unto the people" (Alma 13:1). Presumably he is speaking here of those who held the priesthood in its fulness from Adam to Moses, whom this prophet could have learned of through the brass plates, by independent revelation, and through the traditions and group memory of this branch of American Hebrews. "All of the ancient patriarchs were high priests," Joseph Fielding Smith explained, "but the direction of the Church in those days was by patriarchs."[6] In those early ages, the presiding high priest was "God's chief representative on earth, the one who holds the highest spiritual position in [the Lord's] kingdom in any age. . . . This special designation of the chief spiritual officer of the Church has reference to the administrative position which he holds rather than to the office to which he is ordained in the priesthood."[7]

Continuing from the Nephite text: "And those priests were ordained after the order of his Son, in a manner that thereby the people might know in what manner to look forward to his Son for redemption" (Alma 13:2). The preeminent responsibility of prophets is to bear witness of the Savior, "for the testimony of Jesus is the spirit of prophecy" (Revelation 19:10). Those who preceded the Lord of Light spoke of the redemption and reconciliation that would come through Jesus Christ. They thus pointed toward and anticipated his coming. The messianic age would indeed be the apex, the midpoint, truly the meridian of time. At the same time, all prophets are types and shadows of the Savior. He was called and prepared from before the foundations of this world. So were they. He speaks the truth. So do they. He offers the words of life. So do they. He preaches as one having authority. So do they. He offers his life as a final testament. Such also is required on occasion of those who stand in the prophetic office. Thus the ancient prophets were living messianic prophecies.

FOREORDINATION TO THE PRIESTHOOD

One cannot fully comprehend the boundless and eternal implications of priesthood by examining its purposes and powers as pertaining to this life alone. Priesthood is God's almighty power. Men are not called and ordained to the priesthood in this life without appropriate readiness and preparation, and no person receives the higher priesthood in this second estate who was not called, prepared for, and foreordained to the same in the first estate. Joseph Smith declared: "Every man who has a calling to minister to the inhabitants of the world was ordained to that very purpose in the Grand Council of heaven before this world was. I suppose I was ordained to this very office in that Grand Council."[8] In referring to this statement by the Prophet, President J. Reuben Clark, Jr., said: "I do not know whether we have a right to interpret the Prophet's statement . . . , but I like to think that it does include those of us of lesser calling and lesser stature. . . . I like to think that perhaps in that grand council something at least was said to us indicating what would be expected of us, and empowering us, subject to the re-confirmation here, to do certain things in building up the kingdom of God on earth."[9] In that same spirit, Wilford Woodruff had remarked some seventy years earlier:

> Joseph Smith was ordained before he came here, the same as Jeremiah was. Said the Lord unto him, 'Before you were begotten I knew you,' etc. So do I believe with regard to this people, so do I believe with regard to the apostles, the high priests, seventies and the elders of Israel bearing the holy priesthood, I believe they were ordained before they came here; and I believe the God of Israel has raised them up, and has watched over them from their youth, and has carried them through all the scenes of life both seen and unseen, and has prepared them as instruments in his hands to take this kingdom and bear it off. If this be so, what manner of men ought we to be? If anything under the heavens should humble men before the Lord and before one another, it should be the fact that we have been called of God.[10]

Alma's discourse on priesthood continued: "And this is the manner after which they were ordained—being called and prepared from the foundation of the world according to the foreknowledge of God, on account of their exceeding faith and good works" (Alma 13:3). We are prone to say in the Church that in the premortal existence we walked by sight but now we walk by faith. This is only partly true. Though in that pristine sphere we saw the Gods and surely conversed with them; though we had the plan of salvation, the gospel of God the Father, presented to us and heard the noble and great ones attest to its veracity; though we walked by knowledge in that estate, still *faith* was required to be obedient and thereby to qualify for the blessings of the Father. There was a gradation of faithfulness among the spirits. There were many who were "noble and great" (Abraham 3:22), implying that there were those spirits who were less great and less noble, perhaps some even ignoble. Those men who demonstrated the "exceeding faith and good works" that Alma discusses were ordained there to receive the priesthood here. This is the doctrine of foreordination. It is based upon a man's faithfulness in premortality and God's foreknowledge, that is, God's infinite capacity to have the past, present, and future before him as "one eternal 'now.'"[11] Joseph Fielding Smith observed: "In regard to the holding of the priesthood in pre-existence, I will say that there was an organization there just as well as an organization here, and men there held authority. *Men chosen to positions of trust in the spirit world held priesthood.*"[12]

Alma noted that individuals were called with a holy calling "on account of their exceeding faith and good works; in the first place"— that is, in the premortal world—"being left to choose good or evil; therefore they having chosen good, and exercising exceedingly great faith, are called with a holy calling" (Alma 13:3). The question arises at this point: Does this call to the priesthood refer to righteousness and subsequent ordination in premortality or mortality? We cannot tell for sure from the context. Alma in fact moves back and forth between the past and the present, and we simply do not always know when he has changed perspectives. The fact is, the principle is true in regard to both spheres: men are called to serve because of faith and obedience—there and here. The faithful "are called with a holy calling, yea, with that holy calling which was prepared with, and according to, a preparatory redemption for such" (Alma 13:3). Men are called to the priesthood to assist in the redemption of souls. They are called to preach and make available what Paul described as "the ministry of reconciliation" (2 Corinthians 5:18). They are called to bless lives—to lighten burdens, to strengthen the feeble knees and lift up the hands that hang down—just as their Master, the great High Priest, is called upon to do.

Priesthood bearers who lived before and after Christ are and have been involved in the work of his ministry; their work is preparatory. They, like the preeminent forerunner, John the Baptist, prepare the way of the Lord. Those prophets and priests who labored before the meridian of time sought to prepare the people for the coming of the Redeemer. In the words of Elder Bruce R. McConkie: "They could preach redemption; they could foretell its coming; but their work was preparatory only. Redemption itself would come through the ministry of Him of whom they were but types and shadows."[13] Those who have lived since that time seek to instruct and warn and exhort the people—all in preparation for his second advent, that final redemption of the earth and its inhabitants.

Alma then offered prophetic insight into this doctrine, insight that readily distinguished foreordination from the false concept of predestination: "And thus they have been called to this holy calling on account of their faith, while others would reject the Spirit of God on account of the hardness of their hearts and blindness of their minds, while, if it had not been for this they might have had as great privilege as their brethren. Or in fine, in the first place they were on the same standing with their brethren" (Alma 13:4–5). The simple truth is that men and women may fall from grace and depart from the living God through sin; in short, many live beneath their privileges. They qualify in the first estate for transcendent earthly blessings but then come into this life, fail to hearken to the voice of the Spirit, and thus traverse the broad roads of the world as natural beings, existing in an uninspired and unregenerated state.

Nephi had spoken centuries earlier of those who harden their hearts. These are they who say in regard to further light and knowledge: "We have received, and we need no more! . . . We have received the word of God, and we need no more of the word of God, for we have enough!" (2 Nephi 28:27, 29.) Alma had similarly spoken: "It is given unto many to know the mysteries of God," but, on the other hand, those who harden their hearts, "the same receiveth the lesser portion of the word" until "they know nothing concerning his mysteries; and then they are taken captive by the devil, and led by his will down to destruction. Now this is what is meant by the chains of hell" (Alma 12:9–11). President Harold B. Lee suggested:

> Despite that calling which is spoken of in the scriptures as "fore-
> ordination," we have another inspired declaration: "Behold, there
> are many called, but few are chosen. . . ." (D&C 121:34). This sug-
> gests that even though we have our free agency here, there are
> many who were foreordained before the world was, to a greater state
> than they have prepared themselves for here. Even though they
> might have been among the noble and great, from among whom

the Father declared he would make his chosen leaders, they may fail of that calling here in mortality.[14]

Alma explained that those who fail to live up to their privileges had been "in the first place" on the "same standing with their brethren" (Alma 13:3, 5). That is, even though no two persons were exactly alike in premortality; even though gifts and talents, abilities and capacities varied infinitely from person to person in this pre-existence, still all had the opportunity to choose the right, to love the truth, and to exercise exceedingly great faith.

This description in the Book of Mormon of foreordination may be the first reference in modern scripture to the doctrine of the premortal existence. Once we grasp this fundamental verity, once our minds have been enlightened to understand the eternal nature of humanity, then we recognize these teachings in Alma 13 (or later in Ether 3, regarding the appearance of the premortal Christ) without difficulty. It may be, however, that few of the Saints in the early years of the restored Church turned initially to the Book of Mormon as a scriptural source for the doctrine of pre-existence. Elder Orson Pratt explained: "I do not think that I should have ever discerned it in [the Book of Mormon], had it not been for the new translation of the Scriptures"—specifically, what we would call the book of Moses—"that throwing so much light and information on the subject, I searched the Book of Mormon to see if there were indications in it that related to the pre-existence of man."[15]

FROM ETERNITY TO ALL ETERNITY

Alma explained that "this high priesthood [was] after the order of [God's] Son, which order was from the foundation of the world; or in other words, being without beginning of days or end of years, being prepared from eternity to all eternity, according to his foreknowledge of all things" (Alma 13:7). Joseph Smith declared: "The Priesthood is an everlasting principle, and existed with God from eternity, and will to eternity, without beginning of days or end of years."[16] In the words of President George Q. Cannon, the priesthood "had no beginning; [it will have] no end. It is [as] eternal as our Father and God, and it extends into the eternities to come, and it is as endless as eternity is endless, and as our God is endless: for it is the power and authority by which our Father and God sits upon His throne and wields the power He does throughout the innumerable worlds over which He exercises dominion."[17] The Holy Priesthood after the order of the Son of God is from eternity to eternity, from everlasting to everlasting, meaning from one existence to the next. It was in operation in the first estate, it blesses lives and seals souls to eternal life in mortality, and it will continue into the world of spirits and beyond, on into the kingdoms of glory wherein dwell kings and queens, priests and priestesses.

The loss of plain and precious truths from the Old and New Testaments had led many to believe that Melchizedek, the great high priest of antiquity, rather than the priesthood, was himself without "beginning of days [or] end of life" (Hebrews 7:3). We learn, however, from the Joseph Smith Translation (JST, Hebrews 7:3) and from the Book of Mormon (Alma 13:8) that it was the order of the priesthood to which Melchizedek was ordained that is endless. "The Melchizedek Priesthood holds the right from the eternal God," Joseph Smith clarified, "and not by descent from father and mother; and that priesthood is as eternal as God Himself, having neither beginning of days nor end of life."[18] Indeed, as Alma pointed out, the priesthood of the Son of God is as eternal as the Son of God. Persons "thus . . . became high priests forever, after the order of the Son, the Only Begotten of the Father, who is without beginning of days or end of years, who is full of grace, equity, and truth. And thus it is. Amen" (Alma 13:9).

ENTERING THE REST OF GOD

It is often the case that the scriptures may be understood on many levels. Words and phrases and doctrinal concepts may mean a number of things, depending upon the context, the audience, and the need at the time. For this reason, it is seldom wise to be overly zealous about exclusive definitions, singular interpretations, formulas, steps, and so on when it comes to comprehending holy writ. We have this principle illustrated in Moroni's recitation to Joseph Smith of the prophecy of Malachi concerning the coming of Elijah. In the midst of quoting numerous passages from the Old and New Testaments, Moroni quoted Malachi 4:5–6 quite differently from how it appears in the King James Version. Did this new rendition invalidate the old one? Are the renditions in our present Bibles inaccurate, or does Moroni's account simply represent another dimension of the prophecy?

Chapter 10—The Holy Order of God

Knowing full well what Moroni had said in 1823, Joseph the Prophet, in an epistle to the Church in 1842, quoted the Malachi passage directly from the King James Version. "I might have rendered a plainer translation to this," he said, "but it is sufficiently plain to suit my purpose as it stands" (D&C 128:18). In discussing this specific example, Elder Bruce R. McConkie said: "Moroni gave an *improved* rendering. All this does is establish that there is more than one way to render a passage, and that the version that the people receive depends upon the spiritual maturity they possess. . . . Thus, we have two versions, both of which accurately portray and give a doctrine of the kingdom. One of them gives it in a way that is intended to open our eyes to something over and beyond and above what, shall we say, the generality of mankind who are not so spiritually endowed are entitled to receive."[19]

Alma 13 teaches us to appreciate that men were foreordained to the priesthood and that we all should walk in the light to live worthy of premortal promises. This is an important realization. It is true, and it is what is intended. At the same time, there appear to be additional messages presenting themselves to us as we read and search and compare. We will illustrate the principle in this and the next section, through a consideration of two main concepts: (1) entering the rest of the Lord, and (2) being received into the holy order of God.

In reading Alma 13 in context—as a part of a larger sermon—we begin to see that the idea of entering the rest of the Lord is a central theme. The word *rest* is mentioned in each of the final four verses of the preceding chapter. It is mentioned five times in chapter 13. It would appear that Alma is trying to point out that it is through the atoning blood of Christ and by the power of the holy priesthood that individuals and congregations are prepared and made ready to enter the rest of God.

In one sense, a person enters the rest of God when he or she gains a testimony of the gospel and is brought out of worldly confusion into the peace and security that comes only from God. In this sense, the rest of God is "the spiritual rest and peace which are born from a settled conviction of the truth in the minds of [individuals]."[20] It is to know the peace of the Spirit, to enjoy the blessing of the Comforter. It is what Jesus promised to disciples when he said, "Come unto me, all ye that

139

labour and are heavy laden, and I will give you rest" (Matthew 11:28). Second, spirits enter the rest of God when they enter paradise, the home of the righteous in the postmortal spirit world at the time of death (see Alma 40:11–12; 60:13). A third dimension of the rest of the Lord is that which follows the Resurrection and Judgment, as we enter the celestial kingdom and receive exaltation. It is interesting that Mormon, speaking to the members of the Church in his day, uses *rest* in at least two ways. "Wherefore," he said, "I would speak unto you that are of the church, that are the peaceable followers of Christ, and that have obtained a sufficient hope by which ye can enter into the rest of the Lord,"—meaning here in mortality—"from this time henceforth until ye shall rest with him in heaven" (Moroni 7:3).

There is yet another sense in which the word *rest* is used in scripture, particularly in the Book of Mormon. This is also the sense in which a modern revelation uses the word:

> And this greater priesthood administereth the gospel and holdeth the key of the mysteries of the kingdom, even the key of the knowledge of God.
>
> Therefore, in the ordinances thereof, the power of godliness is manifest.
>
> And without the ordinances thereof, and the authority of the priesthood, the power of godliness is not manifest unto men in the flesh;
>
> For without this [the power of godliness] no man can see the face of God, even the Father, and live.
>
> Now this Moses plainly taught to the children of Israel in the wilderness, and sought diligently to sanctify his people that they might behold the face of God;
>
> But they hardened their hearts and could not endure his presence; therefore, the Lord in his wrath, for his anger was kindled against them, swore that they should not enter into his rest while in the wilderness, *which rest is the fulness of his glory.*
>
> Therefore, he took Moses out of their midst, and the Holy Priesthood also. (D&C 84:19–25; italics added.)

This is a significant scriptural statement, especially as we consider Alma's remarks to the people in Ammonihah. His invitation for them to enter into the rest of the Lord is built upon the notion that ancient Israel provoked God and proved unworthy of this blessing (see Alma 12:36–37). Moses desired to make available the highest privilege of the priesthood to Israel—the privilege of seeing the face of God, of coming directly into the divine presence. Of the Israelites, Jehovah said, "I have sworn in my wrath, that they shall not enter into my presence, into my rest, in the days of their pilgrimage" (JST, Exodus 34:2). Here the rest of the Lord is equated with being in the personal presence of the Lord while the recipients are still mortal.

It appears that the concept of the "rest of the Lord" is used occasionally in terms of what other scriptures call the Church of the Firstborn (see Hebrews 12:23; D&C 76:54). The Church of the Firstborn is the church of the exalted, an organization of saved souls, a body of believers who have passed the tests of mortality and received the approval of God. They qualify for life in the celestial kingdom, and become co-inheritors with him to all of the blessings of the Firstborn.[21] The phrase *church of the Firstborn* is not found in the Book of Mormon, but it may be that to enter the rest of the Lord is to enter the church of the Firstborn. In speaking of the ancient worthies, Alma said: "They were called after this holy order, and were sanctified, and their garments were washed white through the blood of the Lamb. Now they, after being sanctified by the Holy Ghost, having their garments made white, being pure and spotless before God, could not look upon sin save it were with abhorrence; and there were many, exceedingly great many, who were made pure and entered into the rest of the Lord their God" (Alma 13:11–12).

From one point of view, we can grasp and apply this vital lesson from the past: those of us who magnify our callings in the priesthood are sanctified—made pure and holy—by the renovating powers of the spirit (see D&C 84:33). We come in time to hate sin and to love and cherish righteousness. We are at peace in a troubled and turbulent world. We enter the rest of the Lord. From another perspective, we qualify, through the atonement of Christ, for the highest of priesthood blessings spoken of in the revelations. "These are they who have come to an innumerable company of angels, to the general assembly and church of Enoch, and of the Firstborn." Further, "They who dwell in his presence are the church of the Firstborn" (D&C 76:67, 94). Indeed, the ultimate privileges of God's holy authority are spoken of as follows: "The power and authority of the higher, or Melchizedek Priesthood, is to hold the keys of all the spiritual blessings of the church—to have the privilege of receiving the mysteries of the kingdom of heaven, to have the heavens opened unto them, to commune with the general assembly and church of the Firstborn, and to enjoy the communion and presence of God the Father, and Jesus the mediator of the new covenant" (D&C 107:18–19).

THE HOLY ORDER OF GOD

Related to this doctrine is the second topic that might be viewed from more than one perspective—being received into the holy order of God. We have generally understood that we enter into the holy order of God through receiving the Melchizedek Priesthood, inasmuch as the full name of this sacred authority is *"the Holy Priesthood, after the Order of the Son of God"* (D&C 107:3). At another level, we encounter the holy order of God through receiving the ordinances of the temple, through receiving the endowment and the blessings of eternal marriage.

I would suggest the possibility that the scriptures speak of an additional and ultimate way of entering the holy order—through receiving the promise and seal of eternal life, through receiving what the scriptures and the prophets call the "fulness of the priesthood" (see D&C 124:28). In the book of Moses, the Prophet Joseph Smith's inspired translation of the early chapters of Genesis, he recorded the revelation of the gospel to Adam. We read there of Adam's baptism and spiritual rebirth. "And he heard a voice out of heaven, saying: Thou art baptized with fire, and with the Holy Ghost. This is the record of the Father, and the Son, from henceforth and forever." And now note the language of the scripture: "And *thou art after the order of him who was without beginning of days or end of years,* from all eternity. Behold, thou art one in me, *a son of God;* and thus may all become my sons. Amen" (Moses 6:66–68; italics added). Adam was born again and became through adoption a son of Christ. But there was more. He became, through the powers of the holy priesthood and the ordinances associated therewith, a son of God, meaning the Father. Of this matter Elder Bruce R. McConkie has written:

> As men [and women] pursue the goal of eternal life, they first enter in at the gate of repentance and baptism, thereby taking upon themselves the name of Christ. They then gain power to become his sons and daughters, to be adopted into his family, to be brethren and sisters in his kingdom. Baptism standing alone does not transform them into family members, but it opens the door to such a

blessed relationship; and if men so live as to obtain the Spirit and are in fact born again, then they become members of the Holy Family.

Then, if they press forward with a steadfastness in Christ, keeping the commandments and living by every word that proceedeth forth from the mouth of God, they qualify for celestial marriage, and this gives them power to become the sons [and daughters] of God, meaning the Father. They thus become joint-heirs with Christ who is his natural heir. Those who become sons [and daughters] of God in this sense are the ones who become gods in the world to come (D&C 76:54–60). They have exaltation and godhood because the family unit continues in eternity (D&C 132:19–24).[22]

Again, in referring to the experience of our first parent, President Joseph Fielding Smith wrote: "To Adam, after he was driven from the Garden of Eden, the plan of salvation was revealed, and upon him the *fulness* of the priesthood was conferred."[23] President Ezra Taft Benson, in an address delivered at the Logan Temple Centennial in May of 1984, spoke the following about this order of God:

> The temple is a sacred place, and the ordinances in the temple are of a sacred character. Because of its sacredness we are sometimes reluctant to say anything about the temple to our children and grandchildren.
>
> As a consequence, many do not develop a real desire to go to the temple, or when they go there, they do so without much background to prepare them for the obligations and covenants they enter into.
>
> I believe a proper understanding or background will immeasurably help prepare our youth for the temple. This understanding, I believe, will foster within them a desire to seek their priesthood blessings just as Abraham sought his.
>
> When our Heavenly Father placed Adam and Eve on this earth, He did so with the purpose in mind of teaching them how to regain His presence. Our Father promised a Savior to redeem them from their fallen condition. He gave to them the plan of salvation and told them to teach their children faith in Jesus Christ and repentance. Further, Adam and his posterity were commanded by God to be baptized, to receive the Holy Ghost, and *to enter into the order of the Son of God.*
>
> *To enter into the order of the Son of God is the equivalent today of entering into the fullness of the Melchizedek Priesthood, which is only received in the house of the Lord.*
>
> Because Adam and Eve had complied with these requirements,

God said to them, "Thou art after the order of him who was without beginning of days or end of years, from all eternity to all eternity" (Moses 6:67).[24]

The Prophet Joseph Smith stated in June 1843: "If a man gets a fullness of the priesthood of God he has to get it in the same way that Jesus Christ obtained it, and that was by keeping all the commandments and obeying all the ordinances of the house of the Lord."[25] In the latter part of August in that same year, he said: "Those holding the fulness of the Melchizedek Priesthood are kings and priests of the Most High God, holding the keys of power and blessings."[26]

Thus it may be that in the ultimate sense we enter the holy order of God when we enter that ultimate rest of the Lord, when we receive the fulness of the priesthood, when we gain membership in the church of the Firstborn. Such a blessing may come here or hereafter, for as the Lord declared in a modern revelation: "blessed are they who are faithful and endure, *whether in life or in death,* for they shall inherit eternal life" (D&C 50:5; italics added).

It is in this light that the meaning of a number of related scriptures begins to surface. For example, the order into which Enoch and his people were received (and that which was later conferred upon Melchizedek) is described as follows: "For God having sworn unto Enoch and his seed with an oath by himself; that every one being ordained after this order and calling should have power, by faith, to break mountains, to divide the seas, to dry up waters, to turn them out of their course; . . . to stand in the presence of God." Then, in some cases, people were even taken from the earth because of their righteousness: "And men having this faith, *coming up unto this order of God, were translated and taken up into heaven*" (JST, Genesis 14:30–32; italics added).

After the children of Israel rejected their spiritual privileges at the base of Sinai and after Moses had broken the first set of tablets, Jehovah said to the Lawgiver: "Hew thee two other tables of stone, like unto the first, and I will write upon them also, the words of the law, according as they were written at the first on the tables which thou brakest; but it shall not be according to the first, for I will take away the priesthood out of their midst; therefore *my holy order, and the ordinances thereof, shall not go before them;* for my presence shall not go up in their midst, lest I destroy them" (JST, Exodus 34:1; italics added). In speaking of this "last law," the higher priesthood privilege which Israel lost, Joseph Smith observed: "God cursed the children of Israel because they would not receive the last law from Moses." Or stated another way, "The law revealed to Moses in Horeb never was revealed to the children of Israel as a nation."[27] Similarly, the group of 144,000 seen by John the Revelator in vision—those who in a future day will have the seal of God in their foreheads (see Revelation 7:4–8; D&C 133:18)—"are high priests, *ordained unto the holy order of God* . . . who are ordained out of every nation, kindred, tongue, and people, by the angels to whom is given power over the nations of the earth, *to bring as many as will come to the church of the Firstborn*" (D&C 77:11; italics added).

And so what does all of the above have to do with Alma 13? I feel it to be no stretch of the imagination, no wresting of the scriptures, to suppose that many of the descendants of Lehi were possessors of great knowledge and power, that they sought for and received the mysteries of the kingdom, and thus that many of the Nephite Saints proved worthy of all of the blessings of the house of the Lord. They did so, even as those about whom they read. They built and used temples. President Brigham Young said simply: "The ordinances of the house of God are expressly for the Church of the Firstborn."[28] Thus, in the words of Alma, "there were many, exceedingly great many, who were made pure and entered into the rest of the Lord their God" (Alma 13:12). Alma's appeal to the attainments of the faithful of the past serves as a model and a pattern for his own people and, by extension, as a guide and incentive for modern readers.

MELCHIZEDEK: THE SCRIPTURAL PROTOTYPE

Alma's discussion of the ancients who entered the rest of the Lord narrows at this point as he chooses Melchizedek to illustrate his doctrine. "And now, my brethren," he said, "I would that ye should humble yourselves before God, and bring forth fruit meet for repentance, that ye may also enter into that rest. Yea, humble yourselves even as the people in the days of Melchizedek, who was also a high priest after this same order [the holy order of God] which I have spoken, who also took upon him the high priesthood forever" (Alma 13:13–14). Melchizedek is one of the most enigmatic figures in Judaeo-Christian history. Legends about Melchizedek abound in Jewish traditions, in Christian literature and art, and among the writings of the Qumran sectaries.[29]

In some Jewish and Christian writings, Melchizedek is identified as Shem, the son of Noah, while later traditions hold that he was a descendant of Shem. Others suggest that he was named Melchizedek by God when the priesthood was bestowed upon him.[30] Josephus explained that the city of Salem, over which Melchizedek reigned, later became known as Jerusalem.[31] In writing of Jerusalem, Josephus observed: "He who first built it was a potent man among the Canaanites and is in our tongue called [Melchizedek] the Righteous King, for such he really was; on which account he was [there] the first priest of God, and *first built a temple* [there], and called the city Jerusalem, which was formerly called Salem."[32] And, most important for our study, the legends attest that Melchizedek was both king and priest in Salem (Hebrews 7:1).[33]

As Latter-day Saints, we know a great deal about Melchizedek as a result of these verses in Alma, from Joseph Smith's translation of the fourteenth chapter of Genesis and the fifth and seventh chapters of Hebrews, and from the Prophet Joseph Smith's sermons on the priesthood. Alma tells us that Melchizedek reigned under or in the stead of his father, whose name is not given; that he received tithes from Abraham; that he was king over the land of Salem, initially a people steeped in wickedness; and that through the exercise of mighty faith and through his preaching ministry as a high priest of the holy order, he helped to establish peace and righteousness among his people (see Alma 13:15–18). The scriptures also make clear that Melchizedek is a marvelous type of Christ. His name comes from two Hebrew roots, *Melekh* (king), and *tzedek* (righteousness), Melchi-tzedek meaning literally "king of righteousness" or "my king is righteousness." We know from modern revelation that to honor him as a great high priest and to avoid the too frequent repetition of the sacred name of Deity, the Church in ancient days called the priesthood after his name (see D&C 107:3–4). His was a single-minded existence, a life of devotion to duty, a life that pointed people toward the great High Priest, *the Prince of Peace*. From the Joseph Smith Translation we learn:

> Now Melchizedek was a man of faith, who wrought righteousness; and when a child he feared God, and stopped the mouths of lions, and quenched the violence of fire.
> And thus, having been approved of God, he was ordained an

146

high priest after the order of the covenant which God made with
Enoch,

It being after the order of the Son of God; which order came, not
by man, nor the will of man; neither by father nor mother; neither
by beginning of days nor end of years; but of God;

And it was delivered unto men by the calling of his own voice,
according to his own will, unto as many as believed on his name.
(JST, Genesis 14:26–29.)

In writing his epistle to the Hebrews, Paul spoke of Christ who
"glorified not himself to be made an high priest; but he that said unto
him, Thou art my Son, to day have I begotten thee. As he saith also in
another place, Thou art a priest for ever after the order of Melchisedec"
(Hebrews 5:5–6).

Who in the days of his flesh, when he had offered up prayers and
supplications with strong crying and tears unto him that was able
to save him from death, and was heard in that he feared;

Though he were a Son, yet learned he obedience by the things
which he suffered. (Hebrews 5:7–8.)

Most of us have heard these verses quoted scores of times, particularly verse eight, in reference to the place of obedience and suffering
in the process of the Son of God becoming perfect. There is, however,
a fascinating note at this point on the manuscript page in the Joseph
Smith Translation; it states that verses seven and eight "are a parenthe-
sis alluding to Melchizedek and not to Christ" (see footnote *a* to
Hebrews 5:7 in the LDS Bible). That is to say, Melchizedek, though a
son, learned obedience by the things that he suffered. But is such not
true of Christ? Certainly. As Elder McConkie has suggested, it is true of
both.

The fact is verses 7 and 8 apply to both Melchizedek and to
Christ, because Melchizedek was a prototype of Christ and that
prophet's ministry typified and foreshadowed that of our Lord in
the same sense that the ministry of Moses did. . . . Thus, though the
words of these verses, and particularly those in the 7th verse, had
original application to Melchizedek, they apply with equal and perhaps even greater force to the life and ministry of him through
whom all the promises made to Melchizedek were fulfilled.[34]

And what of the relationship of Melchizedek to Abraham? Alma
mentions simply that Abraham paid tithing to him (Alma 13:15). An

old tradition among the Jews states that "Melchizedek, the king of righteousness, priest of God Most High, and king of Jerusalem, came forth to meet [Abraham]," as Abraham was returning from the war "with bread and wine. And *this high priest instructed Abraham in the laws of the priesthood* and in the Torah."[35] More specifically, a modern revelation informs us that "Esaias . . . lived in the days of Abraham, and was blessed of him—which Abraham received the priesthood from Melchizedek, who received it through the lineage of his fathers, even till Noah" (D&C 84:13–14). It appears that Abraham sought for the same power and authority that Melchizedek possessed, the power to administer endless lives, the fulness of the powers of the priesthood. We read the following from the book of Abraham (1:2):

> And finding there was greater happiness and peace and rest for me, I sought for the blessings of the fathers, and the right whereunto I should be ordained to administer the same; having been myself a follower of righteousness, desiring also to be one who possessed great knowledge, and to be a greater follower of righteousness, and to possess a greater knowledge, and to be a father of many nations, a prince of peace, and desiring to receive instructions, and to keep the commandments of God, I became a rightful heir, a High Priest, holding the right belonging to the fathers.

On 27 August 1843, Joseph Smith offered prophetic commentary on the seventh chapter of Hebrews, Paul's discussion of the place and power of the Melchizedek Priesthood. According to James Burgess, the Prophet said:

> Paul is here treating of three different priesthoods, namely, the priesthood of Aaron, Abraham, and Melchizedek. Abraham's priesthood was of greater power than Levi's, and *Melchizedek's was of greater power than that of Abraham.* . . . I ask: was there any sealing power attending this [Levitical] Priesthood that would admit a man into the presence of God? Oh no, but Abraham's was a more exalted power or priesthood. He could talk and walk with God. And yet consider how great this man [Melchizedek] was when even this patriarch Abraham gave a tenth part of all his spoils and then *received a blessing under the hands of Melchizedek—even the last law or a fulness of the law or priesthood, which constituted him a king and priest after the order of Melchizedek or an endless life.*[36]

According to Elder Franklin D. Richards, the Prophet explained that the power of Melchizedek was "not the power of a prophet, nor apostle, nor patriarch only, but of a king and priest to God, to open the windows of heaven and pour out the peace and law of endless life to man. And no man can attain to the joint heirship with Jesus Christ without being administered to by one having the same power and authority of Melchizedek."[37] In summary, Joseph the Prophet explained: "Abraham says to Melchizedek, I believe all that thou hast taught me concerning the priesthood and the coming of the Son of Man; so Melchizedek ordained Abraham and sent him away. Abraham rejoiced, saying, Now I have a priesthood."[38]

As we have noted already, Alma taught that the people of Salem "did repent; and Melchizedek did establish peace in the land in his days; therefore he was called the prince of peace" (Alma 13:18). More specifically, we are told elsewhere that Melchizedek and his people established Zion and attained a level of transcendent righteousness, even as did Enoch. That is, Melchizedek "obtained peace in Salem, and was called the Prince of peace. And *his people wrought righteousness, and obtained heaven, and sought for the city of Enoch* which God had before taken. . . . And this Melchizedek, having thus established righteousness, was called the king of heaven by his people, or, in other words, the King of peace" (JST, Genesis 14:33–34, 36; italics added). We can thus understand why Alma would close his discussion of Melchizedek in the spirit of tribute: "Now, there were many before him, and also there were many afterwards, but none were greater; therefore, of him they have more particularly made mention" (Alma 13:19).

And so Melchizedek is Alma's prototype, the example, the scriptural illustration. He received the priesthood, magnified callings in the priesthood, and chose to work righteousness; he made it possible for himself and his people to enter into the rest of the Lord through applying the atoning blood of Christ and by virtue of the sealing powers of the priesthood. Paul likewise stressed the importance and example of this faithful soul: "For this Melchizedek was ordained a priest after the order of the Son of God, which order was without father, without mother, without descent, having neither beginning of days, nor end of life. And all those who are ordained unto this priesthood are made like unto the Son of God, abiding a priest continually" (JST, Hebrews 7:3). It is in this context, then, that we see the ultimate reward of faithful service in the priesthood, a reward "according to the oath and covenant which belongeth to the priesthood" (D&C 84:39). Those who abide by the *covenant* of the priesthood, magnify their callings therein, and live by every word of God, eventually receive what Enoch and Melchizedek received: God swears unto them with an *oath,* by his own voice, that the fulness of eternal reward will be theirs (see D&C 84:33–40).

CONCLUSION

I have believed for some time that at certain periods in their history the Nephites were a spiritually sensitive and accomplished people, that they knew their God and enjoyed fellowship with him. I have a witness that the Book of Mormon is intended to do more than present valuable doctrines and principles and precepts, though it would be worth its weight in gold if it did that alone. In addition, the narrative details and encourages encounters with the divine. From Nephi to Moroni we see and hear the steady witness that God is the same yesterday, today, and forever—that he constantly and consistently reveals himself to those who seek him and strive to do his will. In that sense, Alma 13 is more, much more, than a theological exercise; it is the blessed ideal, the goal to which the Saints of the Most High aspire.

Alma is a master teacher. As is so typical of the great prophetic spokesmen of the ages, he warns, instructs, points toward the divine goal and blessings that follow from faithfulness, and gives specific and simple counsel. How are people to qualify to enter into the rest of the Lord in this life and ultimately rest with God hereafter? They are to live their lives with watchfulness and carefulness. Alma encouraged his people to prepare for the coming of the Son of Man, a divine directive that is equally applicable for the Latter-day Saints. Note the timeliness of his counsel, given some eighty years before the birth of Jesus: "And now we only wait to hear the joyful news declared unto us by the mouth of angels, of his coming; for the time cometh, we know not how soon. Would to God that it might be in my day; but let it be sooner or later, in it I will rejoice" (Alma 13:25). Like all of the Lord's mouthpieces, he warned against procrastination. He testified that safety from Satan is to be had through vigilance: "Humble yourselves before the Lord and call on his holy name, and watch and pray continually, that ye may not be tempted above that which ye can bear, and thus be led by the Holy

Spirit, becoming humble, meek, submissive, patient, full of love and all long-suffering" (verse 28).

How are we to qualify to enter the rest of the Lord? It is not through conducting spiritual marathons, not through excessive zeal, not through attempting to run faster than our file leaders. It is "by a godly walk and conversation" (D&C 20:69), by a quiet but steadfast commitment to the Lord, his gospel, and his anointed servants. It is through applying the blood of Christ, putting off the natural man, becoming free from the taints and stains of the world, by enjoying the gifts and fruit of the Spirit. In the words of Alma, it is through "having *faith* on the Lord; having a *hope* that ye shall receive eternal life; having the *love* of God always in your hearts, *that ye may be lifted up at the last day and enter into his rest*" (13:29; italics added). Alma later declared to his son Helaman "that by small and simple things are great things brought to pass" (Alma 37:6). And so it is in regard to the highest of spiritual blessings and the grandest of priesthood privileges—we gain them, in process of time, through acquiring and exemplifying faith, hope, and charity. Only by abiding by principles of righteousness is one entitled to the rights of the priesthood, the powers of heaven (see D&C 121:36).

The Book of Mormon is a vital window to the past. It is, in conjunction with the words of living oracles, a standard against which our present beliefs and practices may be measured. In addition, it is an invitation to come unto Christ and partake of his love and life hereafter. Though this sacred volume is not intended as a procedural handbook—it is Christ centered more than church centered—it makes known precious and profound truths relative to the holy order of God and the manner in which the ancients were sanctified, sealed, and saved. This is not just a lesson in history, for as the revelation declares, "Now this same Priesthood, which was in the beginning, shall be in the end of the world also" (Moses 6:7). What was true for the Former-day Saints is true for the Latter-day Saints. What inspired and motivated them can and should entice us to continued fidelity and devotion. In the words of a modern apostle: "This is the priesthood which we hold. It will bless us as it blessed Melchizedek and Abraham. The priesthood of Almighty God is here."[39]

Notes

1. Bruce R. McConkie, *A New Witness for the Articles of Faith* (Salt Lake City: Deseret Book Co., 1985), pp. 35, 657–58; Joseph Fielding Smith, *Answers to Gospel Questions,* 5 vols. (Salt Lake City: Deseret Book Co., 1957–66), 2:174; Joseph Fielding Smith, *Doctrines of Salvation,* 3 vols., comp. Bruce R. McConkie (Salt Lake city: Bookcraft, 1954–56), 3:104; Joseph Fielding Smith, *The Way to Perfection* (Salt Lake City: Deseret Book Co., 1970), pp. 72–73.

2. Joseph Fielding Smith, *Doctrines of Salvation,* 3:85.

3. McConkie, *New Witness for the Articles of Faith,* p. 311; *The Promised Messiah: the First Coming of Christ* (Salt Lake City: Deseret Book Co., 1978), p. 427; Joseph Fielding Smith, *Answers to Gospel Questions,* 1:123–26.

4. Joseph Smith, *Teachings of the Prophet Joseph Smith,* sel. Joseph Fielding Smith (Salt Lake City: Deseret Book Co., 1976), pp. 180–81; italics added.

5. Noah Webster, *American Dictionary of the English Language,* facsimile of the 1828 edition (San Francisco: Foundation for American Christian Education, 1967), s.v. "forward."

6. Joseph Fielding Smith, *Doctrines of Salvation,* 3:104.

7. Bruce R. McConkie, *Mormon Doctrine,* 2d ed. (Salt Lake City: Bookcraft, 1966), pp. 355–56.

8. Smith, *Teachings,* p. 365.

9. J. Reuben Clark, Jr., in Conference Report, October 1950, pp. 170–71.

10. Wilford Woodruff, *Journal of Discourses,* 26 vols. (London: Latter-day Saints' Book Depot, 1854–86), 21:317.

11. Smith, *Teachings,* p. 220.

12. Joseph Fielding Smith, *Doctrines of Salvation,* 3:81; italics added.

13. McConkie, *Promised Messiah,* p. 451.

14. Harold B. Lee, in Conference Report, October 1973, p. 7.

15. Orson Pratt, in *Journal of Discourses,* 15:249.

16. Smith, *Teachings,* p. 157.

17. George Q. Cannon, *Journal of Discourses,* 15:249.

18. Smith, *Teachings,* p. 323.

19. Bruce R. McConkie, "The Promises Made to the Fathers," in *Studies in Scripture Vol. 3: The Old Testament, Genesis to 2 Samuel,* ed. Kent P. Jackson and Robert L. Millet (Salt Lake City: Deseret Book Co., 1989), pp. 50–51.

20. Joseph F. Smith, *Gospel Doctrine,* 5th ed. (Salt Lake City: Deseret Book Co., 1971), p. 126; see also p. 58.

21. McConkie, *Mormon Doctrine,* pp. 139–40; *Promised Messiah,* p. 47; Joseph Fielding Smith, *Man: His Origin and Destiny* (Salt Lake City: Deseret Book Co., 1954), p. 272; *The Way to Perfection,* p. 208.

22. Bruce R. McConkie, *Doctrinal New Testament Commentary,* 3 vols. (Salt Lake City: Bookcraft, 1965–73), 2:474.

23. Joseph Fielding Smith, *Doctrines of Salvation,* 3:81.

Chapter 10—The Holy Order of God

24. Ezra Taft Benson, "What I Hope You Will Teach Your Children about the Temple," *Ensign,* August 1985, p. 8.

25. Smith, *Teachings,* p. 308.

26. Ibid., p. 323.

27. Ibid., pp. 322–23.

28. Brigham Young, in *Journal of Discourses,* 8:154.

29. John W. Welch, "The Melchizedek Material in Alma 13:13–19," in *By Study and Also by Faith,* 2 vols., ed. John M. Lundquist and Stephen D. Ricks (Salt Lake City: Deseret Book Co. and Provo: F.A.R.M.S., 1990), 2:238–72.

30. Louis Ginzberg, *The Legends of the Jews,* 7 vols. (Philadelphia: The Jewish Publication Society of America, 1937), 1:233; 5:225–26.

31. *Josephus: Complete Works,* trans. William Whiston (Grand Rapids, Mich.: Kregel Publications, 1981), "Antiquities of the Jews," 1.10.3.

32. Josephus, *Complete Works,* "The Wars," 6.10.1.

33. Ginzberg, *Legends of the Jews,* 1:233.

34. *Doctrinal New Testament Commentary,* 3:157; see also *The Promised Messiah,* pp. 450–451.

35. *The Legends of the Jews,* 1:233.

36. Joseph Smith, *The Words of Joseph Smith,* ed. Andrew F. Ehat and Lyndon W. Cook (Provo: BYU Religious Studies Center, 1980), pp. 245–46, italics added; spelling and punctuation corrected.

37. Ibid., p. 245.

38. Smith, *Teachings,* pp. 322–23.

39. Bruce R. McConkie, in Conference Report, October 1977, p. 35.

The Path of Repentance

Alma discovered, to his horror, that his son Corianton had been guilty of sexual sin during his mission to the Zoramites; he had become involved with a harlot named Isabel, a women of degraded character and morals who had contributed to the downfall of many men. Corianton had yielded to moral temptation for the following several reasons, reasons that should cause the Saints of the last days to take note.

1. Corianton had become haughty, had yielded to feelings of self-sufficiency. He had begun to boast in his own strength (see Alma 39:2), to rely less and less on the arm of the Lord and more and more on the arm of flesh. In our day, Corianton might have been heard to say repeatedly, "I can handle it!" Corianton learned through a painful process that each of us is dependent upon the Almighty, not only to ultimately be saved but also to have sufficient strength to resist evil. Alma had pleaded almost a decade earlier with a rebellious people: "Cast off your sins, and [do] not procrastinate the day of your repentance; but *humble yourselves before the Lord, and call on his holy name,* and watch and pray continually, that ye may not be tempted above that which ye can bear" (Alma 13:27–28; italics added).

2. Corianton had forsaken his ministry (see Alma 39:3), had left his duty station. He was not where he had been assigned to be. One who sings "I'll go where you want me to go, dear Lord" (*Hymns,* 1985, no. 270) must not then be guilty of desertion, of negligence and waywardness when the assignment comes. "No man," the Savior declared, "having put his hand to the plough, and looking back, is fit for the kingdom of God" (Luke 9:62).

3. Having begun to associate with the wrong kinds of people, Corianton eventually surrendered to the allurements and pressures to conform to the ways of the worldly. But, Alma scolded, because others gave in to sin was no reason for Corianton to do the same: "This was no excuse for thee, my son. Thou shouldst have tended to the ministry wherewith thou wast entrusted" (Alma 39:3–4).

THE SERIOUSNESS OF SEXUAL TRANSGRESSION

Alma then placed all things in perspective by stressing the seriousness of sexual immorality. He explained that only two sins were greater abominations in the sight of God—the sin against the Holy Ghost and murder, or the shedding of innocent blood. In speaking of the former sin, he taught: "If ye deny the Holy Ghost when it once has had place in you, and ye know that ye deny it, behold, this is a sin which is unpardonable" (Alma 39:6).

"All manner of sin and blasphemy shall be forgiven unto men," Jesus warned, "but the blasphemy against the Holy Ghost shall not be forgiven unto men, . . . neither in this world, neither in the world to come" (Matthew 12:31–32). These are they who "know [God's] power, and have been made partakers thereof, and suffered themselves through the power of the devil to be overcome, and to deny the truth and defy [God's] power—they are they who are the sons of perdition, . . . vessels of wrath," enemies to the cause of truth, "having denied the Holy Spirit after having received it, and having denied the Only Begotten Son of the Father, having crucified him unto themselves and put him to an open shame" (D&C 76:31–35).[1] Joseph Smith declared:

> All sins shall be forgiven, except the sin against the Holy Ghost; for Jesus will save all except the sons of perdition. What must a man do to commit the unpardonable sin? He must receive the Holy Ghost, have the heavens opened unto him, and know God, and then sin against Him. After a man has sinned against the Holy Ghost, there is no repentance for him. He has got to say that the sun does not shine while he sees it; he has got to deny Jesus Christ when the heavens have been opened unto him, and to deny the plan of salvation with his eyes open to the truth of it; and from that time he begins to be an enemy.[2]

The sin against the Holy Ghost is *unpardonable* because it is not covered by the atoning blood of Christ and because no amount of personal suffering on the part of the sinner can atone for the pernicious deed.

"Whosoever murdereth against the light and knowledge of God, it is not easy for him to obtain forgiveness," Alma warned (Alma 39:6). "A murderer," Joseph Smith explained, "one that sheds innocent blood, cannot have forgiveness."[3] Murder is thus referred to as an *unforgivable* sin, a heinous crime against humanity, an offense not covered by the atoning blood of Christ and for which deliverance from hell in the world of spirits is possible only after much personal suffering. "There are sins unto death," wrote Elder Bruce R. McConkie, "meaning spiritual death. There are sins for which there is no forgiveness, neither in this world nor in the world to come. There are sins which utterly and completely preclude the sinner from gaining eternal life. Hence there are sins for which repentance does not operate, sins that the atoning blood of Christ will not wash away, sins for which the sinner must suffer and pay the full penalty personally."[4]

Sexual immorality ranks third in order of serious offenses before God because it, like murder, deals with life. One who tampers with virtue prematurely or inappropriately—outside of marriage—tampers with the powers of life. Elder Boyd K. Packer has taught: "There was provided in our bodies—and this is sacred—a power of creation, a light, so to speak, that has the power to kindle other lights. This gift was to be used only within the sacred bonds of marriage. Through the exercise of this power of creation, a mortal body may be conceived, a spirit enter into it, and a new soul born into this life." Further, this power "is a gift from God our Father. In the righteous exercise of it as in nothing else, we may come close to him." On the other hand, "God has declared in unmistakable language that misery and sorrow will follow the violation of the laws of chastity. . . . Crowning glory awaits you if you live worthily. The loss of the crown may well be punishment enough. Often, very often, we are punished as much by our sins as we are for them."[5]

A PATTERN FOR REPENTANCE

It would appear that much of Corianton's problem was borne of doctrinal ignorance and misunderstanding, particularly concerning the appropriateness of justice and punishment for sin (see Alma 41:1; 42:1). It is fitting, then, that Alma should instruct his son about repentance and point the way back to the path of peace and happiness.

First, having stressed the seriousness of the offense, Alma sought now to ensure that Corianton was experiencing godly sorrow for sin, the kind of sorrow that is an essential element of true repentance. In short, Alma desired that his son experience appropriate guilt—no more than is requisite, but surely no less than is needful to bring about change. Alma observed: "I would to God that ye had not been guilty of so great a crime. I would not dwell upon your crimes, to harrow up your soul, if it were not for your good" (Alma 39:7; compare 2 Corinthians 7:10). Alma later remarked: "And now, my son, I desire that ye should let these things trouble you no more, and only let your sins trouble you, with that trouble which shall bring you down unto repentance" (Alma 42:29). Alma knew only too well the awful agony associated with grievous sin; on the other hand, he understood as few others do how intense pain could be turned to consummate joy, how suffering could make saints out of sinners. Appropriate guilt can and does have a sanctifying effect: it alerts the offender to the spiritual chasm between himself and his Maker and motivates him thereafter to a godly walk and conduct.

"Now my son," Alma continued, "I would that ye should repent and forsake your sins, and go no more after the lusts of your eyes, but cross yourself in all these things" (Alma 39:9). For Corianton to "cross himself" was for him to turn away from evil inclinations, to deny himself of worldly lusts, to work at cross purposes from the natural man, to forsake worldly paths, and to chart and navigate a course of righteousness (see 3 Nephi 12:30). "As well as establishing worthy goals, charting the course prevents one from living an unplanned, haphazard life—a tumbleweed existence."[6] Those desirous of keeping themselves from sinful practices must often change associations, places, and attitudes toward life. Corianton was specifically advised to lean upon his older brothers—Helaman and Shiblon—for support, to look to their example and seek their counsel. "Ye stand in need to be nourished by your brothers," Alma said (Alma 39:10).

Because Corianton's abominable deeds rang so loudly in the ears of the Zoramites, the words of the Nephite missionaries did not have the spiritual appeal or impact they might otherwise have had. "How great iniquity ye brought upon the Zoramites," Alma chastened the errant son, "for when they saw your conduct they would not believe in my words" (Alma 39:11). It was thus incumbent upon Corianton—a major part of his repentance and a key to forgiveness—to make restitution where possible. "Turn to the Lord with all your mind, might, and strength; that ye lead away the hearts of no more to do wickedly; but rather return unto them, and acknowledge your faults and that wrong which ye have done" (Alma 39:13). President Joseph F. Smith asked,

"Does repentance consist of sorrow for wrong doing?" Yes," he answered, "but is this all? By no means."

> True repentance only is acceptable to God, nothing short of it will answer the purpose. Then what is true repentance? True repentance is not only sorrow for sins, and humble penitence and contrition before God, but it involves the necessity of turning away from them, a discontinuance of all evil practices and deeds, a thorough reformation of life, a vital change from evil to good, from vice to virtue, from darkness to light. Not only so, but to make restitution, so far as it is possible, for all the wrongs we have done, to pay our debts, and restore to God and man their rights—that which is due to them from us. This is true repentance, and exercise of the will and all the powers of body and mind is demanded, to complete this glorious work of repentance; then God will accept it.[7]

Indeed, Corianton learned, as do we all, that repentance consists of a major realignment of priorities, a turn from the fleeting, and an acceptance of the permanent. "Seek not after riches nor the vain things of this world," a tender father thus counseled, "for behold, you cannot carry them with you" (Alma 39:14).

No discussion of repentance would be complete without a focus upon the power and saving grace available through the redemptive work of Jesus Christ. And thus it is that Alma set forth in plain and unmistakable language the significance of the timeless and eternal sacrifice available through the blood of him who is man's Advocate with the Father. Alma's testimony (see Alma 39:17–19) is in harmony with that of John the Revelator: Jesus Christ is the Lamb slain from the foundation of the world (see Revelation 13:8). The Book of Mormon provides a restoration of a vital and precious truth, a verity largely absent from the biblical record: the knowledge that Christian prophets have taught Christian doctrine and administered Christian ordinances since the beginning of time. Our Lord's atonement reaches from creation's dawn to millennial splendor; the children of God from Eden to Armageddon can have their sins remitted in the name of the Holy One of Israel. That is, the Atonement applies to "not only those who believed after he came in the meridian of time, in the flesh, but all those from the beginning, even as many as were before he came, who believed in the words of the holy prophets, . . . as well as those who should come after, who should believe in the gifts and callings of God by the Holy Ghost" (D&C 20:26–27).

Chapter 11—The Path of Repentance

THE RETURN OF THE PRODIGAL

Corianton's sin was abhorrent to God and the people of God. It hindered the work of the Lord among the Zoramites and caused deep pain and sorrow for those who knew and loved him. But it was not an unpardonable nor an unforgivable sin. Though it is true that the Holy One cannot look upon sin with the least degree of allowance, it is also true that "he that repents and does the commandments of the Lord shall be forgiven" (D&C 1:31–32; see also Alma 45:16). God the Father is anxious for the return of his children to the path of righteousness and peace, perhaps infinitely more so than we can now perceive. Elder Orson F. Whitney held out this hope for the parents of wandering or wayward children:

> You parents of the wilful and the wayward: Don't give them up. Don't cast them off. They are not utterly lost. The shepherd will find his sheep. They were his before they were yours—long before he entrusted them to your care; and you cannot begin to love them as he loves them. They have but strayed in ignorance from the Path of Right, and God is merciful to ignorance. Only the fulness of knowledge brings the fulness of accountability. Our Heavenly Father is far more merciful, infinitely more charitable, than even the best of his servants, and the Everlasting Gospel is mightier in power to save than our narrow finite minds can comprehend.[8]

President J. Reuben Clark, Jr., observed: "I feel that [the Lord] will give that punishment which is the very least that our transgression will justify. . . . I believe that when it comes to making the rewards for our good conduct, he will give the maximum that it is possible to give."[9]

Alma was not only a concerned father; he was a prophet of God and the president of the Church. His was the gift of discernment and the spirit of prophecy and revelation. He was thus able to judge whether Corianton's repentance was genuine and when his heart was right before God. Knowing these things, it is touching to read these words of Alma to his son: "And now, O my son, ye are called of God to preach the word unto this people. And now, my son, go thy way, declare the word with truth and soberness, that thou mayest bring souls unto repentance, that the great plan of mercy may have claim upon them. And may God grant unto you even according to my words. Amen" (Alma 42:31).

We have every reason to believe that Corianton's repentance was complete, that he "crossed himself" and forsook sinful practices, places, and people, and that he qualified to return to the ministry and to full fellowship among the household of faith. We read of Corianton's labors a year or so later: "Thus ended the nineteenth year of the reign of the judges over the people of Nephi. Yea, and there was continual peace among them, and exceedingly great prosperity in the church because of their heed and diligence which they gave unto the word of God, which was declared unto them by Helaman, and Shiblon, *and Corianton,* and Ammon and his brethren, yea, and by all those who had been ordained by the holy order of God" (Alma 49:29–30; italics added).[10] Truly salvation is free (see 2 Nephi 2:4), freely available, and the Lord's hand is extended to all, such that "whosoever will come may come and partake of the waters of life freely" (Alma 42:27; compare Isaiah 55:1–2).

NOTES

1. There is a sense in which those who have "shed innocent blood" are guilty of the sin against the Holy Ghost. That person who becomes a son of perdition crucifies Christ anew (compare Hebrews 6:4–6). "He gets the spirit of the devil—the same spirit that they had who crucified the Lord of Life—the same spirit that sins against the Holy Ghost" (Joseph Smith, *Teachings of the Prophet Joseph Smith,* sel. Joseph Fielding Smith [Salt Lake City: Deseret Book Company, 1976], p. 358). "The blasphemy against the Holy Ghost, which shall not be forgiven in the world nor out of the world, is in that *ye commit murder wherein ye shed innocent blood, and assent unto my death*" (D&C 132:27; italics added). See also Bruce R. McConkie, *Doctrinal New Testament Commentary,* 3 vols. (Salt Lake City: Bookcraft, 1965–73), 3:116, 345; *The Mortal Messiah: From Bethlehem to Calvary,* 4 vols. (Salt Lake City: Deseret Book Co., 1979–81), 2:216; *A New Witness for the Articles of Faith* (Salt Lake City: Deseret Book Co., 1985), p. 233.

2. Smith, *Teachings,* p. 358.

3. Ibid., p. 339.

4. McConkie, *New Witness for the Articles of Faith,* p. 231.

5. Boyd K. Packer, in Conference Report, April 1972, pp. 136–38.

6. Spencer W. Kimball, *The Miracle of Forgiveness* (Salt Lake City: Bookcraft, 1969), pp. 233–34.

7. Joseph F. Smith, *Gospel Doctrine* (Salt Lake City: Deseret Book Co., 1971), pp. 100–101.

8. Orson F. Whitney, in Conference Report, April 1929, p. 110.

9. J. Reuben Clark, Jr., "As Ye Sow . . . ," address at Brigham Young University, 3 May 1955.

10. Later in the story we read of Corianton busily engaged in the work of the Lord (see Alma 63:10).

Justice, Mercy, and the Life Beyond

It is in the context of a serious father-and-son discussion—counsel by Alma to his errant son Corianton—that we are able to read some of the deepest and most profound doctrine in the Book of Mormon. Because life is at best tenuous; because death is an ever-present reality; and because all men and women must eventually put off this mortal coil and engage a new existence that is, for the most part, strange and unknown, a theological discussion of life after life is welcomed and appreciated. The prophet Alma, recognizing that resurrection—the inseparable union of spirit and body—did not immediately follow death, inquired of the Lord about the state of the soul between death and resurrection. An angel, a citizen himself of the world of spirits, taught Alma about the nature of the afterworld. And it is through Alma's explanation of these things to his son that we become privy to sacred and solemn matters.

BETWEEN DEATH AND RESURRECTION

Before discussing the doctrine of resurrection and the law of restoration—the principle that all people will be raised to that level of glory commensurate with the lives they lived in mortality—Alma turned his attention to a discussion of the postmortal spirit world, a matter he had "inquired diligently of the Lord to know" (Alma 40:9). He explained that, according to what he had been taught by an angel, "the spirits of all men, as soon as they are departed from this mortal body, yea, the spirits[1] of all men, whether they be good or evil, are taken home to that God who gave them life" (Alma 40:11). "Then shall the dust return to the earth as it was," said the Preacher, "and the spirit shall return unto God who gave it" (Ecclesiastes 12:7).

Both of these scriptural preachers were speaking in broadest terms and should not be interpreted to mean that the spirit—at the time of death—goes into the immediate presence of the Lord. President Brigham Young explained that to speak of the spirit returning to the God who gave it means that "when the spirits leave their bodies they are in the presence of our Father and God" in the sense that they "are prepared then to see, hear and understand spiritual things."[2] To go into the "presence" of God is not necessarily to be "placed within a few yards or rods, or within a short distance of his person."[3] President George Q. Cannon explained: "Alma, when he says that 'the spirits of all men, as soon as they are departed from this mortal body, . . . are taken home to that God who gave them life,' has the idea, doubtless, in his mind that our God is omnipresent—not in His own personality but through His minister, the Holy Spirit. He does not intend to convey the idea that they are immediately ushered into the personal presence of God. He evidently uses that phrase in a qualified sense."[4]

The transition from time into eternity is immediate. As the physical self breathes its last breath, the spirit self passes through a veil separating this world from the next. At this point the spirit experiences what might be called a "partial judgment."[5] Those who have been true and faithful to their trust in mortality, Alma explained, are received into *paradise,* "a state of rest, a state of peace, where they shall rest from all their troubles and from all care, and sorrow" (Alma 40:12). As I have written elsewhere, "those things which burdened the obedient—the worldly cares and struggles, the vicissitudes of this life—are shed with the physical body. Paradise is a place where the spirit is free to think and act with a renewed capacity and with the vigor and enthusiasm that characterized one in his prime. Though a person does not rest per se from the work associated with the plan of salvation . . . , at the same time he is delivered from those cares and worries associated with a fallen world and a corrupt body."[6]

Those, on the other hand, who have been wicked on earth—who gave themselves up to the lusts and lasciviousness of the flesh—shall be received into that portion of the spirit world called *hell* or *outer darkness,*[7] a place of "weeping, and wailing, and gnashing of teeth, and this because of their own iniquity, being led captive by the will of the devil" (Alma 40:13). Joseph Smith explained: "The great misery of departed spirits in the world of spirits, where they go after death, is to know that they come short of the glory that others enjoy and that they might have enjoyed themselves, and they are their own accusers."[8] On another occasion the Prophet taught: "A man is his own tormentor and his own condemner. Hence the saying, They shall go into the lake that burns with fire and brimstone. The torment of disappointment in the mind of man is as exquisite as a lake burning with fire and brimstone. I say, so is the torment of man."[9] Hell is both a place—a part of the world of spirits where suffering and sorrow and repentance take place—and a state—a condition of the mind associated with remorseful realization. The righteous remain in paradise and the wicked in hell until the time of their resurrection (see Alma 40:14).[10]

The Doctrine of Resurrection

No doctrine provides a more powerful assurance and comfort to the bereaved than the doctrine of resurrection—the verity that all who have taken physical bodies through birth shall survive death, shall receive those bodies again in the Resurrection. Resurrection is a doctrine as old as the world: it is not a creation of the first-century Christians, nor a belief spawned by the Jews in Babylonian captivity. It was taught to Adam, discussed by Enoch, and testified of by Abraham. Any people through the ages who have gained the understanding of the ministry of the Messiah, who have come to know by revelation of the coming of Jesus Christ, have likewise gained the understanding that Christ would break the bands of death and open the door for all others to be likewise raised from death to life in glorious immortality. That was precisely so with the Nephites. Alma, the noble patriarch, sought to inform and inspire his son on this fundamental principle of the Christian religion.[11]

"The soul shall be restored to the body," Alma explained, "and the body to the soul; yea, and every limb and joint shall be restored to its body; yea, even a hair of the head shall not be lost; but all things shall be restored to their proper and perfect frame" (Alma 40:23; compare 11:43).[12] Joseph Smith provided additional insight into the nature of the Resurrection when he said, "As concerning the resurrection, I will merely say that all men will come from the grave as they lie down, whether old or young; there will not be 'added unto their stature one cubit,' neither taken from it; all will be raised by the power of God, having spirit in their bodies, and not blood."[13] A prophetic successor, President Joseph F. Smith, observed: "The body will come forth as it is laid to rest, for there is no growth or development in the grave. As it is laid down, so will it arise, and changes to perfection will come by the law of restitution. But the spirit will continue to expand and develop, and the body, after the resurrection will develop to the full stature of man."[14]

Alma's discussion of the first resurrection (see Alma 40:16–20) is slightly difficult to follow. At first it appears that Alma was suggesting that the first resurrection consists of the resurrection of all persons—righteous and wicked—who had lived before Christ (see Alma 40:16). Abinadi had clearly stated, however, that the first resurrection would be made up of "the prophets, and all those that have believed in their words, or all those that have kept the commandments of God" (Mosiah 15:22). That is to say, from Abinadi's and Alma's chronological perspective, the first resurrection would be made up of the righteous dead—"an innumerable company of the spirits of the just" (D&C 138:12)—from Adam to Christ. From our perspective in the final dispensation, with information revealed to Joseph Smith, we know that the first resurrection will resume at the time of the Second Coming; the Savior will bring with him the hosts of the righteous dead from the meridian of time to the time of his coming. Finally Alma did give his opinion on the matter—an opinion that is in fact accurate and appropriate—that "the souls and the bodies are reunited, *of the righteous*, at the resurrection of Christ, and his ascension into heaven" (Alma 40:20; italics added).[15]

The Lord has stated in a modern revelation that "the resurrection from the dead is the redemption of the soul" (D&C 88:16). Death is not the end. The grave shall not have won the victory. The prophetic promise is sure. Joseph Smith declared: "All your losses will be made up to you in the resurrection, provided you continue faithful. By the vision of the Almighty I have seen it."[16]

THE DOCTRINE OF RESTORATION

The Resurrection, Alma explained, is but a part of a larger system of restoration: not only shall spirit and body be inseparably united, but all things shall hereafter be restored to the way they were here. In short, our station and reward hereafter shall be directly related to the manner in which we managed our time and spiritual resources while in this life. It is thus ludicrous to suppose that one could hope for a glorious resurrection and transcendent reward hereafter when his or her thoughts and actions in this life were shoddy and superficial. What was to Paul the law of the harvest (see Galatians 6:7: "Whatsoever a man soweth, that shall he also reap") was to Alma the law of restoration. "The plan of restoration," Alma observed, "is requisite with the justice of God; for it is requisite that all things should be restored to their proper order." Further, "it is requisite with the justice of God that men should be judged according to their works; and if their works were good in this life, and the desires of their hearts were good, that they should also, at the last day, be restored unto that which is good," what we would know as exaltation in the highest heaven. "And if their works are evil they shall be restored unto them for evil" (Alma 41:2–4).

Wickedness here never was and never will be happiness here or hereafter. Carnality here never was and never will be spirituality here or hereafter. Charting a course contrary to God and his plan in this life can never lead to spiritual union and joy with him in the life to come (see Alma 41:10–11). Moroni focused the attention of his readers upon the stark reality of the law of restoration in these words: "Do ye suppose that ye shall dwell with [God] under a consciousness of your guilt? Do ye suppose that ye could be happy to dwell with that holy Being, when your souls are racked with a consciousness of guilt that ye have ever abused his laws? Behold, I say unto you that ye would be more miserable to dwell with a holy and just God, under a consciousness of your filthiness before him, than ye would to dwell with the damned souls in hell" (Mormon 9:3–4). A modern revelation thus stated that "they who are not sanctified through the law which I have given unto you, even the law of Christ, must inherit another kingdom, even that of a terrestrial kingdom, or that of a telestial kingdom."

> For he who is not able to abide the law of a celestial kingdom cannot abide a celestial glory. And he who cannot abide the law of a terrestrial kingdom cannot abide a terrestrial glory. And he who cannot abide the law of a telestial kingdom cannot abide a telestial glory; therefore he is not meet for a kingdom of glory. Therefore he must abide a kingdom which is not a kingdom of glory.
>
> They who are of a celestial spirit [in mortality] shall receive [in the Resurrection] the same body which was a natural body; even ye shall receive your bodies, and your glory shall be that glory by which your bodies are quickened. Ye who are quickened by a portion of the celestial glory shall then receive of the same, even a fulness. And they who are quickened by a portion of the terrestrial glory shall then receive of the same, even a fulness. And also they

who are quickened by a portion of the telestial glory shall then receive of the same, even a fulness. (D&C 88:21–24, 28–31.)

In summary, "that which ye do send out [the life we live, the deeds we do] shall return unto you again, and be restored; therefore, the word restoration more fully condemneth the sinner, and justifieth him not at all" (Alma 41:15).

JUSTICE AND MERCY: THE DELICATE BALANCE

To demonstrate the necessity and timelessness of justice and to show that there are always consequences for our transgressions, Alma recounted the story of the fall of Adam and Eve. The Fall brought on the justice of God and resulted in physical and spiritual death, both of which are necessary in the eternal plan of the Father. "Now behold," Alma continued, "it was not expedient that man should be reclaimed from this . . . death, for that would destroy the great plan of happiness" (Alma 42:8). Jacob had noted earlier that "death hath passed upon all men, to fulfil the merciful plan of the great creator" (2 Nephi 9:6). It was necessary for the justice of a God to be meted out in order for the mercy of a God to be extended; as the Fall is the father of the Atonement, so justice paves the way for mercy (see Alma 42:1–13).

The balance of justice and mercy is achieved only in and through a God, only in and through a being in whom there is a perfect balance, through him who is both infinitely just and merciful. The balance is achieved only by him who is sinless and upon whom justice has no claim, through him who has no need of pardoning mercy. Elder Boyd K. Packer beautifully illustrated the role of Christ as Mediator in the following parable:

> There was once a man who wanted something very much. It seemed more important than anything else in his life. In order for him to have his desire, he incurred a great debt.
>
> He had been warned about going into that much debt, and particularly about his creditor. But it seemed so important for him to do what he wanted to do and to have what he wanted right now. He was sure he could pay for it later.
>
> So he signed a contract. He would pay it off some time along the way. He didn't worry too much about it, for the due date seemed such a long time away. He had what he wanted now, and that was what seemed important.

Chapter 12—Justice, Mercy, and the Life Beyond

The creditor was always somewhere in the back of his mind, and he made token payments now and again, thinking somehow that the day of reckoning really would never come.

But as it always does, the day came, and the contract fell due. The debt had not been fully paid. His creditor appeared and demanded payment in full.

Only then did he realize that his creditor not only had the power to repossess all that he owned, but the power to cast him into prison as well.

"I cannot pay you, for I have not the power to do so," he confessed.

"Then," said the creditor, "we will exercise the contract, take your possessions, and you shall go to prison. You agreed to that. It was your choice. You signed the contract, and now it must be enforced."

"Can you not extend the time or forgive the debt?" the debtor begged. "Arrange some way for me to keep what I have and not go to prison. Surely you believe in mercy? Will you not show mercy?"

The creditor replied, "Mercy is always so one-sided. It would serve only you. If I show mercy to you, it will leave me unpaid. It is justice I demand. Do you believe in justice?"

"I believed in justice when I signed the contract," the debtor said. "It was on my side then, for I thought it would protect me. I did not need mercy then, nor think I should need it ever. Justice, I thought, would serve both of us equally as well."

"It is justice that demands that you pay the contract or suffer the penalty," the creditor replied. "That is the law. You have agreed to it and that is the way it must be. Mercy cannot rob justice."

There they were: One meting out justice, the other pleading for mercy. Neither could prevail except at the expense of the other.

"If you do not forgive the debt there will be no mercy," the debtor pleaded.

"If I do, there will be no justice," was the reply.

Both laws, it seemed, could not be served. They are two eternal ideals that appear to contradict one another. Is there no way for justice to be fully served, and mercy also?

There is a way! The law of justice *can* be fully satisfied and mercy *can* be fully extended—but it takes someone else. And so it happened this time.

The debtor had a friend. He came to help. He knew the debtor well. He knew him to be shortsighted. He thought him foolish to have gotten himself into such a predicament. Nevertheless, he wanted to help because he loved him. He stepped between them, faced the creditor, and made this offer:

"I will pay the debt if you will free the debtor from his contract so that he may keep his possessions and not go to prison."

As the creditor was pondering the offer, the mediator added, "You demanded justice. Though he cannot pay you, I will do so. You will have been justly dealt with and can ask no more. It would not be just."

And so the creditor agreed.

The mediator turned then to the debtor. "If I pay your debt, will you accept me as your creditor?"

"Oh yes, yes," cried the debtor. "You save me from prison and show mercy to me."

"Then," said the benefactor, "you will pay the debt to me and I will set the terms. It will not be easy, but it will be possible. I will provide a way. You need not go to prison."

And so it was that the creditor was paid in full. He had been justly dealt with. No contract had been broken.

The debtor, in turn, had been extended mercy. Both laws stood fulfilled. Because there was a mediator, justice had claimed its full share, and mercy was fully satisfied.[17]

The scriptures affirm that "there is one God, and one mediator between God and men, the man Christ Jesus" (1 Timothy 2:5). Mercy comes because of the atonement. Mercy is extended to the penitent (see Alma 42:23). Those who accept Christ as their Benefactor and apply the appropriate price of repentance are delivered from the demands of justice and come to know that freedom and peace available only through him who is the Way, the Truth, and the Life (see John 8:31–32).

CAN GOD CEASE TO BE GOD?

In seeking to dramatize the absolute necessity for God's justice to be meted out where appropriate, Alma spoke to Corianton of a most unusual hypothetical situation. "According to justice," he said, "the plan of redemption could not be brought about, only on conditions of repentance of men in this probationary state, yea, this preparatory state; for except it were for these conditions, mercy could not take effect except it should destroy the work of justice. Now the work of justice could not be destroyed; if so, *God would cease to be God*." Alma explained further that "there is a law given, and a punishment affixed, and a repentance granted; which repentance, mercy claimeth; otherwise, justice claimeth the creature and executeth the law, and the law inflicteth the punishment; if not so, the works of justice would be destroyed, and

Chapter 12—Justice, Mercy, and the Life Beyond

God would cease to be God" (Alma 42:13, 22; italics added; see also verse 25). Some have taken these verses to mean that it is indeed possible for God to cease to be God; that if he should, by some bizarre means, fail to function in perfectness, he would be unseated and removed from his place of preeminence; that the forces in the universe would demand his abdication from the heavenly throne. Such ideas are to some people quite stimulating but are, nonetheless, erroneous and misleading.

Joseph Smith taught, and the scriptures boldly and repeatedly attest to the fact, that God is omnipotent, omniscient, and, by the power of his Holy Spirit, omnipresent. The Prophet taught that "God is the *only supreme governor and independent being* in whom all fulness and perfection dwell; . . . without beginning of days or end of life; and that in him every good gift and every good principle dwell; and that he is the Father of lights; *in him the principle of faith dwells independently,* and he is the object in whom the faith of all other rational and accountable beings center for life and salvation."[18] The Prophet Joseph also stated:

> It is . . . necessary, in order to the exercise of faith in God unto life and salvation, that men should have the idea of the existence of the attribute justice in him; for without the idea of the existence of the attribute justice in the Deity, men could not have confidence sufficient to place themselves under his guidance and directions; for they would be filled with fear and doubt lest the judge of all the earth would not do right, and thus fear or doubt, existing in the mind, would preclude the possibility of the exercise of faith in him for life and salvation. But when the idea of the existence of the attribute justice in the Deity is fairly planted in the mind, it leaves no room for doubt to get into the heart, and the mind is enabled to cast itself upon the Almighty without fear and without doubt, and with the most unshaken confidence, believing that the Judge of all the earth will do right.[19]

The fact of the matter is that God will not nor cannot cease to be God. His title, his status, and his exalted position are forever fixed and immutable. Exalted beings simply do not apostatize! They do not slip! It is contrary to their divine nature to lie or cheat or be anything other than impartial. God is not dependent on others for his godhood, nor can he be impeached. Nor need the Saints of God spend a particle of a second worrying and fretting about the Almighty falling from grace. In fact, for members of the Church to do so is, as the Prophet suggested, to err in doctrine as to the true nature of God and

169

thus fall short of that dynamic faith that leads to life and salvation. Alma's hypothetical case is just that—purely hypothetical. He is arguing toward the impossible to demonstrate the logical certainty of his position—that mercy cannot rob justice. It is as if Alma had said: "To suppose that one can break the laws of God with impunity; to suppose that one can live a life of sin and have the atonement of Christ—the mercy of the Lord—rob justice of its due, is to suppose that which cannot be. It is as absurd as to suppose that God would cease to be God!" Truly, Alma explained, "*God ceaseth not to be God,* and mercy claimeth the penitent, and mercy cometh because of the atonement. . . . For behold, justice exerciseth all his demands, and also mercy claimeth all which is her own; and thus, none but the truly penitent are saved" (Alma 42:23–24; italics added).

NOTES

1. Alma repeatedly used the word *soul* to refer to the spirit (see verses 7, 9, 11, 14, 15, 17, 18, 21, 23). This, of course, is a different usage from the more specific definition of *soul* (the spirit and the body) contained in D&C 88:15; see also 2 Nephi 9:13.
2. Brigham Young, *Journal of Discourses,* 26 vols. (London: Latter-day Saints' Book Depot, 1854–86), 3:368.
3. Orson Pratt, in *Journal of Discourses,* 16:365.
4. George Q. Cannon, *Gospel Truth,* two volumes in one, comp. Jerreld L. Newquist (Salt Lake City: Deseret Book Co., 1987), p. 58.
5. This expression is used by Joseph F. Smith (see *Gospel Doctrine* [Salt Lake City: Deseret Book Co., 1971], pp. 448–49) and is probably what Alma was describing in Alma 40:15 as an initial consignment to happiness or misery before the actual Resurrection.
6. Robert L. Millet and Joseph Fielding McConkie, *The Life Beyond* (Salt Lake City: Bookcraft, 1986), p. 18. For a discussion of the Savior's statement to the thief on the cross, "To day shalt thou be with me in paradise" (Luke 23:43), see *The Life Beyond,* pp. 19–20, 168.
7. With but few exceptions, *outer darkness* refers to hell, the place of suffering and sadness and confrontation in the spirit world (see Alma 34:33; 40:13–14; 41:7; D&C 38:5; 138:22, 30, 57; Isa. 49:9). "So complete is the darkness prevailing in the minds of these spirits, so wholly has gospel light been shut out of their consciences, that they know little or nothing of the plan of salvation, and have little hope within themselves of advancement and progression through the saving grace of Christ" (Bruce R. McConkie, *Mormon Doctrine,* 2nd. ed. [Salt Lake City: Bookcraft, 1966], pp. 551–52).
8. Joseph Smith, *Teachings of the Prophet Joseph Smith,* sel. Joseph Fielding Smith (Salt Lake City: Deseret Book Co., 1976), pp. 310–11.
9. Ibid., p. 357.

Chapter 12—Justice, Mercy, and the Life Beyond

10. The entire spirit world, and not just that portion designated as hell, is appropriately called a "spirit prison" (see D&C 45:17; 138:15, 18, 50; Moses 7:55–57; Smith, *Teachings*, p. 310; Orson Pratt, in *Journal of Discourses*, 1:289–90; Brigham Young, in *Journal of Discourses*, 3:95; Bruce R. McConkie, *Ensign*, August 1976, p. 11). Paradise will be vacated and its residents released to a glorious resurrection at the second coming of Christ. Hell comes to an end at the time of the second resurrection, at the end of the Millennium.

11. Joseph Smith explained that "the fundamental principles of our religion are the testimony of the Apostles and Prophets, concerning Jesus Christ, that He died, was buried, and rose again the third day, and ascended into heaven; and all other things which pertain to our religion are only appendages to it" (Smith, *Teachings*, p. 121; compare 1 Corinthians 15:1–4).

12. Joseph Smith distinguished between the fundamental and nonfundamental elements of the body. "There is no fundamental principle," he taught, "belonging to a human system that ever goes into another in this world or in the world to come; I care not what the theories of men are. We have the testimony that God will raise us up, and he has the power to do it. If anyone supposes that any part of our bodies, that is, the fundamental parts thereof, ever goes into another body, he is mistaken" (*History of The Church of Jesus Christ of Latter-day Saints*, 7 vols., 2d ed. rev., ed. B. H. Roberts [Salt Lake City: The Church of Jesus Christ of Latter-day Saints, 1932–51], 5:339).

13. Smith, *Teachings*, pp. 199–200.

14. *Improvement Era*, June 1904, pp. 623–24; see also *Gospel Doctrine*, pp. 23, 447–48. President Smith's son, Joseph Fielding Smith, commented on these words as follows: "President Smith was in full accord with Amulek and Alma. He taught that the body will be restored as stated in Alma 11:42–45 and 40:22–23. While he expresses the thought that the body will come forth as it was laid down, he also expresses the thought that it will take time to adjust the body from the condition of imperfections. This, of course, is reasonable, but at the same time the length of time to make these adjustments will not cover any appreciable extent of time.

   "President Smith never intended to convey the thought that it would require weeks or months of time in order for the defects to be removed. These changes will come naturally, of course, but *almost instantly*. We cannot look upon it in any other way" (Joseph Fielding Smith, *Doctrines of Salvation*, 3 vols., comp. Bruce R. McConkie [Salt Lake City: Bookcraft, 1954–56], 2:293–94).

15. "It is evident Alma's understanding of the extent of the resurrection at the time the Savior came forth from the dead was limited, therefore he stated only his opinion" (Joseph Fielding Smith, *Answers to Gospel Questions*, 5 vols., comp. Joseph Fielding Smith, Jr. [Salt Lake City: Deseret Book Co., 1957–66], 1:36; see also *Doctrines of Salvation*, 2:300).

16. Smith, *Teachings*, p. 296.

17. Boyd K. Packer, in Conference Report, April 1977, pp. 79–80.

18. Joseph Smith, *Lectures on Faith* (Salt Lake City: Deseret Book Co., 1985), 2:2.

19. Ibid., 4:13. In a limited meaning of the phrase, therefore, God *can* cease to be God in the mind of mortals, but never in an absolute sense. That is to say, if people do not understand that God Almighty possesses all attributes in perfection, they cannot exercise saving faith in him—he ceases to be God to them.

Building Our Lives on Christ

It is often the case that at a time of spiritual crisis the Lord raises up someone to minister to the needs of a wandering generation. In a day when pride afflicted the Nephites and when, because of their own feelings of self-sufficiency, God had left the people "in their own strength" (Helaman 4:13), God called and prepared Nephi and Lehi, sons of Helaman. These two chosen servants, surely unsurpassed in greatness in all the Nephite saga, lived and taught in such a way as to be the means of transforming hundreds of people and leading them out of spiritual darkness into the marvelous light of Christ. At a time when it was obvious that the preservation of the society depended wholly upon cleansing the inner vessel, Nephi yielded up his position as chief judge and, like his great-grandfather Alma, confined himself with his brother Lehi to the work of the ministry (see Alma 4:15–20). The success of these two missionaries seemed to be a direct result of the foundation upon which they built, a doctrinal base founded on the teachings of their father Helaman. This chapter will focus upon the salient doctrines contained in the words of Helaman to his sons just prior to his death—a plea and a commission to build our lives and establish our faith on Jesus Christ, the rock of our salvation.

POWER IN A NAME

The Holy Ghost often speaks to our consciences through the medium of memory. One Book of Mormon prophet-leader after another pleads with his flock to remember: remember what the Lord has done; remember the covenants of the Lord with our fathers; remember the trials and tribulations of our forebears and that the Lord delivered them from captivity. In the spirit of that same call to devotion, Helaman said to his sons:

> Behold, my sons, I desire that ye should remember to keep the commandments of God; and I would that ye should declare unto the people these words. Behold, I have given unto you the names of our first parents who came out of the land of Jerusalem; and this

Chapter 13—Building Our Lives on Christ

> I have done that when you remember your names ye may remember them; and when ye remember them ye may remember their works; and when ye remember their works ye may know how that it is said, and also written, that they were good. (Helaman 5:6.)

We do not know the meanings of the names Lehi and Nephi, but we do know, as Helaman reminded his sons, that the names stood for steadfastness and goodness. Because the first Lehi and Nephi were true to their charge to lead their little branch of Israel out of a wicked world and to initiate a new gospel dispensation in America, because they sacrificed all and forsook the treasures of this world, and because they sought for the Lord and found him, basked in the light of his Spirit and power, and endured the crosses associated with total Christian commitment, their names are and forever will be enshrined among the sanctified. To be named after Nephi or Lehi is to be called and enlisted in the works they performed and the righteousness they brought to pass. One could hardly bear the names of Nephi and Lehi without being motivated by the memory of what they had done. "Therefore, my son," Helaman continued, "I would that ye should do that which is good, that it may be said of you, and also written, even as it has been said and written of them" (Helaman 5:7).

Helaman counseled his sons to glory in their Lord and Redeemer, never in themselves or in their names. "And now my sons," he added, "behold I have somewhat more to desire of you, which desire is, that ye may not do these things that ye may boast, but that ye may do these things to lay up for yourselves a treasure in heaven, yea, which is eternal, and which fadeth not away; yea, that ye may have that precious gift of eternal life, which we have reason to suppose hath been given to our fathers" (Helaman 5:8). Simply stated, we are not assured of the highest heaven in the celestial world because of our parentage, surname, or given name. Ancestry and heritage can guarantee nothing more than a great legacy, a memory, and a motivation to goodness. To be sure, all of us, whether reared in the Church or converts, are under covenant to be true to our shared heritage, to those who went before, who gave their lives that we might enjoy the privileges of Church membership today. We have a moral obligation to be true to our good names, to bear them with dignity and fidelity.

Nephi and Lehi were called to bear a name, however, that was more significant than that of their noble forebears. It is a name that is above every name that is named, whether on earth or in heaven, save only the name of the Almighty Elohim. It is a name that brings joy to the desolate heart, a name that speaks peace to the sorrowing soul. It is a name that falls in hushed and hallowed tones from the lips of Saints and angels, a name that leads true believers on both sides of the veil to glory and honor everlasting. It is the name of the One sent of God to bring salvation, the name of the One who paid an infinite price to ransom us from Satan's grasp. It is the blessed name of Jesus Christ.

We do not fully appreciate the significance of bearing the name of the Lord until we sense what our plight would be had Jesus not redeemed a lost and fallen world. The fall of Adam and Eve, though a fortunate fall and an essential step toward mortality and thus a pillar in the plan of salvation, brought about dramatic changes in the earth and all forms of life on it. Spiritual death represents an alienation from God, in a sense a disinheritance from the royal family. Unless appropriate reconciliation with the family head is made, the blessings and the family name may be lost. That is, unless an atonement, an at-one-ment, is brought to pass, we lose the kind of association, sociality, and family life that the scriptures denominate as eternal life. We are then nameless and familyless, spiritual orphans, and thereby alone in the world. From an eternal perspective we have, in the words of Malachi, neither root nor branch (see 3 Nephi 25:1).

In order to experience those joys and feel that warmth known only in family living, we must be reinstated in the family, literally *re*-deemed, or deemed worthy once again, of the privileges and opportunities of being called sons or daughters of God. Deliverance from this state—redemption from spiritual death—is made available only through the labors of a god, through the majestic ministry of one mightier than death, one upon whom justice had no claims and death had no hold. In order to be released from carnality and restored to righteousness, men and women must exercise saving faith in Jesus Christ and thus receive the blessings of the Atonement; they must put off the natural man through Christ, must crucify the old man of sin (see Romans 6:6) and rise through their Redeemer unto a newness of life (see Mosiah 3:19).

People are not born in mortality into the family of God. Because on earth we are estranged by the Fall from holiness, we must be *adopted* into that divine family. Our compliance with the legal requirements of the laws of adoption is accomplished through subscribing to and receiving what Joseph Smith called the "articles of adoption," the first principles and ordinances of the gospel.[1] As the Savior and foreordained Messiah, Jesus, our Lord, became the "author of eternal salvation unto all them that obey him" (Hebrews 5:9); and the Father's gospel, the gospel of God (see Romans 1:1–3), became his gospel, the gospel of Jesus Christ. Christ is the Father of salvation, the Father of resurrection, and the Father of redemption. He is also the King of kings, and spiritual adoption represents acceptance into his family kingdom.

It is in the spirit of this doctrine—the new birth and the new name—that Helaman again appeals to memory: "O remember, remember, my sons, the words which king Benjamin spake unto his people; yea, remember that there is no other way nor means whereby man can be saved, only through the atoning blood of Jesus Christ, who shall come; yea, remember that he cometh to redeem the world" (Helaman 5:9). More specifically, Benjamin testified that "there shall be no other name given nor any other way nor means whereby salvation can come unto the children of men, only in and through the name of Christ, the Lord Omnipotent" (Mosiah 3:17). Salvation, meaning exaltation and eternal life, cannot come in any other way; it cannot be brought to pass through humanity's devising or genius. There is nothing people can do to save themselves; they can, as we shall discuss shortly, place themselves in a position to be saved by yielding their hearts and focusing their faith on the Master, but they cannot save themselves any more than they can create themselves. And in no other name—not that of the grandest apostle or the mightiest prophet—can this greatest of all gifts be bestowed. Had there been no Christ, had there been no Advocate with the Father, no Mediator, no Intercessor for the children of men, then no amount of good works on the part of fallen man could have made up the difference. As Benjamin declared: "Men drink damnation to their own souls except they humble themselves and become as little children, and believe that salvation was, and is, and is to come, in and through the atoning blood of Christ, the Lord Omnipotent" (Mosiah 3:18).

DELIVERANCE FROM SIN, NOT IN SIN

Helaman calls his sons to remembrance once again, this time to the words of Amulek spoken to Zeezrom the lawyer a half-century earlier (see Alma 11:34–37). "Amulek spake unto Zeezrom . . . that the Lord surely should come to redeem his people, but that he should not come to redeem them in their sins, but to redeem them from their sins" (Helaman 5:10). This is an old issue, much older than Amulek's encounter with Zeezrom. It dates, in fact, to the War in Heaven. Lucifer, a son of the morning, rebelled against the plan of the Father and offered his own amendments: "Behold, here am I," he said, "send me, I will be thy son, and *I will redeem all mankind, that one soul shall not be lost,* and surely I will do it; wherefore, give me thine honor" (Moses 4:1; italics added).

We note that there is no mention in this scriptural passage of coercion, of force, of denied agency. Though such things may have been necessary eventually to bring to pass Lucifer's nefarious purposes, they certainly would not have been a part of his public proclamation or proposal. Instead, Satan simply proposed to save us all. Joseph Smith observed: "The contention in heaven was—Jesus said there would be certain souls that would not be saved; and *the devil said he could save them all,* and laid his plans before the grand council, who gave their vote in favor of Jesus Christ. So the devil rose up in rebellion against God, and was cast down, with all who put up their heads for him."[2] Satan cannot make saints out of untried and untested souls. Salvation cannot come to those who have not experienced temptation, been exposed to sin and spiritual sickness, and overcome it all through the application of divine powers.

Nor can a place in heaven be given to those of us who remain in our sins. Christ came to earth on a search-and-rescue mission; he came to search out those who yearn for higher and greater things than an everlasting residence in this telestial tenement, those who desire more than life itself to be transformed into the image of Christ himself. The atonement of our Lord is infinite in scope. It is endless and eternal, but it has limitations; it cannot save people *in* their sins, meaning it cannot bestow power and glory and eternal life upon those who are unrepentant, unclean, and unprepared for celestial society. It cannot, as Alma explained to Corianton, restore one from debauchery and depravity to purity and holiness or deliver one from mortal wickedness to immortal happiness (see Alma 41). Jesus Christ is a God of justice, just as he is a God of mercy. Though his arms of mercy are forever extended to the sinner, he cannot tolerate sin. To do so would be to go against his very nature. Abinadi thus explained that those who have known the commandments yet rebel against truth and die in their sins "have no part in the first resurrection. . . . For salvation cometh to none such; for the Lord hath redeemed none such; for *he cannot deny himself; for he cannot deny justice* when it has its claim" (Mosiah 15:26–27; italics added).

We might add that salvation does not come to a people who glory in repentance. Repentance is a necessary part of redemption in Christ, but we must always remember and teach our children that prevention is far, far better than redemption. As Joseph Smith counseled: "Repentance is a thing that cannot be trifled with every day. Daily transgression and daily repentance"—that is, constantly returning to the well in search of the cleansing waters when we have not sought to forsake or prevent sinful contacts—"is not that which is pleasing in the sight of God."[3] We could not believe and teach otherwise and claim divine approbation. "The more I see of life," President Harold B. Lee observed, "the more I am convinced that we must impress [the Saints] . . . with the awfulness of sin rather than to content ourselves with merely teaching the way of repentance."[4] "Yes, one can repent of . . . transgression," declared President Ezra Taft Benson. "The miracle of forgiveness is real, and true repentance is accepted of the Lord. But it is not pleasing to the Lord to sow one's wild oats . . . and then expect that planned confession and quick repentance will satisfy the Lord."[5] Any form of what Elder Neal A. Maxwell has called "ritual prodigalism"[6]—a deliberate detour, a programmed and predetermined plan to stray from the path and return eventually and effortlessly—evidences that we are still "in sin" and thus desperately in need of redemption.

Sometimes we tend to focus so much upon the fact that Jesus Christ *died for us* that we do not attend to an equally important facet of his redemptive enterprise—the fact that he also came to *live in us*. It is marvelous beyond the power of expression to contemplate that the Savior can and does forgive our sins. There is no way in our present state to comprehend how and in what manner this miracle of miracles was and is brought to pass. It simply happens. And thanks be to God that it does happen. But we cannot enjoy the full and complete powers of the atonement of Christ until our redemption from sin entails the re-creation of a nature that is foreign to sin. That is to say, Jesus came to cleanse us from guilt and the taints of transgression; he also came to renovate our nature and empower our souls so that we are delivered, in process of time, from the effects and pull of those transgressions. We are not in the ultimate sense, therefore, redeemed from our sins, to use Amulek's and Helaman's words, until those sins have no more power over us. The additional wonder and beauty of the Atonement is that we are not expected to resist sin by willpower and personal resolve alone, though such things are essential; rather, as we come to gain that life which is in Christ—a life that comes as we seek for and cultivate the Spirit of the Lord—we receive that enabling power that extends to us the strength to forsake and overcome, a power that we could not have generated on our own. Elder B. H. Roberts explained that

> after the sins of the past are forgiven, the one so pardoned will doubtless feel the force of sinful habits bearing heavily upon him. . . .
>
> *There is an absolute necessity for some additional sanctifying grace that will strengthen poor human nature, not only to enable it to resist temptation, but also to root out from the heart concupiscence*—the blind tendency or inclination to evil. The heart must be purified, every passion, every propensity made submissive to the will, and the will of man brought into subjection to the will of God.
>
> *Man's natural powers are unequal to this task;* so, I believe, all will testify who have made the experiment. *Mankind stand in some need of a strength superior to any they possess of themselves, to accomplish this work of rendering pure our fallen nature.* Such strength, such power, such a sanctifying grace is conferred on man in being born of the Spirit—in receiving the Holy Ghost. Such, in the main, is its office, its work.[7]

"*I am crucified with Christ,*" the Apostle Paul wrote; "*nevertheless I live; yet not I, but Christ liveth in me:* and the life which I now live in the flesh I live by the faith of the Son of God, who loved me, and gave himself for me" (Galatians 2:20; italics added). As the Lord, through his Spirit, comes to live in us in this manner, we literally take part in an exchange with the Master. "We pray you in Christ's stead," Paul wrote to the Corinthians, "be ye reconciled to God." And now comes his expression of this unspeakable exchange: "For [the Father] *hath made [Christ] to be sin for us, who knew no sin; that we might be made the righteousness of God in him*" (2 Corinthians 5:20–21; italics added). In short, we are redeemed from sin as the Lord takes our sins upon himself and imputes his righteousness to us.

REDEMPTION THROUGH THE POWER OF THE FATHER

Helaman went on to explain by what means or power the Savior could perform his divine labors: "And he hath power given unto him from the Father to redeem them from their sins because of repentance" (Helaman 5:11). In this brief statement is embodied the doctrine of the divine Sonship of Christ. In it is found the reason why Jesus alone could and did put into effect the great plan of mercy. Jesus did what he did because of who he was. He was sinless, but this was not sufficient to allow him to redeem humanity. His was a voluntary offering, but his pure motives alone did not provide the means to make the atoning sacrifice. Jesus was the son of Elohim, the Almighty God. As the son of Elohim, Jesus inherited the powers of life and immortality. He was a man, yet he was more than man. He was human, yet he performed acts that required a superhuman endowment. On the other hand, as the son of Mary, a mortal woman, Jesus was subject to the throes and pulls of this mortal sphere. From Mary he inherited the capacity to suffer and die.

Abinadi taught that the Messiah would be many things—spirit and flesh, God and man, Father and Son (see Mosiah 15:1–4). Only by having such a nature could our Lord surrender to death and also rise from the tomb and win the victory over death. "Therefore doth my Father love me," he stated in Jerusalem, "because I lay down my life, that I might take it again. No man taketh it from me, but I lay it down of myself. I have power to lay it down, and I have power to take it again" (John 10:17–18). Lehi affirmed to Jacob that "there is no flesh that can dwell in the presence of God, save it be through the merits, and mercy, and grace of the Holy Messiah, *who layeth down his life according to the flesh*"—his mortal inheritance—"*and taketh it again by the power of the Spirit*"—his immortal inheritance—"that he may bring to pass the resurrection of the dead, being the first that should rise" (2 Nephi 2:8; italics added).

Christ's divine nature allowed him to do more than bring about the Resurrection and thereby transcend physical death and open the door for all other mortals to eventually do the same. In Helaman's words, "he hath power given unto him from the Father *to redeem them from their sins* because of repentance" (Helaman 5:11; italics added). In a way that is incomprehensible to us, the Son of Man bore the effects of the sins of all the sons and daughters of humankind. In an act of infinite irony, the sinless One became the great sinner (see 2 Corinthians 5:21; Galatians 3:13; Hebrews 2:9) and assumed the awful agony of those burdens in Gethsemane and then again on Calvary. He who had always walked in the light of God's Spirit was left to trod the winepress alone, so very alone and without that comforting and confirming influence that had always been a constant companion. He who had brought life and light to the world was subjected to the powers of death and darkness. He who deserved to suffer least suffered most. In the words of the Prophet Joseph Smith, the Mediator "descended in suffering below that which man can suffer; or, in other words, suffered greater sufferings, and was exposed to more powerful contradictions than any man can be."[8] In doing so our Lord and Master descended below all things (2 Corinthians 8:9; Ephesians 4:8–10; D&C 88:6). Elder Boyd K. Packer has taught:

> Before the crucifixion and afterward, many men have willingly given their lives in selfless acts of heroism. But none faced what the Christ endured. Upon Him was the burden of all human transgression, all human guilt. . . . In choosing He faced the awesome power of the evil one, who was not confined to flesh nor subject to mortal pain. . . . How the Atonement was wrought we do not know. No mortal watched as evil turned away and hid in shame before the light of that pure being. All wickedness could not quench that light. When what was done was done, the ransom had been paid. Both death and hell forsook their claim on all who would repent. Men at last were free. Then every soul who ever lived could choose to touch that light and be redeemed.[9]

Jesus the Christ was able to do for us what we could not do for ourselves because he had been endowed and empowered to do so. C. S. Lewis observed:

> I have heard some people complain that if Jesus was God as well as man, then His sufferings and death lose all value in their eyes, "because it must have been so easy for him." Others may (very rightly) rebuke the ingratitude and ungraciousness of this objection; what staggers me is the misunderstanding it betrays. In one sense, of course, those who make it are right. They have even understated their own case. The perfect submission, the perfect suffering, the perfect death were . . . possible only because He was God. But surely that is a very odd reason for not accepting them? . . . If I am drowning in a rapid river, a man who still has one foot on the bank may give me a hand which saved my life. Ought I to shout back

(between my gasps) "No, it's not fair! You have an advantage! You're keeping one foot on the bank"? That advantage—call it "unfair" if you like—is the only reason why he can be of any use to me. To what will you look for help if you will not look to that which is stronger than yourself?[10]

The power of the Father enabled his Only Begotten to endure the physical, mental, and spiritual anguish associated with bleeding from every pore, suffering "both body and spirit" (D&C 19:18), and bearing up under a load greater than mortal mind can fathom (see Mosiah 3:7).

The blessings of life and light and liberation from a sinful nature—available because of the love and condescension of the Holy One of Israel—come to those who acknowledge their dire condition and turn to Christ through repentance. Lehi thus declared that "redemption cometh in and through the holy Messiah; for he is full of grace and truth. Behold, he offereth himself a sacrifice for sin, to answer the ends of the law, *unto all those who have a broken heart and a contrite spirit; and unto none else can the ends of the law be answered.* Wherefore, how great the importance to make these things known unto the inhabitants of the earth" (2 Nephi 2:6–8; italics added). No message is more central, no pronouncement more poignant. For this reason, as Helaman explained, God "hath sent his angels to declare the tidings of the conditions of repentance, which bringeth [people] unto the power of the Redeemer, unto the salvation of their souls" (Helaman 5:11).

THE ROCK OF OUR REDEEMER

Every person builds a house of faith. We do so knowingly or unknowingly. And every builder soon learns that a good building with bad foundations is worse than useless; it is dangerous. As one Christian writer has observed: "If the stability of buildings depends largely on their foundations, so does the stability of human lives. The search for personal security is a primal instinct, but many fail to find it today. Old familiar landmarks are being obliterated. Moral absolutes which were once thought to be eternal are being abandoned."[11] Thus our house of faith can be no more secure than the foundation upon which it is built. Foolish men build upon the shifting sands of ethics and the marshlands of human philosophies and doctrines. The wise build upon the rock of revelation, heeding carefully the living oracles, lest they be "brought under condemnation . . . and stumble and fall when the storms descend, and the winds blow, and the rains descend, and beat upon their house" (D&C 90:5). All that we do as members of The Church of Jesus Christ of Latter-day Saints must be built upon a foundation of faith and testimony and conversion. When external supports fail us, then our hearts must be riveted upon the things of the Spirit, those internal realities that provide the meaning, the perspective, and the sustenance for all else that matters in life.

A very old story among the Jews holds that during the early stages of construction of the second temple, the builders accidentally discarded the cornerstone. Centuries later, in the midst of a long day of debate, Jesus, seemingly drawing upon this story, spoke of the irony associated with ignoring or dismissing him and his message. "Did ye never read in the scriptures," he asked, "The stone which the builders rejected, the same is become the head of the corner: this is the Lord's doing, and it is marvelous in our eyes"? (Matthew 21:42; compare Psalm 118:22–23; Acts 4:11). Among the Nephites, Jacob prophesied: "I perceive by the workings of the Spirit which is in me, that by the stumbling of the Jews they will reject the stone upon which they might build and have safe foundation" (Jacob 4:15).

It is appropriate, therefore, that the climax of Helaman's commission to his sons contains the following admonition:

> And now, my sons, remember, remember that it is upon the rock of our Redeemer, who is Christ, the Son of God, that ye must build your foundation; that when the devil shall send forth his mighty winds, yea, his shafts in the whirlwind, yea, when all his hail and his mighty storm shall beat upon you, it shall have no power over you to drag you down to the gulf of misery and endless wo, because of the rock upon which ye are built, which is a sure foundation, a foundation whereon if men build they cannot fall. (Helaman 5:12.)

Surely the supreme challenge of this life for those of us who aspire to Christian discipleship is to build our lives on Christ, to erect our house of faith, a divine domicile in which he and his Spirit would be pleased to dwell. There is safety from Satan and his minions only in Christ. There is security only in his word and through his infinite and eternal power.

How, then, do we build on Christ? In a day when the winds are blowing and the waves are beating upon our ship, how do we navigate our course safely into the peaceful harbor? What must we do to have our Savior pilot us through life's tempestuous seas? Amid the babble of voices—enticing voices that threaten to lead us into forbidden paths or that beckon us to labor in secondary causes—how do the Saints of the Most High know the Way, live the Truth, and gain that Life which is abundant? The revelations and the prophets offer us some simple yet far-reaching suggestions:

Treasure up his word. The scriptures are the words of Christ. They contain the warnings and doctrinal teachings of those who were moved upon by the Holy Ghost and who thus spoke with the tongue of angels (see 2 Nephi 31:13; 32:1–3; 33:10). To read and ponder them is to hear the voice of the Master (see D&C 18:34–36). Holy writ has been preserved to bring us to Christ and to establish us upon his doctrine. Those who are serious students of the revelations seek diligently to know and apply scriptural precepts and principles; they can more readily see the hand of God and discern the handiwork of Lucifer. More equipped to sift and sort through the sordid, such persons are more prepared to distinguish the divine from the diabolical, the sacred from the secular.

Mormon explained that "whosoever will may lay hold upon the word of God, which is quick and powerful, which shall divide asunder all the cunning and the snares and the wiles of the devil, and lead the man of Christ in a strait and narrow course across that everlasting gulf of misery which is prepared to engulf the wicked" (Helaman 3:29). The word of God, especially that found in the canon of scripture, allows us to discern and expose those teachings or schools of thought that lead us on intellectual or spiritual detours, to cut through false educational ideas, and to discard spurious notions that may be pleasing to the carnal mind but are in fact destructive to the eternal soul. Further, those who search and study the institutional revelations open themselves more fully to that individual revelation which is promised. Elder Bruce R. McConkie explained to Church leaders that "however talented men may be in administrative matters; however eloquent they may be in expressing their views; however learned they may be in worldly things—they will be denied the sweet whisperings of the Spirit that might have been theirs unless they pay the price of studying, pondering, and praying about the scriptures."[12] Those who are grounded and settled in truth, anchored to the Lord's word, are built upon the rock of Christ. Or, to complete Mormon's thought, those men and women of Christ who manage to lay hold upon the word of God and follow the strait and narrow path, eventually "land their souls, yea, their immortal souls, at the right hand of God in the kingdom of heaven, to sit down with Abraham, and Isaac, and with Jacob, and with all our holy fathers, to go no more out" (Helaman 3:30).

Teach his doctrine. There is a supernal power that accompanies the plain and direct teaching of doctrine. The views and philosophies of men—no matter how pleasingly they are stated or how lofty and timely they may seem—simply cannot engage the soul in the same way that the doctrines of the gospel can. If we teach doctrine, particularly the doctrine of Christ, and if we do so with the power and persuasion of the Holy Ghost, our listeners will be turned to Christ.

The gospel is the glad tidings—the good news—that Christ has come into the world (see 3 Nephi 27; D&C 76:40–42), broken the bands of death, and made eternal life available through faithful obedience to him and his principles and ordinances. The gospel is the doctrine of Christ (see 2 Nephi 31; Jacob 7:6). When we preach the gospel we preach Jesus Christ and him crucified. Other doctrines or programs or policies, no matter their inherent and even obvious value, will have light and power breathed into them only to the degree that they are attached to this fundamental verity.

Sustain his servants. The Savior taught his apostles in the eastern hemisphere, "He that receiveth you receiveth me, and he that receiveth me receiveth him that sent me" (Matthew 10:40). To the Nephites the resurrected Lord said, "Blessed are ye if ye shall give heed unto the words of these twelve whom I have chosen from among you to minister unto you, and to be your servants" (3 Nephi 12:1). To receive the apostles meant to accept them as the mouthpiece of Deity, recognizing their voice as his voice and their authority as his authority. Certainly no one could accept the Father while rejecting the Son, and no one could accept the Son while rejecting those he had commissioned to act in his name. A rejection of Peter, James, Nephi, or any of Jesus' apostolic ministers was at the same time a rejection of Jesus.

There are members who feel they can enjoy a relationship with the Lord independent of his church, separate and apart from the organization established by revelation. There are even those who feel they can stay close to the Lord while they criticize of find fault with the Church and its leaders. They are wrong. They are deceived. They are painfully mistaken and are walking in slippery paths. No person comes fully to the Master who does not acknowledge the mantle worn by his anointed. There is no salvation to be found in Christ independent of his constituted priesthood authorities. In the words of Elder Marvin J. Ashton, "Any Church member not obedient to the leaders of this Church will not have the opportunity to be obedient to the promptings of the Lord."[13]

Trust in and rely on the Lord. There is power in Christ, power not only to create the worlds and divide the seas but also to still the storms of the human heart, to heal the pain of scarred and beaten souls. We must learn to trust in him more and in the arm of flesh less. We must learn to rely on him more and on solutions of humanity less. We must learn to work to our limits and then be willing to seek that grace or enabling power which will make up the difference, that consummate power which indeed makes all the difference. As C. S. Lewis pointed out:

> In one sense, the road back to God is a road of moral effort, of trying harder and harder. But in another sense it is not trying that is ever going to bring us home. All this trying leads up to the vital moment at which you turn to God and say, "You must do this. I can't." Do not, I implore you, start asking yourselves, "Have I reached that moment?" Do not sit down and start watching your own mind to see if it is coming along. That puts a man quite on the wrong track. When the most important things in our life happen we quite often do not know, at the moment, what is going on. A man does not always say to himself, "Hullo! I'm growing up." It is often only when he looks back that he realizes what has happened and recognizes it as what people call "growing up." You can see it even in simple matters. A man who starts anxiously watching to see whether he is going to sleep is very likely to remain wide awake. As well, the thing I am talking of now may not happen to every one in a sudden flash. . . . It may be so gradual that no one could ever point to a particular hour or even a particular year. And what matters is the nature of the change in itself, not how we feel while it is happening. *It is the change from being confident about our own efforts to the state in which we despair of doing anything for ourselves and leave it to God.*
>
> I know the words "leave it to God" can be misunderstood, but they must stay for the moment. *The sense in which a Christian leaves it to God is that he puts all his trust in Christ: trusts that Christ will somehow share with him the perfect human obedience which He carried out from His birth to His crucifixion: that Christ will make the man more like*

Himself and, in a sense, make good his deficiencies. . . . In yet another
sense, handing everything over to Christ does not, of course, mean
that you stop trying. *To trust Him means, of course, trying to do all that
He says.* There would be no sense in saying you trusted a person if
you would not take his advice. Thus if you have really handed yourself over to Him, it must follow that you are trying to obey Him. But
trying in a new way, a less worried way.[14]

The Satanic shafts in the whirlwind may take many forms. They
may come in the form of temptations described by President Joseph F.
Smith: enticements to be immoral, to yield to the "flattery of prominent
men," or to succumb to "false educational ideas."[15] We may be tempted
to judge all things, including the gospel and the Church, through the
lenses of our own academic discipline or professional position. In this
regard Elder Dallin H. Oaks has written:

We can liken the various ways of the world to implements that
can draw water from a worldly well. We need such implements. We
can and do use them to make our way in the world.

But while we are doing this, in our occupations, in our civic
responsibilities, and in our work in other organizations, we must
never forget the Savior's words, "Whosoever drinketh of this water
shall thirst again." Only from Jesus Christ, the Lord and Savior of
this world, can we obtain the living water whose partaker shall
never thirst again, in whom it will be "a well of water springing up
into everlasting life." And we do not obtain that water with worldly
implements.[16]

Whatever may come in the mighty storms that shall beat upon
our houses of faith—and they shall come, as surely as the Lord lives—we
shall be able to withstand and endure, if we are properly grounded.
Satan shall not have power sufficient to drag us down to hell, to that
gulf of misery and woe, if we will have built securely on the rock of our
Redeemer (see Helaman 5:12).

CONCLUSION

There are few gifts of the Spirit of greater worth in a day of doubt
and a time of confusion than the gift of discernment. We have the challenge of not only discerning good from evil, light from darkness, but
also that which matters from that which is of but little value. In a time
like our own when a babble of discordant voices vie for our attention
and seek for our time and interest, it is incumbent upon us to be dis-

cerning, to be discriminating. Some things simply matter more than others. But, in the words of Alma, "there is one thing which is of more importance than they all" (Alma 7:7). That something is the knowledge and testimony of Jesus, the calm certitude that comes by the spirit of revelation. We may know many things, but if we do not know this, our testimony is deficient and our foundation less solid than it might otherwise be. "Upon this rock"—the rock of revelation, the Master said at Caesarea Philippi—"I will build my church"[17] (Matthew 16:18). "And how could it be otherwise?" Elder Bruce R. McConkie asked.

> There is no other foundation upon which the Lord could build his Church and kingdom. The things of God are known only by the power of his Spirit. God stands revealed or he remains forever unknown. No man can know that Jesus is the Lord but by the Holy Ghost.
>
> *Revelation:* Pure, perfect, personal revelation—this is the rock!
>
> *Revelation that Jesus is the Christ:* the plain, wondrous word that comes from God in heaven to man on earth, the word that affirms the divine Sonship of our Lord—this is the rock!
>
> *The testimony of our Lord:* the testimony of Jesus, which is the spirit of prophecy—this is the rock!
>
> All this is the rock, and yet there is more. *Christ is the Rock:* the Rock of Ages, the Stone of Israel, the Sure Foundation—the Lord is our Rock![18]

Truly, as the Apostle Paul testified: "Other foundation can no man lay than that is laid, which is Jesus Christ" (1 Corinthians 3:11).

Save only what is written in scripture, perhaps nowhere do we find the invitation and the challenge to build upon the rock of our Redeemer taught so forcefully as in hymns. Consider the words of E. Mote:

> My hope is built on nothing less
> than Jesus' blood and righteousness;
> no merit of my own I claim,
> but wholly trust in Jesus' name.
> > On Christ, the solid rock, I stand—
> > all other ground is sinking sand.
>
> When weary in this earthly race,
> I rest on his unchanging grace;
> in every wild and stormy gale
> my anchor holds and will not fail.

His vow, his covenant and blood
are my defense against the flood;
when earthly hopes are swept away
he will uphold me on that day.

When the last trumpet's voice shall sound,
O may I then in him be found!
clothed in his righteousness alone,
faultless to stand before his throne.
　　On Christ, the solid rock, I stand—
　　all other ground is sinking sand.[19]

Or ponder the significance of the words of a hymn we frequently sing:

How firm a foundation, ye Saints of the Lord,
Is laid for your faith in his excellent word!
What more can he say than to you he hath said,
Who unto the Savior . . . for refuge have fled?
. . . .

When through fiery trials thy pathway shall lie,
My grace, all sufficient, shall be thy supply.
The flame shall not hurt thee; I only design
Thy dross to consume and thy gold to refine.

E'en down to old age, all my people shall prove
My sov'reign, eternal, unchangeable love;
And then, when gray hair shall their temples adorn,
Like lambs shall they still in my bosom be borne.

The soul that on Jesus hath leaned for repose
I will not, I cannot, desert to his foes;
That soul, though all hell should endeavor to shake,
I'll never, no never, no never forsake!
(*Hymns,* 1985, no. 85.)

Those who accept the invitation to "come unto Christ and be perfected in him" (Moroni 10:32) thus come out of the world, enjoy citizenship with the Saints of the Most High, and erect their houses of faith on "the foundation of the apostles and prophets, Jesus Christ himself being the chief corner stone" (Ephesians 2:19–20).

On Christ's mighty arm we rely. Because of who he is and what he has done, there is no obstacle to eternal life too great to overcome. Because of him our minds may be at peace and our souls may rest.

Chapter 13—Building Our Lives on Christ

NOTES

1. Orson Pratt, *Orson Pratt's Works* (Salt Lake City: Deseret News, 1945), p. 48; Joseph Smith, *Teachings of the Prophet Joseph Smith,* sel. Joseph Fielding Smith (Salt Lake City: Deseret Book Co., 1976), p. 328.

2. Smith, *Teachings,* p. 357.

3. Ibid., p. 148.

4. Harold B. Lee, *Decisions for Successful Living* (Salt Lake City: Deseret Book Co., 1973), p. 88.

5. Ezra Taft Benson, *Teachings of Ezra Taft Benson* (Salt Lake City: Bookcraft, 1988), p. 70.

6. Neal A. Maxwell, in Conference Report, October 1988, pp. 37–41.

7. B. H. Roberts, *The Gospel and Man's Relationship to Deity* (Salt Lake City: Deseret Book Co., 1965), pp. 169–70; italics added.

8. Joseph Smith, *Lectures on Faith* (Salt Lake City: Deseret Book Co., 1985), 5:2.

9. *Let Not Your Heart Be Troubled* (Salt Lake City: Bookcraft, 1991), p. 76.

10. C. S. Lewis, *Mere Christianity* (London: Collins, 1988), p. 61.

11. John Stott, *Life in Christ* (Wheaton, Ill.: Tyndale House, 1991), p. 22.

12. Bruce R. McConkie, *Doctrines of the Restoration: Sermons and Writings of Bruce R. McConkie,* ed. Mark L. McConkie (Salt Lake City: Bookcraft, 1989), p. 238.

13. *The First Area General Conference for Germany* (Salt Lake City: The Church of Jesus Christ of Latter-day Saints, 1974), American Collection, Harold B. Lee Library, p. 23.

14. Lewis, *Mere Christianity,* pp. 128–29; italics added.

15. Joseph F. Smith, *Gospel Doctrine* (Salt Lake City: Deseret Book Co., 1971), p. 313.

16. Dallin H. Oaks, *The Lord's Way* (Salt Lake City: Deseret Book Co., 1991), p. 14.

17. Smith, *Teachings,* p. 274.

18. Bruce R. McConkie, in Conference Report, April 1981, p. 77, italics added.

19. E. Mote in Stott, *Life in Christ,* p. 29.

The Glad Tidings

After at least two days of instruction, worship, and intense spiritual experience, the risen Lord appeared once again to his American Hebrews. His Nephite apostles "were gathered together and were united in mighty prayer and fasting." When Jesus appeared he inquired as to their desires. "Lord," they answered, "we will that thou wouldst tell us the name whereby we shall call this church; for there are disputations among the people concerning this matter" (3 Nephi 27:1–3). It is in this context—the Master's discussion of the name of his church and the central message, the proclamation of the gospel—that the living Christ sets forth some of the most profound doctrine to be found in the entire Book of Mormon.

His Name and His Church

Why disputations should arise among the Nephites concerning the name of the Church is not clear. Since the days of Alma, in which a formal church structure and organization had been established, it appears that the Saints had been called the members of the "Church of Christ" or the "Church of God" (see Mosiah 18:17; 25:18, 23; Alma 4:5; 3 Nephi 26:21). With the end of the Mosaic dispensation and the initiation of the messianic dispensation, a new day had dawned; it was the meridian or focal point of salvation history, the age in which the Lord Omnipotent, the long-awaited Promised Messiah, would "come down from heaven among the children of men, and . . . dwell in a tabernacle of clay" (Mosiah 3:5). We recall that Jesus had earlier bestowed priesthood authority to baptize upon Nephi and the Twelve (see 3 Nephi 11:22) when in fact they already held authority from God to perform the saving ordinances. Likewise, Jesus baptized those who had previously been baptized (see 3 Nephi 19:10–12). But it was a new day, a new light, and a new revelation.[1]

Though the Nephites had held the fulness of the priesthood and had enjoyed the blessings of the everlasting gospel from the days of Lehi and Nephi, still they had observed the law of Moses. That is, they offered sacrifice, just as Adam had done two and a half millennia before, and they conformed to the Law's "myriad moral principles and its endless ethical restrictions."[2] Because the faithful among the Nephites accepted and treasured the blessings of the gospel; because they looked forward with an eye of faith to the coming of the Holy One; because they knew full well the central message of the Law and thus comprehended with certainty the Law as a means to Him who was and is the great End, the law of Moses had become "dead" unto them. They were "alive in Christ because of [their] faith" in him (2 Nephi 25:25) and because they had learned to distinguish tokens from covenants, ritual from religion. Perhaps it was because it was a new era, the beginning of the dispensation of the meridian of time, and they had only recently been initiated anew into the covenants and ordinances that the people had begun to wonder if there was a new or different name by which the congregation of Christians in this new dispensation was to be called and known.

That there may have been some among the Nephites who proposed to name the Church something other than the Church of Jesus Christ is suggested by the Master's words: "Verily, verily, I say unto you, why is it that the people should murmur and dispute because of this thing? Have they not read the scriptures, which say you must take upon you the name of Christ, which is my name? For by this name shall ye be called at the last day; and whoso taketh upon him my name, and endureth to the end, the same shall be saved at the last day" (3 Nephi 27:4–6). Our Lord's words are most instructive. The Church, or body of Christ, is a true and living thing only to the degree that it is imbued and animated by Christ. Like an individual, the Church must take upon it the name of Christ—meaning his divine influence, his attributes, his nature—in order to enjoy his transforming powers. A person who is noble in character, kindly in deed and manner, considerate and compassionate—what the bulk of the Western world would call "Christian" in nature—but who refuses to take upon him the name of Christ (and all that such a commitment entails) is not fully Christ's. He is not a Christian in the total and complete sense. A person who remains in his lost and fallen state, who yields to the enticings of the spirit of the evil one and to the nature of things in a fallen world, is without God in the world (see Alma 41:11) and, as such, is without tie to the family of God.

He is a spiritual orphan, nameless and familyless, in a lone and dreary world. And what of the Church? The Church is made up of people, and to the degree that those congregants are as yet unredeemed and unregenerated, the Church cannot be the light that is so desperately needed in a darkened world, nor can it make available the life and energy that flow from its great Head.

Only the children of Christ will be called by the name of Christ. Only those who have by covenant adoption taken upon them the holy name shall receive the rewards of holiness. "Behold, I say unto you," Alma declared, "that the good shepherd doth call you; yea, and in his own name he doth call you, which is the name of Christ; and if ye will not hearken to the voice of the good shepherd, to the name by which ye are called, behold, ye are not the sheep of the good shepherd. And now if ye are not the sheep of the good shepherd, of what fold are ye? Behold, I say unto you, that the devil is your shepherd, and ye are of his fold" (Alma 5:38–39). In the same way, the Redeemer has taught in a modern revelation: "Behold, Jesus Christ is the name which is given of the Father, and there is none other name given whereby man can be saved; wherefore, all men must take upon them the name which is given of the Father, for in that name shall they be called at the last day; wherefore, if they know not the name by which they are called, they cannot have place in the kingdom of my Father" (D&C 18:23–25).

From the days of Adam, the divine decree has gone forth: "Thou shalt do all that thou doest in the name of the Son, and thou shalt repent and call upon God in the name of the Son forevermore" (Moses 5:8). All things are to be done in his holy name. All things. We are to speak and act, preach and prophesy in the name of the Son. We are to heal the sick and raise the dead in the name of the Son. We are to conduct the business of the Church and perform the ordinances of salvation in the name of the Son. We are to do what we do in the name of Jesus Christ, speaking and acting the way our blessed Master would under similar circumstances. The pattern by which we gauge our actions and direct our labors is not alone the holy scriptures, as vital an instrument as they are in pointing us to the words and works of the Perfect One. More important, the people of God seek to be led by the power of the Holy Ghost, the oldest and most enduring form of living scripture, that sure and certain guide who shows and tells all things that need to be done (see 2 Nephi 32:3, 5).

Through baptism and rebirth we signify, according to Elder Dallin H. Oaks, "our commitment to do all that we can to achieve eternal life in the kingdom of our Father. We are expressing our candidacy for— our determination to strive for—exaltation in the celestial kingdom." Further, we "take upon us [Christ's] name as we publicly profess our belief in him, as we fulfill our obligations as members of his Church, and as we do the work of his kingdom. But there is something beyond these familiar meanings," Elder Oaks continues, "because what we witness [in the sacrament prayers] is not that we *take* upon us his name but that we are *willing* to do so. In this sense, our witness relates to some future event or status whose attainment is not self-assured, but depends on the authority or initiative of the Savior himself."[3] That is, we have presently announced our righteous desires and have entered into a covenant with God, but we have not yet obtained; ours is but a candidacy for exaltation. When the time comes that we have received the fulness of the Father, when we qualify for the highest of eternal rewards, then in the full and perfect sense we shall have the name of Christ sealed upon us forever. King Benjamin thus pleaded with his people: "I would that ye should be steadfast and immovable, always abounding in good works, *that Christ, the Lord God Omnipotent, may seal you his, that you may be brought to heaven, that ye may have everlasting salvation and eternal life*" (Mosiah 5:15; italics added).

The Lord's church, with his name upon it, administers his gospel. It teaches his doctrine and makes available his ordinances. The Church of Jesus Christ is a service agency, established for the blessing and edification of individuals and families. Elder Russell M. Nelson thus observed that "the Church is the way by which the Master accomplishes His work and bestows His glory. Its ordinances and related covenants are the crowning rewards of our membership. While many organizations can offer fellowship and fine instruction, only His church can provide baptism, confirmation, ordination, the sacrament, patriarchal blessings, and the ordinances of the temple—all bestowed by authorized priesthood power. That power is destined to bless all children of our Heavenly Father."[4]

In summary, then, the Savior directed: "Therefore, whatsoever ye shall do, ye shall do it in my name; therefore ye shall call the church in my name; and ye shall call upon the Father in my name that he will bless the church for my sake" (3 Nephi 27:7). We ever pray for the growth and proliferation of the Church of Jesus Christ, which is the kingdom of God on earth. We plead mightily for the expansion of the work of the Lord in all nations and among all kindreds, tongues, and people. We petition the Father in the name of the Son, and when our prayers meet the divine standard, they are offered under the direction of the Holy Ghost. We pray for the church that bears the name of the Son, and we pray for special outpourings of light and power "for Christ's sake," meaning because of or on account of what Christ has done for the Church and, more particularly, for those who constitute the sheep of his fold. We ask sincerely that the judgments of God may be turned away and the mercies of heaven extended, all because of the mediation and intercession of the Holy One of Israel (see Alma 33:11, 16).

BUILT UPON HIS GOSPEL

We learn, however, that although being called after Christ's name is a necessary condition to be his church and people, such is not sufficient. The resurrected Lord stated that "if it be called in my name then it is my church, *if it so be that they are built upon my gospel*" (3 Nephi 27:8; italics added). Anyone can organize a church. Anyone can name that church the Church of Jesus Christ. And yet, as the Master affirms, it will not be his church unless it is built upon his gospel. We will note in this brief section when a church is *not* built upon his gospel and then attend to the principles of Christ's gospel in the next section.

We cannot really be built upon Christ's gospel if we do not believe in the divinity of Jesus Christ. Those who labor tirelessly to lighten burdens or alleviate human suffering, but at the same time deny the fact that Jesus Christ is God, cannot have the lasting impact on society that they could have through drawing upon those spiritual forces that center in the Lord Omnipotent. Those in our day who focus endlessly upon the moral teachings of Jesus but who downplay the divine Sonship miss the mark dramatically.

In the absence of the real thing—the fulness of the gospel—there are many ideas and movements that seek to occupy center stage. Among the more popular tendencies in today's world is to focus upon

Jesus as loving teacher, guide, and moral leader. For some persons, Jesus stands as the preeminent example of kindness, the ultimate illustration of social and interpersonal graciousness and morality. A favorite text for members of this group is the Sermon on the Mount, while their highest aspiration is to live the Golden Rule. A Roman Catholic philosopher has observed: "According to the theological liberal, [the Sermon on the Mount] is the essence of Christianity, and Christ is the best of human teachers and examples. . . . Christianity is essentially ethics. What's missing here?" he asks. "Simply, the essence of Christianity, which is *not* the Sermon on the Mount. When Christianity was proclaimed throughout the world, the proclamation *(kerygma)* was not 'Love your enemies!' but 'Christ is risen!' This was not a new *ideal* but a new *event,* that God became man, died, and rose for our salvation. Christianity is first of all not ideal but real, an event, news, the gospel, the 'good news.' The essence of Christianity is not Christianity; the essence of Christianity is Christ."[5]

For many persons, the doctrine of Christ has been replaced by the ethics of Jesus. Those who insist that ethics must be discussed or taught or enforced point toward the declining moral standards of our day, the increase of drug abuse or teenage pregnancy, and the prevalence of our inhumanity to each other. They contend that if Christianity is to make a difference in the world, we must find ways to transform ethereal theology into religious practice in a decaying society. They thus promote a social gospel, a relevant religion. The problem with a social gospel is that it is inherently and forevermore deficient as far as engaging the real problems of human beings. It almost always focuses on symptoms rather than causes. Ethics is not the essence of the gospel. Ethics is not necessarily righteousness. The very word *ethics* has come to connote socially acceptable standards based on current consensus, as opposed to absolute truths based on God's eternal laws. Ethics is too often to virtue and righteousness what theology is to religion—a pale and wimpy substitute. Indeed, ethics without that virtue that comes through the cleansing powers of the Redeemer is like religion without God, at least the true and living God.

"It is one thing," Elder Bruce R. McConkie has written, "to teach ethical principles, quite another to proclaim the great doctrinal verities, which are the foundation of true Christianity and out of which eternal salvation comes. True it is that salvation is limited to those in whose souls the ethical principles abound, but true it is also that Christian ethics, in the full and saving sense, automatically become a part of the lives of those who first believe Christian doctrines." In summary, "it is only when gospel ethics are tied to gospel doctrines that they rest on a sure and enduring foundation and gain full operation in the lives of the saints."[6]

The Latter-day Saints are occasionally criticized for expending so much of the resources of the Church on missionary work or the construction of temples. Some indicate that the institutional Church should be more involved in leading or officially supporting this or that crusade, in laboring for this or that social cause. "Where is your charity?" they ask. "Of what avail are your noble theological principles?" they inquire. I agree with Bruce Hafen, who pointed out that "the ultimate purpose of the gospel of Jesus Christ is to cause the sons and daughters of God to become as Christ is. Those who see religious purpose only in terms of ethical service in the relationship between man and fellowmen may miss that divinely ordained possibility. It is quite possible to render charitable—even 'Christian'—service without developing deeply ingrained and permanent Christlike character. Paul understood this when he warned against giving all one's goods to feed the poor without charity. . . . *While religious philosophies whose highest aim is social relevance may do much good, they will not ultimately lead people to achieve the highest religious purpose, which is to become as God and Christ are.*"[7] The Savior declared to his Nephite followers, "If it so be that the church is built upon my gospel then will the Father show forth his own works in it" (3 Nephi 27:10). When the Saints of God have been true to their trusts and live worthy of the gifts and influence of the Holy Ghost, then the works of the Father—the works of righteousness, the actions and behaviors of the faithful, including deeds of Christian service—flow forth from regenerate hearts. Those works are not alone the works of mortals but rather the doings of persons who have become new creatures in Christ. Their works are therefore the works of the Lord, for they have been motivated by the power of the Spirit. To the Philippian Saints the Apostle Paul beckoned: "Work out your own salvation with fear and trembling. For *it is God which worketh in you* both to will and to do of his good pleasure" (Philippians 2:12–13; italics added).

Chapter 14—The Glad Tidings

It is true that much of the time we do the works of righteousness simply because they need to be done and not always as a result of some overwhelming spiritual motivation within us. Such efforts attest to our willingness to be obedient, to carry out the will of the Almighty. But along the way we strive in prayer for a change of heart, for the Lord through his Spirit to prompt and direct our labors. Otherwise we spend our days operating merely in terms of expectation and requirement, when we could be operating in terms of pure love and enjoyment. Without the Spirit and power of God providing impetus, meaning, purpose, and staying power for our poor efforts, we begin eventually to experience a type of spiritual burnout; we continue to work to exhaustion, but our hearts are not in it. Though for a season we may serve because of good companionship, out of fear of punishment, because of duty or loyalty, and even as a part of a hope for an eternal reward, "if our service is to be most efficacious, it must be accomplished for the love of God and the love of his children." Laboring "with all of our heart and mind is a high challenge for all of us. Such service must be free of selfish ambition. It must be motivated by only the pure love of Christ."[8]

The Master warned what would happen if we seek to be his but are not built upon his gospel. If our effort "be not built upon my gospel," he said, "and is built upon the works of men, or upon the works of the devil, verily I say unto you they have joy in their works for a season, and by and by the end cometh, and they are hewn down and cast into the fire, from whence there is no return" (3 Nephi 27:11). The works of the devil obviously pertain to carnality and devilishness, what Paul called "the works of the flesh"—such sins as adultery, fornication, idolatry, witchcraft, hatred, strife, and heresy (Galatians 5:19–21). They bring pleasure and telestial titillation for a season, but they result inevitably in shrinkage of the soul, followed in time by bitter loneliness and that awful alienation from things of lasting worth. Indeed, "their works do follow them, for it is because of their works that they are hewn down" (3 Nephi 27:12). God's work and glory is "to bring to pass the immortality and eternal life of man" (Moses 1:39). Our most noble work will be accomplished and our greatest glory and joy will come, to the degree that we are similarly occupied with this overarching objective.

The "works of men" may refer to what we know as honorable

endeavors, worthwhile efforts to improve man and society but labors whose focus are not truly on the Lord or his work and glory. Political agendas, ethical concerns, and environmental issues, all works of men, are good and proper, and we should be involved in them to the degree that our time and circumstances allow. Noble enterprises bring a measure of personal satisfaction. Too often, however, the works of men bring glory to men. More often than not, the works of men hack away at the leaves of the inconsequential while ignoring the spiritual roots of attitudes and behavior. The poignant message of the Savior is that happiness, meaning lasting joy, comes only to those who are built upon his gospel and whose works are really his works. So many people, as C. S. Lewis observed, seek to

> invent some sort of happiness for themselves outside God, apart from God. And out of that hopeless attempt has come nearly all that we call human history—money, poverty, ambition, war, prostitution, classes, slavery—the long terrible story of man trying to find something other than God which will make him happy.
>
> The reason why it can never succeed is [that] . . . *God designed the human machine to run on Himself. He Himself is the fuel our spirits were designed to burn, or the food our spirits were designed to feed on. There is no other. That is why it is just no good asking God to make us happy in our own way without bothering about religion. God cannot give us a happiness and peace apart from Himself,* because it is not there. There is no such thing.[9]

Because we are so very limited in our vision, we are tempted to envy the financial success or holdings or portfolios or real estate of those who spurn the laws and commandments of God. "They look happy and free," Elder Glenn L. Pace remarked, "but don't mistake telestial pleasure for celestial happiness and joy. Don't mistake lack of self-control for freedom. Complete freedom without appropriate restraint makes us slaves to our appetites. Don't envy a lesser and lower life."[10]

"THIS IS THE GOSPEL"

Some things simply matter more than others. Some topics of discussion, even intellectually stimulating ones, must take a back seat to more fundamental verities. It is just so in regard to what the scriptures call the gospel or the doctrine of Christ, those foundational truths associated with the person and powers of Jesus the Messiah. Who he is and what he has done are paramount and central issues; all else, however supplementary, is secondary. If in fact our efforts do not essentially assist the Saints in their quest to come unto Christ, then perhaps a particular program or activity has no place in the Church.

The Church of Jesus Christ of Latter-day Saints is, in the language of the revelation, "the only true and living church upon the face of the whole earth" (D&C 1:30). The true Church administers the gospel; salvation in this day and age will come through the covenants and ordinances administered and made available by the Church or it will come not at all. To speak of coming unto Christ independent of Christ's church or in defiance of his anointed servants is foolishness. It is, however, the gospel that saves (see Romans 1:16) and not the Church per se. Auxiliaries and programs and policies and procedures—though inspired from heaven and essential for the everyday operation and continuing expansion of the Lord's kingdom—are of efficacy, virtue, and force only to the degree that they encourage and motivate the Saints to trust in and serve the Lord and thus receive his matchless mercy and grace.

The word *gospel* literally means "God-news," or "good news." The gospel is the good news that Christ came, that he lived and died, and that he rose again to immortal glory. The gospel is the good news that through Christ we may be cleansed and renewed, transformed into new creatures. The gospel is the good news that through our Savior and Redeemer we can be delivered from death and sin to the abundant life. In short, the gospel is the "glad tidings . . . that he came into the world, even Jesus, to be crucified for the world, and to bear the sins of the world, and to sanctify the world, and to cleanse it from all unrighteousness; that through him all might be saved whom the Father had put into his power and made by him" (D&C 76:40–42). To the Nephites, the risen Lord declared: "Behold I have given unto you my gospel, and this is the gospel which I have given unto you—that I came into the world to do the will of my Father, because my Father sent me" (3 Nephi 27:13).

The gospel is a sacred covenant, a two-way promise between God and man. Christ does for us what we could never, worlds without end, do for ourselves. He offers himself as a ransom for sin; he descends below all things so that he and we might have the privilege of ascending to celestial heights; and he dies and rises from the tomb so that we—in a way that is completely incomprehensible to the finite mind—might likewise come forth from death into resurrected, immortal glory. On our part, we agree to do those things that we can do for ourselves: we make a solemn promise to accept and receive him as our Lord and Savior; to believe on his name and rely wholly upon his merits, mercy, and grace; to accept and receive the principles and ordinances of his gospel; and to strive all the days of our lives to endure faithfully to the end, meaning to keep our covenants and walk in paths of truth and righteousness. "Viewed from our mortal position," Elder Bruce R. McConkie wrote, "the gospel is all that is required to take us back to the Eternal Presence, there to be crowned with glory and honor, immortality and eternal life." He continued: "To gain these greatest of all rewards, two things are required. The first is the atonement by which all men are raised in immortality, with those who believe and obey ascending also unto eternal life. This atoning sacrifice was the work of our Blessed Lord, and he has done his work. The second requisite is obedience on our part to the laws and ordinances of the gospel. Thus *the gospel is, in effect, the atonement. But the gospel is also all of the laws, principles, doctrines, rites, ordinances, acts, powers, authorities, and keys needed to save and exalt fallen man in the highest heaven hereafter.*"[11]

The sufferings of Jesus Christ that began in the Garden of Gethsemane were consummated on the cross. Between noon and 3:00 P.M. on that fateful Friday, all of the agonies of Gethsemane returned, as the Spirit of our Heavenly Father was once again withdrawn from the Suffering Servant.[12] Truly, the lowly Nazarene has trodden the winepress—meaning Gethsemane, or the garden of the oilpress—alone (see D&C 76:107; 88:106; 133:50; Isaiah 63:3). In his own words, that awful agony in the Garden "caused myself, even God, the greatest of all, to tremble because of pain, and to bleed at every pore, and to suffer both body and spirit—and would that I might not drink the bitter cup and shrink—nevertheless, glory be to the Father, and I partook and finished my preparations unto the children of men" (D&C 19:18–19). And as to the final phase of his redemptive labor, his foreordained place on that accursed cross, he explained to the Nephites: "My Father sent me that I might be lifted up upon the cross; and after that I had been lifted up upon the cross, that I might draw all men unto me" (3 Nephi 27:14).

Chapter 14—The Glad Tidings

The scriptures—especially verses thirteen through twenty-two in this marvelous chapter we know as 3 Nephi 27—clearly and consistently teach that the principles of the gospel are as follows:

1. *Faith in the Lord Jesus Christ.* Those who seek to enjoy the benefits of the atonement of Christ must first learn to exercise faith in Christ. They must believe in him, believe that he is, "that he created all things, both in heaven and in earth; believe that he has all wisdom, and all power, both in heaven and in earth; believe that man doth not comprehend all the things which the Lord can comprehend" (Mosiah 4:9). In the *Lectures on Faith* Joseph Smith taught that three things are necessary in order for rational and intelligent beings to exercise saving faith in God or Christ. First, they must accept the idea that God actually exists; they must plant the seed of faith in their hearts and experiment upon (pray over and labor with) the fact that there actually is a Savior (see Alma 32–33). Second, they must have a correct idea of God's character, attributes, and perfections; they must from serious study and personal revelation seek to understand what God is like. Third, they must gain an actual knowledge that the course of life they are pursuing accords with the will of God; they must know that their lives are worthy of divine approbation and thus of the blessings of heaven. The Prophet explained that the latter requisite for faith—the peaceful assurance that we have pleased God—comes only through our willingness to sacrifice all things for the kingdom's sake. Faith in Jesus Christ, the first principle of the gospel, is thus based on evidence. And the more evidence we amass—external and internal—the greater our faith. We may, like the Zoramites, begin with the simple hope that there is a Christ and that salvation is available (see Alma 32:27); but in time that hope can, by the power of the Holy Ghost, ripen into the knowledge that one day we will not only be with Christ but also be *like* him (see Moroni 7:41, 48; 1 John 3:2). The Savior teaches plainly that no persons enter into his rest save their garments are washed in his blood, which cleansing comes by faith and repentance (see 3 Nephi 27:19).

2. *Repentance.* Once we come to know the power, greatness, and perfections of the Lord, we automatically sense our own inadequacies (see Mosiah 4:5). We feel to shrink before the Lord Omnipotent; we cry out for mercy and pardon from the Holy One of Israel. And thus it is that repentance follows on the heels of faith: as we encounter the Mas-

ter, we begin to discern the vast chasm between the divine realm and our own unholy state. Repentance is literally an "afterthought," a "change of mind," a change in perspective and a change in lifestyle. Repentance is the process by which we discard the rags of uncleanness and through Christ begin to adorn ourselves in the robes of righteousness. It is the means by which we incorporate into our lives a power beyond our own, an infinite power that transforms us into new creatures, new creatures in Christ. It is only through "the repentance of all their sins" (3 Nephi 27:19) that the followers of Christ are enabled to go where God and Christ are.

3. *Baptism by water and by fire.* Jesus and his prophets have declared in unmistakable terms that salvation comes only to those who have been born again (see John 3:1–5; Mosiah 27:24–26; Alma 7:14). People must be born again, or born from above, in order to see and enter the kingdom of God. When the Spirit of the Lord brings about a change of heart, takes the veil of darkness and unbelief from our eyes, we are born again to *see* and are thereby enabled to recognize and acknowledge the Lord's church and his servants. We are born again to *enter* the kingdom only as we subscribe to the first principles and ordinances of the gospel, the legal requirements for entrance into Christ's family kingdom. Joseph Smith taught that "baptism is a sign to God, to angels, and to heaven that we do the will of God, and there is no other way beneath the heavens whereby God hath ordained for man to come to Him to be saved, and enter into the Kingdom of God, except faith in Jesus Christ, repentance, and baptism for the remission of sins, and any other course is in vain; then you have the promise of the gift of the Holy Ghost."[13] Baptism becomes the physical token of our acceptance of the atoning graces of our Lord. We go down into the "watery grave" and come forth as initiates, new citizens of the kingdom, even as a sign of our ready acceptance of the Lord's burial in the tomb and his subsequent rise to newness of life in the Resurrection (see Romans 6:3–5).

The baptism of fire takes place as the Holy Ghost, who is a sanctifier, takes from our souls the filth and dross of worldliness. Truly, it is the *reception* of the Holy Ghost by the initiate that results in the sanctification of the soul (see 3 Nephi 27:20). Joseph Smith the Prophet explained, "You might as well baptize a bag of sand as a man, if not done in view of the remission of sins and getting of the Holy Ghost.

Baptism by water is but half a baptism, and is good for nothing without the other half—that is, the baptism of the Holy Ghost."[14] That is to say, "Sins are remitted not in the waters of baptism, as we say in speaking figuratively, but when we receive the Holy Ghost. It is the Holy Spirit of God that erases carnality and brings us into a state of righteousness."[15] Men and women who come unto Christ through the appropriate ordinances are in time "sanctified by the reception of the Holy Ghost" (3 Nephi 27:20), meaning they are made pure and holy. Filth and dross—the elements of the natural world—are burned out of their souls as though by fire, thus giving rise to the expression "the baptism of fire." The Holy Ghost, that *revelator* who is the means by which we come to know the truth, is also a *sanctifier* and thus the means whereby we become people who are just and true. In time, through being sanctified, members of the Church come to abhor sin and cleave unto righteousness (see Alma 13:12).

4. *Enduring to the end.* Disciples of Christ in all ages are instructed to be baptized of water and of fire and then to labor to maintain their worthy standing before God. The scriptures teach that to the degree the Saints of the Most High trust in the will and purposes of God and lean upon his mighty arm, as well as extend themselves in Christian service to the needy, they are able to *retain* that remission of sins from day to day (see Mosiah 4:11–12, 26; Alma 4:13–14). To endure to the end is to remain true to our covenants after baptism, to live the life of a Saint to the best of one's ability throughout the remainder of one's life. The commission is for members of the household of faith to "stand as witnesses of God at all times and in all things, and in all places that ye may be in, even until death, that ye may be redeemed of God, and be numbered with those of the first resurrection, that ye may have eternal life" (Mosiah 18:9). To endure to the end is to be "steadfast and immovable"—the scriptural phrase for spiritual maturity—and to press toward the high prize of eternal life (see Mosiah 5:15; 2 Nephi 31:16, 20; 33:4; D&C 6:13; 14:7). The scriptures plainly affirm that "whoso repenteth and is baptized in [Christ's] name shall be filled; and if he endureth to the end, behold, him will [Christ] hold guiltless before [the] Father at that day when [Christ] shall stand to judge the world" (3 Nephi 27:16).

People of the covenant are able to endure to the end, not just through personal grit and willpower, not just by holding white knuckled-like to the iron rod, but by cultivating the gift and gifts of the Holy Ghost. It is the Spirit that provides direction while we are encircled by the mists of darkness (see 2 Nephi 32:5). It is the Spirit that provides moral courage to proceed along the gospel path while the tauntings and temptations emanating from the great and spacious building ring out loud and clear. And it is the Spirit that brings peace to the weary, hope to the faithful, and the promise of eternal life to those who continue to hunger and thirst after righteousness and are willing to serve God at all hazards.[16]

5. *Resurrection and eternal judgment.* In 1839 Joseph Smith observed that "the doctrines of the Resurrection of the Dead and the Eternal Judgment are necessary to preach among the first principles of the Gospel of Jesus Christ."[17] Through the atonement of Jesus Christ, as an unconditional benefit all men and women will, in a limited sense, be redeemed from spiritual death. They will be raised from the grave and thereafter brought to stand in the presence of the Almighty to be judged according to the deeds done in the body. This principle of the gospel illustrates both the mercy and justice of God. Samuel the Lamanite testified that Christ "surely must die that salvation may come; yea, it behooveth him and becometh expedient that he dieth, to bring to pass the resurrection of the dead, that thereby men may be brought into the presence of the Lord" (Helaman 14:15; see also 2 Nephi 9:15, 21–22; Mormon 9:13). Christ reinforced this doctrinal teaching to his Nephite disciples: "And my Father sent me that I might be lifted up upon the cross; and after that I had been lifted up upon the cross, that I might draw all men unto me, that as I have been lifted up by men even so should men be lifted up [that is, raised from the dead] by the Father, to stand before me, to be judged of their works, whether they be good or whether they be evil—and for this cause have I been lifted up; therefore according to the power of the Father I will draw all men unto me, that they may be judged according to their works" (3 Nephi 27:14–15).

WHAT GOSPEL SHALL WE TEACH?

The Book of Mormon is said to contain the fulness of the gospel (see D&C 20:9; 27:5; 35:12, 17; 42:12). Some have wondered how the Lord and his prophets could state this, when in fact the Book of Mormon contains no specific reference to such matters as eternal marriage, degrees of glory in the Resurrection, vicarious work for the dead, and so forth. Again, let us focus upon what the gospel is. The Book of Mormon contains the fulness of the gospel in the sense that it teaches the doctrine of redemption—that salvation is in Christ and in him alone—and the principles of the gospel (faith, repentance, rebirth, enduring, resurrection, and judgment) more plainly and persuasively than any other book of scripture. The Book of Mormon does not necessarily contain the fulness of gospel doctrine. Rather, it is a sacred repository of eternal truth relative to the most fundamental and far-reaching doctrine of all— the doctrine of Christ.[18]

We have received a divine commission from our Lord to teach one another the doctrine of the kingdom (see D&C 88:77). What is it that we should teach? Above and beyond all that might be said in sermons and lessons and seminars and discussions, what should be the walk and talk of the Latter-day Saints? Simply stated, we are to teach the gospel. Our primary message, like Paul's, must be "Jesus Christ and him crucified" (1 Corinthians 2:2). If we have any hope of preserving the faith of our fathers among our people, of building firmly on the rock of revelation and the doctrines Joseph Smith taught, we must ground and settle ourselves in Jesus Christ and his atoning sacrifice. We must, of course, teach all the doctrines of the gospel when it is appropriate to do so. But above all, we must see to it that "we talk of Christ, we rejoice in Christ, we preach of Christ, we prophesy of Christ, . . . that our children may know to what source they may look for a remission of their sins" (2 Nephi 25:26). "Truth, glorious truth, proclaims there is . . . a Mediator," Elder Boyd K. Packer testified. "Through Him mercy can be fully extended to each of us without offending the eternal law of justice. *This truth is the very root of Christian doctrine. You may know much about the gospel as it branches out from there, but if you only know the branches and those branches do not touch that root, if they have been cut free from that truth, there will be no life nor substance nor redemption in them.*"[19]

We frequently hear mention made of the fact that the gospel is universal, that Mormonism welcomes and embodies all that is true and good and ennobling. From this perspective, then, the gospel embraces the truths of the sciences, of the arts, and of great literature. Would it not follow, then, that no matter what we taught in the meetings of the

Church, so long as it was true, was the gospel? If a man should address the congregation in sacrament meeting and speak for twenty minutes on the laws of motion or the process of photosynthesis, would he then be preaching the gospel? If a woman should decide to speak at length to her Spiritual Living class on the laws of genetics or the manner in which sentences may be properly diagrammed, would she then be bearing witness of the gospel? Certainly not. For although in a rather broad sense the gospel may be said to contain all truth, it should be clear that the constant and consistent witness of scripture is that only those truths tied to the doctrine of Christ have power to touch and lift and transform human souls. Of these truths the Holy Ghost will bear testimony; when preached by that Spirit, they result in mutual edification of speaker and listener.

In 1984 Henry B. Eyring, Commissioner of the Church Educational System, delivered an address to Church educators. He spoke soberly of the "sea of filth" that today's youth encounter and of the absolute necessity for solid and sound gospel instruction in an effort to immunize the youth against the ways of the world.

> Now I would like to say this: There are two views of the gospel—both true. They make a terrific difference in the power of your teaching. One view is that the gospel is all truth. It is. The gospel is truth. With that view I could teach pretty well anything true in a classroom, and I would be teaching the gospel. The other view is that the gospel is the principles, commandments, and ordinances which, if kept, conformed with, and accepted, will lead to eternal life. That is also true.
>
> When I choose which of these views I will let dominate my teaching, I take a great step. If I take the view that the gospel is all truth, rather than that it is the ordinances and principles and commandments which, if kept, conformed with, and accepted, lead to eternal life, I have already nearly taken myself out of the contest to help a student withstand the sea of filth. Why? Because he needs to have his eyes focused on light, and that means not truth in some abstract sense but the joy of keeping the commandments and conforming with the principles and accepting the ordinances of the gospel of Jesus Christ. If I decide I will not make that my primary vision of the gospel, I am already out of the contest to help my student with his capacity to see good and to want and desire it in the midst of filth.[20]

CONCLUSION

The Master summarized the gospel or doctrine of Christ for us and beautifully elucidated each of the principles of that gospel:

> And no unclean thing can enter into [God's] kingdom; therefore nothing entereth into his rest save it be those who have washed their garments in my blood, because of their faith, and the repentance of all their sins, and their faithfulness unto the end.
>
> Now this is the commandment: Repent, all ye ends of the earth, and come unto me and be baptized in my name, that ye may be sanctified by the reception of the Holy Ghost, that ye may stand spotless before me at the last day.
>
> Verily, verily, I say unto you, this is my gospel; and ye know the things that ye must do in my church; for the works which ye have seen me do that shall ye also do; for that which ye have seen me do even that shall ye do;
>
> Therefore, if ye do these things blessed are ye, for ye shall be lifted up at the last day. (3 Nephi 27:19–22.)

These matters are sacred. They are among the mysteries of the kingdom, meaning they are to be known and understood only by revelation from God.[21] I have a personal witness to the effect that other great and marvelous things, further mysteries, are made known unto us not as we wade in the morass of the unknown or the esoteric, but rather as we ponder upon, teach from, and focus on those plain and precious truths we know as the principles of the gospel. Profundity thus grows naturally out of simplicity.

Just thirteen days before his death, Elder Bruce R. McConkie affirmed the vital importance of teaching the doctrine of atonement. "Now the atonement of Christ," he stated, "is the most basic and fundamental doctrine of the gospel, and it is the least understood of all our revealed truths. Many of us have a superficial knowledge and rely upon the Lord and his goodness to see us through the trials and perils of life. But if we are to have faith like Enoch and Elijah we must believe what they believed, know what they knew, and live as they lived. May I invite you to join with me in gaining a sound and sure knowledge of the Atonement. We must cast aside the philosophies of men and the wisdom of the wise and hearken to that Spirit which is given to us to guide us into all truth. We must search the scriptures, acccepting them as the mind and will and voice of the Lord and the very power of God unto salvation."²² The gospel is the glad tidings concerning the infinite and eternal atoning sacrifice of the Lord Jesus Christ. The Atonement is central. It is the hub of the wheel; all other matters are spokes at best.

The good news is that we can be changed, be converted, become different people in and through Christ. The good news is that we can come to perceive an entirely new realm of reality, a realm unknown to the world at large. It is a new life, a new life in Christ. In a time of stress and great uncertainty, thanks be to God for the peace and joy of the Spirit that can come to us through Christ and his gospel. In a day when we encounter somber and soul-stirring headlines on almost every page of the newspaper, God be praised that the good news of the gospel has been restored in our day through modern witnesses of Christ. "In the world ye shall have tribulation," the Master acknowledged, "but be of good cheer; I have overcome the world" (John 16:33). Christ our Lord has overcome the world, and he has opened the door and made available to us the power to do the same. And surely there could be no better news, no more joyful tidings, than that.

NOTES

1. See Joseph Fielding Smith, *Doctrines of Salvation*, 3 vols., comp. Bruce R. McConkie (Salt Lake City: Bookcraft, 1954–56), 2:336.
2. Bruce R. McConkie, *The Promised Messiah: The First Coming of Christ* (Salt Lake City: Deseret Book Co., 1979), p. 427.
3. Dallin H Oaks, in Conference Report, April 1985, pp. 104–105; italics in original.
4. Russell M. Nelson, in Conference Report, April 1990, p. 20.
5. Peter Kreeft, *Back to Virtue* (San Francisco: Ignatius Press, 1992), p. 83; italics in original.
6. Bruce R. McConkie, *A New Witness for the Articles of Faith* (Salt Lake City: Deseret Book Co., 1985),pp. 699–700.
7. Bruce C. Hafen, *The Broken Heart* (Salt Lake City: Deseret Book Co., 1989), pp. 196–97; italics added.
8. Dallin H. Oaks, in Conference Report, October 1984, pp. 14–16.
9. C. S. Lewis, *Mere Christianity* (New York: Macmillan Company, 1952), pp. 53–54; italics added.
10. Glenn L. Pace, in Conference Report, October 1987, p. 49.
11. McConkie, *A New Witness for the Articles of Faith*, p. 134; italics added.
12. See Matthew 27:46; James E. Talmage, *Jesus the Christ*, 3d edition (Salt Lake City: The Church of Jesus Christ of Latter-day Saints, 1916), p. 661; Bruce R. McConkie, in Conference Report, April 1985, p. 10; *The Mortal Messiah: From Bethlehem to Calvary*, 4 vols. (Salt Lake City: Deseret Book Co., 1979–81), 4:224, 226; Brigham Young, in

Chapter 14—The Glad Tidings

Journal of Discourses, 26 vols. (London: Latter-day Saints' Book Depot, 1854–86), 3:205–6.

13. Joseph Smith, *Teachings of the Prophet Joseph Smith,* sel. Joseph Fielding Smith (Salt Lake City: Deseret Book Co., 1976), p. 198.

14. Ibid., p. 314.

15. McConkie, *A New Witness for the Articles of Faith,* p. 290; see also p. 239; compare 2 Nephi 31:17; Moroni 6:4.

16. See Smith, *Teachings of the Prophet Joseph Smith,* p. 150.

17. Ibid., p. 149; see also p. 365.

18. See Ezra Taft Benson, *A Witness and a Warning* (Salt Lake City: Deseret Book Co., 1988), pp. 18–19.

19. Boyd K. Packer, in Conference Report, April 1977, p. 80; italics added.

20. Henry B. Eyring, "Eyes to See, Ears to Hear," Church Educational System Symposium, August 1984, p. 11.

21. See Harold B. Lee, *Ye Are the Light of the World* (Salt Lake City: Deseret Book Co., 1974), p. 211.

22. McConkie, in Conference Report, April 1985, p. 11.

CHAPTER 15

The House of Israel: From Everlasting to Everlasting

Several years ago I was startled by a question from a bright young woman in a rather large introductory Book of Mormon class. We were near the end of the Book of Mormon. She said, essentially, "Brother Millet, you continue to use a phrase that I don't understand. Maybe others in the class have the same problem. You keep referring to 'the house of Israel.' What do you mean?" For a full ten seconds I stood in wonder. It never occurred to me that at this point in the two-semester course I needed to define and describe something so fundamental. I made a brief explanation during the period and asked her to see me after class. I discovered that she was an A student, had been raised in the Church, had completed four years of seminary, and had a pretty good knowledge of the gospel.

Sometime later in a large Book of Mormon class for returned missionaries, a young man raised his hand during the middle of our discussion of the Savior's teachings in 3 Nephi concerning the destiny of Israel. He asked: "Brother Millet, I don't mean to be disrespectful or irreverent in any way, but I need to know: What difference does it make if I am of the house of Israel? Why does it matter that my patriarchal blessing says that I am of the tribe of Ephraim?" During this same class period, I asked the class: "How many of you are adopted into the house of Israel?" Of the eighty members of the class, perhaps sixty raised their hands, evidencing their own misunderstandings concerning patriarchal declarations of lineage.

These instances and others that might be cited illustrate what I sense to be a particular problem among many Latter-day Saints. I sense frequently among young and old a lack of covenant consciousness, not necessarily in regard to the covenants and ordinances required for salvation, but rather a lack of appropriate kinship and identity with ancient Israel and with the fathers—Abraham, Isaac, and Jacob—and the responsibilities we have inherited from them.

In our democratic and egalitarian society—in a time when equality and brotherhood are all important—I fear that we are losing a feel for what it means to be a covenant people, what it means to be a chosen people. Too many even among the Latter-day Saints cry out that such sentiments are parochial and primitive, that they lead to exclusivism and racism. Others contend that to emphasize Israel's chosen status is to denigrate and degrade others not designated as Israel.

I am convinced that careful and prayerful study of scripture—particularly the Old Testament and the Book of Mormon—will not only bring people to understand in their minds the origins and destiny of the descendants of Jacob, but also will cause them to know in their hearts what it means to come to earth through a chosen lineage and what God would have them do to be a light to the world. I feel that the words of the Lord to ancient Israel should be received by modern Israel with sobriety and humility, but they *must* be received and believed if we are to realize our potential to become a holy people and a royal priesthood. Jehovah spoke millennia ago of "Israel, whom I have chosen" (Isaiah 44:1) and assured the Israelites that "you only have I known of all the families of the earth" (Amos 3:2; compare Isaiah 45:4). This chapter will deal with the house of Israel—its place and mission in the earth, how and why God has chosen that lineage, and what things lie ahead for the people that God delights to call his "peculiar treasure." The subject is vast and obviously worthy of volumes, but it will be helpful to briefly touch upon the crucial elements in understanding Israel's past, present, and future.

ISRAEL IN PREMORTALITY

Zenos' allegory of the olive tree draws to a close as the millennial day witnesses the gathering of Israel in great numbers by the chosen servants and as the Gentiles join with Israel to constitute one royal family. "And thus they labored, with all diligence, according to the commandments of the Lord of the vineyard, even until the bad had been cast away out of the vineyard, and the Lord had preserved unto himself that the trees had become again the natural fruit; and they became like unto one body; and the fruits were equal; and *the Lord of the vineyard had preserved unto himself the natural fruit, which was most precious unto him from the beginning*" (Jacob 5:74; italics added). I believe this to be a reference to Jehovah's love and tender regard for Israel that stretches beyond her mortal origins and sojournings and reaches back to the premortal day wherein certain souls qualified for a select status.

Following our birth as spirits, being endowed with agency, each of the spirit sons and daughters of God grew and developed and progressed according to their desires for truth and righteousness. "Being subject to law," Elder Bruce R. McConkie wrote, "and having their agency, all the spirits of men, while yet in the Eternal Presence, developed aptitudes, talents, capacities, and abilities of every sort, kind, and degree. During the long expanse of life that then was, an infinite variety of talents and abilities came into being. As the ages rolled, no two spirits remained alike. . . . Abraham and Moses and all of the prophets sought and obtained the talent for spirituality. Mary and Eve were two of the greatest spirit daughters of the Father. *The whole house of Israel, known and segregated out from their fellows, was inclined toward spiritual things.*"[1]

Perhaps the greatest foreordination—based on premortal faithfulness—is foreordination to lineage and family: certain individuals come to earth through a designated channel, through a lineage that entitles them to remarkable blessings but also carries with it burdens and responsibilities. As a people, therefore, we enjoy what my colleague Brent L. Top calls "a type of collective foreordination—a selection of spirits to form an entire favored group or lineage." "Although it is a collective foreordination," he adds, "it is nonetheless based on individual premortal faithfulness and spiritual capacity."[2] In the words of Elder Melvin J. Ballard, Israel is "a group of souls tested, tried, and proven before they were born into the world. . . . Through this lineage were to come the true and tried souls that had demonstrated their righteousness in the spirit world before they came here."[3]

"Remember the days of old," Moses counseled his people, "consider the years of many generations: ask thy father, and he will shew thee: thy elders, and they will tell thee. When the most High divided to the nations their inheritance, when he separated the sons of Adam, he set the bounds of the people *according to the number of the children of Israel.* For the Lord's portion is his people; Jacob is the lot of his inheritance" (Deuteronomy 32:7–9; italics added). In speaking to the Athenians, the Apostle Paul declared: "God that made the world and all things therein . . . hath made of one blood all nations of men for to dwell on all the face of the earth, and *hath determined the times before appointed, and the bounds of their habitation"* (Acts 17:24, 26; italics added). President Harold B. Lee explained:

> Those born to the lineage of Jacob, who was later to be called Israel, and his posterity, who were known as the children of Israel, were born into the most illustrious lineage of any of those who came upon the earth as mortal beings. All these rewards were seemingly promised, or foreordained, before the world was. Surely these matters must have been determined by the kind of lives we had lived in that premortal spirit world. Some may question these assumptions, but at the same time they will accept without any question the belief that each one of us will be judged when we leave this earth according to his or her deeds during our lives here in mortality. Isn't it just as reasonable to believe that what we have received here in this earth [life] was given to each of us according to the merits of our conduct before we came here?[4]

It thus appears that the declaration of lineage by patriarchs is as much a statement about who and what we *were* as it is about who we are now and what we may become. There are those people, of course, who believe otherwise, those who propose that premortality has little or nothing to do with mortality and that there is no tie between faithfulness there and lineage and station here. To believe in any other way, they contend, is racist, sexist, and exclusionary. Despite the cleverness of the posture and the egalitarian-sounding nature of such a perspective, it is my firm belief that such views are doctrinally defenseless and even potentially hazardous. If there is no relationship between the first estate and the second, why, as President Lee might well have asked, should I believe that there is any relationship between what I do here and what I will receive hereafter? Our task as parents and teachers and students of the gospel is not simply to win friends and influence people through avoiding, watering down, or in some cases even denying what are "hard sayings" or difficult doctrines. Truth is not established by consensus or by popularity.

Who are we, then? President Lee answered: "You are all the sons and daughters of God. Your spirits were created and lived as organized intelligences before the world was. You have been blessed to have a physical body because of your obedience to certain commandments in that premortal state. You are now born into a family to which you have come, into the nations through which you have come, as a reward for the kind of lives you lived before you came here and at a time in the world's history, as the apostle Paul taught the men of Athens and as the Lord revealed to Moses, determined by the faithfulness of each of those who lived before this world was created."[5]

And yet a person's coming to earth through a chosen or favored lineage is a blessing entailing a burden. "Once we know who we are," Elder Russell M. Nelson said, "and the royal lineage of which we are a part, our actions and directions in life will be more appropriate to our inheritance."[6] Years ago a wise man wrote of the burdens of chosenness and of why it is that God had selected a particular people as his own:

> A man will rise and demand, "By what right does God choose one race or people above another?" I like that form of the question. It is much better than asking by what right God degrades one people beneath another, although that is implied. God's grading is always upward. If he raises up a nation, it is that other nations may be raised up through its ministry. If he exalts a great man, an apostle of liberty or science or faith, it is that He might raise a degraded people to a better condition. The divine selection is not [alone] a prize, a compliment paid to the man or the race—it is a burden imposed. To appoint a Chosen people is not a pandering to the racial vanity of a "superior people," it is a yoke bound upon the necks of those who are chosen for a special service.

In short, God "hath made [Israel] great for what He is going to make [Israel] do."[7]

ISRAEL IN MORTALITY: THE SCATTERING AND GATHERING

Those of Israel who follow the Light of Christ in this life will be led eventually to the higher light of the Holy Ghost and will come to know the Lord and come unto him. In time they come to know of their noble heritage and of the royal blood that flows through their veins. They come to earth with a predisposition to receive the truth, with an inner attraction to the message of the gospel. "My sheep hear my voice," the Master said, "and I know them, and they follow me" (John 10:27). Those chosen to come to the earth through the favored lineage "are especially endowed at birth with spiritual talents. It is easier for them to believe the gospel than it is for the generality of mankind. Every living soul comes into this world with sufficient talent to believe and be saved, but the Lord's sheep, as a reward for their devotion when they dwelt in his presence, enjoy greater spiritual endowments than their fellows."[8] "The blood of Israel has flowed in the veins of the children of men," Wilford Woodruff declared, "mixed among the Gentile nations, and when they have heard the sound of the Gospel of Christ it has been like vivid lightening to them; it has opened their understandings, enlarged their minds, and enabled them to see the things of God. They have been born of the Spirit, and then they could behold the kingdom of God."[9]

And yet chosenness implies a succession of choices. Those who became Israel before the world was, those who were *called* in that pristine existence, must exercise wisdom and prudence and discernment in this life before they become truly *chosen* to enjoy the privilege of ruling and reigning in the house of Israel forever. It was of such that Alma spoke when he declared that many people who were foreordained to receive transcendent privileges do not enjoy "as great privilege as their brethren" because in mortality the former choose to "reject the spirit of God on account of the hardness of their hearts and blindness of their minds" (Alma 13:4). The scriptures thus teach that "there are many called, but few are chosen" (D&C 121:34). "This suggests," President Harold B. Lee explained, "that even though we have our free agency here, there are many who were foreordained before the world was, to a greater state than they have prepared themselves for here. Even though they might have been among the noble and great, from among whom the Father declared he would make his chosen leaders, they may fail of that calling here in mortality."[10] And so the vivid and harsh reality is that lineage and ancestry alone do not qualify one for a divine family inheritance. To use Paul's language, "they are not all Israel, which are of Israel: neither, because they are the seed of Abraham, are they all children" (Romans 9:6–7). In fact, as Nephi reminded us, only those who receive the gospel and commit themselves by obedience and continued faithfulness to the Mediator of that covenant are really covenant people. "As many of the gentiles as will repent are the covenant people of the Lord," he said; "and as many of the Jews as will not repent shall be cast off; for the Lord covenanteth with none save it be with them that repent and believe in his Son, who is the Holy One of Israel" (2 Nephi 30:2).

Both the Old Testament and the Book of Mormon—and it is particularly in the latter volume that we see the pattern clearly—set forth in consistent detail the reasons why over the generations Israel has been scattered and how it is they are to be gathered. Speaking on behalf of Jehovah, Moses warned ancient Israel that if they should reject their God they would be scattered among the nations, dispersed among the Gentiles. "If thou wilt not hearken to the voice of the Lord thy God," he said, "to observe to do all his commandments and his statutes which I command thee this day, . . . [you will be] removed into all the kingdoms of the earth . . . ; and ye shall be plucked from off the land whither thou goest to possess it. And the Lord shall scatter thee among all people, from the one end of the earth even unto the other; and there thou shalt serve other gods, which neither thou nor thy fathers have known" (Deuteronomy 28:15, 25, 63–64). The Lord spoke in a similar vein through Jeremiah more than half a millennium later: "Because your fathers have forsaken me, saith the Lord, and have walked after other gods, and have served them, and have worshipped them, and have forsaken me, and have not kept my law; and ye have done worse than your fathers . . . : therefore I will cast you out of this land into a land that ye know not, . . . where I will not shew you favour" (Jeremiah 16:11–13). The people of God became scattered—alienated from Jehovah and the ways of righteousness, lost as to their identity as covenant representatives, and displaced from the lands set aside for their inheritance—because they forsook the God of Abraham, Isaac, and Jacob and partook of the worship and ways of unholy men.

Though Israel is generally scattered because of her apostasy, we should also point out that the Lord scatters certain branches of his chosen people to the nethermost parts of the earth in order to accomplish his purposes—to spread the blood and influence of Abraham throughout the globe (see 1 Nephi 17:36–38; 21:1; 2 Nephi 10:20–22). Through this means all the families of the earth will be blessed eventually—either through being of the blood of Abraham themselves or through being ministered unto by the blood of Abraham—with the right to the gospel, the priesthood, and eternal life (see Abraham 2:8–11).

On the other hand, the *gathering* of Israel is accomplished through repentance and turning to the Lord. Individuals were gathered in ancient days when they aligned themselves with the people of God, with those who practiced the religion of Jehovah and received the ordinances of salvation. They were gathered when they gained a sense of tribal identity, when they came to know who they were and whose they were. They were gathered when they congregated with the Former-day Saints, when they settled on those lands designated as promised lands— lands set apart as sacred sites for people of promise. The hope of the chosen people from Adam to Isaac, as well as the longing of the house of Israel from Joseph to Malachi, was to be reunited with their God and to enjoy fellowship with those of the household of faith. "But now thus saith the Lord that created thee, O Jacob," Isaiah recorded, "and he that formed thee, O Israel, Fear not: for I have redeemed thee, I have called thee by thy name; thou art mine."

> When thou passest through the waters, I will be with thee; and through the rivers, they shall not overflow thee; when thou walkest through the fire, thou shalt not be burned; neither shall the flame kindle upon thee.
>
> For I am the Lord thy God, the Holy One of Israel, thy Saviour. . . .
>
> Since thou wast precious in my sight, thou hast been honourable, and I have loved thee: therefore will I give men for thee, and people for thy life.
>
> Fear not: for I am with thee: I will bring thy seed from the east, and gather thee from the west; I will say to the north, Give up; and to the south, Keep not back: bring my sons from far, and my daughters from the ends of the earth. (Isaiah 43:1–6.)

"Ye shall be gathered one by one, O ye children of Israel," Isaiah declared (Isaiah 27:12). The call to the dispersed of Israel has been and ever will be the same: "Turn, O backsliding children, saith the Lord," through Jeremiah; "for I am married unto you: and I will take you one of a city, and two of a family, and I will bring you to Zion" (Jeremiah 3:14). That is to say, gathering is accomplished through individual conversion, through faith and repentance and baptism and confirmation, through, as we shall see shortly, the receipt of and obedience to the ordinances of the holy temple.

Indeed, the Old Testament and Book of Mormon prophets longed for the day when the scattered remnants of Israel—those lost as to their identity and lost as to their relationship with the true Messiah and his church and kingdom—would be a part of a work that would cause all former gatherings to pale into insignificance. Jeremiah recorded: "Therefore, behold, the days come, saith the Lord, that it shall no more be said,

The Lord liveth, that brought up the children of Israel out of the land of Egypt; but, The Lord liveth, that brought up the children of Israel from the land of the north, and from all the lands whither he had driven them." And how is such a phenomenal gathering to be accomplished? Jehovah answers: "Behold, I will send for many fishers, saith the Lord, and they shall fish them; and after will I send for many hunters, and they shall hunt them from every mountain, and from every hill, and out of the holes of the rocks" (Jeremiah 16:14–16). That is, through the great missionary work of the Church, the elders and sisters—the Lord's legal administrators in the great proselyting program—seek and teach and baptize and thereby gather the strangers home.

And so people are gathered into the fold of God through learning the doctrine of Christ and subscribing to the principles and ordinances of his gospel. They learn through scripture and through patriarchal and prophetic pronouncement of their kinship with or, in rare instances today, of their adoption into the house of Israel. The crowning tie to Israel, however, comes only by the worthy reception of the blessings of the temple, through being endowed and sealed into the holy order of God (see D&C 131:1–4). "What was the [ultimate] object," Joseph Smith asked, "of gathering the Jews, or the people of God, in any age of the world?" He then answered: "The main object was to build unto the Lord a house whereby He could reveal unto His people the ordinances of His house and the glories of His kingdom, and teach the people the way of salvation; for there are certain ordinances and principles that, when they are taught and practiced, must be done in a place or house built for that purpose."[11] "Missionary work," Elder Russell M. Nelson observed, "is only the beginning" to the blessings of Abraham, Isaac, and Jacob. "The fulfillment, the consummation, of these blessings comes as those who have entered the waters of baptism perfect their lives to the point that they may enter the holy temple. Receiving an endowment there seals members of the Church to the Abrahamic Covenant."[12]

JOSEPH SMITH: A MODERN ABRAHAM

In September of 1823 the angel Moroni appeared to the Prophet Joseph Smith. "This messenger proclaimed himself," Joseph wrote to John Wentworth, "to be an angel of God, sent to bring the joyful tidings that the covenant which God made with ancient Israel was at hand to be fulfilled, that the preparatory work for the second coming of the Messiah was speedily to commence; that the time was at hand for the Gospel in all its fulness to be preached in power, unto all nations that a people might be prepared for the Millennial reign. I was informed that I was chosen to be an instrument in the hands of God to bring about some of His purposes in this glorious dispensation."[13] Joseph of old prophesied that his latter-day namesake would be a "choice seer," one who would be raised up by God to bring the people of the last days to the knowledge of the covenants that God had made with the ancient fathers (see 2 Nephi 3:7; 1 Nephi 13:26). The name Joseph is a blessed and significant name. Whether taken from the Hebrew word *Yasaf,* which means "to add," or from the word *Asaph,* meaning "to gather," one senses that the latter-day seer was destined to perform a monumental labor in regard to the fulfillment of the Abrahamic covenant in the final dispensation.

Joseph Smith was a descendant of Abraham. By lineage he had a right to the priesthood, the gospel, and eternal life (see Abraham 2:8–11). In a revelation received on 6 December 1832, the Savior said: "Thus saith the Lord unto you, with whom the priesthood hath continued through the lineage of your fathers—for ye are lawful heirs, according to the flesh, and have been hid from the world with Christ in God—therefore your life and the priesthood have remained, and must needs remain through you and your lineage until the restoration of all things spoken by the mouths of all the holy prophets since the world began" (D&C 86:8–10). President Brigham Young stated:

> It was decreed in the counsels of eternity, long before the foundations of the earth were laid, that he [Joseph Smith] should be the man, in the last dispensation of this world, to bring forth the word of God to the people, and receive the fulness of the keys and power of the Priesthood of the Son of God. The Lord had his eye upon him, and upon his father, and upon his father's fathers, and upon their progenitors clear back to Abraham, and from Abraham to the flood, from the flood to Enoch, and from Enoch to Adam. He has watched that family and that blood as it has circulated from its fountain to the birth of that man.[14]

President Young declared on another occasion: "You have heard Joseph say that the people did not know him; he had his eyes on . . .

blood-relations. Some have supposed that he meant spirit, but it was the blood-relation. This is it that he referred to. His descent to Joseph that was sold into Egypt was direct, and the blood was pure in him. That is why the Lord chose him and we are pure when this blood-strain from Ephraim comes down pure. The decrees of the Almighty will be exalted—that blood which was in him was pure and he had the sole right and lawful power, as he was the legal heir to the blood that has been on the earth and has come down through a pure lineage. The union of various ancestors kept that blood pure. There is a great deal the people do not understand, and many of the Latter-day Saints have to learn all about it."[15]

What is true in regard to the Prophet's lineage, his right to the priesthood and the gospel, and his duty in regard to the salvation of the world, is equally true for other members of the Lord's church. The Lord spoke of his Latter-day Saints as "a remnant of Jacob, and those who are heirs according to the covenant" (D&C 52:2). "Awake, awake; put on thy strength, O Zion," Isaiah recorded; "put on thy beautiful garments, O Jerusalem, the holy city" (Isaiah 52:1). A modern revelation provides our finest commentary on this passage and explains that Jehovah "had reference to those whom God should call in the last days, who should hold the power of priesthood to bring again Zion, and the redemption of Israel; and to put on her strength is to put on the authority of the priesthood, which she, Zion, has a right to by lineage; and to return to that power which she had lost" (D&C 113:8). The Lord also encouraged Israel through Isaiah to shake herself from the dust and loose herself from the bands about her neck (see Isaiah 52:2). That is, "the scattered remnants are exhorted to return to the Lord from whence they have fallen; which if they do, the promise of the Lord is that he will speak to them, or give them revelation." In so doing, Israel rids herself of "the curses of God upon her," her "scattered condition among the Gentiles" (D&C 113:10).

Joseph Smith became a "father of the faithful" of this dispensation, the means by which the chosen lineage could be identified, gathered, organized as family units, and sealed forevermore into the house of Israel to their God. The patriarch in the early days of the restored Church, Joseph Smith, Sr., blessed his son as follows: "A marvelous work and a wonder has the Lord wrought by thy hand, even that which shall prepare the way for the remnants of his people to come in among the Gentiles, with their fulness, as the tribes of Israel are restored. I bless thee with the blessings of thy Fathers Abraham, Isaac and Jacob; and even the blessings of thy father Joseph, the son of Jacob. Behold, he looked after his posterity in the last days, when they should be scattered and driven by the Gentiles."[16]

On 3 April 1836 Moses, Elias, and Elijah appeared in the Kirtland Temple and restored priesthood keys of inestimable worth, keys that formalized much of the labor that had been under way since the organization of the Church (see D&C 110). Moses restored the keys of the gathering of Israel, including the right of presidency and directing powers needed to gather the ten lost tribes. Elias committed unto Joseph and Oliver the dispensation of the gospel of Abraham, making it possible that through those first elders all generations after them would be blessed. That is, Elias restored the keys necessary to organize eternal family units in the patriarchal order through the new and everlasting covenant of marriage. Elijah restored the keys necessary to bind and seal those family units for eternity, as well as the power to legitimize all priesthood ordinances and give them efficacy, virtue, and force in and after the Resurrection.[17] Thus through the coming of Elijah and his prophetic colleagues in Kirtland, the promises made to the fathers—the promises of the gospel, the priesthood, and the possibility of eternal life granted to Abraham, Isaac, and Jacob—are planted in our hearts, the hearts of the children (see D&C 2). More specifically, because of what took place through Joseph Smith in Kirtland in 1836, the desire of our hearts to have all the blessings enjoyed by the ancients can be realized. And because of the spirit of Elijah moving upon the faithful, there comes also a desire to make those same blessings available for our more immediate fathers through family history and vicarious temple ordinances. Through Joseph Smith the blessings of Abraham, Isaac, and Jacob are available to all who will join the Church and prove worthy of the blessings of the temple. Jehovah's plea through Isaiah that the people of the covenant become a light to the nations, that they might be his "salvation unto the end of the earth" (Isaiah 49:6), is thus realized through the restoration of the gospel. Thereby, as the Prophet himself declared, "the election of the promised seed still continues, and in the last days they shall have the priesthood restored unto them, and they shall be 'saviors on Mount Zion.'"[18] Because Joseph Smith was the head of this dispensation and its modern Abraham, Brigham Young could appropriately say of his predecessor: "Joseph is a father to Ephraim and to all Israel in these last days."[19]

The Lord has repeatedly affirmed the special status of the Latter-day Prophet-leader: "As I said unto Abraham concerning the kindreds of the earth, even so I say unto my servant Joseph: In thee and in thy seed shall the kindred of the earth be blessed" (D&C 124:58). Further: "Abraham received promises concerning his seed, and of the fruit of his loins—from whose loins ye are, namely, my servant Joseph—which were to continue so long as they were in the world; and as touching Abraham and his seed, out of the world they should continue; both in the world and out of the world should they continue as innumerable as the stars; or, if ye were to count the sand upon the seashore ye could not number them. This promise is yours also, because ye are of Abraham" (D&C 132:30–31).

THE MILLENNIAL GATHERING OF ISRAEL

Both the Old Testament and the Book of Mormon attest to the fact that a significant part of the drama we know as the gathering of Israel will be millennial, brought to pass after the second coming of Jesus Christ. Between now and then we shall see marvelous things on the earth in regard to the people of Israel coming unto their Lord and King and thereafter unto the lands of their inheritance. We have witnessed already the phenomenal gathering of many thousands of the seed of Lehi (of the tribe of Joseph) into the Church, and this is but the beginning. We have stood in awe as descendants of Jacob around the globe have been found, identified, taught, and converted to the faith of their fathers, and yet we have seen but the tip of the iceberg. Our missionaries shall soon enter into lands wherein pockets of Israelites will be baptized and confirmed and where patriarchs shall declare lineage through such tribes as Issachar, Zebulun, Gad, Asher, and Naphtali.

A major conversion of the Jews will take place near the time of the coming of the Lord in glory. "And it shall come to pass in that day," Jehovah said through Zechariah, "that I will seek to destroy all the nations that come against Jerusalem. And I will pour upon the house of David, and upon the inhabitants of Jerusalem, the spirit of grace and of supplications: and they shall look upon me whom they have pierced, and they shall mourn for him, as one mourneth for his only son, and shall be in bitterness for him, as one that is in bitterness for his first-born. . . . And one shall say unto him, What are these wounds in thine hands? Then he shall answer, Those with which I was wounded in the house of my friends" (Zechariah 12:9–10; 13:6). A modern revelation provides a more detailed description of this poignant moment in our Lord's dealings with his own. Having set his foot on the Mount of Olives and the mountain having cleaved in twain, "then shall the Jews look upon me," the Lord prophesies, "and say: What are these wounds in thine hands and in thy feet? Then shall they know that I am the Lord; for I will say unto them: These wounds are the wounds with which I was wounded in the house of my friends. I am he who was lifted up. I am Jesus that was crucified. I am the Son of God. And then shall they weep because of their iniquities; then shall they lament because they persecuted their king" (D&C 45:48–53). Prior to this time Jews from around the globe will already have investigated the message of the Restoration, entered into the covenant gospel, and come home to the God of Abraham, Isaac, and Jacob. They will not only have come to acknowledge Jesus as an honorable prophet-teacher, but will confess him as Lord and God, as Messiah. Their garments will have been "washed in the blood of the Lamb" (Ether 13:11). But at the time the Master appears at Olivet, the conversion of a nation will begin. "That is to say, the Jews 'shall begin to believe in Christ' [2 Nephi 30:7] before he comes the second time. Some of them will accept the gospel and forsake the traditions of their fathers; a few will find in Jesus the fulfillment of their Messianic hopes; but their nation as a whole, their people as the distinct body that they now are in all nations, the Jews as a unit shall not, at that time, accept the word of truth. But a beginning will be made; a foundation will be laid; and then Christ will come and usher in the millennial year of his redeemed."[20]

In 721 B.C. the Assyrians under Shalmaneser took the ten northern tribes captive. According to tradition, these Israelites escaped as they were being taken northward and scattered themselves throughout different parts of the earth. They were never again heard of and came thereafter to be known as the "lost tribes." Nephi explained to his brothers early in the Book of Mormon story that "the house of Israel, sooner or later, will be scattered upon all the face of the earth, and also among all nations. And behold, there are many"—note that he is here making reference to the ten northern tribes—"who are already lost from the knowledge of those who are at Jerusalem. Yea, the more part of all the tribes have been led away; and they are scattered to and fro upon the isles of the sea; and whither they are none of us knoweth, save that we know that they have been led away" (1 Nephi 22:3–4). Nephi's use of the word "lost" is most interesting. The tribes are lost "from the knowledge of those who are at Jerusalem." Let me here refer to a statement made by President George Q. Cannon in 1890. After having quoted at length from 2 Nephi 30 regarding the final gathering of Israel from among the nations, President Cannon said:

> This prediction plainly foreshadows that which is now taking place, and which has been taking place for some years. "As many of the Gentiles as will repent," the prophet says,"are the covenant people of the Lord." By virtue of this promise which God has made, we are His covenant people. Though of Gentile descent, and numbered among the Gentile nations, by and through our obedience to the Gospel of the Son of God we become incorporated, so to speak, among His covenant people and are numbered with them. We say frequently that we are descendants of the house of Israel. This is undoubtedly true. . . . *Our ancestors were of the house of Israel but they mingled with the Gentiles and became lost, that is, they became lost so far as being recognized as of the house of Israel, and the blood of our forefathers was mingled with the blood of the Gentile nations.* We have been gathered out from those nations by the preaching of the gospel of the Son of God. The Lord has made precious promises unto us that every blessing, and every gift, and every power necessary for salvation and for exaltation to His Kingdom shall be given unto us in common with those who are more particularly known as the covenant people of the Lord.[21]

Mormon teaches that in the last days all of the twelve tribes will come to Christ through accepting the Book of Mormon and the restored gospel (see Mormon 3:17–22). Will such persons gather into the true Church from the north? Yes. And they shall also come, as the scriptures attest, from the south and the east and the west (see Isaiah 43:5–6; 3 Nephi 20:13). In fact, it just may be that the idea of gathering from "the lands of the north" is simply a reference to a return from all parts of the earth. For example, Jehovah, speaking through Zechariah, called forth to his chosen but scattered people: "Come! Come! Flee from the land of the north, declares the Lord, for I have scattered you to the four winds of heaven" (New International Version, Zechariah 2:6).

As we have indicated, the work of the Father—the work of gathering Israel into the fold—though begun in the early nineteenth century, will continue into and through the Millennium. The missionary effort begun in our time will accelerate at a pace that we cannot now comprehend. This is why the Book of Mormon speaks of the work of the Father "commencing" during the Millennium. In the millennial day "shall the power of heaven come down among them; and I also will be in the midst," the resurrected Lord stated. "And then shall the work of the Father commence at that day, even when this gospel shall be preached among the remnant of this people. Verily I say unto you, at that day shall the work of the Father commence among all the dispersed of my people, yea, even the tribes which have been lost, which the Father hath led away out of Jerusalem" (3 Nephi 21:25–26; compare 2 Nephi 30:7–15).

We are prone to speak of there being no death during the thousand years. Let us be more precise. The Saints shall live to the age of a tree, the age of one hundred (see Isaiah 65:20; D&C 43:32; 63:51; 101:30–31), before they are changed in the twinkling of an eye from mortality to resurrected immortality. On the other hand, and presumably in speaking of terrestrial persons, Joseph Smith said: "There will be wicked men on the earth during the thousand years. The heathen nations who will not come up to worship will be visited with the judgments of God, and must eventually be destroyed from the earth."[22] "There will be need for the preaching of the gospel after the millennium is brought in," President Joseph Fielding Smith explained, "until all men are either converted or pass away. In the course of the thousand years all men will either come into the Church, or kingdom of God, or they will die and pass away."[23] Or, as Elder Bruce R. McConkie has described this process: "There will be many churches on earth when the Millennium begins. False worship will continue among those whose desires are good, 'who are honorable men of the earth,' but who have been 'blinded by the craftiness of men.' (D&C 76:75.) Plagues will rest upon them until they repent and believe the gospel or are destroyed, as the Prophet said. It follows that missionary work will continue into the Millennium until all who remain are converted. Then 'the earth shall be full of the knowledge of the Lord as the waters cover the sea.' (Isaiah

11:9.) Then every living soul on earth will belong to The Church of Jesus Christ of Latter-day Saints."[24]

In that glorious era of peace and righteousness, the dispersed of Israel shall receive the message of the Restoration, read and believe the Book of Mormon, traverse the "highway of righteousness" (Isaiah 35:8) into the true Church, and take their place beside their kinsmen in the household of faith. The revelation declares that "their enemies shall become a prey unto them" (D&C 133:28). This means that the enemies of Israel—the wicked and carnal elements of a fallen world—will have been destroyed by the glory and power of the Second Coming. "For the time speedily cometh," Nephi prophesied, "that the Lord God shall cause a great division among the people, and the wicked will he destroy; and he will spare his people, yea, even if it so be that he must destroy the wicked by fire" (2 Nephi 30:10; compare 1 Nephi 22:17). There will have been "an entire separation of the righteous and the wicked"; the enemies of the chosen people will be no more, because the Lord will have sent forth his angels "to pluck out the wicked and cast them into unquenchable fire" (D&C 63:54). Truly, "such of the gathering of Israel as has come to pass so far is but the gleam of a star that soon will be hidden by the splendor of the sun in full blaze; truly, the magnitude and grandeur and glory of the gathering is yet to be."[25]

One of the most graphic prophetic statements about Israel in the Millennium is contained in the writings of Zenos, one of the prophets of the brass plates. In speaking of what appears to be the millennial day, Zenos taught:

> And there began to be the natural fruit again in the vineyard; and the natural branches began to grow and thrive exceedingly; and the wild branches began to be plucked off and to be cast away; and they did keep the root and the top thereof equal, according to the strength thereof.
>
> And thus they labored, with all diligence, according to the commandments of the Lord of the vineyard, even until the bad had been cast away out of the vineyard, and the Lord had preserved unto himself that the trees had become again the natural fruit; and they became like unto one body; and the fruits were equal; and the Lord of the vineyard had preserved unto himself the natural fruit, which was most precious unto him from the beginning. (Jacob 5:73–74.)

In that glorious day, the promise of God to his chosen seed will be well on the way to fulfillment. Paul's words, spoken in the meridian of time, will then have particular application and fulfillment. "As many of you as have been baptized into Christ," he observed, "have put on Christ. There is neither Jew nor Greek, there is neither bond nor free, there is neither male nor female; for ye are all one in Christ Jesus. And if ye be Christ's then are ye Abraham's seed, and heirs according to the promise" (Galatians 3:27–29). All those who come unto Christ, who is the Holy One of Israel, shall, under Christ, rule and reign in the house of Israel forever. In the millennial day the Lord Jehovah will reign personally upon the earth (see Articles of Faith 1:10). More specifically, "Christ and the resurrected Saints will reign over the earth during the thousand years. They will not probably dwell upon the earth, but will visit it when they please, or when it is necessary to govern it."[26] In that day he shall preside as King of kings and Lord of lords: Israel's Good Shepherd shall be with them and minister to them in everlasting splendor.

The blossoming and ultimate fulfillment of the everlasting covenant restored through Joseph Smith shall be millennial. The principles and ordinances of the gospel, the "articles of adoption"[27] by which men and women are received into the royal family and given a rightful place in the house of Israel, shall continue during the thousand years. "During the Millennium," a modern apostle has written,

> Children will be named and blessed by the elders of the kingdom. When those of the rising generation arrive at the years of accountability, they will be baptized in water and of the Spirit by legal administrators appointed so to act. Priesthood will be conferred upon young and old, and they will be ordained to offices therein as the needs of the ministry and their own salvation require. At the appropriate time each person will receive his patriarchal blessing, we suppose from the natural patriarch who presides in his family, as it was in Adamic days and as it was when Jacob blessed his sons. The saints will receive their endowments in the temples of the Lord, and they will receive the blessings of celestial marriage at their holy altars. And all the faithful will have their callings and elections made sure and will be sealed up unto that eternal life which will come to them when they reach the age of a tree.[28]

"Behold," Jeremiah wrote, "the days come, saith the Lord, that I will make a new covenant with the house of Israel, and with the house of Judah."

Not according to the covenant that I made with their fathers in the day that I took them by the hand to bring them out of the land of Egypt; which my covenant they brake, although I was an husband unto them, saith the Lord:

But this shall be the covenant that I will make with the house of Israel; after those days, saith the Lord, I will put my law in their inward parts, and write it in their hearts; and will be their God, and they shall be my people.

And they shall teach no more every man his neighbour, and every man his brother, saying, Know the Lord: for they shall all know me, from the least of them unto the greatest of them, saith the Lord: for I will forgive their iniquity, and I will remember their sin no more. (Jeremiah 31:31–34.)

"How is this to be done?" Joseph Smith asked. "It is to be done by this sealing power, and the other Comforter spoken of, which will be manifest by revelation."[29]

CONCLUSION

"When the Lord shall come," a modern revelation explains, "he shall reveal all things—things which have passed, and hidden things which no man knew, things of the earth, by which it was made, and the purpose and the end thereof—things most precious, things that are above, and things that are beneath, things that are in the earth, and upon the earth, and in heaven" (D&C 101:32–34). When the Lion of the tribe of Judah finally unseals the scrolls containing "the revealed will, mysteries, and the works of God," even "the hidden things of his economy concerning this earth during the seven thousand years of its continuance, or its temporal existence" (D&C 77:6; compare Revelation 5:1), surely we shall one and all come to know of his peculiar dealings with Israel, of the strange but masterful manner in which he has moved upon and through his covenant people in mysterious ways his wonders to perform.

And so, to those who have come unto Christ through the everlasting covenant, we echo the words of Mormon: "Know ye that ye are of the house of Israel" (Mormon 7:2). Or as Jesus explained to the Nephites: "Ye are the children of the prophets; and ye are of the house of Israel; and ye are of the covenant which the Father made with your fathers, saying unto Abraham: And in thy seed shall all the kindreds of the earth be blessed" (3 Nephi 20:25).

Chapter 15—The House of Israel: From Everlasting to Everlasting

NOTES

1. Bruce R. McConkie, *The Mortal Messiah: From Bethlehem to Calvary,* 4 vols. (Salt Lake City: Deseret Book Co., 1979–81), 1:23; italics added.

2. Brent L. Top, *The Life Before* (Salt Lake City: Bookcraft, 1988), p. 144.

3. From Melvin J. Ballard, "The Three Degrees of Glory," in *Melvin J. Ballard: Crusader for Righteousness* (Salt Lake City: Bookcraft, 1966), pp. 218–19.

4. Harold B. Lee, in Conference Report, October 1973, pp. 7–8.

5. Ibid., p. 7.

6. Russell M. Nelson, "Thanks for the Covenant," Brigham Young University devotional address, 22 November 1988, typescript, p. 8.

7. See W. J. Cameron, "Is There a Chosen People?" in James H. Anderson, *God's Covenant Race* (Salt Lake City: Deseret News Press, 1938), pp. 300–302.

8. Bruce R. McConkie, *A New Witness for the Articles of Faith* (Salt Lake City: Deseret Book Co., 1985), p. 34.

9. Wilford Woodruff, in *Journal of Discourses,* 26 vols. (London: Latter-day Saints' Book Depot, 1854–86), 15:11.

10. Harold B. Lee, in Conference Report, October 1973, p. 7.

11. Joseph Smith, *Teachings of the Prophet Joseph Smith,* sel. Joseph Fielding Smith (Salt Lake City: Deseret Book Co., 1976), pp. 307–8.

12. Nelson, "Thanks for the Covenant," p. 7.

13. Joseph Smith, *History of the Church of Jesus Christ of Latter-day Saints,* 7 vols., ed. B. H. Roberts (Salt Lake City: Deseret Book Co., 1957), 4:536–37.

14. Brigham Young, *Journal of Discourses,* 7:289–90.

15. Brigham Young, in *Utah Genealogical and Historical Magazine,* 11:107.

16. Joseph Smith, Sr., in Joseph F. McConkie, *His Name Shall Be Joseph* (Salt Lake City: Hawkes Publishing, 1980), p. 103.

17. See Smith, *Teachings of the Prophet Joseph Smith,* p. 172.

18. Ibid., p. 189.

19. Journal History, 9 April 1837.

20. Bruce R. McConkie, *The Millennial Messiah* (Salt Lake City: Deseret Book Co., 1982), pp. 228–29.

21. George Q. Cannon, address delivered at the Tabernacle in Salt Lake City, 12 January 1890, in *Collected Discourses* (B. H. S. Publishing, 1988), 2:2–3; italics added.

22. Smith, *Teachings of the Prophet Joseph Smith,* pp. 268–69; compare Zechariah 14.

23. Joseph Fielding Smith, *Doctrines of Salvation,* 3 vols., comp. Bruce R. McConkie (Salt Lake City: Bookcraft, 1954–56), 1:86.

24. McConkie, *The Millennial Messiah,* p. 652.

25. Ibid., p. 196.

26. Smith, *Teachings of the Prophet Joseph Smith,* p. 268.

27. See ibid., p. 328; *Orson Pratt's Works* (Salt Lake City: Parker Pratt Robison, 1965), pp. 46–48.

28. McConkie, *The Millennial Messiah,* pp. 673–74.

29. Smith, *Teachings of the Prophet Joseph Smith,* p. 149.

CHAPTER 16

Growing in the Pure Love of Christ

A fundamental part of gospel living is love—love for God and love for our fellowman. Those who come out of the world into the true Church, forsake their sins, and take upon themselves the name of Christ, covenant to live a life consistent with the doctrines and principles espoused and exemplified by the Master. They covenant to be Christians. They covenant to love. To those who have gotten onto the strait and narrow path that leads to eternal life, Nephi counsels: "Wherefore, ye must press forward with a steadfastness in Christ, having a perfect brightness of hope, and *a love of God and of all men*. Wherefore, if ye shall press forward, feasting upon the word of Christ, and endure to the end, behold, thus saith the Father: Ye shall have eternal life" (2 Nephi 31:20; italics added). In this single phrase, "love of God," we see both divine and human initiative.

GOD'S LOVE FOR US

Godlike love begins with and centers in and emanates from God. The Apostle John wrote that "God is love; and he that dwelleth in love dwelleth in God, and God in him" (1 John 4:16). Our Heavenly Father and his Only Begotten Son, Jesus Christ, possess in perfection all of the attributes of godliness, including charity. They love purely, absolutely, and perfectly. Moroni, speaking to the Savior, said: "And again, I remember that thou hast said that thou hast loved the world, even unto the laying down of thy life for the world, that thou mightest take it again to prepare a place for the children of men. And now I know that *this love that thou hast had for the children of men is charity*" (Ether 12:33–34; italics added). Pure love comes from a pure source, from God. It begins with God, is extended by him to man, and sheds "itself abroad in the hearts of the children of men" (1 Nephi 11:22). As we shall see, we are able to love others purely only as we seek for and partake of the love of God ourselves. As the Prophet Joseph Smith explained, "Love is one of the chief characteristics of Deity, and ought to be manifested by those who aspire to be the sons of God."[1] One of the greatest evidences of the Father's love for us is in the gift of his Beloved Son. The prophet Nephi, having desired to receive the same manifestation that his father, Lehi, had been given, was shown a vision of a rod of iron, a strait and narrow path, and a large and spacious building. In addition, he beheld a tree whose beauty was "far beyond, yea, exceeding of all beauty; and the whiteness thereof did exceed the whiteness of the driven snow" (1 Nephi 11:8). Lehi had explained that the fruit "was most sweet, above all that [he] ever before tasted." Further, "it filled [his] soul with exceedingly great joy" (1 Nephi 8:11–12). Nephi concluded from his visionary experience that the tree represented "the love of God, which sheddeth itself abroad in the hearts of the children of men; wherefore, it is the most desirable above all things." Nephi's guide, an angel, added, "Yea, and the most joyous to the soul" (1 Nephi 11:22–23).

It is worth noting that earlier in this same chapter the Spirit had asked Nephi, "Believest thou that thy father saw the tree of which he has spoken?" Nephi answered, "Yea, thou knowest that I believe all the words of my father." And then the Spirit exulted: "Hosanna to the Lord, the most high God; for he is God over all the earth, yea, even above all. And *blessed art thou, Nephi, because thou believest in the Son of the most high God.* . . . And behold," the Spirit continued, "this thing shall be given unto thee for *a sign,* that after thou hast beheld *the tree* which bore the fruit which thy father tasted, thou shalt also behold *a man* descending out of heaven, and him shall ye witness; and after ye have witnessed him *ye shall bear record that it is the Son of God"* (1 Nephi 11:4–7; italics added). This tree was more than an abstract principle, more than a vague, albeit divine, sentiment. The tree was a doctrinal symbol, a "sign" of an even greater reality—a type of him whose branches provide shade from the scorching rays of sin and ignorance. This was a messianic message, a poignant prophecy of him toward whom all men and women press on that path leading eventually to life eternal. Truly God the Father "so loved the world, that he gave his only begotten Son, that whosoever believeth in him should not perish, but have everlasting life" (John 3:16; compare 1 John 4:9; D&C 34:3).

OUR LOVE FOR GOD

John the Beloved observed that we love God because he first loved us (see 1 John 4:10, 19). "To love God with all your heart, soul, mind, and strength," President Ezra Taft Benson has taught, "is all-consuming and all-encompassing. . . . The breadth, depth, and height of this love of God extend into every facet of one's life. Our desires, be they spiritual or temporal, should be rooted in a love of the Lord."[2] As we live in a manner that allows the Spirit to be with us regularly, we begin to see things as they really are. Our love for God grows as we begin to sense his goodness to us, as we become aware of his involvement in our lives, and as we begin to acknowledge his hand in all that is noble and good and worthy.

There are times when our love for God is almost consuming. Such feelings may come in prayer as we sense through the Spirit a closeness to the Almighty. Sometimes such feelings of gratitude come as we sing "Because I Have Been Given Much," "I Stand All Amazed," "How Great Thou Art" (*Hymns,* 1985, nos. 219, 193, 86), or any number of hymns that allow our souls to express praise or thanksgiving. Sometimes a love of the Lord burns within us as we hear and feel the power of the word as it is preached by one who does so under the direction of the Holy Ghost. As we feel charity in the form of a pure love for the Lord, we may, like Alma, feel to "sing the song of redeeming love" (Alma 5:26). To sing the song of redeeming love is to joy in the matchless majesty of God's goodness, to know the wonder of his love. It is to sense and know that the Lord is intimately involved with his children and that he cares, really cares, about their well-being. Jacob surely sang the song of redeeming love when he exulted in the wisdom of God, the greatness and justice of God, the mercy of God, the goodness of God, and the holiness of God (see 2 Nephi 9).

Elder George F. Richards sought to explain the ineffable sense of love and gratitude that one can feel for his Lord and Savior: "More than forty years ago I had a dream which I am sure was from the Lord. In this dream I was in the presence of my Savior as he stood in mid-air. He spoke no word to me, but *my love for him was such that I have not words to explain. I know that no mortal man can love the Lord as I experienced that love for the Savior unless God reveals it to him.* I would have remained in his presence, but there was a power drawing me away from him. As a result of that dream, I had this feeling that no matter what might be required of my hands, what the gospel might entail unto me, I would do what I should be asked to do even to the laying down of my life. . . .

If only I can be with my Savior and have that same sense of love that I had in that dream, it will be the goal of my existence, the desire of my life."³ In that same spirit, Joseph Smith explained that following his first vision, "my soul was filled with love, and for many days I could rejoice with great joy, and the Lord was with me."⁴

It is not only those who have seen the Lord and have enjoyed a personal appearance, dream, or vision who feel the desire to sing the song of redeeming love. All those who have had the burdens of sin, the weight of guilt, and the agonies of bitterness, hostility, or pain removed by the Great Physician shout praises to the Holy One of Israel. They know that pure love of Christ. Nephi wrote: "My God hath been my support; he hath led me through mine afflictions in the wilderness; and he hath preserved me upon the waters of the great deep. He hath filled me with his love, even unto the consuming of my flesh" (2 Nephi 4:20–21). And perhaps nowhere in holy writ do we find a more glorious expression of love and gratitude and praise of the Almighty than in the words of Ammon, son of Mosiah. "Blessed be the name of our God," he exulted to his brothers following the miraculous conversion of thousands of Lamanites; "let us sing to his praise, yea, let us give thanks to his holy name, for he doth work righteousness forever. . . . Yea, we have reason to praise him forever, for he is the Most High God, and has loosed our brethren from the chains of hell. . . . Behold, who can glory too much in the Lord? Yea, who can say too much of his great power, and of his mercy, and of his long-suffering towards the children of men? Behold, I say unto you, I cannot say the smallest part which I feel" (Alma 26:8, 14, 16).

OUR LOVE FOR OTHERS

One dramatic evidence of apostasy in the world today is a growing sense of indifference toward and among the sons and daughters of God. "Because iniquity shall abound," the Savior taught before his death, "the love of men shall wax cold" (Joseph Smith—Matthew 1:30; compare D&C 45:27). "It is one evidence," the Prophet Joseph Smith explained, "that men are unacquainted with the principles of godliness to behold the contraction of affectionate feelings and lack of charity in the world." On the other hand, those who come unto Christ become as Christ. They partake of his divine nature, receive his attributes, and come to love as he loves. *"The nearer we get to our Heavenly Father,"* the modern seer went on to say, *"the more we are disposed to look with compassion on perishing souls; we feel that we want to take them upon our shoulders, and cast their sins behind our backs."*[5]

Ethical deeds, works of faith, acts of kindness toward others—these are so much more effective and pure when grounded in the love of Deity, when the source of the goodness is the Holy One. As we begin to become new creatures in Christ, we begin to serve out of proper motives. Nephi wrote that the Lord does not do anything "save it be for the benefit of the world; for he loveth the world, even that he layeth down his own life that he may draw all men unto him." He then asked: "Hath he commanded any that they should not partake of his salvation? Behold I say unto you, Nay; but he hath given it free for all men." Nephi then explained that it must be on the basis of this same motivation—this charity, or "pure love of Christ"—that the people of the Lord labor in order for Zion to be established. Those who practice priestcraft, he observed, "preach and set themselves up for a light unto the world, that they may get gain and praise of the world; but they seek not the welfare of Zion." It is in this context that we learn of charity as the antidote to priestcraft, the preventive medicine and the solution to improper or perverted desires: "The Lord God hath given a commandment that all men should have charity, which charity is love. And except they should have charity they were nothing. Wherefore, if they should have charity they would not suffer the laborer in Zion to perish. But the laborer in Zion shall labor for Zion; for if they labor for money they shall perish" (2 Nephi 26:24–31).

Both Mormon (see Moroni 7:45–48) and Paul (see 1 Corinthians 13:1–13) wrote of charity as the greatest of all the fruits of the Spirit, the one that shall endure forever. Both of them described the charitable person as one who:

1. *Suffers long, bears all things.* He or she is endowed with a portion of the love of God and thus, to some degree, with the patience and perspective of God toward people and circumstances. Their vision of here and now (the present) is greatly affected by their glimpse of there and then (the future). It was by means of this pure love of Christ, which followed their spiritual rebirth (Mosiah 28:3), that Alma and the sons of

234

Mosiah were able to bear the burdens that were placed upon them, even persecution and rejection.

2. *Is kind.* Charity motivates to goodness, to benevolence and sensitivity toward the needs of others. People are their business. It was by means of this pure love of Christ that Ammon, son of Mosiah, was able to extend himself, kindly and lovingly, in the service of Lamoni and his household, to win their hearts, and to be an instrument in their conversion to the truths of the gospel (see Alma 17–19).

3. *Envies not.* Those who love the Lord and are filled with his love are much less prone to concern themselves with the acquisitions or accolades of others. Their joy is full in Christ (see D&C 101:36). They find happiness in simple pleasures and delight in God's goodness to them. It is by means of this pure love of Christ, this anchor to the soul, that people are able to ignore the tauntings and temptations of those who chant and proselyte from the great and spacious building (see 1 Nephi 8).

4. *Is not puffed up, seeks not his or her own.* The charitable person seeks diligently to turn attention away from self and toward God. He or she eagerly acknowledges the hand of the Lord in all things and is hesitant to take personal credit for accomplishments. Such a one is void of pride. Mormon spoke of a time when many of the Nephites were lifted up in pride, so much so that they proved a major stumbling block to the Church, and the Church began to fail in its progress. At the same time, in this day of inequality and wickedness, there were others who, filled with the love of God, were "abasing themselves, succoring those who stood in need of their succor, such as imparting their substance to the poor and the needy, feeding the hungry, and suffering all manner of afflictions, for Christ's sake, who should come according to the spirit of prophecy" (Alma 4:13).

5. *Is not easily provoked.* Those filled with the love of Christ are meek; theirs is a quiet but pervasive poise under provocation. Because the Lord has begun to remake their hearts, they do not experience anger and thus do not express it. Because of their trust in the Almighty and because of the power and perspective of the love that flows from him, Alma and Amulek were able to bear viewing the hideous scene of women and children being sent to the flames because of their acceptance of the truth. Like their Master would do over a century later on

another hemisphere, they stood with meek majesty before the tauntings and assaults of the unholy (see Alma 14).

6. *Thinks no evil.* Their minds are on things of righteousness, their desires directed toward that which builds and strengthens and encourages. They have no secret agenda, no private yearnings for personal aggrandizement, only a heart focused on the Lord and his kingdom. "Behold," Nephi declared, "my soul delighteth in the things of the Lord; and my heart pondereth continually upon the things which I have seen and heard" (2 Nephi 4:16).

7. *Rejoices not in iniquity, but rejoices in the truth.* The charitable person is repulsed by sin, though anxious to fellowship and lift the sinner; is pained by the waywardness of the world; and labors tirelessly to extend gospel assistance to those who stray from the path of peace. At the same time, this person delights in the Spirit, in goodness, and in noble accomplishments and discoveries, no matter the source. Filled with a portion of the Lord's love, this person, like the people of Benjamin, has no more disposition to do evil but rather to do good continually (see Mosiah 5:2). Though possessed with love for the wayward, he or she cannot look upon sin save it be with abhorrence (see Alma 13:12).

8. *Believes all things.* It is not that one possessed of charity is naive or gullible, simply open to truth. He or she enjoys the spiritual gift of a believing heart and has little or no difficulty in accepting the words and following the counsel of those called to direct the destiny of the Church. Because charitable persons are believing in nature, all things work together for their good (see D&C 90:24). Like Sam, son of Lehi, the charitable person readily believes on the testimony of one who knows (see 1 Nephi 2:17; compare D&C 46:13–14).

9. *Hopes all things.* Theirs is a hope in Christ, a quiet but dynamic assurance that, first, even though one is imperfect, he or she is on a course pleasing to the Lord and that, second, eternal life is at the end of the path. "What is it that ye shall hope for?" Mormon asked the humble followers of Christ. "Behold I say unto you that ye shall have hope through the atonement of Christ and the power of his resurrection, to be raised unto life eternal" (Moroni 7:41).

10. *Endures all things.* No matter what the true follower of Christ is required to pass through, he or she proceeds as called. Neither the

shame of the world nor the threat of physical death can deter one who is bent upon enjoying the love of God everlastingly. "If ye shall press forward, Nephi wrote, "feasting upon the word of Christ, and endure to the end, behold, thus saith the Father: Ye shall have eternal life" (2 Nephi 31:20).

The greatest acts of charity come through the giving of oneself. Though there are times when presentations of money or food or material goods will meet a pressing need, the enduring need for sacrifice of self remains. "Never did the Savior give in expectation," President Spencer W. Kimball explained.

> I know of no case in his life in which there was an exchange. He was always the giver, seldom the recipient. Never did he give shoes, hose, or a vehicle; never did he give perfume, a shirt, or a fur wrap. His gifts were of such a nature that the recipient could hardly exchange or return the value. His gifts were rare ones: eyes to the blind, ears to the deaf, and legs to the lame; cleanliness to the unclean, wholeness to the infirm, and breath to the lifeless. His gifts were opportunity to the downtrodden, freedom to the oppressed, light in the darkness, forgiveness to the repentant, hope to the despairing. His friends gave him shelter, food, and love. He gave them of himself, his love, his service, his life. The wise men brought him gold and frankincense. He gave them and all their fellow mortals resurrection, salvation, and eternal life. We should strive to give as he gave. To give of oneself is a holy gift.[6]

It should go without saying that disciples of Christ ought to love one another. They have in common those things that matter most in life. Their view of reality, their goals and ambitions, their hopes and dreams for here and hereafter—all these things they share with members of the Church far and wide. They are welded together, clothed in the bond of charity, that mantle "which is the bond of perfectness and peace" (D&C 88:125). The expression of the love of God is not to be limited, however, to the household of faith (see D&C 121:45). We have a duty beyond the fold as well, and the Holy Spirit, which is the source of pure love, expands our vision to see and feel as we ought. Joseph Smith said: "A man filled with the love of God is not content with blessing his family alone, but ranges through the whole world, anxious to bless the whole human race."[7] On another occasion the Prophet declared: "There is a love from God that should be exercised toward those of our faith, who walk uprightly, which is peculiar to itself, but it is without prejudice; *it also gives scope to the mind, which enables us to conduct ourselves with greater liberality towards all that are not of our faith, than what they exercise towards one another. These principles approximate nearer to the mind of God, because it is like God, or Godlike."*[8] President Ezra Taft Benson thus observed that "we must develop a love for people. Our hearts must go out to them in the pure love of the gospel, in a desire to lift them, to build them up, to point them to a higher, finer, life and eventually to exaltation in the celestial kingdom of God."[9]

The Book of Mormon provides a companion witness of the eternal fact that love of man is vitally related to love of God, that when we are in the service of our fellow beings we are only in the service of our God (see Mosiah 2:17). President Harold B. Lee related a personal experience that brought this truth home to him in a powerful manner: "Just before the dedication of the Los Angeles Temple, something new happened in my life when, along about three or four o'clock in the morning, I enjoyed an experience that I think was not a dream, but it must have been a vision. It seemed that I was witnessing a great spiritual gathering, where men and women were standing up, two or three at a time, and speaking in tongues. The spirit was so unusual. I seemed to hear the voice of President David O. McKay say, 'If you want to love God, you have to learn to love and serve the people. That is the way to show your love for God.' "[10]

Indeed, the Book of Mormon writers affirm that service is essential to salvation. Benjamin taught that caring for the temporal and spiritual needs of the poor, for example, was inextricably tied to receiving the full blessings of the atonement of Christ. Having witnessed the marvelous manner in which the Spirit of the Lord pricked the hearts of those who hearkened to the words of his sermon; having listened as they called upon the name of the Lord for forgiveness of sin; having observed the people as their souls were transformed from guilt and remorse to joy and peace and love, Benjamin then explained how the Saints are enabled through service to remain clean before God. "And now, *for the sake of . . . retaining a remission of your sins from day to day,* that ye may walk guiltless before God—I would that *ye should impart of your substance to the poor,* every man according to that which he hath, such as feeding the hungry, clothing the naked, visiting the sick and administering to their relief, both spiritually and temporally, according to their wants" (Mosiah 4:26; italics added). Mormon likewise spoke of a time in the days of Alma when the Saints were "abasing themselves, succoring those who stood in need of their succor, such as imparting their substance to the poor and the needy, . . . thus retaining a remission of their sins" (Alma 4:13–14).

OBSTACLES TO CHARITY

Because charity is so vital to the perfection of human nature and the growth of the kingdom of God, Satan labors incessantly to establish barriers or obstacles to the receipt and practice of this highest of spiritual endowments. There are things that get in the way, that dam the flow of love from God to man, from man to God, and from man to man. Some of these include:

1. *Preoccupation with self.* One who is preoccupied with self is unable to feel the pure love of Christ and, by extension, to extend that love to others. "The final and crowning virtue of the divine character," President Ezra Taft Benson explained, "is charity, or the pure love of Christ" (see Moroni 7:47). "If we would truly seek to be more like our Savior and Master, learning to love as He loves should be our highest goal. . . . The world today speaks a great deal about love, and it is sought for by many. But the pure love of Christ differs greatly from what the world thinks of love. Charity never seeks selfish gratification. The pure love of Christ seeks only the eternal growth and joy of others."[11] The Savior's commission to "love thy neighbor as thyself" has little to do with loving oneself; it has much to do with loving others as one would desire to be loved, to fulfill the Golden Rule as given by the Master in the sermon at Galilee and at Bountiful (see Matthew 14:12; 3 Nephi 14:12). There is no divine directive to spend time developing self-love or becoming obsessed with self-esteem. Rather, the irony of the ages is to be found in the principle that only as one loses his life does he find it (see Matthew 16:25).

2. *Dishonesty.* Only as we open ourselves to the truth, strive to know the truth, and then live in harmony with that truth can we grow in godlike love. In Dostoyevski's classic work *The Brothers Karamazov*, Zossima says to Feodor:

> A man who lies to himself and who listens to his own lies gets to
> a point where he can't distinguish any truth in himself or in those

around him, and so loses all respect for himself and for others. Having no respect for anyone, he ceases to love, and to occupy and distract himself without love. He becomes a prey to his passions and gives himself up to coarse pleasures, . . . and all this from continual lying to people and to himself. A man who lies to himself can be more easily offended than anyone else. For it is sometimes very pleasant to take offense, isn't it? And yet he knows that no one has offended him and that he has invented the offense himself, that he has lied just for the beauty of it, that he has exaggerated just to make himself look big and important, that he has fastened on a phrase and made a mountain out of a molehill—he knows it all and yet is the first to take offense, he finds pleasure in it and feels mightily satisfied with himself, and so reaches the point of real enmity.[12]

On the other hand, those persons who, like Helaman's two thousand stripling warriors, are true at all times to themselves, to their values, to their witness, and to others (see Alma 53:20) come to know that true love that emanates from God and feel the need to be true to him. Of the Ammonites, the Nephite record states that they were "distinguished for their zeal towards God, and also towards men; for *they were perfectly honest and upright in all things*." Now note what follows: "And they were firm in the faith of Christ, even unto the end" (Alma 27:27; italics added).

3. *Immorality*. Wickedness weakens love. Surely if godlike love is a fruit of the Spirit and bestowed as a result of faithfulness, then continuing in sin prevents one from receiving and giving such love. Sexual immorality, for example, prostitutes those God-given powers that are so intimately connected with the fountains of human life. Thus sexual expression outside the bonds of marriage estranges rather than builds and strengthens. Lust is a pitiful substitute for pure love, that expression and commitment that bind and seal throughout time and eternity. Jacob chastened his people, particularly the fathers and husbands, for their infidelity. "Ye have broken the hearts of your tender wives, and lost the confidence of your children," he said, "because of your bad examples before them; and the sobbings of their hearts ascend up to God against you" (Jacob 2:35). The people of God are thus commanded to bridle all their passions so that they may be filled with love (see Alma 38:12).

4. *Harshness, crudeness, and insensitivity*. Though not mentioned specifically in the Book of Mormon as obstacles to charity, these vices

do much to deaden mankind to things of worth. It is not just the blatant immorality on the screen, in books, and in the lyrics of modern music that prove to be soul destroying. Man's inhumanity to man in the form of bitter sarcasm, perpetual insults, and the increasing fascination with brutality and violence works upon the heart and mind to desensitize people to people and to those sweet feelings of tenderness and gentility that encourage and evidence love. Whenever the crude, the rough, or the harsh characterize language and interpersonal relations in any given culture, then the people of that culture are on the high road to destruction: they are offending and alienating the Spirit of the Lord. The Book of Mormon prophets stressed again and again that hardened hearts are simply unable to perceive and then receive the quiet whisperings of the Spirit (see 2 Nephi 33:2; Alma 13:4; 40:13). In time, what love they do have will be lost, and their crudeness will be transformed and translated into perversion and murder. They shall become like the Nephites who, within four centuries after the coming of Christ, were described by Mormon as being "without civilization," "without order and without mercy," "without principle and past feeling" (Moroni 9:11, 18, 20). "For the Spirit of the Lord will not always strive with man. And when the Spirit ceaseth to strive with man then cometh speedy destruction" (2 Nephi 26:11; compare Helaman 13:8; Ether 2:15).

CHARITY AS A FRUIT OF THE SPIRIT

Charity is a fruit of the Spirit. It is bestowed by God. One does not "work on" his charity any more than he might work on his prophecy, dreams, visions, or discernment. Charity is that "more excellent way" (see 1 Corinthians 12:31) that comes by and through the Holy Ghost as one of the gifts of God. It is true that we have a responsibility to give of ourselves in service to others as a part of our covenantal obligation as Christians (see Mosiah 18:8–10; James 2:8). It is true that service is essential to salvation. But service and charity are not necessarily the same. Charity is "the highest, noblest, strongest kind of love, not merely affection; the pure love of Christ. It is never used to denote alms or deeds or benevolence, although it may be a prompting motive" (LDS Bible Dictionary, s.v. "Charity," p. 632). Charity is a fruit of the Spirit that motivates us to greater goodness, specifically greater service and compassion for others. In a manner of speaking, we can serve people without loving them, but we cannot truly love them (as the Lord does) without serving them. Bruce C. Hafen has written: "Our own internally generated compassion for the needs of others is a crucial indication of our desire to be followers of the Savior. . . . For that reason, we must be reaching out to others even as we reach out to God, rather than waiting to respond to others' needs until our charitable instincts are quickened by the Spirit. But even then, charity in its full-blown sense is 'bestowed upon' Christ's righteous followers. Its source, like all other blessings of the Atonement, is the grace of God."[13]

When Benjamin challenged his people (and us) to be spiritually reborn, to put off the natural man and become a saint through the atonement of Christ, he further instructed us to become as little children—"submissive, meek, humble, patient, *full of love,* willing to submit to all things which the Lord seeth fit to inflict" upon us (Mosiah 3:19; italics added). Likewise, Alma warned the people of Ammonihah against procrastination: "Humble yourselves before the Lord, and call on his holy name, and watch and pray continually, that ye may not be tempted above that which ye can bear, *and thus be led by the Holy Spirit, becoming humble, meek, submissive, patient, full of love and all long-suffering;* having faith on the Lord; having a hope that ye shall receive eternal life; *having the love of God always in your hearts,* that ye may be lifted up at the last day and enter into his rest" (Alma 13:28; italics added).

It is, of course, Mormon who provides the clearest scriptural statement as to how to acquire charity. "Wherefore, my beloved brethren," he writes, *"pray unto the Father with all the energy of heart, that ye may be filled with this love,* which he hath bestowed upon all who are true followers of his Son, Jesus Christ; that ye may become the sons of God; that when he shall appear we shall be like him, for we shall see him as he is; that we may have this hope; that we may be purified even as he is pure" (Moroni 7:48; italics added). We see from this profound pronouncement, then, that the purpose of charity is not just to motivate us to Christian service (as important as that is), but also to sanctify us from sin and prepare us to be not only with God but like him (see Ether 12:34). In Mormon's words, those who become sons and daughters of Jesus Christ by applying the atoning blood of the Savior and having been born again as to the things of righteousness are the ones upon whom the Lord bestows this gift.

President George Q. Cannon spoke of the failure of the Latter-day Saints to seek after the fruits and gifts of the Spirit. "We find, even among those who have embraced the Gospel," he observed, "hearts of unbelief."

> How many of you, my brethren and sisters, are seeking for these gifts that God has promised to bestow? How many of you, when you bow before your Heavenly Father in your family circle or in your secret places, contend for these gifts to be bestowed upon you? How many of you ask the Father, in the name of Jesus, to manifest Himself to you through these powers and these gifts? Or do you go along day by day like a door turning on its hinges, without having any feeling on the subject, without exercising any faith whatever; content to be baptized and be members of the Church, and to rest there, thinking that your salvation is secure because you have done this? I say to you, in the name of the Lord, as one of His servants, that you have need to repent of this. You have need to repent of your hardness of heart, of your indifference, and of your careless-ness. There is not that diligence, there is not that faith, there is not that seeking for the power of God that there should be among a people who have received the precious promises we have. . . . I say to you that it is our duty to avail ourselves of the privileges which God has placed within our reach. . . .
>
> I feel to bear testimony to you, my brethren and sisters, . . . that God is the same today as He was yesterday; that God is willing to bestow these gifts upon His children. . . . If any of us are imperfect, it is our duty to pray for the gift that will make us perfect. *Have I imperfections? I am full of them. What is my duty? To pray to God to give me the gifts that will correct these imperfections. If I am an angry man, it is my duty to pray for charity, which suffereth long and is kind. Am I an envious man? It is my duty to seek for charity, which envieth not. So with all the gifts of the Gospel.* They are intended for this purpose. No man ought to say, "Oh, I cannot help this; it is my nature." He is not justified in it, for the reason that God has promised to give strength to correct these things, and to give gifts that will eradicate them. If a man lack wisdom, it is his duty to ask God for wisdom. The same with everything else. That is the design of God concern-ing His Church. He wants His Saints to be perfected in the truth. For this purpose He gives these gifts, and bestows them upon those who seek after them, in order that they may be a perfect people upon the face of the earth, notwithstanding their many weaknesses, because

God has promised to give the gifts that are necessary for their perfection.[14]

The Spirit of God sanctifies—it cleanses and purges the human heart. The Spirit does far more, however, than remove uncleanness. It also fills. It fills one with a holy element, with a sacred presence that motivates to a godly walk and goodly works. Such persons filled with the Holy Ghost (and with charity) do not necessarily plan out how they will perform the works of righteousness; they do not always plot and design which deeds and what actions are to be done in every situation. Rather, they embody righteousness. They are goodness. Good works flow from a regenerate heart and evidence their commitment to their Lord and Master. Yes, these persons do have agency. Indeed, they are free, because they have given themselves up to the Lord and his purposes. They choose to do good, but their choices are motivated by the Spirit of the Lord. They live in a world of turmoil but are at peace. They may exist in a society steeped in anxiety and uncertainty, but they are at rest. They may live among persons on all sides who are frightened, but they are secure, for charity, or perfect love, casts out all fear (see Moroni 8:16; 1 John 4:18).

So where do we go from here? We have discussed the ideal. We have seen that the prophets and the Lord challenge us to see to it that our labors are motivated by the pure love of Christ. But what do we do if for the time being our motives for service are less than the highest? Of course we are to strive to do what is right, even if our hearts have not been fully changed. Of course we are to do our home and visiting teaching, even if our motivation for now is more in terms of inspection than divine expectation and spontaneous service. Saints cannot remain stagnant. They cannot sit idly by while others perform the labors of the kingdom. They certainly are not justified in doing wrong because they are as yet unregenerated. At the same time, our task is to seek regularly and consistently for that Spirit which gives life and light and substance and consequence to our deeds. Our assignment is not to run faster than we have strength, to labor harder than we have means, or to be truer than true. Our zeal for righteousness must always be tempered and appropriate and must be accompanied with wisdom. Zion is established "in process of time" (Moses 7:21), and with but few exceptions, the pure in heart become so in like manner. In short, we do the work of the kingdom, but we pray constantly for a purification of our motives and a sanctification of our desires.

CHARITY AS A KEY TO ENDURING TO THE END

The Apostle Peter taught that charity prevents a multitude of sins (see JST, 1 Peter 4:8). It is not just that one filled with charity is too busy to sin. Rather, the possession of charity is an evidence of the presence and enduring influence of the Holy Ghost, that moral monitor given by the Father to warn, reprove, correct, prick, sanctify, encourage, and comfort. Mormon taught that charity provides the spiritual strength and fortitude that enable one to endure faithfully to the end. "The first fruits of repentance is baptism," he taught; "and baptism cometh by faith unto the fulfilling the commandments; and the fulfilling the commandments bringeth remission of sins; and the remission of sins bringeth meekness, and lowliness of heart; and because of meekness and lowliness of heart cometh *the visitation of the Holy Ghost, which Comforter filleth with hope and perfect love, which love endureth by diligence unto prayer, until the end shall come, when all the saints shall dwell with God"* (Moroni 8:25–26; italics added). Stated simply, remission of sins brings the influence of the Comforter, which in turn brings the gifts and fruit of the Spirit, preeminent among which is charity. And charity enables us to endure faithfully to the end. Perhaps this is what Joseph Smith meant when he said: *"Until we have perfect love we are liable to fall and when we have a testimony that our names are sealed in the Lamb's book of life we have perfect love and then it is impossible for false Christs to deceive us."*[15] Those who possess charity are less prone to have their heads turned by the allurements of a fallen world, less willing to loosen their grasp of the iron rod, on things of enduring worth, in order to embrace the trappings of Babylon. There are but few things we may depend on with absolute assurance. Elder Jeffrey R. Holland observed:

> Life has its share of some fear and some failure. Sometimes things fall short, don't quite measure up. Sometimes in both personal and public life, we are seemingly left without strength to go on. Sometimes people fail us, or economics and circumstance fail us, and life with its hardship and heartache can leave us feeling very alone.
>
> But when such difficult moments come to us, I testify that there is one thing which will never, ever fail us. One thing alone will stand the test of all time, of all tribulation, all trouble, and all trans-

gression. One thing only never faileth—and that is the pure love of Christ. . . .

"If ye have not charity, ye are nothing" (Moroni 7:46). Only the pure love of Christ will see us through. It is Christ's love which suffereth long, and is kind. It is Christ's love which is not puffed up nor easily provoked. Only his pure love enables him—and us—to bear all things, believe all things, hope all things, and endure all things. (See Moroni 7:45.)[16]

Indeed, as Mormon and Paul wrote, charity endures forever. It never fails (see Moroni 7:46–47; 1 Corinthians 13:8). Though there may come a day when such gifts of the Spirit as prophecy or tongues or knowledge will have served their useful function, charity—the pure love of Christ—will still be in operation, burning brightly in the hearts and souls of the sons and daughters of Almighty God. "When that which is perfect is come" (1 Corinthians 13: 10), the true followers of Jesus Christ will have become like unto him who is the embodiment of love. They will be filled with charity, which is everlasting love (see Moroni 8:17).

CONCLUSION

I have come to believe that the Lord's barometer of righteousness is the heart. No matter the depth of our knowledge, the efficiency of our administration, the charisma with which we influence and lead people—no matter how well we do what we do, of much greater significance in the eternal scheme of things is who we are and what we feel toward God and toward our fellowman. It is so easy to be distracted from what matters most, to focus on things—on goals, on excellence programs, on statistics—when in reality it is people that counts. I am convinced that people are more important than goals, more important than private or corporative endeavors. People are more important than the attainment of some form of success. God is in the business of people. And so must we be.

In summary, we do not come to love as the Lord loves merely because we work hard at it. True it is that we must serve others and concern ourselves with others' needs more than with our own. And true it is that the disciple is expected to bear the burdens and take up the cross of Christian fellowship. But that service and outreach cannot have lasting impact, nor can it result in the quiet peace and rest in the giver, unless and until it is motivated from on high. We come to know the cleansing and regenerating power of our Savior only through acknowledging our fallen nature, calling upon Him who is mighty to save, and, in the language of the Book of Mormon prophets, relying wholly upon his merits and mercy and grace (see 2 Nephi 2:8; 31:19; Moroni 6:4). That forgiveness which comes from Christ evidences and conveys his perfect love, and, in process of time, empowers us to love in like manner.

We must pray for forgiveness, for cleansing, for reconciliation with the Father through the Son. And we must pray for charity. We must plead for it. We must ask with all the energy of heart to be so endowed. As we do so, I testify that there will come moments of surpassing import, sublime moments that matter, moments in which our whole souls seem to reach out to others with a kind of fellowship and affection that we would not otherwise know. I have felt that love. I have tasted of its sweet fruit. It is beyond anything earthly, above and beyond anything that mortal man can explain or produce. One of the greatest regrets of my life is that such moments do not come with the regularity and frequency that I would desire.

Such love settles the hearts of individuals. It provides moral courage to those who must face difficult challenges. It unites and seals husbands, wives, and children and grants them a foretaste of eternal life. It welds classes and congregations and wards and stakes in a union that is the foundation for that "highest order of priesthood society" we know as Zion.[17] And, once again, it comes from that Lord who is the Source of all that is godlike. To the degree that we trust in that Lord and yield our hearts unto him (see Helaman 3:35), "I am persuaded," with the Apostle Paul, "that neither death, nor life, nor angels, nor principalities, nor powers, nor things present, nor things to come, nor height, nor depth, nor any other creature, shall be able to separate us from the love of God, which is in Christ Jesus our Lord" (Romans 8:38–39).

NOTES

1. Joseph Smith, *Teachings of the Prophet Joseph Smith,* sel. Joseph Fielding Smith (Salt Lake City: Deseret Book Co., 1976), p. 174.

2. Ezra Taft Benson, *Teachings of Ezra Taft Benson* (Salt Lake City: Bookcraft, 1988), p. 349.

3. George F. Richards, cited by Spencer W. Kimball in Conference Report, April 1974, pp. 173–74; italics added.

4. Joseph Smith, from 1832 account, in Milton V. Backman, Jr., *Joseph Smith's First Vision* (Salt Lake City: Bookcraft, 1971), p. 157.

5. Smith, *Teachings of the Prophet Joseph Smith,* pp. 240–41; italics added.

6. Spencer W. Kimball, *Teachings of Spencer W. Kimball* (Salt Lake City: Bookcraft, 1982), pp. 246–47.

7. Smith, *Teachings of the Prophet Joseph Smith,* p. 174.

8. Ibid., p. 147; italics added.

9. Ezra Taft Benson, *Come Unto Christ* (Salt Lake City: Deseret Book Co., 1983), p. 96.

10. David O. McKay, *Stand Ye in Holy Places* (Salt Lake City: Deseret Book Co., 1974), p. 189.

11. Ezra Taft Benson, *Teachings of Ezra Taft Benson,* p. 275.

12. Fyodor Dostoyevski, *The Brothers Karamazov* (Garden City, New York: Literary Guild of America, 1953), p. 47.

13. Bruce C. Hafen, *The Broken Heart* (Salt Lake City: Deseret Book Co., 1989), pp. 195–96.

14. *Millennial Star,* vol. 56 [1894], pp. 260–61; italics added.

15. Smith, *Teachings of the Prophet Joseph Smith,* p. 9.

16. Jeffrey R. Holland, in Conference Report, October 1989, pp. 32–33.

17. See Spencer W. Kimball, Conference Report, October 1977, p. 125; compare 4 Nephi 1:15.

The Salvation of Little Children

The eighth chapter of Moroni contains an epistle of Mormon, written to his son, Moroni, soon after Moroni's call to the ministry. The epistle begins with Mormon's encouragement and his expression of confidence in his son. "I am mindful of you always in my prayers," Mormon declares, "continually praying unto God the Father in the name of his Holy Child, Jesus, that he, through his infinite goodness and grace, will keep you through the endurance of faith on his name to the end" (Moroni 8:3). But this epistle was not written solely as an expression of a father's satisfaction on behalf of a faithful son. Rather, Mormon had learned of disputations among the Nephites concerning the baptism of little children. His letter was a powerful appeal to root out and remove such heresy from among the Saints, as well as an explanation as to why such doctrine was abominable and abhorrent to that Lord who loves little children perfectly.

Nephi beheld in vision that because plain and precious truths would be taken away or kept back from the earliest biblical records, "an exceedingly great many" people would stumble and fall, and many thereby would wander in doctrinal darkness, eventually becoming subject to the snares of Satan (1 Nephi 13:20–42). Some of the most critical verities of salvation to be lifted or twisted from their pristine purity are the truths dealing with the Creation, the Fall, and the Atonement. If by no other means than by virtue of the clarity and power in which these doctrines are proclaimed and stressed in the Book of Mormon and the Joseph Smith Translation of the Bible, we know that such matters were taught more plainly in the early ages of this world. A misunderstanding of the nature of the fall of Adam, for example, has led to some of the most serious heresies and perversions in religious history. Without the exalting knowledge of such matters as the Fall as a foreordained act, a God-inspired and predesigned plan for the perpetuation and preservation of the human family—parent to the atonement of Christ—men and women struggle helplessly to find meaning in the involvement of our first parents in Eden. Others allegorize or spiritualize away the plain meanings of the scriptures regarding the Fall and thus cloud in mystery the true purposes behind the Atonement. When revelation is wanting, when unillumined man seeks for understanding of heavenly and eternal matters, he is left to his own resources—to the powers of reason and the limitations of the human intellect.

One of the most influential philosopher-theologians in Christian history was St. Augustine (350–430 A.D.), a man whose writings and teachings have had a marked impact on the formulation of both Catholic and Protestant beliefs. A historian's description of Augustine's thought on the doctrine of "original sin" follows: "The first man, Adam, set the pattern for all future life of men. Adam, he taught, committed sin and thus handed on to all men the effects of this sin. He corrupted the entire human race, so that all men are condemned to sin for all times. Adam's sin, therefore, is hereditary. But God can reform corrupted man by his grace. . . .

"Thus man, a creation of the all-ruling power of the universe, created out of nothing, inherits the weaknesses and sins of the first man. He must pay the price for this sin. But the all-ruling can and does select some men for forgiveness and leaves others to the natural results of Adam's sins. Man is lost forever unless the Creator of the universe chooses to save him."[1]

The false doctrine of original sin is thus based upon the notion that Adam and Eve's disobedience was an act of overt rebellion against the Almighty, an attempt to usurp the knowledge available only to the gods. How much more ennobling and soul satisfying is the true doctrine of the Fall, the assurance that Adam—also known as Michael, the prince and archangel—"fell that men might be; and men are, that they might have joy" (2 Nephi 2:25). How much more gratifying it is to know that through the atonement of Christ, the act of redemption on the part of the "Lamb slain from the foundation of the world" (Revelation 13:8), *"men will be punished for their own sins, and not for Adam's transgression"* (Articles of Faith 1:2; italics added). One wonders what a difference it would make in the Christian world if the following simple yet profound truths from Joseph Smith's translation of Genesis had not been lost from the Bible:

> And [God] called upon our father Adam by his own voice, say-

ing: I am God; I made the world, and men before they were in the flesh.

And he also said unto him: If thou wilt turn unto me, and hearken unto my voice, and believe, and repent of all thy transgressions, and be baptized, even in water, in the name of mine Only Begotten Son, who is full of grace and truth, which is Jesus Christ, the only name which shall be given under heaven, whereby salvation shall come unto the children of men, ye shall receive the gift of the Holy Ghost, asking all things in his name, and whatsoever ye shall ask, it shall be given you.

And our father Adam spake unto the Lord, and said: Why is it that men must repent and be baptized in water? And the Lord said unto Adam: Behold *I have forgiven thee thy transgression in the Garden of Eden.*

Hence came the saying abroad among the people, that the Son of God hath atoned for original guilt, wherein the sins of the parents cannot be answered upon the heads of the children, for they are whole from the foundation of the world. (Moses 6:51–54; italics added.)

An equally vicious falsehood that follows on the heretical heels of original sin is the moral depravity of man and his complete inability to choose good over evil. As an illustration, from the views of Augustine:

The conception of individual freedom was denied by Saint Augustine. According to him, mankind was free in Adam, but since Adam chose to sin, he lost freedom not only for himself, but for all men and for all time. Now no one is free, but all are bound to sin, are slaves of evil. But God makes a choice among men of those whom he will save and those whom he will permit to be destroyed because of sin. This choice is not influenced by an act of an individual man, but is determined only by what God wants.

In Augustine we find both fatalism and predestination as far as the individual man is concerned. With Adam there was no fatalism. He was free. But God knew even then how Adam would act, knew he would sin. Thus, from the beginning God made up his mind whom he would save. These were predestined from the first to salvation, and all the rest were predestined to eternal punishment.[2]

Reasoning of this sort may well have come from reading such passages as Romans 7 without the clarifying lenses provided by the Prophet Joseph Smith. To read this particular chapter in the New Testament, for example, is to conclude that Paul the apostle (and thus all men by extension) was a depraved and helpless creature who muddled in sin as a result of a carnal nature, an evildoer with little or no hope of deliverance. The Joseph Smith Translation of Romans 7 presents a significantly different picture of Paul and of all men; it might well be called "Paul: Before and after the Atonement" or "The Power of Christ to Change Men's Souls." The King James Version has Paul introspecting as follows: "I am carnal, sold under sin. For that which I do I allow not: for what I would, that do I not; but what I hate, that do I." Further, "For I know that in me (that is, in my flesh,) dwelleth no good thing: for to will is present with me; but how to perform that which is good I find not" (Romans 7:14–15, 18). The Joseph Smith Translation lays stress where Paul surely intended it: upon the fact that through the atonement of Christ man is made free from the pull and stain of sin. "When I was under the law [of Moses], I was yet carnal, sold under sin. *But now I am spiritual; for that which I am commanded to do, I do; and that which I am commanded not to allow, I allow not. For what I know is not right I would not do; for that which is sin, I hate.*" Finally, "For I know that in me, that is, in my flesh, dwelleth no good thing; for to will is present with me, but to perform that which is good I find not, *only in Christ*" (JST, Romans 7:14–16, 19; italics added). The testimony of Lehi is a confirming witness to this principle of truth: "Adam fell that men might be; and men are, that they might have joy. And the Messiah cometh in the fulness of time, that he may redeem the children of men from the fall. And *because that they are redeemed from the fall they have become free forever, knowing good from evil; to act for themselves and not be acted upon*" (2 Nephi 2:25–26; italics added; compare Helaman 14:30).

THE PRACTICE OF INFANT BAPTISM

One who chooses to believe in the depravity of man via transmission of the "original sin" is only a stone's throw removed from a practice that would absolve man from the supposed stain of Eden as early as possible. Infant baptism is thus the result of a major doctrinal misunderstanding, a lack of appreciation for the full impact of Christ's atonement upon mankind. A form of this false practice seems to predate the Christian era by many centuries. The Lord Jehovah spoke to his servant Abraham of a number of the theological errors of the day, some of which appear to be tied to ignorance of the true nature and scope of the Atonement. "And it came to pass, that Abram fell on his face, and called upon the name of the Lord. And God talked with him,

Chapter 17—The Salvation of Little Children

saying, My people have gone astray from my precepts, and have not kept mine ordinances, which I gave unto their fathers; and they have not observed mine anointing, and the burial, or baptism wherewith I commanded them; but have turned from the commandment, and *taken unto themselves the washing of children,* and the blood of sprinkling; and have said that the blood of the righteous Abel was shed for sins;[3] and *have not known wherein they are accountable before me*" (JST, Genesis 17:3–7; italics added).

This passage clearly demonstrates the inseparable relationship between the Atonement and accountability. Simply stated, the atonement of Jesus Christ—the greatest act of love and intercession in all eternity—defines the bounds and limits of accountability. One of the unconditional benefits of the Atonement is the fact that no man or woman will be held responsible for or denied blessings related to a law whose adoption and application were beyond their power. This is the principle underlying the doctrine concerning the salvation of little children who die. They are simply not accountable for their deeds and therefore are not required as children to participate in those gospel ordinances prepared for accountable persons.

The question of the innocence of children was also a matter that arose in discussions between the Christians and the Jews in the meridian of time. Paul emphasized that the law of circumcision and "the tradition [should] be done away, which saith that little children are unholy; for it was had among the Jews" (D&C 74:6). Joseph Smith's translation of the Bible is a witness that Jesus had taught concerning the innocent status of children. "Take heed that ye despise not one of these little ones," the Master said, "for I say unto you, That in heaven their angels [spirits] do always behold the face of my Father which is in heaven. For the Son of man is come to save that which was lost and to call sinners to repentance; but *these little ones have no need of repentance, and I will save them*" (JST, Matthew 18:10–11; italics added; compare 19:13).

During the period of the Great Apostasy (after the first century of the Christian era) the doctrine of infant baptism again reared its ugly head. Elder James E. Talmage has written, "There is no authentic record of infant baptism having been practiced during the first two centuries after Christ, and the custom probably did not become general before

253

the fifth century; from the time last named until the Reformation, however, it was accepted by the dominant church organization."[4] Elsewhere Elder Talmage observed: "Not only was the form of the baptismal rite radically changed [during the time of the Apostasy], but the application of the ordinance was perverted. The practice of administering baptism to infants was recognized as orthodox in the third century and was doubtless of earlier origin. In a prolonged disputation as to whether it was safe to postpone the baptism of infants until the eighth day after birth—in deference to the Jewish custom of performing circumcision on that day—it was generally decided that such delay would be dangerous, as jeopardizing the future well-being of the child should it die before attaining the age of eight days, and that baptism ought to be administered as soon after birth as possible."[5]

It is worth noting that this perverse practice was introduced in the Americas by approximately the same period. Quoting and expounding upon the Lord's words to him, Mormon instructed Moroni as follows:

1. The Lord came into the world not to call the righteous but sinners to repentance (see Moroni 8:8). The immediate application of this principle is, of course, in regard to little children, the only ones, save Jesus only, who live without sin. To say that the whole need no physician (compare Mark 2:17) is to say that redemption from sin is only requisite for those who are under the bondage of sin. All others, especially those who suppose they have no sin (see John 9:41; Romans 3:23; 1 John 1:8), are in dire need of that safety and security that come only in and through the atoning blood of Christ.

2. Little children are whole, for they are not capable of committing sin (see Moroni 8:8). A modern revelation affirms that little children "are redeemed from the foundation of the world through mine Only Begotten," meaning that this dimension of the Atonement has been in effect as an integral part of the plan of salvation from the time of our premortal existence. "Wherefore, they cannot sin, for power is not given unto Satan to tempt little children, until they begin to become accountable before me" (D&C 29:46–47). It is not that children cannot do things that are evil or that under other circumstances would be called sinful. They certainly can do such things. What the revelations seem to be teaching is that their actions are covered by the merciful ministry of our Master. It is in this sense that they cannot sin. Thus

Chapter 17—The Salvation of Little Children

"little children are holy, being sanctified through the atonement of Jesus Christ" (D&C 74:7).

3. The "curse of Adam" is taken from children in Christ so that it has no power over them (see Moroni 8:8). What is called here the "curse of Adam" is presumably the effects of the Fall. In one sense, the curse of Adam, meaning an original sin or "original guilt" (Moses 6:54), is taken away from all men and women; that is, Adam and Eve's transgression in Eden was forgiven them (see Moses 6:53), and no person is held responsible for something our first parents did (see Articles of Faith 1:2). In another sense, the curse of Adam, meaning the fallen nature that comes as a direct result of the Fall (see 1 Nephi 10:6; 2 Nephi 2:21; Alma 42:6–12; Ether 3:2), is taken away from children as an unconditional benefit of the atonement of Christ (see Mosiah 3:16).

4. The law of circumcision is done away in Christ (see Moroni 8:8). Circumcision was instituted in the days of Abraham as a token of the covenant God made with the "father of the faithful" and his posterity. It signified, among other things, that male children were to be circumcised at *eight days* as a token and reminder that children are not accountable until they are *eight years* of age (see JST, Genesis 17:11; compare D&C 68:25). Mormon taught that with the atoning sacrifice accomplished, circumcision is no longer required as a part of the Abrahamic covenant (see Moroni 8:8).

5. It is solemn mockery before God to baptize children; to do so is to deny the mercies and atoning power of Christ, as well as the power of the Holy Spirit (Moroni 8:9, 20, 23). That is, to baptize children is to ignore, to shun, to deny outright what had been taught from the beginning of time by prophets and seers—"that the Son of God hath atoned for original guilt" (Moses 6:54).

6. The leaders of the Church should teach parents that they must repent and be baptized, to humble themselves as their little children (Moroni 8:10). The Savior's command for us to "become as little children" (Matthew 18:3) is not alone a call to humility and submission (see Mosiah 3:19); in addition, it is a call to become clean, to become innocent, to be justified by virtue of the blood of Christ, through the sanctifying powers of the Holy Ghost. Children are not innocent because they are good by nature. Benjamin taught, "As in Adam, or by nature, they

fall"; thankfully "the blood of Christ atoneth for their sins" (Mosiah 3:16). Children are innocent because the Lord decreed that they are so.

In a modern revelation the Lord declared: "Every spirit of man was innocent in the beginning; and God having redeemed man from the fall, men became again, in their infant state, innocent before God" (D&C 93:38). How do persons become "*again,* in their infant state, innocent before God"? Does this not have reference to the fact that men and women left the premortal existence clean and free from sin through the powers of the Atonement and that, in addition, they become innocent in regard to law and sin as infants through that same Atonement? Elder Orson Pratt asked: "Why was the Lamb considered as 'slain from the foundation of the world?' . . . The very fact that the atonement which was to be made in a future world, was considered as already having been made, seems to show that there were those who had sinned, and who stood in need of the atonement. The nature of the sufferings of Christ was such that it could redeem the spirits of men as well as their bodies. . . . All the spirits when they come here are innocent, that is, if they have ever committed sins, they have repented and obtained forgiveness through faith in the future sacrifice of the Lamb."[6]

7. The ordinance of baptism appropriately follows the principle of repentance. Since little children, through Christ, are in no need of repentance, they are in no need of baptism (see Moroni 8:11, 19, 25). It makes little sense to symbolize a child's rise from spiritual death to life. Little children are alive in Christ—free from the sins of the sinful world (verses 12, 22). Elder Bruce R. McConkie taught: "Spiritual death passes upon all men when they become accountable for their sins. Being thus subject to sin they die spiritually; they die as pertaining to the things of the Spirit; they die as pertaining to the things of righteousness; they are cast out of the presence of God."[7]

8. Any who suppose that children are in need of baptism are devoid of faith (see Moroni 8:14). That is, they do not believe what Christ has done or what he can do for little children, or for that matter, for all others. It is impossible to exercise saving faith in that which is untrue (see Alma 32:21) or in that of which we are completely ignorant. Faith is based upon evidence or assurance (see JST, Hebrews 11:1).

9. Because a belief in infant baptism demonstrates a significant departure from the faith of Jesus Christ, any who continue in this belief

shall perish eventually as pertaining to the things of righteousness (see Moroni 8:16). Truly, it is only in and through our Lord and Savior and his holy name that salvation comes (see Mosiah 3:17; see also Acts 4:12; Moses 6:52).

10. All children are alike in regard to the atonement of Christ (see Moroni 8:17, 19, 22). To borrow Nephi's words, all children, "black and white, bond and free, male and female, . . . are alike unto God" (2 Nephi 26:33).[8]

11. All little children are alive in Christ, as are those "that are without the law. For the power of redemption cometh on all them that have no law" (Moroni 8:22). There are two groups of people in scripture who are referred to as those who "died without law." The first group are the heathen nations, those who will not receive the fulness of gospel light and understanding and who thereby qualify for a terrestrial inheritance (see D&C 45:54; 76:72). The other group are those who never have an opportunity to receive the gospel in this life but who would have done so if the opportunity had presented itself (see D&C 137:7–8). As Jacob explained: "Where there is no law given there is no punishment; and where there is no punishment there is no condemnation; and where there is no condemnation the mercies of the Holy One of Israel have claim upon them, because of the atonement; for they are delivered by the power of him. For the atonement satisfieth the demands of [God's] justice upon all those who have not the law given to them" (2 Nephi 9:25–26). Truly as Benjamin declared, Christ's blood "atoneth for the sins of those who have fallen by the transgression of Adam, who have died not knowing the will of God concerning them, or who have ignorantly sinned" (Mosiah 3:11). Or, as Abinadi testified, those who "died before Christ came, in their ignorance, not having salvation declared unto them" are those who "have part in the first resurrection" (Mosiah 15:24).

12. To baptize children is to deny the mercies of Christ and the power of his Holy Spirit, to put "trust in dead works" (Moroni 8:23). Dead works are works not animated or motivated by the power of the Spirit, works that are neither God-ordained nor God-approved. In short, to baptize children is to perform ordinances that not only do not channel power from the heavens to the earth and manifest the powers of godliness (see D&C 84:20), but also tend to block that divine power

through trifling with sacred things. In this sense, infant baptism is worse than false; it is perverse. Joseph Smith summarized the issue concisely: "The doctrine of baptizing children, or sprinkling them, or they must welter in hell, is a doctrine not true, not supported in Holy Writ, and is not consistent with the character of God."[9]

RELATED QUESTIONS

There are a number of questions that arise through a discussion of the salvation of little children. For some of these we have adequate answers in scripture or through the teachings of latter-day prophets and apostles. For others, we are left to wait patiently upon the Lord for further light and knowledge. For example:

• *Why do some children die and others live?* Lacking a memory of what went before and in some cases having only a general outline of what will come hereafter, we as Latter-day Saints rest secure in the knowledge that God is our Father, that he is intimately acquainted with each of us, that he knows the end from the beginning, and that he will arrange premortal, mortal, and postmortal conditions for our eternal best interest. We rest secure in the knowledge that God knows what is best for each of us and that he will bring to pass those conditions that will maximize our growth and further our opportunities for exaltation. "We must assume that the Lord knows and arranges beforehand who shall be taken in infancy and who shall remain on earth to undergo whatever tests are needed in their cases."[10]

An eye of faith provides us with a heavenly perspective, a divinely discriminating view of things as God sees them. Joseph the seer asked, "Why is it that infants, innocent children, are taken away from us, especially those that seem to be the most intelligent and interesting?" He reflected upon the waywardness of the world and provided at least a partial answer to this most difficult question: "The strongest reasons that present themselves to my mind are these: This world is a very wicked world; and it is a proverb that the 'world grows weaker and wiser'; if that is the case, the world grows more wicked and corrupt. In the earlier ages of the world a righteous man, and a man of God and of intelligence, had a better chance to do good, to be believed and received than at the present day; but in these days such a man is opposed and persecuted by most of the inhabitants of the earth, and he has much sorrow to pass through here." Then, evidencing the perspective of those who see with the eye of faith, the Prophet added, "*The Lord takes many away even in infancy, that they may escape the envy of man, and the sorrows and evils of this present world; they were too pure, too lovely, to live on earth; therefore, if rightly considered, instead of mourning we have reason to rejoice as they are delivered from evil, and we shall soon have them again.*" Finally, he concluded: "The only difference between the old and young dying is, one lives longer in heaven and eternal light and glory than the other, and is freed a little sooner from this miserable wicked world. Notwithstanding all this glory, we for a moment lose sight of it, and mourn the loss, but we do not mourn as those without hope."[11]

In commenting upon the Prophet's remarks, Elder Bruce R. McConkie said: "There are certain spirits who come into this life only to receive bodies; for reasons that we do not know, but which are known in the infinite wisdom of the Eternal Father, they do not need the testing, probationary experiences of mortality. We come here for two great reasons—the first, to get a body; the second, to be tried, examined, schooled, and tested under mortal circumstances, to take a different type of probationary test than we underwent in the pre-mortal life. There are some of the children of our Father, however, who come to earth to get a body—for that reason solely. They do not need the testings of this mortality."[12]

• *What of the mentally deficient?* What is to become of those who are not capable of distinguishing completely between good and evil, those who never come to comprehend sin and grasp the miracle of forgiveness through the atoning blood of Christ? What is the disposition of the Lord with regard to those who never arrive mentally at the age of accountability, those who are in some way deficient in understanding of these vital matters? The revelations of the Restoration are not silent here. To six elders of the Church in September of 1830 the Lord explained: "Little children are redeemed from the foundation of the world through mine Only Begotten; wherefore, they cannot sin, for power is not given unto Satan to tempt little children, until they begin to become accountable before me; for it is given unto them even as I will, according to mine own pleasure, that great things may be required at the hand of their fathers." All who have knowledge have been commanded to repent. Of them who have "no understanding" the Lord has said, "it remaineth in me to do according as it is written" (D&C 29:46–50; italics added; compare D&C 68:25–28).

Elder Bruce R. McConkie has written the following concerning the status of the mentally deficient: "It is with them as it is with little children. They never arrive at the years of accountability and are considered as though they were little children. If because of some physical deficiency, or for some other reason unknown to us, they never mature in the spiritual or moral sense, then they never become accountable for sins. They need no baptism; they are alive in Christ; and they will receive, inherit, and possess in eternity on the same basis as do all children."[13]

• *Joseph Smith taught that "all children who die before they arrive at the years of accountability are saved in the celestial kingdom of heaven" (D&C 137:110). The word used is saved. Will they be exalted?* First of all, with but few exceptions (see, for example, D&C 76:43–44, 87; 132:17)[14] the word *salvation,* as used in scripture, means exaltation or eternal life (see, for example, Mosiah 3:18; 4:6–8; 15:26–27; Alma 9:28; 11:40; 34:37; 3 Nephi 18:32; D&C 6:13; 14:7; Abraham 2:11). Secondly, it is worth noting that Abinadi declares in his sermon to the priests of Noah that "little children also have eternal life" (Mosiah 15:25). Joseph Smith himself stated that "children will be enthroned in the presence of God and the Lamb; . . . they will there enjoy the fulness of that light, glory, and intelligence, which is prepared in the Celestial Kingdom."[15]

• *Will children who die ever be tested?* Let us reason on this matter, leaning heavily upon the wisdom of the prophets for support. A righteous man or woman cannot take a backward step spiritually after death; in short, the righteous have completed their days of probation in mortality. It was Amulek who informed us that our disposition here will be our disposition hereafter (see Alma 34:32–35). Such is the case with regard to little children. They were pure in this existence, will be pure in the world of spirits, and will come forth in the resurrection of the pure in heart at the appropriate time. At the time of the second coming of Christ, wickedness will be cleansed from the face of the earth. The great Millennium will be ushered in with power, and then Satan and his hosts will be bound by the righteousness of the people (see 1 Nephi 22:26). During this glorious era of enlightenment, the earth shall be given to the righteous "for an inheritance; and they shall multiply and wax strong, and *their children shall grow up without sin unto salvation*" (D&C 45:58; emphasis added). But will not the devil be loosed at the end of the Millennium, some may ask? Could not those who had left mortality without trial be tested during that "little season"? Certainly not, for these children will already have come forth from the graves as resurrected and immortal beings. How could such persons—whose salvation is already assured—possibly be tested? To reason otherwise is to place God and all exalted beings in peril of apostasy. In the words of President Joseph Fielding Smith: "Satan will be loosed to gather his forces after the millennium. The people who will be tempted, will be [mortal] people living on this earth, and they will have every opportunity to accept the gospel or reject it. Satan will have nothing to do whatever with little children, or grown people who have received their resurrection and entered into the celestial kingdom. *Satan cannot tempt little children in this life, nor in the spirit world, nor after the resurrection. Little children who die before reaching the years of accountability will not be tempted.*"[16]

At this point it is helpful to consider the tender words of Mormon: "Behold, I speak with boldness, having authority from God; and I fear not what man can do; for perfect love casteth out all fear. And I am filled with charity, which is everlasting love; wherefore, all children are alike unto me; wherefore, I love little children with a perfect love; and they are all alike and partakers of salvation" (Moroni 8:16–17). We trust that God will eventually reveal more of the particulars of this doctrine to the Church through his appointed servants in days to come. In the meantime, however, we are under obligation to believe and teach that which we have received from an omniscient and all-loving God.

• *What is the status of children in and after the Resurrection?* It is a marvelous thing to consider that a seer has walked among us and that seers continue to grace the earth in this final gospel dispensation. We need to feel profoundly grateful to God our Father for sending the Prophet Joseph Smith, one who communed with Jehovah and was schooled in the mysteries of the kingdom of Jehovah. Joseph has brought comfort and consolation and comprehension to man in this day regarding the ever-present phenomenon of death and the little-understood world beyond the grave. In speaking of the status of children in the Resurrection, the Prophet taught in 1842: "As concerning the resurrection, I will merely say that all men will come from the grave as they lie down, whether old or young; there will not be 'added unto their stature one cubit,' neither taken from it; all will be raised by the power of God, having spirit in their bodies, and not blood."[17] Some two years later, in the King Follett discourse, he repeated the same doctrine; he delivered the comforting assurance to grieving parents who had lost little ones that they would again enjoy the companionship of their children and that these tiny ones would not grow in the grave but would come forth as they had been laid to rest—as children.[18]

Some confusion arose over the years after the Prophet Joseph Smith's death concerning his teachings on the status of children in the Resurrection. Some people erroneously claimed that the Prophet had taught that children would be resurrected as children and never grow but would remain in that state through all eternity. President Joseph F. Smith collected testimonies and affidavits from a number of persons who had heard the King Follett sermon, and it was his powerful witness that Joseph Smith, Jr., had taught the truth but had been misunderstood by some. President Smith spoke in 1895 at the funeral of Daniel W. Grant, the child of Heber J. Grant:

> Under these circumstances, our beloved friends who are now deprived of their little one, have great cause for joy and rejoicing, even in the midst of the deep sorrow that they feel at the loss of their little one for a time. They know he is all right; they have the assurance that their little one has passed away without sin. Such children are in the bosom of the Father. They will inherit their glory and their exaltation, and they will not be deprived of the blessings that belong to them; . . . all that could have been obtained and enjoyed by them if they had been permitted to live in the flesh will be provided for them hereafter. They will lose nothing by being taken away from us in this way.
>
> This is a consolation to me. Joseph Smith, the Prophet, was the promulgator under God of these principles. He was in touch with the heavens. God revealed himself unto him, and made known unto him the principles that lie before us, and which are comprised in the everlasting gospel. Joseph Smith declared that the mother who laid down her little child, being deprived of the privilege, the joy, and the satisfaction of bringing it up to manhood or womanhood in this world, would after the resurrection, have all the joy, satisfaction and pleasure, and even more than it would have been

possible to have had in mortality, in seeing her child grow to the full measure of the stature of its spirit. If this be true, and I believe it, what a consolation it is. . . . It matters not whether these tabernacles mature in this world, or have to wait and mature in the world to come, according to the word of the Prophet Joseph Smith, the body will develop, either in time or in eternity, to the full stature of the spirit, and when the mother is deprived of the pleasure and joy of rearing her babe to manhood or womanhood in this life, through the hand of death, that privilege will be renewed to her hereafter, and she will enjoy it to a fuller fruition than it would be possible for her to do here. When she does it there, it will be with certain knowledge that the results will be without failure; whereas here, the results are unknown until after we have passed the test.[19]

Children will come forth from the grave as children, be raised to maturity by worthy parents, and be entitled to receive all of the ordinances of salvation that eventuate in the everlasting continuation of the family unit.[20] There are no joys of more transcendent beauty than family joys and surely no sorrows more poignant than family sorrows. God lives in the family unit and knows family feelings. He has provided a means—through the mediation of his Only Begotten—whereby families may be reunited and affections renewed. "All your losses will be made up to you in the resurrection," the Prophet Joseph Smith declared, "provided you continue faithful. By the vision of the Almighty I have seen it."[21]

CONCLUSION

Little children shall live! What more perfect evidence of an omniscient and all-loving God than the doctrine that proclaims that little children who die are heirs of celestial glory! From these no blessings shall be withheld and from such no opportunities will be denied. The testimony of the Book of Mormon and the latter-day oracles is certain and clear: children who die before the time of accountability shall come forth in the resurrection of the just and go on to enjoy all of the privileges associated with eternal life and the family unit. In speaking of the fruits of this everlasting principle—the doctrine that little children shall be saved—a modern apostle has written:

> Truly it is one of the sweetest and most soul-satisfying doctrines of the gospel! It is also one of the greatest evidences of the divine mission of the Prophet Joseph Smith. In his day the fiery evange-

lists of Christendom were thundering from their pulpits that the road to hell is paved with the skulls of infants not a span long because careless parents had neglected to have their offspring baptized. Joseph Smith's statements, as recorded in the Book of Mormon and latter-day revelation, came as a refreshing breeze of pure truth: little children shall be saved. Thanks be to God for the revelations of his mind where these innocent and pure souls are concerned![22]

NOTES

1. S. E. Frost, *The Basic Teachings of the Great Philosophers* (New York: The New Home Library, 1942), p. 63.

2. Frost, *Basic Teachings*, pp. 150–51. See also Martin Luther's debate with Erasmus the humanist on the nature of free will in Martin Luther, *The Bondage of the Will*, trans. Henry Cole (Grand Rapids, Michigan: Baker Book House, 1976).

3. This is a particularly interesting heresy. It may well be that the Apostle Paul had reference to this problem in Hebrews 12:24.

4. James E. Talmage, *The Articles of Faith* (Salt Lake City: Deseret Book Co., 1975), p. 126.

5. James E. Talmage, *The Great Apostasy* (Salt Lake City: Deseret Book Co., 1973), p. 119.

6. Orson Pratt, in *The Seer*, vol. 1, no. 4, April 1853, pp. 54–56.

7. Bruce R. McConkie, *The Promised Messiah: The First Coming of Christ* (Salt Lake City: Deseret Book Co., 1979), pp. 349–50.

8. See also Joseph Fielding Smith, *Doctrines of Salvation*, 3 vols., comp. Bruce R. McConkie (Salt Lake City: Bookcraft, 1954–56), 2:53, 55.

9. Joseph Smith, *Teachings of the Prophet Joseph Smith*, sel. Joseph Fielding Smith (Salt Lake City: Deseret Book Co., 1976), p. 197.

10. Bruce R. McConkie, expressing the sentiments of Joseph Fielding Smith, in "The Salvation of Little Children," *Ensign*, April 1977, p. 6.

11. Smith, *Teachings*, pp. 196–97.

12. From an address at the funeral of Rebecca Adams, 28 October 1967, typescript, pp. 2–3.

13. McConkie, "The Salvation of Little Children," p. 6; see also Joseph Fielding Smith, *Doctrines of Salvation*, 2:55–56.

14. See also Smith, *Teachings*, p. 12.

15. Ibid., p. 200. Some have suggested that the doctrinal context for the Prophet Joseph Smith's statement about the salvation of little children is verses 7–9, that is, that those children *who would have received the gospel had they been afforded the opportunity in this life* shall receive all of the blessings of exaltation. Surely much more remains to be revealed in regard to this glorious concept.

16. Joseph Fielding Smith, *Doctrines of Salvation*, 2:56–57; italics added; compare McConkie, "The Salvation of Little Children," p. 6.

Chapter 17—The Salvation of Little Children

17. Smith, *Teachings*, pp. 199–200.

18. Joseph Smith, *History of The Church of Jesus Christ of Latter-day Saints*, 7 vols., 2d ed., rev., ed. B. H. Roberts (Salt Lake City: The Church of Jesus Christ of Latter-day Saints, 1932–51), 6:316.

19. Joseph F. Smith, *Gospel Doctrine* (Salt Lake City: Deseret Book Co., 1971), pp. 452–54; see also an article in the *Improvement Era*, June 1904. For President Smith's discussion of the misunderstanding of Joseph's original teachings, see a sermon entitled "Status of Children in the Resurrection," remarks at a temple fast meeting held in February of 1918, in *Improvement Era*, May 1918, pp. 567–74; cited also in *Messages of the First Presidency*, 6 vols., comp. James R. Clark (Salt Lake City: Bookcraft, 1965–75), 5:91–98.

20. See Joseph Fielding Smith, *Doctrines of Salvation*, 2:54; McConkie, "The Salvation of Little Children," p. 5.

21. Smith, *Teachings*, p. 296.

22. McConkie, "The Salvation of Little Children," p. 7.

The Christian Backgrounds of the Nephite Culture

For some time now, various students of the Book of Mormon have focused upon Israelite antecedents of Nephite society, the manner in which the culture and religious practices of ancient Israel underlie so much within the Book of Mormon. This chapter will focus on the *Christian* nature of what the Nephites believed and practiced, a worldview driven and directed by their faith in Jesus Christ and their adherence to the principles, ordinances, and teachings of his everlasting gospel.

A WINDOW TO THE PAST

Of Joseph Smith and all those who are called as president of the Church, the Savior said: "The duty of the president of the office of the High Priesthood is to preside over the whole church, and to be like unto Moses—behold, here is wisdom; yea, to be a seer, a revelator, a translator, and a prophet, having all the gifts of God which he bestows upon the head of the church" (D&C 107:91–92; see also 21:1; 124:125). Joseph Smith not only stands as the head of this final dispensation but also is the "choice seer" among the fruit of the loins of Joseph (2 Nephi 3:7). A seer, Ammon explained to King Limhi, is a prophet and a revelator also (see Mosiah 8:16).

"A gift which is greater can no man have," he went on to say, "except he should possess the power of God, which no man can; yet a man may have great power given him from God. But *a seer can know of things which are past, and also of things which are to come, and by them shall all things be revealed, or, rather, shall secret things be made manifest, and hidden things shall come to light, and things which are not known shall be made known by them.* . . . Thus God has provided a means that man, through faith, might work mighty miracles; therefore he becometh a great benefit to his fellow beings" (Mosiah 8:16–18; italics added).

I am particularly interested in the seer's role of making known things *past.* Ponder for a moment on what we have come to know about the past as a result of the ministry of seers in these last days. Through what has been revealed by means of the Book of Mormon, the revelations in the Doctrine and Covenants, the Prophet's translation of the King James Bible, the Book of Abraham, and other inspired prophetic commentary, we sit as it were with a great Urim and Thummim before us, gazing upon the scenes of days gone by. It just may be that the Lord revealed to Joseph Smith as much or more pertaining to the *past* than he did in regard to the future.

Surely there could be no truth of greater worth, no insight from the Restoration of more precious value, than the idea of an eternal gospel. That is to say, because of the supplementary scriptures of the Restoration, we know that Christian prophets have declared Christian doctrine and administered Christian ordinances since the dawn of time. Adam and Eve were taught the gospel. They were commanded to do all that they did in the name of the Son (see Moses 5:8). They prayed to the Father in the name of the Son, repented of their sins, were baptized by immersion, received the gift of the Holy Ghost, were married for eternity, and entered into the Holy Order of the Son of God. They knew, and they taught their children and their grandchildren, the plan of salvation and the eternal fact that redemption would be wrought through the shedding of the blood of the Son of Man (see Moses 5:1–9; 6:51–68). And what was true of our first parents was also true of Abel and Seth and Enoch and Melchizedek and Abraham. They had the gospel. They knew the Lord, taught his doctrine, and officiated as legal administrators in his earthly kingdom. Isaac, Israel, Joseph, and all the patriarchs enjoyed personal revelation and communion with their Maker. Samuel, Nathan, and those from Isaiah to Malachi in the Old World and from Nephi to Moroni in the New—all these prophets held the Melchizedek Priesthood.[1] We cannot be sure to what degree the generality of the people enjoyed the full blessings of the gospel or the priesthood, but that such powers were present on earth is evident through the revelations.

"We cannot believe," Joseph Smith stated, "that the ancients in all ages were so ignorant of the system of heaven as many suppose, since all that were ever saved, were saved through the power of this great plan of redemption, as much before the coming of Christ as since; if not, God has had different plans in operation (if we may so express it), to bring men back to dwell with Himself; and this we cannot believe, since there has been no change in the constitution of man since he fell. . . . It will be noticed that, according to Paul (see Galatians 3:8), the Gospel was preached to Abraham. We would like to be informed in what name the Gospel was then preached, whether it was in the name of Christ or some other name. If in any other name, was it the Gospel? And if it was the Gospel, and that preached in the name of Christ, had it any ordinances? If not, was it the Gospel?"[2] Further, "Now taking it for granted that the scriptures say what they mean and mean what they say, we have sufficient grounds to go on and prove from the Bible that *the gospel has always been the same; the ordinances to fulfill its requirements, the same, and the officers to officiate, the same;* and the signs and fruits resulting from the promises, the same." The Prophet then continues with an illustration of this principle: "Therefore, as Noah was a preacher of righteousness he must have been baptized and ordained to the priesthood by the laying on of the hands."[3]

In a revelation given to Joseph Smith in January of 1841, the Lord explained: "Your anointings, and your washings, and your baptisms for the dead, and your solemn assemblies . . . are ordained by the ordinance of *my holy house, which my people are always commanded to build unto my holy name*" (D&C 124:39; italics added). In that light it is worth noting that the explanation for figure 3 in the Hypocephalus (Facsimile 2) in our Book of Abraham reads as follows: "Is made to represent God, sitting upon his throne, clothed with power and authority; with a crown of eternal light upon his head; representing also *the grand Key-words of the Holy Priesthood, as revealed to Adam in the Garden of Eden, as also to Seth, Noah, Melchizedek, Abraham, and all to whom the priesthood was revealed*" (italics added).

In one of the most informative statements in our literature on the principle that the gospel message and ordinances are forever the same, Elder Bruce R. McConkie declared:

> The everlasting gospel; the eternal priesthood; the identical ordinances of salvation and exaltation; the never-varying doctrines of salvation; the same Church and kingdom; the keys of the kingdom, which alone can seal men up unto eternal life—all these have always been the same in all ages; and it shall be so everlastingly on this earth and all earths to all eternity. These things we know by latter-day revelation.
>
> Once we know these things, the door is open to an understanding of the fragmentary slivers of information in the Bible. By combining the Book of Mormon, the Doctrine and Covenants, and the

Pearl of Great Price, we have at least a thousand passages that let us know what prevailed among the Lord's people in the Old World.

Did they have the fulness of the everlasting gospel at all times? Yes. There was not a period of ten minutes from the days of Adam to the appearing of the Lord Jesus in the land Bountiful when the gospel—as we have it, in its eternal fulness—was not on earth.

Do not let the fact that the performances of the Mosaic law were administered by the Aaronic Priesthood confuse you on this matter. Where the Melchizedek Priesthood is, there is the fulness of the gospel; and all the prophets held the Melchizedek Priesthood.

Was there baptism in the days of ancient Israel? The answer is in the Joseph Smith Translation of the Bible and in the Book of Mormon. The record of the first six hundred years of Nephite history is simply a true and plain account of how things were in ancient Israel from the days of Moses downward.

Was there a Church anciently, and if so, how was it organized and regulated? There was not so much as the twinkling of an eye during the whole so-called pre-Christian Era when the Church of Jesus Christ was not upon the earth, organized basically in the same way it now is. Melchizedek belonged to the Church; Laban was a member; so also was Lehi, long before he left Jerusalem.

There was always apostolic power. The Melchizedek Priesthood always directed the course of the Aaronic Priesthood. All of the prophets held a position in the hierarchy of the day. Celestial marriage has always existed. Indeed, such is the heart and core of the Abrahamic covenant. Elias and Elijah came to restore this ancient order and to give the sealing power, which gives it eternal efficacy.

People ask, Did they have the gift of the Holy Ghost before the day of Pentecost? As the Lord lives, they were so endowed—such is part of the gospel—and those so gifted wrought miracles and sought and obtained a city whose builder and maker is God.

I have often wished the history of ancient Israel could have passed through the editing and prophetic hands of Mormon. If so, it would read like the Book of Mormon, but I suppose that was the way it read in the first instance anyway.[4]

If I may be so bold as to qualify Elder McConkie's statement, let me suggest again that although the priesthood and its blessings, including the ordinances of the temple, were enjoyed by the prophets and by groups of people during the ages from Moses to John the Baptist, they may not have been a part of the religious lives of the generality of the people. Elder McConkie has written elsewhere concerning God's taking Moses and the holy priesthood out of the midst of Israel: "That is, he took the Melchizedek Priesthood, which administers the gospel, out of their midst in the sense that *it did not continue and pass from one priesthood holder to another in the normal and usual sense of the word.* The keys of the priesthood were taken away with Moses so that *any future priesthood ordinations required special divine authorization.*"⁵ In the words of President Joseph Fielding Smith, "In Israel, *the common people, the people generally, did not exercise the functions of priesthood in its fulness,* but were confined in their labors and ministrations very largely to the Aaronic Priesthood."⁶

What is true for the ancient Israelites may be only partially true for the Nephites. Because the priesthood of administration among ancient Israel was the Aaronic, the people as a body did not enjoy the transcendent privileges that come with the higher priesthood. For example, the average person's contact with temple worship probably consisted of sacrificial offerings made by the designated priests in their behalf. The Nephites, on the other hand, had the higher priesthood. It governed the Church and kingdom in America. "This greater priesthood," a modern revelation sets forth, "administereth the gospel and holdeth the key of the mysteries of the kingdom, even the key of the knowledge of God" (D&C 84:19). Stated another way, "the power and authority of the higher, or Melchizedek Priesthood, is to hold the keys of all the spiritual blessings of the church—to have the privilege of receiving the mysteries of the kingdom of heaven, to have the heavens opened unto them, to commune with the general assembly and church of the Firstborn, and to enjoy the communion and presence of God the Father, and Jesus the mediator of the new covenant" (D&C 107:18–19). Though all of the Nephites obviously did not live worthy of such privileges, many did. Thus Jacob wrote of his people: "We . . . had many revelations, and the spirit of much prophecy; wherefore, we knew of Christ and his kingdom, which should come. Wherefore we labored diligently among our people, that we might persuade them to come unto Christ, and partake of the goodness of God, that they might enter into his rest" (Jacob 1:6–7). Though the text is silent on the matter, I would suppose that temple worship for the Nephites was much like that of our own day; that is, the people were taught the doctrines of salvation, entered into sacred covenants, and participated in binding ordinances in holy places.

Chapter 18—The Christian Backgrounds of the Nephite Culture

Modern revelation provides, as it were, an interpretive lens, a key to understanding the Bible. Much of what we know about the Bible is clear to us because of the Book of Mormon, the Joseph Smith Translation, the Doctrine and Covenants, and the Pearl of Great Price. Some people, however, are hesitant to "read into" the biblical record what we know from modern revelation, feeling that to do so is to compromise the integrity or unique contribution of the Bible itself. In response to this posture, let me suggest an analogy. If one were eager to locate a valuable site, should he utilize a map that is deficient in detail or inaccurate in layout, simply because the map had been in the family for generations and was highly prized? Should he choose to ignore the precious information to be had on a more reliable or complete map if such were made available? Of course, the whole matter is inextricably tied to the question of whether the traveler is sincerely desirous of reaching his destination: maps have real value only to the degree that they guide us to a desired location. In fact, would a scholar in any discipline choose to maintain a position or defend a point of view when subsequent and available research has shed further (and perhaps clarifying) information on the subject? To do so would represent at best naivete and at worst shoddy and irresponsible scholarship, and in some cases even a distortion of things as they really were and are. Indeed, reading one scriptural record in the light of another is the prophetic pattern. It is exactly what Matthew and Paul and other New Testament prophets and apostles do in regard to the Old Testament. Who in the world, for example, could make sense of scores of the Psalms without superimposing the life and and teachings and atoning work of Jesus the Messiah?

In that spirit, and knowing what we do about the everlasting nature of the gospel, the Church and kingdom, and the principles and ordinances pertaining thereto, I suggest that it is perfectly appropriate and perhaps even incumbent upon us to make doctrinal inferences about personalities and events in scripture when details may be lacking. For example, I know that Eve and Sarah and Rebekah were baptized, that Jacob received the temple endowment, and that Micah and Malachi stood in the prophetic office by divine call and not because they assumed that role on their own. I know that Nephi, son of Lehi, was baptized by water and received the gift of the Holy Ghost, as well as the high priesthood, although an account of the same is not stated directly in the Nephite record. These are valid inferences, based upon principles of doctrine and priesthood government. Because of what has been made known through Joseph Smith, we know what it takes to operate the kingdom of God and what things the people of God must do to comply.

At the same time, I suggest that it may not be as safe (or doctrinally sound) to make indiscriminate historical inferences about the Book of Mormon, based upon what some people feel they know about the contemporary Old World. For example, biblical scholars might suggest that the doctrine of resurrection is not to be found in pre-exilic Israelite thought. But the Book of Mormon demonstrates otherwise: there were people living some five to six centuries before Christ who had a certain conviction that "our flesh must waste away and die; nevertheless, in our bodies we shall see God" (2 Nephi 9:4). Others may conclude that deeper doctrinal sections on the Godhead, for example, reflect more of Joseph Smith's nineteenth century worldview than the theology of a pre-exilic branch of Israel. But we might draw those conclusions only if we use as our template, our standard of measurement, what we know of the Old Testament or what is known of other contemporary cultures. Reading modern revelation into the ancient revelations is one thing, but reading what we think we know about ancient Israel into the Book of Mormon story is something else entirely. The former is essential; we are expected to do so. The latter may in some cases be helpful, but we must use caution and discernment. We always do well to consider carefully the source and thus the doctrinal reliability of whatever interpretive keys we choose to employ in understanding scripture.

The Nephites and the Law of Moses

Let us turn to a specific example to illustrate my point, the matter of the Nephites living the law of Moses. Early in the story, Nephi and his brothers risked their lives to obtain the brass plates, which, we are told, contained the Law (see 1 Nephi 4:16). Later we are informed that the Nephites "did observe to keep the judgments, and the statutes, and the commandments of the Lord in all things, according to the law of Moses" (2 Nephi 5:10). But what does this mean? To what degree did the Nephites observe and keep the law of Moses? Let us first consider the matter of animal sacrifice. Did the Nephites officiate in what we would term Levitical rituals? Were they under a religious obligation that required the intricate system of sacrifices given to ancient Israel under the Law, and did they perform daily sacrifices? We begin with the realization that the Nephites held the Melchizedek Priesthood and enjoyed the fulness of the gospel. As we have noted, Joseph Smith explained that all the prophets—presumably this would include Lehi and his Nephite successors—held the Melchizedek Priesthood.[7] Further, we have no indication in the Book of Mormon that there were any Levites among the Nephites. Elder B. H. Roberts has pointed out:

> In order to offer sacrifices and administer in the other ordinances of the law of Moses (which the Nephites were commanded to observe), it was necessary, of course, that they have a priesthood, and this they had; but not the priesthood after the order of Aaron; for that was a priesthood that could only properly be held by Aaron's family and the tribe of Levi. . . .
>
> That [the] higher priesthood was competent to act in administering the ordinances under what is known as the law of Moses, is evident from the fact that it so administered before the Aaronic or Levitical priesthood power was given; and the fact that there was given to the household of Aaron and the tribe of Levi a special priesthood, by no means detracts from the right and power of the higher or Melchizedek Priesthood to officiate in the ordinances of the law of Moses; for certainly the higher order of priesthood may officiate in the functions of the lower, when necessity requires it.[8]

Further, President Joseph Fielding Smith taught: "The Nephites did not officiate under the authority of the Aaronic Priesthood. They were not descendants of Aaron, and there were no Levites among them. There is no evidence that they held the Aaronic Priesthood until after the ministry of the resurrected Lord among them. . . . [The] higher priesthood can officiate in every ordinance of the gospel, and Jacob and Joseph for instance, were consecrated priests and teachers after this [Melchizedek] order."[9] That is to say, *priest* and *teacher* (2 Nephi 5:26; Jacob 1:17–18) are words descriptive of ministerial duties in the higher priesthood rather than specific offices in the Aaronic.

As we know, the ordinance of animal sacrifice did not originate with Moses or Aaron. Rather, our first parents were commanded to "worship the Lord their God, and . . . offer the firstlings of their flocks, for an offering unto the Lord." An angel explained to Adam the doctrinal significance of those offerings: they served as an ever present reminder of the coming of the great and last sacrifice in the meridian of time (see Moses 5:5–8). My suggestion is that Nephite sacrifice was after this order—the ancient gospel order—rather than the Aaronic order and that the Nephite offerings were of the "simple sacrifice" variety rather than the kinds of offerings described in Exodus, Leviticus, Numbers, and Deuteronomy. Interestingly enough, the prophets Samuel (see 1 Samuel 7:9) and Elijah (see 1 Kings 18), both holders of the Melchizedek Priesthood, officiated in sacrificial ordinances, and there is no indication from the biblical text that anyone witnessing their labors questioned their authority to do so. Thus Elder Bruce R. McConkie could write: "We cannot always tell . . . whether specific sacrificial rites performed in Israel were part of the Mosaic system or whether they were the same ordinances performed by Adam and Abraham as part of the gospel law itself. Further, it appears that some of the ritualistic performances varied from time to time, according to the special needs of the people and the changing circumstances in which they found themselves. Even the Book of Mormon does not help us in these respects. We know the Nephites offered sacrifices and kept the law of Moses. Since they held the Melchizedek Priesthood and there were no Levites among them, we suppose *their sacrifices were those that antedated the ministry of Moses.*"[10]

Other than sacrifice, to what degree did the Nephites observe and keep the law of Moses? I suggest the possibility that the Nephites may not have lived under what the scriptures call the "law of carnal commandments." I believe they lived the law of Moses in the sense that they followed the laws and ordinances of the everlasting gospel, observed simple animal sacrifice, kept the Ten Commandments, and were obedient to principles and standards of justice, equity, and reparation. I do not perceive that the Nephites were ever required to observe dietary laws, laws of purification, or the rather elaborate system of sacrificial offerings. To argue for such things—even for the daily sacrifices— is to argue from textual silence and to make inferences from an Old Testament culture and life that in my mind were foreign to the Nephites and certainly below their spiritual standing. Elder McConkie has thus written that since the Nephites "had the fulness of the gospel itself, *they kept the law of Moses in the sense that they conformed to its myriad moral principles and its endless ethical restrictions.* We suppose this would be one of the reasons Nephi was able to say, 'The law hath become dead unto us.' (2 Nephi 25:25.) *There is, at least, no intimation in the Book of Mormon that the Nephites offered the daily sacrifices required by the law or that they held the various feasts that were part of the religious life of their Old World kinsmen.*"[11]

If it is argued, as some people do, that the Book of Mormon does not contain specific reference to such matters because Mormon, the fourth-century-A.D. prophet-editor lived well beyond the time of the Law's fulfillment, then we ought to ask why such matters are not mentioned in more detail in the unabridged small plates of Nephi. For that matter, animal sacrifice is not mentioned by a Nephite prophet-writer on the small plates after 1 Nephi 7:22, thus causing us to wonder how prominent a place sacrificial offerings really were in the private or community lives of the Nephites. Early on the plates of Mormon (Mormon's abridgment of the large plates), we are told that the people of Benjamin, in "go[ing] up to the temple to hear" their king's final address, took "the firstlings of their flocks, that they might offer sacrifice and burnt offerings according to the law of Moses" (Mosiah 2:3). (It is worth noting that a similar language is used to describe Adam's offerings: "And [God] gave unto them commandments, that they should worship the Lord their God, and should offer the firstlings of their flocks, for an offering unto the Lord" [Moses 5:5].) Thereafter no mention is made of a blood offering on the part of the Nephites until after the death of Christ, at which time the Lord himself commanded that they be replaced by a broken heart and contrite spirit (see 3 Nephi 9:19–20). This commandment suggests that sacrifices had been offered from the beginning and throughout Nephite history, but again I wonder if perhaps these were not merely the simple sacrifices that antedated the giving of the Law.

Though, as we suggested earlier, Lehi was a member of the Church before he left for America, the Jerusalem of his day was in apostasy. The Jews had defiled themselves; they had trampled under their feet the God of their fathers and his prophetic spokesmen and had dishonored the covenant obligations of his gospel. Laman and Lemuel are perhaps our best illustration of what many of the Jews of 600 B.C. were like: they refused to acknowledge their own faithlessness (see 1 Nephi 17:22), were obsessed with this world's goods (see 1 Nephi 17:21), were possessed of a murderous disposition towards any and all who opposed them (see 1 Nephi 2:13; 16:37; 17:44), and denied outright the spirit of prophecy and revelation (see 1 Nephi 15:8–9). It is out of this morass of spiritual infidelity that the Lehite colony was led to the New World. Nephi observed: "I, Nephi, have not taught [my people] many things concerning the manner of the Jews; for their works were works of darkness, and their doings were doings of abominations" (2 Nephi 25:2). Lehi and his family were called to forsake the wickedness of their homeland and establish a new dispensation of the gospel in another hemisphere.

How and to what degree the Mulekites—who came to America at about the same time the Nephite colony first arrived—continued their Israelite way of life is not known. The people of Zarahemla were certainly Jews, inasmuch as Mulek was the son of Zedekiah, king of Judah. It appears that they were, like so many in the land they had left behind, in an apostate condition. "Their language had become corrupted; and they had brought no records with them; and they denied the being of their Creator" (Omni 1:17). We do know that after they had united with Mosiah and his people, they constituted a large percentage of the Nephite population (see Mosiah 25:2; compare Omni 1:5). Surely in joining with the people of Mosiah and becoming Nephites themselves, they would have adopted the teachings of the Nephite prophets and thus accepted the doctrine of Christ.

It is interesting to consider Abinadi's rebuke of Noah and his court some four and a half centuries after Nephi. Abinadi asked the priests, "What teach ye this people? And they said: We teach the law of Moses. And again he said unto them: If ye teach the law of Moses why do ye not keep it?" One would expect Abinadi at that point to lash out against such things as their failure to offer appropriate sacrifices, keep kosher laws, or attend the required feasts and festivals. Instead, he asked: "*Why do ye set your hearts upon riches? Why do ye commit whoredoms and spend your strength with harlots, yea, and cause this people to commit sin,* that the Lord has cause to send me to prophesy against this people, yea, even a great evil against this people?" Abinadi inquired: "Doth salvation come by the law of Moses? What say ye? And they answered and said that salvation did come by the law of Moses. But now Abinadi said unto them"—and note these words—"*I know if ye keep the commandments of God ye shall be saved.*" He then began to read the Ten Commandments to the priests, to chide them for not living them and teaching them to the people, and to prophesy destruction if they did not repent of their sinful ways (see Mosiah 12:27–13:26; italics added). Note that his chastisement for their not observing the law of Moses is a condemnation for not keeping the Ten Commandments as well as the laws of decency and morality associated with gospel living.

Abinadi went on to say that it was expedient for the Nephites to keep the law of Moses for a time but that eventually the Law would be fulfilled in Christ. He testified that salvation did *not* come by the Law alone and that if there were no atonement of Christ all mankind would be lost forever, notwithstanding the Law and all that appertains to it. I am fascinated by what follows. It is as if Abinadi then spoke not of the Law's relation to his people (the Nephites) but rather of why the Law was given to the wayward Israelites in the days of Moses. "And now I say unto you that it was expedient that there should be a law given *to the children of Israel,* yea, even a very strict law; for *they* were a stiffnecked people, quick to do iniquity, and slow to remember the Lord their God; therefore there was a law given *them,* yea, a law of performances and of ordinances, a law which *they* were to observe strictly from day to day, to keep *them* in remembrance of God and *their* duty towards him. But behold, I say unto you, that all these things were types of things to come. And now, *did they understand the law?* I say unto you, Nay, *they did not understand the law; and this because of the hardness of their hearts;* for they understood not that there could not any man be saved except it were through the redemption of God" (Mosiah 13:27–32; italics added; compare Mosiah 3:14). It is as though Abinadi was contrasting the blind faithlessness of an earlier group of Israelites with those Nephites who knew full well what the Law was about, what it pointed toward, and why it was given.

In describing the faith of the Anti-Nephi-Lehies, Mormon wrote: "They did keep the law of Moses; for it was expedient that they should keep the law of Moses as yet, for it was not all fulfilled." Not *all* fulfilled? Could there be a sense in which *a part* of the Law was fulfilled in the lives of believing Nephites, inasmuch as they looked forward with faith to its fulfillment? "But notwithstanding the law of Moses, they did look forward to the coming of Christ, considering that the law of Moses was a type of his coming, and believing that they must keep those outward performances until the time that he should be revealed unto them. Now they did not suppose that salvation came by the law of Moses; but the law of Moses did serve to strengthen their faith in Christ; and thus they did retain a hope through faith, unto eternal salvation, relying upon the spirit of prophecy, which spake of those things to come" (Alma 25:15–16). In other words, those who lived the Law with an eye toward Jesus Christ as its fulfillment and realization were demonstrating their ability to abide a celestial law, thus qualifying them for exaltation.[12] Or, as Jacob stated: "We worship the Father in [Christ's] name. And for this intent we keep the law of Moses, it pointing our souls to him; and for this cause it is sanctified unto us for righteousness" (Jacob 4:5).

In describing the ancient Israelites who rejected the fulness of the gospel—and from whom Moses and the keys of the Melchizedek Priesthood were taken—a modern revelation states: "And the lesser priesthood continued, which priesthood holdeth the key of the ministering of angels and the preparatory gospel; which gospel is the gospel of repentance and of baptism, and the remission of sins, and the law of carnal commandments, which the Lord in his wrath caused to continue with the house of Aaron among the children of Israel until John" (D&C 84:23–27). Please note that it is the *Aaronic* Priesthood that is associated with the law of carnal commandments. In writing of the manner in which the ancient Levitical priest performed his annual labors in the Holy of Holies, Paul observed that into this sacred realm of the sanctuary "went the high priest alone once every year, not without blood, which he offered for himself, and for the errors of the people . . . which was a figure [or type] for the time then present, in which were offered both gifts and sacrifices, that could not make him that did the service perfect, as pertaining to the conscience; which stood [JST, *consisted*] only in *meats and drinks, and divers washings, and carnal ordinances, imposed on them until the time of reformation*" (Hebrews 9:7–10; italics added). I believe that many of the Nephites had basked in the knowledge and blessings of the atonement of Christ and the fulness of the ordinances of salvation from the beginning; that is, they had participated early on in such a reformation or restoration of the everlasting gospel. Like Christ, the High Priest of their profession, they were "after the similitude of Melchizedek" rather than "after the law of a carnal commandment." The order under which they functioned was "after the power of an endless life" (Hebrews 7:15–16).[13]

In summary, from my perspective the Nephites observed and kept the Law in the same spirit that Jehovah counseled the people through Malachi: "Remember ye the law of Moses my servant, which I commanded unto him in Horeb for all Israel, with the statutes and judgments." What was that law? In the very next verse comes the following: "Behold, I will send you Elijah the prophet before the coming of the great and dreadful day of the Lord: and he shall turn the heart of the fathers to the children, and the heart of the children to their fathers, lest I come and smite the earth with a curse" (Malachi 4:4–6; 3 Nephi 25:4–6). Joseph Smith taught that "God cursed the children of Israel because they would not receive the last law from Moses." Further, "The law revealed to Moses in Horeb never was revealed to the children of Israel as a nation."[14] It appears to me that the law of Moses referred to in this passage is what the Prophet described as "the last law, or a fulness of the law or priesthood which constitutes [a man] a king and priest after the order of Melchizedek or an endless life."[15]

THE PERSON AND WORK OF THE MESSIAH

Another major area in which I sense a large chasm between the Israelite world of sixth century B.C. and the beliefs of the Nephites is in regard to the person and work of the Messiah. If the Old Testament is any type of guide as to what the people of ancient Israel understood concerning the Messiah, we conclude that very few grasped the reality and even the necessity of a Savior or Redeemer. The fact is, of the thirty-nine occurrences of the Hebrew word *Mashiah* (that is, "anointed one") in the Old Testament, most refer to the Israelite king. One, interestingly, refers to Cyrus the Persian (see Isaiah 45:1).Whether many of the plain and precious details concerning the coming to earth of Jesus Christ have been taken away or kept back from our present Old Testament (see 1 Nephi 13:26), or whether the people of the day were in general so wicked and perverse as to be unworthy of receiving such prophetic detail, we cannot know for sure. Whatever the reason, the Messiah of sixth century B.C. Jerusalem and the Messiah of the Book of Mormon peoples are very different.

Early in the narrative of the small plates, Nephi wrote: "It came to pass after my father had made an end of speaking the words of his dream, and also of exhorting [Laman and Lemuel] to all diligence, he spake unto them concerning the Jews—that after they should be destroyed, even that great city Jerusalem, and many be carried away captive into Babylon, according to the own due time of the Lord, they should return again, yea, even be brought back out of captivity; and after they should be brought back out of captivity they should possess again the land of their inheritance. Yea, even six hundred years from the time that my father left Jerusalem, *a prophet would the Lord God raise up among the Jews—even a Messiah, or, in other words, a Savior of the world"* (1 Nephi 10:2–4; italics added). That the Nephites understood that this Messiah would be much more than a great teacher or a political ruler is obvious from the Book of Mormon text. The Messiah would recover or gather his chosen people (see 2 Nephi 6:14), come as the Lamb of God to redeem the people (see 1 Nephi 10:14; 12:18; 2 Nephi 2:6–8), be slain (see 1 Nephi 10:11), and rise from the dead (see 2 Nephi 25:14). Further, that the Messiah or Savior would be none other than the Lord God Omnipotent, Jehovah of the patriarchs, is made known early in the Nephite record; such knowledge, by the way, was an important part of that gospel-centered and Christ-centered scriptural and historical record we know as the brass plates (see 1 Nephi 19:10–12). More specifically, the Book of Mormon affirms that saving faith in God can come only through a knowledge and acceptance of the doctrine of the divine Sonship of Christ. Nephi wrote: "And it came to pass after I, Nephi, having heard all the words of my father, concerning the things which he saw in a vision, and also the things which he spake by the power of the Holy Ghost, *which power he received by faith on the Son of God—and the Son of God was the Messiah who should come*—I, Nephi, was desirous also that I might see, and hear, and know of these things, by the power of the Holy Ghost, which is the gift of God unto all those who diligently seek him, as well in times of old as in the time that he should manifest himself unto the children of men" (1 Nephi 10:17; italics added). In short, spiritual power derives from the doctrine of the divine Sonship.

Almost entirely missing from the Old Testament (and, no doubt, from the world of sixth century B.C. Jerusalem) is an additional doctrinal detail so plainly taught in the Book of Mormon—that the Messiah would be the literal Son of God the Father (see 1 Nephi 11:6, 24). The angel's discussion of the condescension of God (see 1 Nephi 11), both of the Father and the Son, gets right to the heart of the matter. The Almighty Elohim condescended in the sense that he joined with a mortal woman to bring forth the Savior and Redeemer of mankind. Jesus of Nazareth condescended in the sense that he left his throne divine to come to earth to extend the blessings of redemption to the fallen and unredeemed sons and daughters of Adam and Eve. The brass plates served as a powerful testimony to the Nephites of the divine Sonship of Christ. Zenos prayed: "And thou didst hear me because of mine afflictions and my sincerity; and it is because of thy Son that thou hast been thus merciful unto me, therefore I will cry unto thee in all mine afflictions, for in thee is my joy; for thou hast turned thy judgments away from me, because of thy Son" (Alma 33:11). Zenock also prayed: "Thou art angry, O Lord, with this people, because they will not understand thy mercies which thou hast bestowed upon them because of thy Son" (Alma 33:16). In short, the Nephites came to understand a dimension of the messianic word—that the Messiah would have power given to him by his exalted sire to carry out his intercessory role (see 2 Nephi 2:8; Mosiah 15:8; Helaman 5:11)—that had been known by the faithful from the beginning but had been lost because of unbelief.

To cite just one example of what was known about God and Christ by the ancient Israelites who believed, notice the following from the Prophet Joseph Smith's inspired translation of the Bible, a section of what we know now as Moses 1. After Moses had stood in the presence of God; after he had "beheld the world and the ends thereof, and all the children of men which are, and which were created"; and after Satan had come tempting, demanding that Moses worship him as the Son of God, the account continues: "Blessed be the name of my God," Moses exulted, "for his Spirit hath not altogether withdrawn from me, or else where is thy glory, for it is darkness unto me? And I can judge between thee and God; for God said unto me: Worship God, for him only shalt thou serve. Get thee hence, Satan; deceive me not; for God said unto me: *Thou art after the similitude of mine Only Begotten.*" And now note this important statement from the Lawgiver: "And he also gave me commandments when he called unto me out of the burning bush [see Exodus 3], saying: *Call upon God in the name of mine Only Begotten, and worship me*" (Moses 1:8–17; italics added). And just as Moses was instructed to call upon the Father in the name of the Son, so also were the Nephites given the same divine direction (see 2 Nephi 25:16; Jacob 4:5).

After his prophetic call, Lehi "went forth among the people, and began to prophesy and to declare unto them concerning the things which he had both seen and heard"—namely that Jerusalem should be destroyed and that many should perish by the sword and others be carried away captive into Babylon. "And it came to pass that the Jews did mock him because of the things which he testified of them; for he truly testified of their wickedness and their abomination; and he testified that the things which he saw and heard, and also the things which he read in the book, manifested plainly of *the coming of a Messiah, and also the redemption of the world.*" What follows is most instructive: "And *when the Jews heard these things they were angry with him;* yea, even as with the prophets of old, whom they had cast out, and stoned, and slain; *and they also sought his life, that they might take it away*" (1 Nephi 1:13, 18–20; italics added). Two of those prophets of old who had lost their lives because of their messianic witness, who had spoken plainly concerning the coming of a Savior, included Zenos (see Helaman 8:19) and Zenock (see Alma 33:17). Later in the Nephite saga, Abinadi would be burned to death because he dared to tell the people "of their wickedness and abominations" and because he "prophesied of many things which are to come, yea, even the coming of Christ" (Mosiah 7:26). In that light, we find that the major anti-Christs in the Book of Mormon perpetuated the spirit and unbelief of the Jews in 600 B.C. Jerusalem. Specifically, they taught that there is no need for redemption and thus for a Savior (see Jacob 7:9; Alma 1:4; 21:6; 30:17–18), no need for repentance (see Alma 15:15; 30:16–17), that personal merit rather than divine grace determine one's standing before God (see Alma 1:4; 30:17), and that the law of Moses is sufficient in itself and needs no addenda and certainly no fulfillment (see Jacob 7:7; compare 1 Nephi 17:22; 2 Nephi 25:27).

We really cannot tell from the text itself just how much the average Nephite knew of the Messiah, but one thing is certain: the Nephite prophecies (supplemented by the oracles from the brass plates) were clear and direct and powerful, much more so than what we find in our present Old Testament. If indeed the clarity of the Nephite prophecies is any indication of what would have been known by the people, it appears to me that the Nephite concept of the Messiah as Savior-Redeemer was worlds ahead of that had by the people in ancient Israel. Repeating Jacob's words in regard to his people, "We . . . had many revelations, and the spirit of much prophecy; wherefore, *we knew of Christ and his kingdom, which should come"* (Jacob 1:6; italics added; see also 4:4–5).

GOD, MAN, AND THE LAW

The world of Lehi was also the world of Jeremiah, Ezekiel, Daniel, Habakkuk, and Zephaniah. It was a wicked world, one which had rejected and murdered the true prophets (see 1 Nephi 7:14; Jacob 4:14), created and rewarded the false ones (see Jeremiah 23), and thus cut the lifeline between themselves and the Spirit of God. Jehovah's repeated accusation against ancient Israel was that they did not *know* their God, meaning not that they did not understand cognitively the name or nature of Deity (though they were sorely lacking here as well) but that there was not that sense of closeness, that covenant loyalty that ought to characterize the relationship between a husband and a wife (see Hosea 4:1; 6:6).

Though scholars generally contend that the synagogue as an institution did not originate until the Babylonian exile, the word *synagogue* is used throughout the Book of Mormon. It is "quite probable that at its inception the synagogue did not refer to an actual building but to a group or community of individuals who met together for worship and religious purposes."[16] The word may have been used to connote simply a "congregation" or "assembly" of believers. Nephi testified that the blessings of the gospel are freely available and that God has not commanded any to "depart out of the synagogues, or out of the houses of worship" (2 Nephi 26:26). It seems that the latter phrase—"houses of worship"—is descriptive of the former—"the synagogues." Mormon wrote that "Alma and Amulek went forth preaching repentance to the people in their temples, and in their sanctuaries, and also in their synagogues, which were built after the manner of the Jews" (Alma 16:13). We also learn that apostate groups like the Amalekites, the Nehors, and the Zoramites built their own synagogues (see Alma 21:4, 6; 31:12; 32:2). That there were synagogues after the coming of Christ to the Nephites is also clear. The Master makes reference to hypocrites praying in the synagogue to be heard of men (see 3 Nephi 13:5), and he also asks that transgressors not be cast out of the synagogues (see 3 Nephi 18:32). Finally, Moroni adds the interesting detail that the teachings of his father, Mormon, on faith, hope, and charity were delivered "as he taught them in the synagogue which they had built for the place of worship" (Moroni 7:1). Though the synagogues themselves may have been conducted "after the manner of the Jews," it may be that the word *synagogue* referred to places of worship, what we would equate with church houses. The word may be used in the Book of Mormon much as it is used in modern revelation, in which the word synagogue seems to denote congregations or churches (see D&C 63:31; 66:7; 68:1).

The people of Lehi's Old World had confused ritual with religion; the quest for holiness was rejected in favor of a strict adherence to the sterile letter of the Law. The burnt offerings no longer represented the whole-soul offering of the human heart. Man's relationship to God had begun to be associated with his strict conformity to ordinance and statute. "Man walked through this life along the road God had put before him," E. R. Goodenough has written, "a road which was itself the light and law of God, and God above rewarded him for doing so. Man was concerned with proper observances to show respect to God, and with proper attitudes and acts toward his fellow men, but apart from honoring God, he looked to God only for the divine rod and staff to guide him and help him when he was weak." Within four centuries this way of life ripened into what we come to know as Halachic or Talmudic or Rabbinic or Pharisaic Judaism, a way of life that "implied a kosher table, exact observances of Sabbaths and Festivals," and so on. This approach to the godly life was an alternative to the "vertical path by which man climbs to God and even to a share in divine nature." It was a "legal religion where man walks a horizontal path through this world according to God's instructions."[17]

In short, in the days of Lehi the concept that man could know the mind and will of God and could be led by his Spirit was all but gone. Laman and Lemuel, who "knew not the dealings of that God who had created them" (1 Nephi 2:12), mocked the visions and revelations of their father and younger brother as foolishness and deceit and rejected the way of holiness with which Lehi sought to guide and govern his colony (see 1 Nephi 2:11–13; 16:37; 17:44). They had hardened their hearts and refused to receive the word of the Lord from the Spirit, from the audible voice of God, as well as from an angel. They were no longer susceptible to those personal promptings or feelings from above (see 1 Nephi 3:29; 16:39; 17:45). I suggest that in this sense they were no different from their callous colleagues in Jerusalem. After Lehi had described his vision of the tree of life, the rod of iron, and the large and spacious building, and after he had spoken to his sons concerning the destiny of the house of Israel, Laman and Lemuel indicated to Nephi that they could not understand Lehi's words concerning "the natural branches of the olive tree, and also concerning the Gentiles. And I [Nephi] said unto them: Have ye inquired of the Lord?" Their answer speaks volumes as to the climate from which they had come, a climate they had imbibed and now embodied: *"We have not; for the Lord maketh no such thing known unto us."* That is to say, they did not believe they could know such things. They did not believe they could receive revelation, because presumably they did not believe in revelation. Nephi scolded with these words: "How is it that ye do not keep the commandments of the Lord? How is it that ye will perish, because of the hardness of your hearts? Do ye not remember the things which the Lord hath said?—If ye will not harden your hearts, and ask me in faith, believing that ye shall receive, with diligence in keeping my commandments, surely these things shall be made known unto you" (1 Nephi 15:7–11; italics added; compare JST, Matthew 7:14; JST, Luke 16:21 for insight into the Jews in New Testament times).

In speaking of a world (sixth century B.C.) that he had never known personally but one about which he must have heard a great deal, Jacob said: "The Jews were a stiffnecked people; and they despised the words of plainness, and killed the prophets, and sought for things that they could not understand. Wherefore, because of their blindness, which blindness came by looking beyond the mark, they must needs fall; for God hath taken away his plainness from them, and delivered unto them many things which they cannot understand, because they desired it. And because they desired it God hath done it, that they may stumble" (Jacob 4:14). In the words of Elder Dean L. Larsen, ancient Israel was "apparently afflicted with a pseudosophistication and a snobbishness that gave them a false sense of superiority over those who came among them with the Lord's words of plainness. *They went beyond*

the mark of prudence and obviously failed to stay within the circle of funda-
mental gospel truths which provide a basis for faith. They must have reveled in
speculative and theoretical matters that obscured for them the fundamental
spiritual truths. As they became infatuated with these 'things that they could
not understand,' their comprehension of and faith in the redeeming role of a
true Messiah were lost, and the purpose of life became confused."[18] On the
other hand, those people who, like Lehi and the faithful of his company, prayerfully searched the scriptures and sought for understanding
through the power of the Holy Ghost stayed within the bounds of propriety and pressed toward the mark—and the Mark was Christ. "Wherefore," Nephi wrote, "I shall prophesy according to the plainness which
hath been with me from the time that I came out from Jerusalem with
my father; for behold, my soul delighteth in plainness unto my people,
that they may learn" (2 Nephi 25:4; compare 25:7; 31:3; 33:6). Such
plainness would not have come from his Jewish counterparts in
Jerusalem, but rather by another means. "Having great desires to know
of the mysteries of God," he had written earlier, "wherefore, *I did cry*
unto the Lord; and behold he did visit me, and did soften my heart that I did
believe all the words which had been spoken by my father; wherefore, I did
not rebel against him like unto my brothers" (1 Nephi 2:16; italics
added). In stark contrast to the agnostic spirit that characterized his
times, Nephi came to know (and taught his people) that God "is the
same yesterday, to-day, and forever; and the way is prepared for all men
from the foundation of the world, if it so be that they repent and come
unto him. For he that diligently seeketh shall find; and the mysteries of
God shall be unfolded unto them, by the power of the Holy Ghost, as
well in these times as in times of old, and as well in times of old as in
times to come; wherefore, the course of the Lord is one eternal round"
(1 Nephi 10:18–19; Alma 12:9–11).

CONCLUSION

The philosopher Karl Jaspers spoke of the sixth century B.C. as the
"axial period" because, as one writer has indicated, "in this century
human consciousness all over the world began turning, as if it were on
its axis, and facing itself. Consciousness became self-conscious, or reflec-
tive. This happened independently at approximately the same time all
over the world. It was either a coincidence or a plot, either chance or

divine providence. The more we look," he concluded, "the less it looks like chance."[19] More than likely, the Spirit of God was being poured out upon all flesh, as Joel had prophesied (see Joel 2:27–29), and persons all about the globe were beginning to rise out of relative obscurity and out of darkness. Lehi was called to leave darkness behind him, come into the light, and spread that light to a foreign soil. It is in that context—a restoration of the gospel and thus a rejection of apostate Jewry, through the scattering of a branch of Israel—that the Book of Mormon story commences. Though there can be no doubt that the Nephites brought much of their culture with them, there is no question in my mind that they left a great deal of it behind.

The Nephites were Jews. They were Jews in the sense that they were nationals, from the kingdom of Judah (see 2 Nephi 30:4; 33:8). They were, however, recipients of the fulness of the gospel of Jesus Christ. Thus they were Christians. The Nephites were Jews in the same manner that the Apostle Paul was a Jew. Like Paul, they felt a sense of personal gratitude for their heritage and rejoiced in the promises of God to Abraham, Isaac, and Jacob. Like Paul, as Christians they basked in the greater light of the covenant gospel. Like Paul, they had little reason to stay themselves completely to the means when they knew the End, and little reason to be absorbed with the prophecy when they were consumed in its Fulfillment.

My reading of the Book of Mormon reveals a group of Former-day Saints who enjoyed transcendent spiritual blessings. They built temples, not to perform work for the dead (for such was not done until the ministry of Christ to the world of spirits), nor primarily to offer animal sacrifices, but to receive the covenants and ordinances of exaltation. As President Brigham Young pointed out, "The ordinances of the house of God are expressly for the Church of the Firstborn."[20] The faithful descendants of Lehi had the veil parted and saw the visions of heaven. They knew the Lord, enjoyed his ministration, and received from him the assurance of eternal life. Many of the Nephites were received into the "holy order of God," meaning the "order of the Son of God." That is, they entered into the fulness of the Melchizedek Priesthood, which is only received in the house of the Lord.[21]

It is my view that their religious life was richly informed by the fulness of the gospel. I feel no need to distinguish between the theology of Nephi and the theology of Mormon, inasmuch as they worshiped the same Lord and lived in conformity with the same gospel laws. Time is basically irrelevant to a people who have vision. The Nephites lived as though Christ had already come (see Jarom 1:11; Mosiah 3:13; 16:6; Alma 24:13; 39:17–19); they lived in perfect anticipation of his atoning sacrifice, and thus for them the grand *prophecy* was *history*. They lived in the Mosaic dispensation, but they enjoyed the full blessings of the Messiah as though the glorious light of the Messianic dispensation had already burst upon them. In that sense, they were blessed, even as those unto whom the mortal Messiah or the resurrected Redeemer would appear in person (see 2 Nephi 2:4). The Book of Mormon was written by a people who knew and experienced the mysteries of godliness. Perhaps this is one of the reasons it carries such a supernal spirit, a power all its own. One day we will see what a mighty civilization inhabited the Americas, and then perhaps we shall appreciate what marvelous spiritual heights they reached and thus what transcendent standards they set for those of us who now read and ponder upon their record.

NOTES

1. Joseph Smith, *Teachings of the Prophet Joseph Smith,* sel. Joseph Fielding Smith (Salt Lake City: Deseret Book Co., 1976), pp. 180–81.
2. Ibid., pp. 59–60; see also D&C 20:25–27.
3. Smith, *Teachings,* p. 264; italics added; see also pp. 168, 308.
4. Bruce R. McConkie, "The Bible: A Sealed Book," in *Doctrines of the Restoration,* ed. Mark L. McConkie (Salt Lake City: Bookcraft, 1989), pp. 292–93.
5. Bruce R. McConkie, *The Mortal Messiah: From Bethlehem to Calvary,* 4 vols. (Salt Lake City: Deseret Book Co., 1979–81), 1:60; italics added.
6. Joseph Fielding Smith, *Doctrines of Salvation,* 3 vols., comp. Bruce R. McConkie (Salt Lake City: Bookcraft, 1954–56), 3:85; italics added.
7. Smith, *Teachings,* pp. 180–81.
8. B. H. Roberts, *New Witnesses for God* (Salt Lake City: The Deseret News, 1909), 2:252–54.
9. Joseph Fielding Smith, *Doctrines of Salvation,* 3:87; see also *Answers to Gospel Questions,* 5 vols. (Salt Lake City: Deseret Book Co., 1957–66), 1:123–26; Bruce R. McConkie, *The Promised Messiah: The First Coming of Christ* (Salt Lake City: Deseret Book Co., 1979), p. 427; *A New Witness for the Articles of Faith* (Salt Lake City: Deseret Book Co., 1985), p. 311.
10. McConkie, *Promised Messiah,* p. 427; italics added.
11. Ibid., p. 427; italics added.

Chapter 18—The Christian Backgrounds of the Nephite Culture

12. See McConkie, *Promised Messiah,* p. 416; *Mortal Messiah* 1:74, 76.

13. See also Smith, *Teachings,* pp. 322–23.

14. Ibid.

15. Joseph Smith, *The Words of Joseph Smith,* ed. Andrew E. Ehat and Lyndon W. Cook (Provo: BYU Religious Studies Center, 1980), p. 246, spelling and punctuation modernized.

16. Eric M. Meyers, "Synagogue," in *Anchor Bible Dictionary,* 6 vols., ed. David Noel Freedman (New York: Doubleday, 1992), 6:251; see also A. J. Saldarini, "Synagogue," in *Harper's Bible Dictionary,* ed. Paul J. Achtemeier (San Francisco: Harper & Row, Publishers, 1985), p. 1007.

17. E. R. Goodenough, in *Jewish Symbols in the Greco-Roman Period,* ed. and abr. Jacob Neusner (Princeton, NJ: Princeton University Press, 1988), pp. 20–22.

18. Dean L. Larsen, in Conference Report, October 1987, p. 12; italics added.

19. Peter Kreeft, *Back to Virtue* (San Francisco: Ignatius Press, 1992), pp. 50–51.

20. Brigham Young, in *Journal of Discourses,* 26 vols. (London: Latter-day Saints' Book Depot, 1854–86), 8:154.

21. Ezra Taft Benson, *Ensign,* August 1985, p. 8; see also Smith, *Teachings,* pp. 323–24.

CHAPTER 19

The Book of Mormon, Historicity, and Faith

My memories of the first class I took in a doctoral program in religion at an eastern university are still very much intact. It was a course entitled "Seminar in Biblical Studies" and dealt with scripture, canon, interpretation, authorship, eschatology, prophecy, and like subjects. We were but weeks into the seminar when the professor was confronted by a question from a fundamentalist Baptist student on the reality of miracles among Moses and the children of Israel. The response was polite but brief: "Well," the professor said, "I'm not going to state my own position on the matter in this class. Let me just say that I feel it doesn't really matter whether the Israelites crossed the Red Sea as a result of Moses' parting that body of water in a miraculous way, or whether they actually tiptoed across the waters of the Reed Sea. What matters is that the Israelites then and thereafter saw it as an act of divine intervention, and the event became a foundation for a people's faith for centuries."

About a year later I found myself in a similar setting, this time in a seminar entitled "Critical Studies of the New Testament," the first half of a two-semester encounter with biblical criticism. The composition of the class made for fascinating conversation: a Reform Jew, two Methodists, two Southern Baptists, a Roman Catholic, a Nazarene, and a Latter-day Saint. By the time we had begun studying the passion narratives in the Gospels, the question of "historical events" versus "faith events" had been raised. The professor stressed the importance of "myth" and emphasized that such events as the miracles and bodily resurrection of Jesus—because in them the narrative detaches itself from the ordinary limitations of time and space so that the supernatural breaks into human history—should be relegated to the category of faith events or sacred story. And then came the interesting phrase: "Now, whether Jesus of Nazareth came back to life—literally rose from the dead—is immaterial. What matters is that the Christians thought he did. And the whole Christian movement is founded upon this faith event."

Perhaps one can appreciate how I felt when I read an article writ-

290

ten by a non-Mormon a few years ago in which he suggested that we Latter-day Saints tend to concern ourselves with all the wrong things. "Whether or not Joseph Smith actually saw God and Christ in a grove of trees is not really crucial," he essentially said. "What matters is that young Joseph thought he did." There was a haunting familiarity about the words and the sentiments. Other prominent Latter-day Saints have described the First Vision as mythical, a vital and significant movement in Mormonism's past upon which so many things turn, and yet a "faith event" that may or may not represent an actual historical occurrence. More recently, it seems fashionable by some to doubt and debate the historicity of the Book of Mormon; to speak of the contents of the Nephite record as "doctrinal fiction"; to question the reality of Book of Mormon personalities or places; or to identify "anachronisms" in the book, specifically doctrines or principles that they feel reflect more of Joseph Smith and the nineteenth century than antiquity. Others go so far as to deny outright the reality of plates, angels, or authentic witnesses. These are interesting times indeed.

Though not a secular history of the Nephites per se, the Book of Mormon is a sacred chronicle, or to use Elder Boyd K. Packer's language, "the saga of a message."[1] The book claims to be historical. Joseph Smith said it was a history. He even went so far as to suggest that one of the major characters of the story, Moroni, appeared to him and delivered golden plates upon which the Nephite narrative was etched. Now, in regard to the historicity of the book, it seems to me that only three possibilities exist: Joseph Smith told the truth, did not know the truth, or told a lie. If Joseph Smith merely thought there were Nephites and supposed that such persons as Nephi and Jacob and Mormon and Moroni wrote things that they did not, then he was deluded or remarkably imaginative. He is to be pitied, not revered. If, on the other hand, the Prophet was solely responsible for the perpetuation of the Book of Mormon story—if he created the notion of a Moroni, of the golden plates and Urim and Thummim, and of a thousand-year-old story of a people who inhabited ancient America, knowing full well that such things never existed—then he was a deceiver pure and simple. He and the work he set in motion are to be feared, not followed. No matter the intensity of his labor, his own personal magnetism, or the literary value of his embellished epic, the work is a hoax and the word of the New

York farm boy is not be trusted in matters of spiritual certainty any more than Hawthorne or Dostoyevski.

My colleague Stephen D. Ricks addressed himself to those who question the historicity of the Book of Mormon. He spoke of a "view of the Book of Mormon" that "accepts its inspiration but rejects its historicity, viewing it as inspired in some sense or senses, but not the product of antiquity, coming, rather, from the pen of Joseph Smith."

> But if the Book of Mormon was simply a spiritual manifesto of Joseph, why could he not have chosen some other genre than one that appears to be making specific historical claims? One thinks, for instance, of the Doctrine and Covenants. Further, it is precisely the internal claims of the Book of Mormon as divine history that gives it its normative religious value (a value maintained in the Doctrine and Covenants, since the individual sections claim to be revelations from God). If the Book of Mormon is simply an unhistorical yarn, even a deeply religious one, it would have no more normative, sacramental value for me (impelling me, that is, to repent, be baptized, and live an upright life before God) than would the Sermons of Wesley or the *Imitation of Christ* of Thomas á Kempis, and perhaps less, since these latter make no claims to the intervention of the divine, while the Book of Mormon does.[2]

One who chooses to assume the posture that the Book of Mormon is doctrinal fiction must come face to face with the issues and implications that automatically flow from such a stance; to pick up one end of this historical-theological stick is to pick up the other.

The "expansionist" position of the Book of Mormon history is what some have assumed to be a middle-of-the-road posture. It propounds the view that the Book of Mormon represents an ancient core source mediated through a modern prophet. I feel this is basically an effort to have it both ways, to contend that certain sections of the Nephite record are ancient, while certain identifiable portions are unmistakably nineteenth century, reflecting the culture, language, and theological worldview of Joseph Smith. Any reference to such matters as the Fall, Atonement, Resurrection, new birth, or Godhead before the time of Christ are seen to be anachronistic— evidencing theological perspectives obviously out of place—perspectives that were written into the narrative by the translator but would not originally have been on the plates themselves. For example, any discussion of resurrection or atonement through Jesus Christ in the writings of Lehi or Jacob would be classified as expansion text, inasmuch as such notions are not to be found among the pre-exilic Jews, at least according to the extant materials we have, such as our present Old Testament or other Near Eastern documents. But, Ricks has observed,

> If we use the Bible or other documents from the ancient Near East as the standard, this seems an implied admission that the Book of Mormon has no independent evidentiary value as an ancient document. It also seems to imply that what can be known about pre-exilic Israelite religion is already to be found in the extant sources, principally the Bible. If this is the case, and nothing not previously known will be accepted, what unique contribution can a new document make? This reminds me of the reply falsely attributed to Umar when asked why he wished to burn the library at Alexandria: "If it is already in the Qur'an, we have no need of the book; if it is not in the Qur'an, then it is suspect of heresy and ought for that reason to be destroyed." But can we be so certain that we know that what can be known about pre-exilic Israelite religion is available in the extant sources? . . . Are we authorized to believe that Israelite religion before the exile is given its complete account in the Bible and other available documents? I, for one, am not so certain.[3]

Nor am I. Nor can I grasp how one can deal with a major inconsistency in the reasoning of such a position. Why is it, for example, that God can reveal to the Lehites how to construct a ship and cross the ocean, but that same God cannot reveal to them the plan of salvation, together with Christian doctrines of the Creation, Fall, Atonement, and redemption through bodily resurrection? Why is it that God can speak to Abinadi, call him to ministerial service, send him to Noah and his priests, and yet not make known to that same prophet the doctrines of the condescension of Jehovah and the ministry of Christ as the Father and the Son? Why is it that God can raise up a mighty prophet-king like Benjamin, can inspire that holy man to gather his people for a large covenant renewal ceremony (an occasion, by the way, that according to expansionists bears the mark of Israelite antiquity), and yet not reveal doctrine to him—doctrine pertaining to the natural man, the coming of the Lord Omnipotent, and the necessity for the new birth? The selectivity is not even subtle.

We need not jump to interpretive extremes because the language found in the Book of Mormon (including that from the Isaiah sections or the Savior's sermon in 3 Nephi) reflects Joseph Smith's language.

Well of course it does! The Book of Mormon is translation literature: practically every word in the book is from the English language. For Joseph Smith to use the English language with which he and the people of his day were familiar in recording the translation is historically consistent. On the other hand, to create the doctrine (or to place it in the mouths of Lehi or Benjamin or Abinadi) is unacceptable. The latter is tantamount to deceit and misrepresentation; it is, as we have said, to claim that the doctrines and principles are of ancient date (which the record itself declares) when, in fact, they are a fabrication (albeit an "inspired" fabrication) of a nineteenth-century man. I feel we have every reason to believe that the Book of Mormon came *through* Joseph Smith, not from him. Because certain theological matters were discussed in the nineteenth century does not preclude their revelation or discussion in antiquity. Unless. Unless we deny one of the most fundamental principles of the Restoration, one discussed in our previous chapter— Christ's eternal gospel, the knowledge that Christian prophets have taught Christian doctrine and administered Christian ordinances since the days of Adam.

Too often the real issue—the subtle but certain undergirding assumption of those who question the historicity of the Book of Mormon in whole or in part—is a denial of the supernatural, a refusal to admit the role of divine intervention in the form of revelation and miracles and predictive prophecy. It is the tendency, unfortunately, to adopt uncritically the secular presuppositions and methodologies of those who have neither faith nor direction. "It should be noted," Stephen E. Robinson observed, "that the rejection of predictive prophecy is characteristic of the secular approach to the scriptures, for the exclusion of any supernatural agency (including God) from human affairs is fundamental to the methodology of most biblical scholarship."

> The naturalistic approach gives scholars from different religious backgrounds common controls and perspectives relative to the data and eliminates arguments over subjective beliefs not verifiable by the historical-critical method. However, there is a cost to using the naturalistic approach, for one can never mention God, revelation, priesthood, prophecy, etc., as having objective existence or as being part of the evidence or as being possible causes of the observable effects.
>
> . . . If one starts with the *a priori* that the claims of Joseph and the Book of Mormon to predictive prophecy are not to be accepted,

then that *a priori* is bound to force a conclusion that where the Book of Mormon contains predictive prophecy it is not authentic and must therefore be an "expansion." But clearly, this conclusion flows not from the evidence but from the *a priori* assumption. If one allows the possibility that God might have revealed future events and doctrines to Nephi, Abinadi or Samuel the Lamanite, then the so-called anachronisms disappear and this part of the argument for "expansion" collapses.

Naturalistic explanations are often useful in evaluating empirical data, but when the question asked involves empirical categories, such as "Is the Book of Mormon what it purports to be?" it begs the question to adopt a method whose first assumption is that the Book cannot be what it claims to be. This points out a crucial logical difficulty in using this method in either attacking or defending the Church.[4]

I candidly admit to caution rather than eagerness when it comes to applying many of the principles of biblical criticism to the Book of Mormon. The quest for the historical Jesus of Nazareth has led thousands to the demythologization and thus the de-deification of Jesus the Christ. "It would be incredibly naive," Robinson noted, "to believe that biblical criticism brings us closer to the Christ of faith. After two hundred years of refining its methods, biblical scholarship has despaired of knowing the real Jesus, except for a few crumbs, and has declared the Christ pictured in scripture to be a creation of the early church."[5] Our faith as well as our approaches to the study of the Bible or the Book of Mormon must not be held hostage by the latest trends and fads in biblical scholarship; our testimony of historical events must not be at the mercy of what we know and can read in sources external to either the Book of Mormon or the witness of revelation. In the words of Elder Orson F. Whitney, "We have no right to take the theories of men, however scholarly, however learned, and set them up as a standard, and try to make the Gospel bow down to them; making of them an iron bedstead upon which God's truth, if not long enough, must be stretched out, or if too long, must be chopped off—anything to make it fit into the system of men's thoughts and theories! On the contrary," he instructed the Saints, "we should hold up the Gospel as the standard of truth, and measure thereby the theories and opinions of men."[6]

Professor Paul Hedengren of the philosophy department at

Brigham Young University made a specific request of those studying the historicity of the Book of Mormon.

> If someone wishes to consider the Book of Mormon as other than historical, do not make subtle this deviation from its obvious historical structure as some have done to the Bible. Make the deviation bold so that it is clear and unmistakable. Do not take the book Joseph Smith had printed in 1830 and say that its truths are not historical but are of some other type, for the simple logical structure of the sentences in it falsifies this claim. Instead create from the Book of Mormon another book which asserts what the Book of Mormon simply reports to have asserted. If someone claims that actually no one said what the Book of Mormon claims someone to have said, but these actually unspoken utterances are true, let them compose a book of these sentences without the historical reports of these sentences being said. Do not say in this new book, "Jesus said to some Nephites, 'Blessed are the meek.'" Simply say in this new book, "Blessed are the meek." In doing this the person will not have to overlook or ignore the historical claims taken to be either false or inessential.

In summary, "If we deny the historicity of the Book of Mormon or consider it unessential, let us compose a book in which claims are not inherently historical and attend to whatever truths we may find there. But in no case, let us say of the new book we compose that it is either the book Joseph Smith had printed in 1830 or that it is the Book of Mormon, for it is neither."[7]

I believe that in regard to faith (and thus faithfulness and adherence to a cause) it matters very much whether there is an actual event, an objective occurrence toward which we look and upon which we build our faith. One cannot exercise saving faith in something untrue (see Alma 32:21) or that did not happen, no matter how sweet the story, how sincere the originator or author, or how committed the followers. Though it is true that great literature, whether historically true or untrue, may lift and strengthen in its own way and even contain great moral lessons, such works cannot result in the spiritual transformation of the soul as only scripture can do. Scripture becomes a divine channel by which personal revelation comes, a significant means by which we may hear the voice of the Lord (see D&C 18:34–36). The power of the word, whether spoken or written, is in its source—even God our Father and his Son, Jesus Christ. We are able to exercise faith in a principle or doctrine taught by real people who were moved upon by the power of the Holy Ghost, actual persons in time and space whose interactions with the Lord and his Spirit were genuine and true and whose spiritual growth we may imitate. Huck Finn may have given the world some sage advice, but his words cannot sanctify. Even the sweet testimonies of Demetrius the slave and Marcellus the Roman centurion from Lloyd Douglas's *The Robe* cannot enliven the soul in the same way that the teachings of Alma to Corianton or the letters of Mormon to Moroni do. There is a difference, a big difference. "Doctrinal fiction" may be entertaining. Its characters may demonstrate wisdom and their lives provide noble examples. But doctrinal fiction cannot engage the sons and daughters of God as does "the will of the Lord, . . . the mind of the Lord, . . . the word of the Lord, . . . the voice of the Lord, and the power of God unto salvation" (D&C 68:4).

In regard to the resurrection of Jesus—and the principle surely applies to the First Vision or to the Book of Mormon—one non-LDS theologian has observed:

> There is an excellent objective ground to which to tie the religion that Jesus sets forth. Final validation of this can only come experientially [that is, as Latter-day Saints would say, by personal revelation]. But it is desperately important not to put ourselves in such a position that the event-nature of the resurrection depends wholly upon "the faith." It's the other way around. The faith has its starting point in the event, the objective event, and only by the appropriation of this objective event do we discover the final validity of it.
>
> The Christian faith is built upon the Gospel that is "good news," and there is no news, good or bad, of something that didn't happen. I personally am much disturbed by certain contemporary movements in theology which seem to imply that we can have the faith regardless of whether anything happened or not. I believe absolutely that the whole Christian faith is premised upon the fact that at a certain point of time under Pontius Pilate a certain man died and was buried and three days later rose from the dead. If in some way you could demonstrate to me that Jesus never lived, died, or rose again, then I would have to say I have no right to my faith.[8]

Faith in Jesus as a type of timeless Galilean guru is at best deficient and at worst perverse. Faith in his moral teachings or in a Christian ethical code alone produce lovely terrestrial labors but superficial and fleeting commitment. As C. S. Lewis observed: "I am trying here to prevent anyone saying the really foolish thing that people often say about Him: 'I'm ready to accept Jesus as a great moral teacher, but I don't accept His claim to be God.' That is the one thing we must not say. A man who was merely a man and said the sort of things Jesus said would not be a great moral teacher. He would either be a lunatic—on a level with the man who says he is a poached egg—or else he would be the Devil of Hell. You must make your choice. Either this man was, and is, the Son of God: or else a madman or something worse. You can shut Him up for a fool, you can spit at Him and kill Him as a demon; or you can fall at His feet and call Him Lord and God. But let us not come with any patronising nonsense about His being a great human teacher. He has not left that open to us. He did not intend to."⁹

Our faith in Christ is grounded in the work of redemption that was accomplished in a specific garden and on a designated cross in a particular moment in our earth's history. It is not the exact site that matters so much as it is that there was such a site. If Jesus did not in reality suffer and bleed and die and rise from the tomb, then we are spiritually doomed, no matter how committed we may be to the "faith event" celebrated by the first-century Christians. And so it is in regard to the occasion in Palmyra. It matters very much that the Eternal Father and His Only Begotten did appear to a young boy in a grove of trees in New York state. Exactly where the Sacred Grove is, as well as what specific trees or ground were hallowed by the theophany, is much less significant. If Joseph Smith did not see in vision the Father and the Son, if the First Vision was only the "sweet dreams" of a naive boy, then no amount of goodness and civility on the part of the Latter-day Saints will save us. And so it is in regard to the people and events and teachings of the Book of Mormon. That there was a Nephi and an Alma and a Gidgiddoni is vital to the story and, in my view, to the relevance and truthfulness of the Book of Mormon. That the prophetic oracles from Lehi to Samuel preached and prophesied of Christ and taught and administered his gospel is vital in establishing the dispensational concept restored through Joseph Smith; these items reveal far more about the way things are and have been among the people of God in all ages than they do about the way things were in the nineteenth century.

There is room in the Church for all types and shapes and sizes of people, and certainly all of us are at differing stages of intellectual development and spiritual maturity. Further, there are myriad doctrinal issues over which discussion and debate may lead to diverse conclusions, particularly in matters that have not been fully clarified in scripture or by prophets. At the same time, there are certain well-defined truths—matters pertaining to the divine Sonship of Christ, the reality of the Atonement, the appearance of the Father and the Son in 1820, and the truthfulness of the Book of Mormon—that, in the uncompromising language of President J. Reuben Clark, Jr., "must stand, unchanged, unmodified, without dilution, excuse, apology, or avoidance; they may not be explained away or submerged. Without these two great beliefs"—the reality of the Resurrection and Atonement and the divine call of Joseph Smith—"the Church would cease to be the Church." Further, "any individual who does not accept the fulness of these doctrines as to Jesus of Nazareth or as to the restoration of the Gospel and Holy Priesthood, is not a Latter-day Saint."[10]

I have often sensed that ours is not the task to shift the Church about with its history, practices, and beliefs—as though the divine institution was on casters—in order to get it into the path of moving persons who desire a religion that conforms with their own private beliefs or attends to their own misgivings or doubts. At a time of intellectual explosion but of spiritual and moral corrosion, I am persuaded that no Latter-day Saint needs to surrender cherished values to live in a modern world; that a member of the Church need not fall prey to the growing "alternate voices" offering alternative explanations for our foundational events and institutions; and that one can have implicit trust in the Church and its leaders without sacrificing or compromising anything. In the end, as we have been counseled repeatedly, the reality of golden plates and Cumorah and angels may be known only by an independent and individual revelation. Such an experience, as well as the reinforcing and renewing ones thereafter, comes to those who demonstrate patience and faith. "The finished mosaic of the history of the Restoration," Elder Neal A. Maxwell taught, "will be larger and more varied as more pieces of tile emerge, adjusting a sequence here or enlarging there a sector of our understanding." "There may even be," he added, "a few pieces of the tile which, for the moment, do not seem to fit. We can wait, as we must." One day, he promised, "the final mosaic of the Restoration will be resplendent, reflecting divine design. . . . At the perfect day, we will see that we have been a part of things too wonderful for us. Part of the marvel and the wonder of God's 'marvelous work and a wonder' will be how perfect Divinity mercifully used us—imperfect humanity. Meanwhile, amid the human dissonance, those with ears to hear will follow the beckoning sounds of a certain trumpet."[11]

NOTES

1. Boyd K. Packer, in Conference Report, April 1986, p. 74.

2. Stephen D. Ricks, "The Historicity of the Book of Mormon: Perspectives and Problems," unpublished manuscript, December 1988.

3. Ibid.

4. Stephen E. Robinson, "The Expanded Book of Mormon?" in *Second Nephi: The Doctrinal Structure*, ed. Monte S. Nyman and Charles D. Tate, Jr. (Provo, Utah: Religious Studies Center, Brigham Young University, 1989), pp. 393–94.

5. Ibid., p. 395.

6. Orson F. Whitney, in Conference Report, April 1915, p. 100.

7. Paul Hedengren, "The Book of Mormon As an Ancient Document," unpublished manuscript, 20 Sept. 1986.

8. John Warwick Montgomery, *History and Christianity* (San Bernardino, California: Here's Life Publishers, 1983), pp. 107–108.

9. C. S. Lewis, *Mere Christianity* (New York: MacMillan Company, 1952), pp. 55–56.

10. J. Reuben Clark, Jr., "The Charted Course of the Church in Education," *J. Reuben Clark, Selected Papers*, ed. David H. Yarn, Jr. (Provo, Utah: Brigham Young University Press, 1984), p. 245.

11. Neal A. Maxwell, in Conference Report, October 1984, pp. 11–12.

The Sanctifying Power of the Book of Mormon

We are witnessing the dawning of a brighter day in the Church. A modern prophet has sounded a trump that will have an everlasting impact upon the Church and thus upon all the world. It is as though we have had a gift sitting under the Christmas tree for many Yuletide seasons—from all appearances a gift not unlike other items under the tree—but, because of what seemed to be more pressing or otherwise distracting business, some of us have been unable and thus unwilling to open it. It lingers. It beckons to be opened. Now, finally as a result of a dramatic and repeated invitation to do so, we are beginning to remove the wrapping. We are the beneficiaries of a clear and certain sound, an unmistakable prophetic voice, that beckons us to engage the eternal. Thus the Saints of the Most High in greater numbers have begun to have joy and rejoicing in that which God has given to us in these latter days. "For what doth it profit a man if a gift is bestowed upon him, and he receive not the gift? Behold, he rejoices not in that which is given unto him, neither rejoices in him who is the giver of the gift" (D&C 88:33).

BEING TRUE TO THE RESTORATION

The Lord extended a warning to the early Saints: "Your minds in times past have been darkened, because of unbelief, and because you have treated lightly the things you have received—which vanity and unbelief have brought the whole church under condemnation." Vanity implies lightness, emptiness, lack of substance. The unbelief was surely not a failure to accept the fact that God had opened a new dispensation; an unwillingness to receive the words of a modern seer; a rejection of angelic ministrants or the priesthood and powers they have restored. No, the vanity and unbelief consisted of trifling with that which they had received, of not holding up before the world the banner or ensign of the Restoration. "And this condemnation," the Lord continued, "resteth upon the children of Zion, even all. And they shall remain under this condemnation until they repent and remember the new covenant, even the Book of Mormon and the former commandments which I have given them" (D&C 84:54–58).

The Saints had certainly been instructed and warned before this time to take more seriously the things they had received. Thomas B. Marsh had been counseled: "Lift up your heart and rejoice, for the hour of your mission is come; and your tongue shall be loosed, and you shall declare glad tidings of great joy unto this generation." What, specifically, was Brother Marsh to teach? What were those glad tidings? *"You shall declare the things which have been revealed to my servant, Joseph Smith, Jun."* (D&C 31:3–4; italics added). In a revelation directed to the Shakers, the Lord gave specific instruction concerning the preparation and schooling of Leman Copley, a recent convert from the Shakers: "My servant Leman shall be ordained unto this work, that he may reason with them [his former people, the Shakers], *not according to that which he has received of them, but according to that which shall be taught him by you, my servants*; and by so doing I will bless him, otherwise he shall not prosper" (D&C 49:4; italics added). There is a remarkable lesson for us here. Leman Copley's missionary approach was to be based not upon what he had learned as a Shaker but upon what he had learned as a Latter-day Saint. In short, his assignment was not to establish common ground and glory in similarities; rather, he was to be true to the truth, to declare with boldness what had been delivered to earth by revelation in this final dispensation of grace. By being true to the Restoration, he would be prospered in his proselyting as well as his personal life.

A later incident in Church history further illustrates the power of this principle. Elder Parley P. Pratt writes of an occasion wherein the Prophet Joseph Smith and Sidney Rigdon addressed a large congregation in the East:

> While visiting with brother Joseph in Philadelphia, a very large church was opened for him to preach in, and about three thousand people assembled to hear him. Brother Rigdon spoke first, and dwelt on the Gospel, illustrating his doctrine by the Bible. When he was through, brother Joseph arose like a lion about to roar; and being full of the Holy Ghost, spoke in great power, bearing testimony of the visions he had seen, the ministering of angels which he had enjoyed; and how he had found the plates of the Book of Mormon, and translated them by the gift and power of God. He commenced by saying: "If nobody else had the courage to testify

of so glorious a message from Heaven, and of the finding of so glorious a record, he felt to do it in justice to the people, and leave the event with God."

This was no time to declare a message that any other minister from any other church might deliver. This was no occasion for sharing and seeking to establish doctrine from the Bible. Joseph's work was and is a new and independent revelation, his witness an independent witness. The result of Joseph Smith's sermon in Philadelphia? "The entire congregation were astounded; electrified, as it were, and overwhelmed with the sense of the truth and power by which he spoke, and the wonders which he related. A lasting impression was made; many souls were gathered into the fold. And I bear witness," Brother Pratt concluded, "that he, by his faithful and powerful testimony, cleared his garments of their blood. Multitudes were baptized in Philadelphia and in the regions around."[1]

In the words of Robert J. Matthews, we must guard against the tendency to live in the past, to remain one dispensation behind. "One of the problems in the Meridian of Time with the Jews and for a while with Paul," he has observed, "was that they were just one dispensation behind the times." That is, before his conversion, Paul—and most of the Jews of his day—refused a current revelation in the name of allegiance to an ancient one. Brother Matthews continued: "When Paul made that change in his own life he became useful to the then current work of the Lord, and all his past learning and experience were channelled into the proper dispensation in which he lived. How is it with us?"

> What about our individual thinking? Have we really caught the spirit of the restoration, or do we still measure the Book of Mormon by the text of the Bible and the traditions of the manuscripts? Do we measure Joseph Smith's revelations by the traditions and canons of the world? Do we accept the JST as revealed words from a living prophet, or do we neglect it because it is not supported by the fragmentary, altered, manuscripts left over from earlier dispensations?
> ... We do not want to be a dispensation behind in these things.
> ... Let's utilize our academic skills and knowledge to promote the things of the restoration so as to make certain the road we travel both collectively and individually leads forward to the New Jerusalem, and not back to Athens, or to Rome.[2]

WHAT IS THE CONDEMNATION?

Then what is the condemnation? What is the scourge, the judgment? How is it that the Lord says the Latter-day Saints as a people are under his divine censure and reprimand? For one thing, because of our near neglect of the Book of Mormon, we are not possessed of the spirit of testimony, the spirit of conversion, as we might otherwise have been. In a broader sense, I believe the condemnation that rests upon the Latter-day Saints is a loss of spiritual power, a loss of blessings, a loss of perspective about eternal possibilities. Perhaps we have not enjoyed the revelations, the divine direction, the sweet promptings of the Spirit that might have been ours. We have not been the recipients of the fruit of the Spirit—"love, joy, peace, longsuffering, gentleness, goodness, faith, meekness, temperance" (Galatians 5:22–23)—as we could have been. Surely we have not enjoyed the understanding, the light and truth, the lens of pure intelligence that is so readily accessible.

In too many cases our minds and hearts have not been shaped and prepared by the Book of Mormon, by its lessons and logic, testimony and transforming power, and thus too often the judgment and discernment so essential to perceiving the false doctrines of the world, and even the irrelevant, have not been as strong as they might have been. Because we have not immersed and washed ourselves in those living waters that flow from the Book of Mormon, we have not enjoyed faith like the ancients, that faith which strengthens resolve and provides courage and peace in a time of unrest. So much of the stress and fear and apprehension and exhaustion that now exist in society is so very unnecessary; ours could be the right to that lifting and liberating Spirit that produces hope and peace and rest. Though the light of the fulness of the everlasting gospel has begun to break forth into a world of darkness (see D&C 45:28), yet too often we walk in darkness at noonday, or at least we traverse the path of life in twilight when we might bask in the bright light of the Son. "There is no doubt," stated President Brigham Young, "if a person lives according to the revelations given to God's people, he may have the Spirit of the Lord to signify to him His will, and to guide and to direct him in the discharge of his duties, in his temporal as well as his spiritual exercises. I am satisfied, however, that in this respect, we live far beneath our privileges."[3]

In summary, we have denied ourselves supernal privileges because we have taken lightly the new covenant—another testament of Jesus Christ. "Our homes are not as strong," President Ezra Taft Benson has warned, "unless we are using [the Book of Mormon] to bring our children to Christ. Our families may be corrupted by worldly trends and teachings unless we know how to use the book to expose and combat the falsehoods in socialism, organic evolution, rationalism, humanism, and so forth. Our missionaries are not as effective unless they are 'hissing forth' with it. . . . Our Church classes are not as spirit-filled unless we hold it up as a standard." In short, "we have not been using the Book of Mormon as we should."[4] That is the *description*. The *prescription* is straightforward: "I will forgive you of your sins with this commandment—that you remain steadfast in your minds in solemnity and the spirit of prayer, *in bearing testimony to all the world of those things which are communicated unto you*" (D&C 84:61; italics added).

WRITTEN FOR OUR DAY

We are given little indication in the biblical record that the prophet-writers delivered and preserved their messages for any day other than their own. There is no doubt that Isaiah, Jeremiah, Ezekiel, Daniel, Malachi, Peter, Paul, John, and others spoke of the distant future; by the power of the Spirit, they saw and described the doings of peoples of another time and place. Their words were given to the people of their own time. Their words have and will yet find application and fulfillment for future times. And yet we never see a particular prophet from the stick of Judah addressing himself directly to those who will one day read his pronouncements.

How very different is the Book of Mormon. It was prepared and preserved by men with seeric vision who wrote and spoke to us; they saw and knew our day and addressed themselves to specific issues that a people in the last days would confront. The poignant words of Moroni alert us to the contemporary relevance of the Book of Mormon: "Behold, I speak unto you as if ye were present, and yet ye are not. But behold, Jesus Christ hath shown you unto me, and I know your doing" (Mormon 8:35). Later Moroni said: "Behold, I speak unto you as though I spake from the dead; for I know that ye shall have my words" (Mormon 9:30). In the words of President Benson, the Book of Mormon "was written for our day. *The Nephites never had the book; neither did the*

Lamanites of ancient times. It was meant for us. Mormon wrote near the end of the Nephite civilization. Under the inspiration of God, who sees all things from the beginning, he abridged centuries of records, choosing the stories, speeches, and events that would be most helpful to us. . . . If they saw our day, and chose those things which would be of greatest worth to us, is not that how we should study the Book of Mormon? We should constantly ask ourselves, 'Why did the Lord inspire Mormon (or Moroni or Alma) to include that in his record? What lesson can I learn from that to help me live in this day and age.'"⁵

Do I desire to know how to handle wayward children; how to deal justly yet mercifully with transgressors; how to bear pure testimony; how to teach and preach in such a manner that people cannot go away unaffected; how to detect the enemies of Christ and how to withstand those who seek to destroy my faith; how to discern and expose secret combinations that seek to destroy the works of the Lamb of God; how to deal properly with persecution and anti-Mormonism; and how to establish Zion? Then I must search and study the Book of Mormon.

Do I desire to know more about how to avoid pride and the perils of the prosperity cycle; how to avoid priestcraft and acquire and embody charity, the pure love of Christ; how my sins may be remitted and how I can know when they have been forgiven; how to retain a remission of sins from day to day; how to come unto Christ, receive his holy name, partake of his goodness and love, be sanctified by his Spirit, and eventually be sealed to him? Do I desire to know how to prepare for the second coming of the Son of Man? Then I must search and study the Book of Mormon. This volume of holy writ is without equal. It is the most relevant and pertinent book available to mankind today.

I love the Bible, especially as clarified by the Joseph Smith Translation. I teach the Old and New Testaments and find joy in doing so. They contain numerous witnesses of our Lord and Savior. I cherish the Doctrine and Covenants, glory in its plain and pure doctrinal pronouncements and clarifications, and feel a deep sense of gratitude and thanksgiving for this "capstone of our religion."⁶ The Pearl of Great Price is exactly what its name implies; it is worth more than silver and gold. It is an inspired collection of some of the unique Latter-day Saint doctrines and messages. It bears a powerful witness of Christ's eternal gospel, of the restoration in the last days, and of the divine calling of the Prophet Joseph Smith.

And yet the Book of Mormon is different from the other books of scripture. They are true and they are inspired. They come from God. But the Book of Mormon has a spirit all its own. "Not all truths are of equal value," President Benson has taught, "nor are all scriptures of the same worth." Further this modern prophet explains: "It is not just that the Book of Mormon teaches us truth, though it indeed does that. It is not just that the Book of Mormon bears testimony of Christ, though it indeed does that, too. But there is something more. There is a power in the book which will begin to flow into your lives the moment you begin a serious study of the book. You will find greater power to resist temptation. You will find the power to avoid deception. You will find the power to stay on the strait and narrow path. The scriptures are called 'the words of life' (D&C 84:85), and nowhere is that more true than it is of the Book of Mormon. When you begin to hunger and thirst after those words, you will find life in greater and greater abundance."[7] This surely is what the Prophet Joseph Smith meant when he taught that a person could get nearer to God by abiding by the precepts of the Book of Mormon than by any other book.[8]

But there is more. The Book of Mormon is far more than a theological treatise, more than a collection of great doctrinal sermons. (It would be worth its weight in gold even if that was all it were!) It is not just a book that helps us feel good; it is a heavenly document that has been given to help us *be* good. It is as if the Nephite prophet-leaders were beckoning and pleading to us from the dust: "We sought for the Lord. We found him. We applied the gospel of Jesus Christ and have partaken of its sweet fruits. We know the joy of our redemption and have felt to sing the song of redeeming love. And now, O reader, go and do thou likewise!" The Book of Mormon is not only an invitation to come unto Christ, but a pattern for the accomplishment of that consummate privilege. That invitation is extended to all mankind, the rank and file as well as the prophets and apostles. The Book of Mormon does more than teach with plainness and persuasion the effects of the Fall and the absolute necessity for an atonement; it cries out to us that unless we acknowledge our fallen state, put off the natural man, apply the atoning blood of Christ, and be born again, we can never be with or become like our Lord, worlds without end. Nor can we ever hope to establish Zion, a society of the pure in heart. Stated differently, this volume is not just a book about religion. It *is* religion. Thus saith the Lord: "They shall remain under this condemnation until they repent and remember the new covenant, even the Book of Mormon and the former commandments which I have given them, *not only to say, but to do* according to that which I have written—that they may bring forth fruit meet for their Father's kingdom; otherwise there remaineth a scourge and judgment to be poured out upon the children of Zion" (D&C 84:57–58; italics added). Our challenge, therefore, is not just to read and study the Book of Mormon; we must live it and accept and apply its doctrines and philosophy.

SALVATION IS AT STAKE

Through the generations following the planting of the Lehite colony in America, there came leader after leader, prophets and kings who led this branch of Israel in truth and righteousness. Though they were inspired by a singular cause, their styles and their approaches to leadership no doubt varied. One thing, however, one symbol and type remained constant: the military leaders among the Nephites wielded the sword of Laban in the defense of their people. That sword was a sign, an ensign, a banner and ever-present reminder that only through the Lord's divine assistance can individuals or nations be delivered from their enemies. It stood for something else as well—the price to be paid for scriptural and thus spiritual literacy. The future Nephites would need the plates of brass to preserve their language and their religious integrity. But there was an impediment, a wicked man who blocked the way. God thus commanded that this man's blood be shed in order that the sacred record could be obtained by Nephi. The scriptures are always bought with a price (see 1 Nephi 3).

And so it is in regard to the Book of Mormon itself. Too much effort has been expended over too many centuries, too much blood has been shed, too many tears have watered the pillows, too many prayers have ascended to the ears of the Lord of Sabaoth, too great a price has been paid for the Book of Mormon record to be destroyed. Or discarded. Or ignored. No, it must not be ignored, either by the Latter-day Saints (the present custodians of the stick of Joseph) or by a world that desperately needs its message and transforming power. No less than God himself has borne solemn witness of the Book of Mormon. To Oliver Cowdery, who was raised up to serve as scribe in the translation, the Lord affirmed: "I tell thee, that thou mayest know that there is none else save God that knowest thy thoughts and the intents of thy heart. I tell thee these things as a witness unto thee—that *the words or the work which thou hast been writing are true*" (D&C 6:16–17; italics added; compare 18:2). The Almighty set his own seal of truthfulness upon the Nephite record by an oath when he said: "And he [Joseph Smith] has translated the book, even that part which I have commanded him, and *as your Lord and your God liveth it is true*" (D&C 17:6; italics added). In the words of a modern apostle: "This is God's testimony of the Book of Mormon. In it Deity himself has laid his godhood on the line. Either the book is true or God ceases to be God. There neither is nor can be any more formal or powerful language known to men or gods."[9] "Do eternal consequences rest upon our response to this book?" President Ezra Taft Benson asked. He answered: "Yes, either to our blessing or our condemnation."[10]

Elder Bruce R. McConkie stated:

> The plain fact is that salvation itself is at stake in this matter. If the Book of Mormon is true—if it is a volume of holy scripture, if it contains the mind and will and voice of the Lord to all men, if it is a divine witness of the prophetic call of Joseph Smith—then to accept it and believe its doctrines is to be saved, and to reject it and walk contrary to its teachings is to be damned.
>
> Let this message be sounded in every ear with an angelic trump; let it roll round the earth in resounding claps of never-ending thunder; let it be whispered in every heart by the still, small voice. Those who believe the Book of Mormon and accept Joseph Smith as a prophet thereby open the door to salvation; those who reject the book outright or who simply fail to learn its message and believe its teachings never so much as begin to travel that course along the strait and narrow path that leads to eternal life.[11]

Elder McConkie further wrote: "No man—great or small, wise or ignorant, theologian or atheist—no man who lives on the earth in the last days can be saved in the kingdom of heaven unless and until he comes to know, by the power of the Holy Ghost, that this holy book is the mind and will and voice of God to the world. . . . Men will stand or fall—eternally—because of what they think of the Book of Mormon."[12]

Such language may sound overly harsh. To some it may even be offensive. And yet this is exactly what the Book of Mormon itself declares. Nephi closed his testimony as follows:

> And now, my beloved brethren, and also Jew, and all ye ends of the earth, hearken unto these words and believe in Christ; and if ye believe not in these words believe in Christ. And if ye shall believe in Christ ye will believe in these words, for they are the words of Christ, and he hath given them unto me; and they teach all men that they should do good.
>
> And if they are not the words of Christ, judge ye—for Christ will show unto you, with power and great glory, that they are his words, at the last day; and you and I shall stand face to face before his bar; and ye shall know that I have been commanded of him to write these things, notwithstanding my weakness.
>
> And I pray the Father in the name of Christ that many of us, if not all, may be saved in his kingdom at that great and last day.
>
> And now, my beloved brethren, all those who are of the house of Israel, and all ye ends of the earth, I speak unto you as the voice of one crying from the dust: Farewell until that great day shall come.
>
> And you that will not partake of the goodness of God, and respect the words of the Jews, and also my words, and the words which shall proceed forth out of the mouth of the Lamb of God, behold, I bid you an everlasting farewell, for these words shall condemn you at the last day.
>
> For what I seal on earth, shall be brought against you at the judgment bar; for thus hath the Lord commanded me, and I must obey. Amen. (2 Nephi 33:10–15.)

Moroni delivered a similar testimony, a solemn and sacred witness of the truthfulness of his own words and of the everlasting significance of the Book of Mormon.

"And now I, Moroni, bid farewell unto the Gentiles, yea, and also unto my brethren whom I love, until we shall meet before the judgment-seat of Christ, where all men shall know that my garments are not spotted with your blood. And then shall ye know that I have seen Jesus, and that he hath talked with me face to face, and that he told me in plain humility, even as a man telleth another in mine own language, concerning these things" (Ether 12:38–39).

Chapter 20—The Sanctifying Power of the Book of Mormon

And now I speak unto all the ends of the earth—that if the day cometh that the power and gifts of God shall be done away among you, it shall be because of unbelief.

And wo be unto the children of men if this be the case; for there shall be none that doeth good among you, no not one. For if there be one among you that doeth good, he shall work by the power and gifts of God.

And wo unto them who shall do these things away and die, for they die in their sins, and they cannot be saved in the kingdom of God; and I speak it according to the words of Christ; and I lie not.

And I exhort you to remember these things; for the time speedily cometh that ye shall know that I lie not, for ye shall see me at the bar of God; and the Lord God will say unto you: Did I not declare my words unto you, which were written by this man, like as one crying from the dead, yea, even as one speaking out of the dust?

I declare these things unto the fulfilling of the prophecies. And behold, they shall proceed forth out of the mouth of the everlasting God; and his word shall hiss forth from generation to generation.

And God shall show unto you, that that which I have written is true. (Moroni 10:24–29.)

For those outside the faith, the Book of Mormon demands a decision. It forces an issue. One cannot simply dismiss it with a wave of the hand and a turn of the head; it must be explained. Thus, as Elder Bruce R. McConkie explained, "the time is long past for quibbling about words and for hurling unsavory epithets against the Latter-day Saints. These are deep and solemn and ponderous matters. We need not think we can trifle with sacred things and escape the wrath of a just God. Either the Book of Mormon is true, or it is false; either it came from God, or it was spawned in the infernal realms. It declares plainly that all men must accept it as pure scripture or they will lose their souls. It is not and cannot be simply another treatise on religion; it either came from heaven or from hell. And it is time for all those who seek salvation to find out for themselves whether it is of the Lord or of Lucifer."[13] And as far as members of the Church are concerned, President Ezra Taft Benson has declared boldly: "Every Latter-day Saint should make the study of this book a lifetime pursuit. Otherwise he is placing his soul in jeopardy and neglecting that which could give spiritual and intellectual unity to his whole life."[14]

THE SAINTS, THE BOOK, AND THE FUTURE

So here we are today. In compliance with the prophetic mandate, tens of thousands of Latter-day Saints across the world have begun to search and pray and teach from the Book of Mormon. Because of their study of the Book of Mormon, many Saints have already begun to find answers to some of their problems; many have come alive to the scriptures and have begun to understand many of the more mysterious passages in the Bible. Many have begun to feel that sometimes subtle but certain transforming influence that flows from the Book of Mormon—they have begun to sense its sanctifying power. Theirs is a greater yearning for righteousness and the things of the Spirit, a heightened sensitivity to people and feelings, and a corresponding abhorrence for the sins of the world. Many have come to the point where they honestly and truly desire to surrender to the Lord and his ways, to know and abide by his will, and to keep an eye single to his glory. For such devotees of the Book of Mormon, surely the condemnation spoken of in D&C 84 is no more.

I believe that this pattern will continue and this movement will grow. In regard to the future, President Benson said:

> I have a vision of homes alerted, of classes alive, and of pulpits aflame with the spirit of Book of Mormon messages. I have a vision of home teachers and visiting teachers, ward and branch officers, and stake and mission leaders counseling our people out of the most correct of any book on earth—the Book of Mormon.
>
> I have a vision of artists putting into film, drama, literature, music, and paintings great themes and great characters from the Book of Mormon.
>
> I have a vision of thousands of missionaries going into the mission field with hundreds of passages memorized from the Book of Mormon so that they might feed the needs of a spiritually famished world.
>
> I have a vision of the whole Church getting nearer to God by abiding by the precepts of the Book of Mormon.
>
> Indeed, I have a vision of flooding the earth with the Book of Mormon.[15]

The day is within reach when the Lord's words—as found in the Book of Mormon—shall hiss forth unto the ends of the earth for a standard unto the Lord's people, the house of Israel (2 Nephi 29:2). The covenant people of the Lord who are scattered among the nations shall respond to that voice from the dust that speaks with a familiar spirit. Multitudes of our Father's children shall gather to Christ and thereafter to the lands of their inheritance through the Book of Mormon. All nations shall, as the ancients foresaw, gather to the mountain of the Lord's house—to the stakes of Zion and to the covenants and ordinances of the holy temple—in preparation for the establishment of the New Jerusalem. And the Book of Mormon shall play an integral role in that process. We note, from the Prophet Joseph Smith's inspired translation of the Bible, the role the Book of Mormon will play in the final winding-up scenes:

> And the Lord said unto Enoch: As I live, even so will I come in the last days, in the days of wickedness and vengeance, to fulfil the oath which I have made unto you concerning the children of Noah;
> And the day shall come that the earth shall rest, but before that day the heavens shall be darkened, and a veil of darkness shall cover the earth; and the heavens shall shake, and also the earth; and great tribulations shall be among the children of men, but my people will I preserve;
> And righteousness will I send down out of heaven; and *truth will I send forth out of the earth, to bear testimony of mine Only Begotten*; his resurrection from the dead; yea, and also the resurrection of all men; and righteousness and truth will I cause to sweep the earth as with a flood, to gather out mine elect from the four quarters of the earth, unto a place which I shall prepare, an Holy City, that my people may gird up their loins, and be looking forth for the time of my coming; for there shall be my tabernacle, and it shall be called Zion, a New Jerusalem. (Moses 7:60–62; italics added.)

But such a scene shall not come to pass without opposition. Ignorance and prejudice now abound among the indifferent and the ungodly, just as love and light and pure religion shall abound among those who accept and build their lives upon the Book of Mormon and modern revelation. Antipathy to Joseph Smith, to the Book of Mormon, and to the Latter-day Saints shall increase. But amid it all, the work of the Lord, with the Book of Mormon held high as an ensign to the nations, shall go forward. As Moroni explained to Joseph Smith: "Those who are not built upon the Rock shall seek to overthrow this church; but it will increase the more [it is] opposed."[16]

I sense that we are not too far removed from a deeply significant era in this final dispensation, a time seen in vision by Nephi: "And it came to pass that I beheld that the great mother of abominations did gather together multitudes upon the face of all the earth, among all the nations of the Gentiles, to fight against the Lamb of God. And it came to pass that I, Nephi, beheld the power of the Lamb of God, that it descended upon the saints of the church of the Lamb, and upon the covenant people of the Lord, who were scattered upon all the face of the earth; and they were armed with righteousness and with the power of God in great glory" (1 Nephi 14:14).

I know that the Book of Mormon is the word of God. I know that the Lord God is its author. It speaks peace and joy to my soul. It is a quiet, steadying influence in my life. Many of our longings for another time and place, those vague but powerful feelings that we have wandered from a more exalted sphere, are satisfied and soothed when we read the Book of Mormon. Reading it is like coming home. It is a gift of God that we are expected to receive, understand, and experience. I feel a deep sense of kinship with its writers, particularly Mormon and Moroni. I know that they are as concerned now, if not more, with what is done with their book than when they etched their messages onto the golden plates some sixteen centuries ago. I know, by the whisperings of the Holy Ghost to my soul, that the Almighty expects us to read and teach from the Book of Mormon and to devote significant time to the consideration and application of the doctrines and principles it contains.

The scriptures testify that perilous times lie ahead, that wickedness will widen and malevolence multiply, before the Son of Man sets his foot upon this earth to reign as King of kings and Lord of lords. Before the time arrives when the proud and the wicked are burned as stubble, it is absolutely essential that those who call themselves after Christ's name and seek to acquire the divine nature stand and remain in holy places. Only the sanctified—those Saints who have yielded their hearts unto God (see Helaman 3:35), who have an eye single to the glory of God (see D&C 88:67–68), and who, like God, have come to abhor sin (see Alma 13:12)—will be able to withstand the tauntings and pulls of the worldly-wise who beckon and belittle from the great and spacious building. It is my conviction that the Book of Mormon will be one of the few mainstays to which we can rivet ourselves, one of the few constants and standards in a relativistic world, one of the few ensigns around which a weary people can rally in that future day when demons and mischievous mortals join hands to destroy the faithful. Truly, those who "treasure" up the word of the Lord "shall not be deceived" (Joseph Smith—Matthew 1:37).

God grant that we might be wise in the day of our probation. God grant us strength in our sacred care and keeping of the timely and timeless Book of Mormon. Then, having done all in this regard, we shall rest our souls everlastingly with those who paid such a dear price to preserve and bring it forth.

Notes

1. Parley P. Pratt, *Autobiography of Parley P. Pratt,* (Salt Lake City: Deseret Book Co., 1976), pp. 298–99.

2. Robert J. Matthews, "What Is a Religious Education?" address to Brigham Young University religious education faculty, 31 August 1989, pp. 16–17.

3. Brigham Young, in *Journal of Discourses,* 26 vols. (London: Latter-day Saints' Book Depot, 1854–86), 12:104.

4. Ezra Taft Benson, *A Witness and a Warning* (Salt Lake City: Deseret Book Co., 1988), p. 6.

5. Ibid., pp. 19–20; italics added.

6. Ibid., p. 30.

7. Ibid., pp. 10, 21–22.

8. Joseph Smith, *Teachings of the Prophet Joseph Smith,* sel. Joseph Fielding Smith (Salt Lake City: Deseret Book Co., 1976), p. 194; introduction to the Book of Mormon.

9. Bruce R. McConkie, in Conference Report, April 1982, p. 50.

10. Benson, *Witness and a Warning,* p. 7.

11. Bruce R. McConkie, in Conference Report, October 1983, p. 104.

12. Bruce R. McConkie, *The Millennial Messiah: The Second Coming of the Son of Man* (Salt Lake City: Deseret Book Co., 1982), p. 147.

13. McConkie, in Conference Report, October 1983, pp. 105–6.

14. Benson, *Witness and a Warning,* pp. 7–8.

15. Ezra Taft Benson, in Conference Report, October 1988, pp. 4–5.

16. *Messenger and Advocate,* October 1835, 2:199;.cited in Francis W. Kirkham, *A New Witness for Christ in America* (Independence, Mo.: Zion's Printing, 1942), p. 100.

SCRIPTURE INDEX

Scripture Index

Scripture Index

Scripture Index

2:2, p. 132
2:11, p. 132
2:23–24, p. 23
2:35, p. 240
4:4–5, p. 283
4:5, pp. 22, 118, 122, 278, 282
4:13, pp. 49, 87
4:14, pp. 283, 285
4:15, p. 182
5, p. 25
5:73–74, p. 226
5:74, p. 211
6:4–5, p. 31
6:7, p. 57
6:13, p. 47
7:2, p. 48
7:4, p. 48
7:5, pp. 54, 60
7:6, pp. 48, 49, 184
7:6–7, p. 116
7:7, pp. 49, 51, 282
7:7–9, p. 50
7:8, pp. 55, 60
7:9, p. 282
7:10–11, pp. 51, 55
7:11, p. 60
7:12, p. 55
7:13, p. 52
7:13–14, p. 57
7:15, p. 57
7:17–18, p. 58
7:19, p. 58
7:22, p. 60

Enos
1:11, p. 55

Jarom
1:11, pp. 114, 118, 288

Omni
1:5, p. 276
1:17, pp. 20, 27–28, 276
1:22, p. 22
1:25, p. 70

Words of Mormon
1:12–18, p. 70

Mosiah
1:3, p. 20
1:4, p. 26
1:11–12, p. 71
1:18, p. 132
2:3, p. 275
2:9, p. 71
2:17, p. 238
3:5, pp. 13–14, 190
3:5–9, p. 118
3:7, pp. 14, 94, 181
3:8, p. 122
3:11, pp. 65, 95, 257
3:13, p. 288
3:14, p. 277
3:15, p. 118
3:16, pp. 81, 126, 255, 256
3:17, pp. 175, 257
3:18, pp. 175, 260
3:18–19, p. 83
3:19, pp. 74, 174, 242, 255
4:2–3, p. 17
4:3, p. 10
4:5, p. 201
4:6–8, p. 260
4:9, p. 201
4:11–12, p. 203
4:23, p. 96
4:26: pp. 203, 238
5:1–15, p. 123
5:2, pp. 105, 236
5:3, pp. 51, 107
5:6, pp. 108–9
5:7–8, p. 109
5:15, pp. 193, 203
7:26, p. 282
7:26–28, p. 125
7:41, p. 201
7:48, p. 201
8:16, p. 266
8:16–18, p. 266
11:20, p. 115
11:21–12:7, p. 115
12:11–24, p. 22
12:17–27, p. 115
12:20, p. 115

Scripture Index

34:33, pp. 96, 170
34:37, p. 260
36, p. 109
37:4, p. 45
37:6, p. 151
37:8, p. 20
37:27–32, p. 40
37:46, p. 37
38:12, p. 240
39:2, p. 154
39:3, p. 154
39:3–4, p. 154
39:6, p. 155
39:7, p. 157
39:9, p. 157
39:10, p. 57, 157
39:11, p. 157
39:13, p. 157
39:14, p. 158
39:17–19, pp. 158, 288
40, p. 125
40:7, p. 170
40:9, pp. 161, 170
40:11, pp. 161, 170
40:11–12, p. 140
40:11–14, p. 92
40:12, p. 162
40:13, pp. 162, 241
40:13–14, p. 170
40:14, pp. 163, 170
40:15, p. 170
40:16, p. 164
40:16–20, p. 164
40:17, p. 170
40:18, p. 170
40:20, p. 164
40:21, p. 170
40:22–23, p. 171
40:23, pp. 163, 170
40:26, p. 88
41, p. 176
41:1, pp. 50–51, 126, 156
41:2–4, p. 165
41:3, p. 95
41:7, p. 170
41:10–11, pp. 74, 165

41:11, p. 191
41:15, p. 166
42, pp. 3, 127
42:1, p. 156
42:1–13, p. 166
42:2–10, p. 22
42:6–12, p. 255
42:8, p. 166
42:9, p. 88
42:13, p. 169
42:22, p. 169
42:23, p. 168
42:23–24, p. 170
42:25, p. 169
42:27, p. 160
42:29, p. 157
42:31, p. 159
45:16, p. 159
45:19, p. 23
45:22, p. 131
46:11–27, p. 35–36
46:24–26, p. 22
49:29–30, p. 160
53:20, p. 240
60:13, p. 140
63:10, p. 160

Helaman
1–2, p. 40
3:13–15, p. 21
3:29, pp. 18, 183
3:30, p. 184
3:35, pp. 247, 314
4:13, p. 172
5:6, p. 173
5:7, p. 173
5:8, p. 173
5:9, p. 175
5:10, p. 176
5:11, pp. 179, 181, 281
5:12, pp. 60, 182, 185
6:10, p. 113
6:26–27, p. 40
8:12–23, p. 124
8:14–15, pp. 23, 37
8:16–17, pp. 22, 42

Scripture Index

74:7, p. 255
76, pp. 89, 126
76:11–19, p. 9
76:23–24, p. 80
76:31–35, p. 155
76:40–41, pp. 89, 91
76:40–42, pp. 48, 184, 199
76:43–44, p. 260
76:50–80, p. 125
76:53, p. 52
76:54, pp. 111, 141
76:54–60, pp. 142–43
76:58, p. 111
76:58–59, p. 80
76:67, p. 141
76:72, pp. 126, 257
76:75, p. 225
76:81–106, p. 126
76:85, p. 125
76:87, p. 260
76:94, p. 141
76:103, p. 97
76:103–6, pp. 96, 97
76:107, p. 200
77:6, p. 228
77:11, p. 145
82:3, p. 96
84, p. 312
84:13–14, p. 148
84:19, p. 270
84:19–25, p. 140
84:19–27, p. 131
84:20, p. 257
84:23–27, p. 278
84:27, p. 118
84:33, pp. 43, 141
84:33–40, p. 150
84:39, p. 150
84:42–50, pp. 79–80
84:45–48, p. 76
84:49–50, p. 76
84:54–58, pp. 301–302
84:54–61, p. 84
84:57, p. 3
84:57–58, p. 307
84:61, p. 305

84:85, p. 307
86:8–10, p. 219
88:6, pp. 93, 180
88:6–13, p. 79
88:15, p. 170
88:16, p. 164
88:21–24, p. 166
88:27, pp. 39, 62
88:28–31, p. 166
88:33, p. 301
88:35, p. 92
88:50, p. 79
88:67, p. 98
88:67–68, p. 314
88:77, p. 205
88:100–101, p. 125
88:102, p. 92
88:106, p. 200
88:125, p. 237
90:5, p. 182
90:24, p. 236
93:4, p. 124
93:12–14, p. 124
93:13, p. 110
93:24, p. 48
93:38, p. 256
95:6, p. 96
101:30–31, p. 225
101:32–34, p. 228
101:36, p. 235
107:3, p. 142
107:3–4, p. 146
107:18–19, pp. 142, 270
107:91–92, p. 266
109:24–33, p. 58
110:2, p. 221
113:8, p. 220
113:10, p. 220
121:34, pp. 136, 215
121:36, p. 151
121:42, p. 50
121:45, p. 237
124:28, p. 142
124:39, p. 268
124:58, p. 222
124:125, p. 266

Scripture Index

128:18, p. 139
131:1–4, p. 218
132:17, p. 260
132:19–24, p. 143
132:27, p. 160
132:30–31, p. 222
132:39, p. 132
133:18, p. 145
133:28, p. 226
133:50, p. 200
135:5, p. 128
137:7–8, p. 257
137:7–9, pp. 95, 126
137:10, p. 126
137:110, p. 260
138:1–11, p. 9
138:12, p. 164
138:12–19, p. 121
138:15, p. 171
138:18, p. 171
138:22, p. 170
138:30, p. 170
138:50, p. 171
138:57, p. 170

Moses
1, p. 281
1:4–6, p. 123
1:8–17, p. 281
1:11, p. 77
1:30, p. 101
1:31–33, p. 122
1:32–33, p. 123
1:32–35, p. 89
1:39, p. 197
2:22, p. 63
2:28, p. 63
3:9, p. 39
3:17, p. 64
4:1, pp. 38–39, 176
4:1–4, p. 38
4:4, p. 39
5, p. 114
5:1–9, p. 267
5:5, p. 275
5:5–8, pp. 39, 274

5:8, pp. 192, 267
5:9–11, p. 40
5:11, p. 64
5:13, pp. 74, 75
5:16–55, p. 41
6:7, p. 151
6:48, pp. 40, 64
6:49, p. 75
6:51–52, p. 123
6:51–54, pp. 250–51
6:51–60, p. 88
6:51–68, p. 267
6:52, p. 257
6:53, pp. 72, 255
6:54, pp. 72, 126, 255
6:55, pp. 72, 81
6:58–59, pp. 40, 99
6:59, pp. 63, 130
6:59–61, p. 103
6:63, pp. 15, 51
6:64–65, pp. 103, 106
6:66–68, p. 142
6:67, p. 143–44
7:21, pp. 84, 244
7:28–32, p. 12
7:30, p. 122
7:55–56, p. 88
7:55–57, p. 171
7:60–62, p. 313

Joseph Smith–Matthew
1:30, p. 233
1:37, p. 315

Abraham
1:2, p. 148
1:2–3, p. 132
2:8–11, pp. 132, 216, 219
2:11, p. 260
3:22, p. 135
3:22–23, p. 80
Facsimile 2, p. 268

Articles of Faith
1:2, pp. 65, 72, 250, 255
1:3, p. 89
1:10, pp. 62, 227

SUBJECT INDEX

Aaron (son of Mosiah), 22

Aaron, sons of, 131

Aaronic Priesthood, 131, 270, 273, 278

Abinadi: studied ancient scriptures, 22; on the fallen state of man, 74–75; before Noah's high priests, 115–18, 276; prophesied of Christ, 118–22; on the Father and Son, 123–25; on the first resurrection, 125–27, 164, 257; killed, 125, 127–28, 282; testified of Atonement, 127; on those who die in their sins, 177; on why law of Moses was given to Israelites, 277

Abraham: known by Book of Mormon prophets, 22; had prophetic vision of Christ, 42; learned from Melchizedek, 147–48; on theological errors, 252–53

Abrahamic covenant, 218, 255

Accusations of false doctrine, 49

Adam: blood of, 63; was "quickened in the inner man," 106; became a son of God, 142; curse of, 255

Adam and Eve: known by Book of Mormon prophets, 22; as amortal, 62; knowledge of, 67; story of, figurative or literal, 66–67; transgression of, 250–51; were taught gospel of Christ, 267. *See also* Fall of Adam and Eve

Adoption into family of Christ, 174–75

Adultery, 52

Alexandria, library of, 293

Allegory of Zenos, 31, 211, 226

Alma the Younger: taught about ancient prophets, 22–23, 37, 43–44; quoted Zenos and

Zenoch, 29–30; struck Korihor dumb, 56; on spiritual rebirth, 101, 109; converted Zeezrom, 104–5; conversion of, 109, 110–11; on the Atonement, 130, 158; on the priesthood, 132, 134–36, 138; on "entering into the rest of the Lord," 139–40, 145; told of works of the faithful, 145; exemplified Melchizedek, 145–46, 149, 150–51; counseled Corianton, 156–58; on postmortal existence, 161–63; on resurrection and restoration, 163–65; on laws, punishments, and repentance, 168–70; on hearkening to the good shepherd, 192; on foreordained privileges, 215; as example of charity, 235–36; on acquiring charity, 242

Amaleki, 22

Ammon, 106, 233, 235, 266

Ammonites, honesty of, 240

Amulek, 22, 96, 104–5, 130, 235–36

Anachronisms, 291–92

Ancient prophets: knew of Christ and Atonement, 118–22; knew of plan of salvation, 267–68

Anti-Christs: Sherem as example of, 47–59; characteristics of, 48–52; sign-seekers as, 52–53, 56–57; in 600 B.C. Jerusalem, 282

Anti-Nephi-Lehies, 277

Articles of adoption, 104, 123, 173, 227. *See also* Rebirth

Ashton, Marvin J., 185

Atonement: as part of condescension of Christ, 14; taught by Book of Mormon prophets, 40, 88, 118–122, 158; denial of, by anti-Christs, 48, 282; little children saved through, 82, 254–55; infinite nature of, 89–90; remits sin, 158; saves from spiritual death, 174–75; cannot save men in sin, 176; misunderstood, 249–50; defines limits of accountability, 253; taught throughout antiquity, 118–22, 267. *See also* Jesus Christ

Ballard, Melvin J., 212
Baptism, 101–2, 202–3, 256. *See also* Infant baptism
Believing heart, 236
Benjamin, King: received explanation of condescension of God, 13–14; on record-keeping, 26; sermon of, 70–71; on natural man, 74, 83; on innocence of children, 81, 242, 256; knew of Christ's suffering, 94; on becoming children of Christ, 108–9; on taking on name of Christ, 175; on being sealed as Christ's, 193; on service, 238; on acquiring charity, 242; on Atonement, 257; people of, 275
Benson, Ezra Taft: on scriptures not being of same worth, 4; on Book of Mormon, 6, 47, 59, 84–85, 305–6, 307, 309, 311, 312; on God the Father as father of Jesus Christ, 12; on need for Christ, 70; on pride, 78–79, 97; on Christ changing lives, 83–84; on process of conversion, 110–11; on Melchizedek Priesthood, 143–44; on repentance, 177; on love of the Lord, 232; on love for all people, 238; on selfishness vs. charity, 239
Bible: compared to brass plates, 28;

lacking in information, 38–42; contains portion of God's revelations, 44; understanding, via modern revelation, 271; written for own time, 305
Biblical criticism, 294–95
Blood: as medium of mortality, 63; of Christ, 103
Book of Mormon: author's testimony of, 1–5, 314; as doctrinal standard of Church, 2–3; motivates to do good, 4, 312; will convert more than the Bible, 4; as witness of Christ, 6–7, 47; as proof of other scriptures, 6–7; 1830 edition of, 12; 1937 edition of, 13, 19; exposes enemies of Christ, 47; written for us today, 59, 305, 306; encourages encounters with the divine, 150, 307; contains fullness of gospel of Christ, 204–5, 288; worldly views of, 291–94; historicity of, 291–99; truthfulness of, 298; neglected by Saints, 304–5; has spirit of its own, 307, 312; opposition to, 313; important to the gathering of Israel, 313; authors of, testify of, 310–11
Brass plates: contents of, 20; origins of, 23–24; written in Egyptian, 26–27; included ministry of Messiah, 28; as part of doctrinal restoration, 44–45; preserved Nephites' religious integrity, 308
Bruce, F. F., 7

Cain, 40–41
Campbellite preacher, story of, 56–57
Cameron, W. J., 214
Cannon, George Q.: on endless

Subject Index

Elias, 221

Elijah, 221

Endowment, temple, 218

Endurance to the end, 203–4; 236–37

Enoch, 144, 149, 150

Enos, 55, 110

"Entering the rest of the Lord," 54, 139–41, 151

Eternal perspective, 107–8

Ethics, 195–96

Expansionist theory, 292, 295

Eyring, Henry B., 206

Eziah, 24–25

Faith: lacking in Anti-Christs, 49–51, 53; building a house of, 181–82; in Christ, 201; in Atonement, 256; lack of, in accepting Book of Mormon, 294; exercised in truth, 296–97

Fall of Adam and Eve: as taught by Lehi, 39; description of, 64–68; effects of, 71–73; brought sin into world, 75; doesn't affect children, 80–82; misunderstood, 249–51

Fallen man. *See* Natural man

False doctrine: accusations of, 49; preached by ignorant, 97–98

Family of Christ, 108–9, 191–92. *See also* Church of Christ; Church of Jesus Christ of Latter-Day Saints; Former-day Saints

First estate, 213

First Vision, 298

Flattery, 48–49

Forbidden fruit, 64

Foreordination: of priesthood, 133–36; to lineage and family, 212; collective, 212; is no guarantee to earth-life success, 215

Form criticism, 7

Former-day Saints, 132, 287. *See also* Church of Christ

Foundation, built on rock of Christ, 181–82, 186–88

Fountain of living waters, 17. *See also* Tree of life

Frost, S. E., 250, 251

Gadianton robbers, 40–41

Garment renting, 35–36

Gifts of the Spirit, 243–44, 245

God the Father: condescension of, 12; love of, is the gift of his Son, 16, 231; as literal father of Christ, 89; gave authority to Son, 122–23

Godhead, 13, 19, 29

Good news. *See* Gospel

Good works, 196–97, 244

Goodenough, E. R., 284

Gospel: principles of, 91–92, 201–4, 207; truths essence of Christ's church, 194–95; as good news, 199, 208; fullness of, 204–5, 273, 287–88; everlasting, 268–69. *See also* Church of Christ; Church of Jesus Christ of Latter-day Saints

Grand Council, 134

Grant, Daniel W., 262–63

Great Apostasy, 253

Hedengren, Paul, 296

Helaman: and naming of Lehi and Nephi, 172; counseled sons, 173; on remembrance, 175–76; on Sonship of Christ, 179; on building foundation on rock of Christ, 182

Hell. *See* Outer darkness

Hafen, Bruce C., 196, 242

Hardened hearts, 136, 241

Higher priesthood. *See* Melchizedek Priesthood

Subject Index

Holland, Jeffrey, R., 245–46
Holy Ghost: as interpreter of Lehi's
vision, 10; does not attend natural man, 75; refining influence
of, 79; as rebirth of spirit, 102;
brings remittance of sins,
102–4; cleansing power of,
105–6; as revelator, 107; as
"midwife of salvation," 112;
sins against, 155–56; enables us
to overcome sin, 178; as baptism by fire, 202–3; enables us
to endure to the end, 203–4; as
sanctifier, 244; brings gifts of
the Spirit, 245; as moral monitor, 245; ancient church
endowed with, 269
Holy Order of God, 142–45, 149–51.
See also Melchizedek Priesthood
Hope in Christ, 236
House of Israel: gathering of, 87,
216–18, 223–25, 313; adoption
into, 210; misunderstanding of,
210; as chosen people, 211; has
predisposition to receive gospel
truths, 214–15; scattering of,
216; comprised of Latter-day
Saints, 220; enemies of,
destroyed, 226; are those who
come unto Christ, 228. *See also*
Israel
"How Firm a Foundation," 188
Hypocephalus, 268

"I Stand All Amazed," 13
Immorality. *See* Sexual immorality
Independence of natural man, 77
Infant baptism, 249, 253–58
Inferences, gospel and historical,
271–72
Innocent before God, 256. *See also*
Children
Isaiah, teachings of: quoted by Book
of Mormon prophets, 23;

taught by Nephi and Jacob,
33–35; taught by Abinadi, 115,
118–22, 127; on the house of
Israel, 87, 211, 217, 220–21; on
the suffering of the Savior, 200;
on the Millennium, 225–26
Israel: destiny of, 3; kingdoms of,
24; children of, unworthy of
higher priesthood, 130–31;
priesthood of, 270; concept of
Messiah of, 282–83; strict
adherence to law of, 284. *See
also* House of Israel
Israelites: language of, 27; influence
of, in Americas unknown, 276

Jacob: taught from ancient
prophets and brass plates, 22,
33–34, 99; on allegory of Zenos,
31; on the Atonement, 40, 91,
95, 98–99; and Sherem, 47–60;
steadfast in truth, 54; testified
of Christ, 55; on house of
Israel, 87; on plan of salvation,
88; praised Christ, 90; on judgments, 92–93; on crucifixion
and suffering of Christ, 93;
warned Saints, 96–97; warned
the learned, 97; qualities of, 98;
on power and authority of
higher priesthood, 270; on the
Jews, 285
Jacob (Israel), 22, 35–36, 222
Jeremiah, 216, 217–18, 227–28
Jerusalem of 600 B.C., 275–76
Jesus Christ: doctrine of, in Book of
Mormon, 2; Book of Mormon
declares, Eternal God, 7; as
God, 13; as mortal and immortal, 12–14, 18–19, 89, 124–25,
179; as tree in Lehi's vision,
15–17; seen by Abraham, 42,
252–53; existence of, denied by
anti-Christs, 48; as judge,

335

92–93, 95; suffering and crucifixion of, 93, 94, 119–20,
179–80, 200; Jacob speaks
name of, 99; on being born
again, 103–4; family of, 108–9;
mission of, prophesied by Abinadi, 118–22; as creator, 122;
invested with power by the
Father, 123; as just and merciful, 166–68; as mediator,
166–68; power of, 169; taking
name of, 173–74, 192–94;
enabling power from, to overcome sin, 178; redeems man
from sins, 179; as rock for foundation, 182, 186–88; responsibilities of followers of, 183–85;
trust and rely on, 185–86;
named church among
Nephites, 190–94; Nephites
knew of, 191; more than great
moral teacher, 194–95; pure
love of, motivates to service,
197; good news of, 199; exercising faith in, 201; on the resurrection and judgment, 204;
doctrine of, 206; on gospel
principles, 207; as fulfiller of
law of Moses, 277–78; not
understood by ancient Israel,
282–83; truthfulness of, 298;
bore witness of Book of Mormon, 309. *See also* Atonement;
Gospel; Plan of Salvation;
Rebirth; Resurrection
Jews, 222–23, 275–76, 282, 285,
287. *See also* House of Israel
Joseph, significance of name, 219
Joseph of old, 35–36, 41–42
Joseph Smith Translation: as
restored ancient scripture, 38,
269; on fall of Lucifer, 38–39;
on Creation, 39; on Fall and
Atonement, 40, 250–51; on ori-

gins of secret combinations, 41;
contains Joseph of old's
prophecies, 42; on
Melchizedek, 43–44, 146–47,
149; on rebirth, 105; on
ancient Israelites losing privileges, 131, 141; on Melchizedek
priesthood, 138; on Holy Order
of God, 144; on charity, 245;
on Romans 7, 252; on children
and accountability, 253, 255;
on faith, 256; of Moses 1,
281–82; on role of the Book of
Mormon, 313
Judaism, 284
Judgment, eternal, 92, 162, 204
Justice, 166–68

Kimball, Spencer W., 79, 237
Kindness, 235
King Follett sermon, 82, 262
Korihor, 56
Kreeft, Peter, 195, 286

Laman and Lemuel, 284–85
Lamoni, King, 106, 109, 110–11
Larsen, Dean L., 285
Latter-day Saints. *See* Church of
Jesus Christ of Latter-day Saints
Law of carnal commandments, 274
Law of Moses: sufficient for anti-
Christs, 51–52, 282; and the
Nephites, 113–15, 190–91, 272,
274–75; cannot save alone,
116–17; as law of carnal com-
mandments, 118; as kept by
priests of Noah, 276–77; to be
fulfilled, 277–78; last, never
revealed to children of Israel,
279
Learned, warning to, 97
Lee, Harold B.: on foreordination
and free agency, 136–37; on
refraining from sin, 177; on lin-

eage foreordained, 213; on first
estate affecting second estate,
213–14; on foreordained righteous people failing in mortality, 215; vision of, 238
Lehi: vision of, 8, 10–18, 231, 285;
on fall of Adam, 22, 39–40,
63–64, 252; quoted Joseph of
old, 23, 41–42; on redemption
through Messiah, 181; seed of,
222; left darkness behind, 287
Lehi (son of Helaman), 172–73
Lesser priesthood. *See* Aaronic
Priesthood
Levites, none in Americas, 113–14,
131, 273, 278
Lewis, C. S.: on fallen man, 76; on
natural man, 77; on pride, 79;
on Christianity, 85; on happiness from God, 198; on Christ
as God, 180–81, 298; on
putting trust in God, 185–86
Light of Christ, 79
Limhi, 125
Lineage of Nephite nation, 113–14
Logan Temple Centennial, 143–44
Lost tribes of Israel. *See* House of
Israel, gathering of
Love of God: as gift of Christ, 16,
231; how to express, 232
Lucifer. *See* Satan
Ludlow, Daniel H., 26

Malachi, 32–33
Map analogy, 271
Marsh, Thomas B., 302
Martyrdom, 124–25, 127–28
Mary, mother of Christ, 12–14, 18,
19, 89
Matthews, Robert J., 38, 303
Maxwell, Neal A.: on sign-seekers
and adultery, 52–53; on
Christ's suffering, 94; on ritual

prodigalism, 177; on history of
the Restoration, 299–300
McConkie, Bruce R.: as author of
Millennial Messiah, 2; on con-
verting power of Book of Mormon, 4; on condescension of
God the Father, 12; on Christ
in all things, 15; on Zenos,
25–26; on brass plates, 27, 29;
on prophets quoting one
another, 32–33; on Bible as part
of revealed truths, 44; on doctrinal restoration, 45; on death,
58; on limited knowledge of
Creation, 66; on figurative
aspects of Fall, 66–67; on Fall
and Atonement, 68, 90–91; on
temporal and spiritual death,
73–74, 256; on remittance of
sins, 102, 203; on process of
conversion, 110; on Nephites
observing law of Moses,
114–15, 274–75; on the
"Mosaic standards," 116; on
plan of salvation, 117; on
Christ invested with Father's
power, 123; on first resurrection, 125–26; on priesthood
among the Nephites, 131, 133;
on preparatory work of priesthood, 135–36; on scripture
variants, 137; on becoming co-
heirs with Christ, 142–43; on
Melchizedek as prototype of
Christ, 147; on leaders studying
the scriptures, 183; on foundation of church on Christ, 187;
on gospel ethics and doctrine,
195–96; on Atonement and
obedience, 200, 207–8; on premortal house of Israel, 212; on
the Millennium, 225, 227; on
infant death, 258, 259; on
mentally deficient, 260; on

little children, 263–64; on everlasting gospel, 268–69; on Melchizedek priesthood in ancient Israel, 269–70; on sacrifice among Nephites, 274; on "salvation at stake," 309; on God's testimony of Book of Mormon, 309; on truthfulness of Book of Mormon, 311

Meekness, 235–36

Melchizedek: taught about by Book of Mormon prophets, 22, 43–44, 145–46, 149–50; ministry of, 146–47; taught Abraham, 147–48

Melchizedek Priesthood: ancient prophets held, 130–32, 267, 269–70, 273, 287; eternal nature of, 138; power and authority of, 141 *See also* Holy Order of God

Mentally deficient, 259–60

Mercy, 166–68

Messiah: of Book of Mormon, 279; of Old Testament, 279, 280; Nephite concept of, 282–83. *See also* Jesus Christ

Millennium: and the gathering of Israel, 222; missionary work during, 225; enemies of house of Israel killed before, 226; what will pass during, 227, 260–61

Millet, Robert L., testimony of, 314

"Ministry of reconciliation," 135

Missionary work, 218, 225

Montgomery, John Warwick, 297

Moral depravity of man, 251–52

Mormon: on Moses, 23; on origins of secret combinations, 40–41; on laying hold of word of God, 183–84; on charity, 234–37, 242–43, 245, 246; on pride, 235; on service, 238; on unfeeling Nephites, 241; on infant

baptism, 249; on children, 254, 261; on Anti-Nephi-Lehies, 277; on synagogues, 283–84; spoke to our day, 305–6

Moroni: on Joseph and Jacob, 22, 35–36; on law of restoration, 165; appeared to Joseph Smith, 218–19; on Christ's love for all, 230; testified of Book of Mormon, 310–11

Moses: spoken of by Book of Mormon prophets, 23, 36–37; Holy Order revealed to, 144–45; on house of Israel, 212, 216; restored keys for gathering of house of Israel, 221. *See also* Law of Moses

Mote, E., 187

Mountains as meeting places, 9

Murder, 155–56

Mysteries of God, 67, 228

Name of Jesus Christ: taking on, 174, 190–94; gospel preached in, in antiquity, 267–68

Names, 172–74

Natural man: defined, 74–75; characteristics of, 76–79; arguments against doctrine of, 79–82; as good, 80

Nehor, 48

Nelson, Russell M., 193, 214, 218

Nephi (son of Lehi): sought Lehi's vision and interpretation, 8–10, 231; had own vision interpreted, 10–18; exhibited faith in Christ, 14–15, 18; taught from ancient prophets, 22–23, 36–37; saw Bible not as extensive as brass plates, 28; on destiny of Israel, 30–31; wrote like Malachi, 32–33; on "entering the gate," 102; taught law of Moses, 113; on covenant people, 215; on the lost tribes, 223–24; felt love of God, 233, 286; on pure love of Christ, 234; as example of charity, 236; on the Messiah, 280; chastised brothers, 285; bore testimony of Book of Mormon, 310; on power of God, 314

Nephi (son of Helaman), 22, 42, 172–73

Nephites: as Christians, 132; had higher priesthood, 270; living law of Moses, 272; and sacrifice, 273–74, 275; and their knowledge of the Atonement and plan of salvation, 278–79; as Christians and Jews, 287; understanding of the Messiah, 280

Neum, 24–25, 29

Nicodemus, 103

Noah, 22

Noah, King, priests of, 115–17, 125, 127–28, 276–77

Noordtzij, A., 36–37

Nourishment, Sherem received, 57

Nyman, Monte S., 33

Oaks, Dallin H., 65, 95–96, 186, 193

Old Testament, inferences about, 271–72. *See also* Bible

Olive vineyard allegory. *See* Allegory of Zenos

Original sin theory, 250–52

Outer darkness, 162, 170

Pace, Glen L., 198

Packer, Boyd K.: on sexual immorality, 156; on parable of debtor and creditor, 166–68; on Christ's ransom for our sins, 180; on Christ as mediator, 205

Parable: of the path, 8–11; of debtor and creditor, 166–68

Paradise, 162

Patience, 234

Paul: and the allegory of Zenos, 31; on putting on the new man, 84; on baptism, 102; conversion of, 109, 110–11; on similarities of Christ and Melchizedek, 147; praised Melchizedek, 149; on redemption from sin, 178; on bounds of habitation, 212–13; on being "one in Christ," 227; on charity, 234–37, 246; on love of God, 247; on nature of man, 251–52; on law of circumcision, 253; Nephites were like, 287

Plan of salvation, 88, 122–23

Postmortal existence, 161–62

Pratt, Orson, 63, 105–6, 137, 256

Pratt, Parley P., 302–3

Prayer, 243–44, 247

Preaching the gospel, 184, 205–6. *See also* Missionary work

Predictive prophecy, 294–95

Premortal existence, 134, 211–14

Pride, 78, 235

Priesthood: among the Nephites, 130–32; of ancient high priests, 132–33; foreordination to, 133–37; as everlasting principle, 137–38, 151; entering the rest of the Lord through, 140–42; fullness of, 142–45. *See also* Melchizedek Priesthood; Aaronic Priesthood

Prophecy, 21, 41–42

Prophets, nonbiblical, 24–25. *See also* Zenos, Zenock, Neum, Ezias

"Quickening in the inner man," 106–7. *See also* Rebirth

Subject Index

Spiritual death, 256
Steadfastness in gospel, 60
Stott, 181
Stripling warriors, 240
Sustaining servants of Lord, 184–85
Sword of Laban, 308
Symbolism: of tree of life, 15–16, 231; of "fountain of living waters", 17; of "marvelous type," 37; of sword of Laban, 308
Synagogue in Book of Mormon, 283–84

Talmage, James E., 11, 253
Taylor, John, 108
Temple work, 218
Telestial glory, 165–66
Terrestrial: order of Edenic earth, 62; resurrection, 126; glory, 165
The Brothers Karamazov, 239
Theological errors, 249–58
Top, Brent L., 212
Tower of Babel, 22
Traditions, oral, 21
Transgression, 65. *See* Fall; Sin; Repentance
Tree of life, 15–17, 231
Truths, eternal, 299

Vision of the Glories, 89
Visions, defined, 8

War in heaven, 176

Warnings, 96–97
Whitney, Orson F., 71, 159, 295
Woodruff, Wilford, 134, 215
Word of God. *See* Scriptures
Works of men, 195–98

Young, Brigham: on plan of salvation, 71; church people as natural man, 76; nature of natural man, 77, 80; on body and spirit, 81; on sin, 84; on Atonement, 85; on how Holy Ghost reveals treasures, 107; on Christ sweating blood, 120; on Church of the Firstborn, 145; on spirit returning to God, 161–62; on lineage of Joseph Smith, 219–220, 222; on living beneath our privileges, 304

Zarahemla, people of, were Jews, 276
Zeezrom, 104–5
Zenock, 24–25, 29, 30, 281, 282
Zenos: as nonbiblical prophet, 24–26; testified of Christ, 30; on prayer, 30; on destiny of Israel, 30–32; allegory of, 31, 211; as quoted by Nephi and Malachi, 33; on Israel in the Millennium, 226; on mercy of the Savior, 281; killed, 282
Zoramites, hindered by Corianton, 157, 159